Dublin

"All you've got to do is decide to go and the hardest part is over.

So go!"

TONY WHEELER, COFOUNDER – LONELY PLANET

Contents

Plan Your Trip 4

Welcome to Dublin 4
Dublin's Top 10 6
What's New 13
Need to Know 14
First Time Dublin 16
Top Itineraries 18
If You Like...................20
Month By Month...........24
Travel With Kids...........28
Like a Local 30
For Free 32
Eating **33**
Drinking & Nightlife...**37**
Entertainment **41**
Shopping.................... **45**
Sports & Activities **47**

Explore Dublin 50

Grafton Street & St Stephen's Green...54
Merrion Square & Around.......................88
Temple Bar..................105
Kilmainham & the Liberties.................121
North of the Liffey...... 142
Docklands 164
The Southside 170
Day Trips from Dublin **178**
Sleeping **198**

Understand Dublin 209

Dublin Today...............210
History.........................212
Literary Dublin............224
Musical Dublin 230
Architecture................233
The Irish Way of Life... 238

Survival Guide 241

Transport 242
Directory A–Z 247
Index 258

Dublin Maps 265

ANNEMARIE MCCARTHY/LONELY PLANET ©

FAITHIE/SHUTTERSTOCK ©

THEATRE ARCHITECT: DANIEL LIBESKIND. GRAND CANAL SQUARE DESIGNER: MARTHA SCHWARTZ.

(left) **Jam Art Factory p119** Browse in this quirky souvenir shop.

(above) **Bord Gais Energy Theatre p169** A magnificent auditorium.

(right) **Trinity College p201** Ireland's most prestigious university.

AITORMMFOTO/SHUTTERSTOCK ©

North of the Liffey p142
Temple Bar p105
Docklands p164
Kilmainham & the Liberties p121
Grafton Street & St Stephens Green p54
Merrion Square & Around p88
The Southside p170

Welcome to Dublin

A small capital with a huge reputation, Dublin has a mix of heritage and hedonism that will not disappoint. All you have to do is show up.

Layers of History

Dublin has been in the news since the 9th century, and while traces of its Viking past have been largely washed away, the city is a living museum of its history since then, with medieval castles and cathedrals on display alongside the architectural splendours of its 18th-century heyday, when Dublin was the most handsome Georgian city of the British Empire and a fine reflection of the aspirations of its most privileged citizens. How power was wrested from their hands is another story, and you'll learn that one in its museums and on its walking tours.

Personality goes a Long Way

Dubliners will admit theirs isn't the prettiest city, but will remind you that pretty things are as easy to like as they are to forget…before showing you the showstopper Georgian bits to prove that Dublin has a fine line in sophisticated elegance. True love is demonstrated with brutal unsentimentality round here, but they'll go soft at the knees when talking about the character and personality of the 'greatest city in the world, if you ignore all the others'. Garrulous, amiable and witty, Dubliners at their ease are the greatest hosts of all, a charismatic bunch with compelling soul and sociability.

A Few Scoops

Even in these times of green juices and heart-monitoring apps, the pub remains the alpha and omega of social interaction in Dublin. The city's relationship with alcohol is complex and conflicted but, at its very best, a night out in the pub is the perfect social lubricant and one of the highlights of a visit to Dublin. Every Dubliner has their favourite haunt, from the never-changing traditional pub to whatever new opening is bringing in the beautiful people. With more than 1000 of them spread about the city, you'll be spoilt for choice.

All the World Is Dublin

For as long as it's been around, Dublin has looked beyond Irish shores for inspiration. Once the second city of the (British) Empire, Dublin has always maintained a pretty cosmopolitan outlook and in the last three decades has conspicuously embraced diversity and multiculturalism. You'll hear languages and eat foods from all four corners of the globe, and while it used to be said that 'real' Dubs had to be born within the canals like their parents and grandparents before them, these days you're just as likely to meet a Dub whose parents were born in Warsaw, Lagos, Cairo or Beijing.

Why I Love Dublin

By Fionn Davenport, Writer

At Dublin Airport I get into a taxi. Within 10 minutes the driver and I know everything about each other. Where we were born, where we grew up, which football team we support. He gives me his potted view of why Irish politics is a waste of space, and I tell him what I liked about whatever destination I've just been to. That's Dublin for you, a city that dispenses with formalities and gets down to the nitty-gritty of everyday existence. We may never see each other again, but in that moment we are friends.

For more about our writers, see p288

Top: Georgian-style house on Mountjoy Square (p151)

Dublin's Top 10

1

A Dublin Pub (p168)

1 'A good puzzle would be to cross Dublin without passing a pub', mused Leopold Bloom in James Joyce's *Ulysses*. A conundrum, given there's at least one on every street, but the answer is simple: go into each one you find. Over a hundred years later, the centre of all social life in Dublin remains the bar. There are more than 700, from traditional boozers, such as John Mulligan's (pictured; p168), to the trendiest watering holes. It's where you'll meet Dubliners at their convivial, easy-going best and get a sense of what makes this city tick.

☆ ***Docklands***

Trinity College (p56)

2 Since its foundation in 1592, Trinity College has become one of the world's most famous universities; it's the alma mater of Swift, Wilde and Beckett; it's where you'll find the most beautiful library in the whole country and the home of the world's most famous illuminated Gospel, the *Book of Kells*. Its 16 hectares are an oasis of aesthetic elegance, its cobbled quadrangles lined with handsome neoclassical buildings that lend an air of magisterial calm to the campus, evident as soon as you walk through Front Arch.

◉ ***Grafton Street & St Stephen's Green***

DERICK HUDSON/SHUTTERSTOCK ©

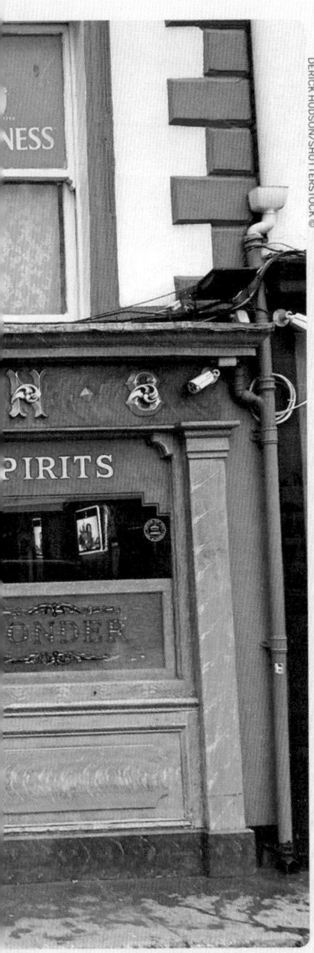

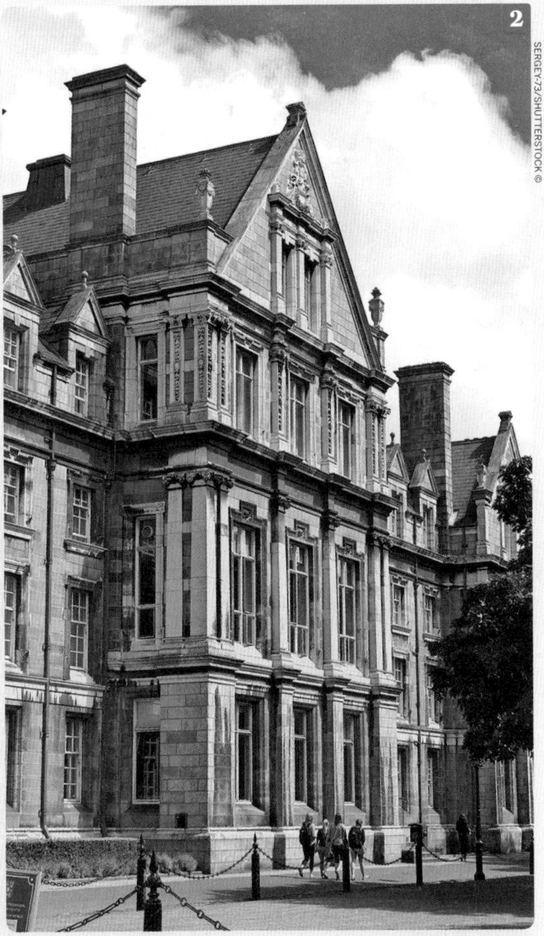

2

SERGEY-73/SHUTTERSTOCK ©

3

4

National Museum of Ireland *(p90)*

3 The artefacts of a nation are to be found in this eminent institution, which opened in 1890 with a fine collection of coins, medals and Irish antiquities. The collection has grown significantly since then, and now numbers in excess of four million objects split across three separate museum buildings, including prehistoric archaeological finds and Celtic and medieval treasures, an extensive folklore collection, and the stuffed beasts and skeletons of the natural history section.

Merrion Square & Around

Hugh Lane Gallery, Dublin *(p144)*

4 Hanging on the walls of a magnificent Georgian pile is arguably the city's finest collection of modern and contemporary art, which runs the gamut from impressionist masterpieces (Degas, Monet, Manet et al) to Irish artists such as Dorothy Cross and Sean Scully. The gallery's extra-special treat is Dublin-born Francis Bacon's actual London studio (pictured), brought over piece by piece and painstakingly reassembled in all its glorious mess – you can't step inside it but you can observe exactly how the artist lived and worked, down to the minute details.

North of the Liffey

Dining Scene *(p74)*

5 It was unthinkable less than two decades ago, but Dublin's foodie scene is now one of the city's major highlights. There are restaurants to suit every taste and budget, but the most exciting ones are the places – such as Richmond – that have led the way in defining Modern Irish cuisine, a catholic style that uses the basic ingredients and recipes of Irish cuisine and infuses them with influences from virtually every other cuisine in the world.

ABOVE: PLATED DISH FROM RESTAURANT PATRICK GUILBAUD (P102).

Grafton Street & St Stephen's Green

Kilmainham Gaol *(p129)*

6 Ireland's struggle for independence was a bloody and tempestuous journey, and this forbidding prison on the western edge of the city played a role in it for nearly 150 years, as the forced temporary home of many a rebel and revolutionary. Unoccupied since 1924, it is now a museum with an enthralling exhibit on the history of Irish nationalism. The guided tour of its grim cells and corridors is highly memorable and it finishes in the yard where the leaders of the failed 1916 Easter Rising were executed.

Kilmainham & the Liberties

Guinness Storehouse *(p123)*

7 One of the world's most famous beer brands is Guinness, as inextricably linked with Dublin as James Joyce and... no, we can't think of anything else. An old fermentation plant in the St James's Gate Brewery has been converted into a seven-storey museum devoted to the beer, the company's history, how the beer is made and how it became the brand it is today. The top floor is an atrium bar, where you put the theory to the test and drink a pint; just below it is an excellent spot for lunch.

Kilmainham & the Liberties

6

SALVADOR MANIQUIZ/SHUTTERSTOCK ©

COURTESY DIAGEO ©

BARRY MASON/ALAMY STOCK PHOTO ©

Chester Beatty Library *(p64)*

8 Alfred Chester Beatty was a mining magnate with exceedingly good taste, and the fruit of his aesthetic sensibility is gathered in this remarkable museum. Books, manuscripts and scrolls were his particular love, and his collection includes one of the world's finest gatherings of Qu'rans, the finest collection of Chinese jade books in existence, and some of the earliest biblical parchments ever found. The remainder of the collection is fleshed out with tablets, paintings, furniture and other beautiful objets d'art.

Grafton Street & St Stephen's Green

St Stephen's Green *(p66)*

9 Dublin is blessed with green spaces, but none is so popular or so beloved by its citizens as St Stephen's Green, whose main entrance is through an arch at the southern end of Grafton St. When the sun burns through the cloud cover, virtually every blade of grass is occupied, by students, lovers and workers on a break. Many a business meeting is conducted along its pathways, which run by flower gardens, playgrounds and old Victorian bandstands.

Grafton Street & St Stephen's Green

9

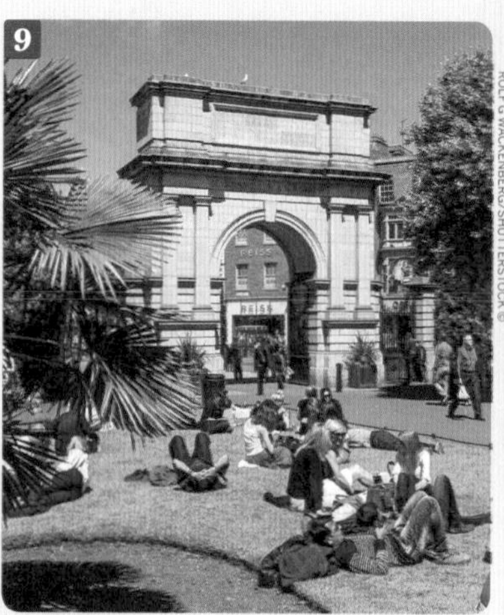

ROLF G WACKENBERG/SHUTTERSTOCK ©

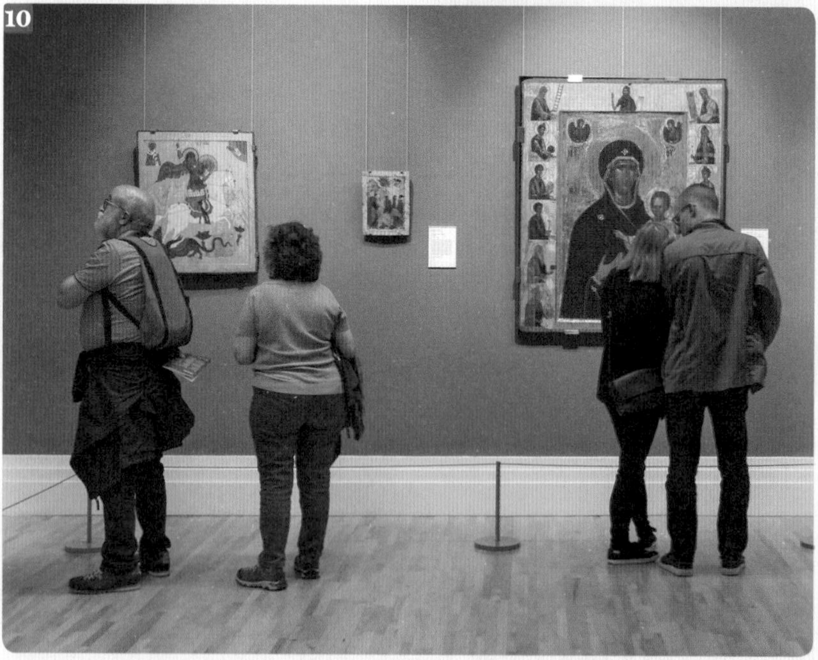
10

SALVADOR MANIQUIZ/SHUTTERSTOCK ©

National Gallery *(p94)*

10 The State's art collection is an impressive one, a history of art spread across six centuries and 54 separate galleries, which have just reopened after a major refurbishment. The marquee names include Goya, Caravaggio and Van Gogh, but no less impressive are the paintings by luminaries such as Orpen, Reynolds and Van Dongen. Don't miss the paintings by Jack B Yeats, or the seasonal exhibit of watercolours by JMW Turner; as you find your way there, you'll pass the odd Rembrandt, Velázquez and Vermeer.

Merrion Square & Around

What's New

5000 New Beds

After more than a decade of stagnation, Dublin is building hotels. More than 5000 new beds are scheduled to be available by 2020. Already open are Aloft Dublin City (p205) and the Iveagh Garden Hotel (p202), with a bunch more to come.

14 Henrietta Street

Dublin's most complete Georgian street is home to this refurbished townhouse, now a museum showcasing the history of the dwelling, from its construction in the 1740s as an elegant family home to its dereliction in the late 19th and early 20th centuries. (p149)

Museum of Literature Ireland

Newman House is now home to this museum, an interactive exploration of the country's rich literary heritage; the new museum includes Joyce's notes for *Ulysses*. (p68)

Vaults Live

This permanent theatre attraction in the Liberties tells tales of Dublin's more gruesome history. (p140)

Bottomless Brunch

The bottomless brunch has arrived in Dublin, with a bunch of places offering limitless drinks (usually mimosas or Bellinis) for a fixed price – try Bow Lane (p74), Cleaver East (p113) or Thundercut Alley (p158).

Seamus Heaney: Listen Now Again

This exhibition dedicated to the poet is in situ in the new Bank of Ireland Cultural & Heritage Centre until 2021. (p68)

Luke Kelly Sculptures

The 35th anniversary of the beloved folk singer's death in January 2019 saw the addition of two sculptures to the cityscape – the first on South King St (p70) and another on Sheriff St (p166) on the northside, where Kelly was born in 1940.

Distillery District

In Dublin, whiskey is what gin is virtually everywhere else, with a handful of new distilleries opening up in the city's very own whiskey quarter, the Liberties. Teeling Distillery (p133) was the trailblazer, but has been followed by the Pearse Lyons Distillery (p133), the Dublin Liberties Distillery (p133) and Roe & Co (p133).

Perfect Pizza

Dublin has rediscovered the pleasure of the perfect pizza – with a handful of spots vying for the title of the city's very best, including newcomers Pi Pizza (p73), Boco (p157) and Manifesto (p172), who join stalwarts Paulie's Pizza (p167).

The Ivy

The first Irish outpost of the Soho landmark restaurant branched out and landed in Dublin in 2018 to much chi-chi fanfare, though tales of staff disaffection have tempered the enthusiasm somewhat – but not quite enough to shorten the booking queues. (p75)

For more recommendations and reviews, see **lonelyplanet.com/ireland/dublin**

Need to Know

For more information, see Survival Guide (p241)

Currency
euro (€)

Language
English

Visas
Not required for citizens of Australia, New Zealand, the USA or Canada, or citizens of European nations that belong to the European Economic Area (EEA).

Money
ATMs are widespread. Credit cards (with PIN) are widely accepted in restaurants, hotels and shops.

Mobile Phones
All European and Australasian mobile phones work in Dublin, as do North American phones not locked to a local network. Check with your provider. Prepaid SIM cards start from €20.

Time
Western European Time (UTC/GMT November to March; plus one hour April to October)

Tourist Information
Visit Dublin Centre (www.visitdublin.com; 25 Suffolk St; 9am-5.30pm Mon-Sat, 10.30am-3pm Sun; all city centre) General visitor information on Dublin and Ireland, as well as an accommodation and booking service.

Daily Costs

Budget under €150
- Dorm bed: €16–28
- Cheap meal in cafe or pub: €15–25
- Bus ticket: up to €2.85
- Some museums: free
- Pint: €5.50–7

Midrange €150–250
- Budget hotel double: €100–150
- Midrange hotel or townhouse double: €130–250
- Lunch or dinner in midrange restaurant: €30–40
- Guided tours and admission to paid attractions: €20

Top End over €250
- Double in top-end hotel: from €250
- Dinner in top-end restaurant: €60–120

Advance Planning

Two months before Book accommodation, especially for summer. Purchase tickets for major live gigs, especially big-name touring musicians and comedians.

Two weeks before Secure accommodation in low season. Book weekend performances for main theatres, and Friday or Saturday night reservations at top-end restaurants.

One week before Book weekend tables at the trendiest or most popular restaurants.

Useful Websites

- All The Food (www.allthefood.ie) Up-to-date restaurant reviews for Dublin.
- Dublin Tourism (www.visitdublin.com) Official website of Dublin Tourism.
- Dublintown (www.dublintown.ie) Comprehensive list of events and goings-on.
- Failte Ireland (www.discoverireland.ie) Official tourist-board website.
- Lonely Planet (www.lonelyplanet.com/ireland/dublin) Destination information, hotel bookings, traveller forum and more.
- Old Dublin Town (www.olddublintown.com) Haphazard-looking website that's an excellent info resource for this city in flux.

WHEN TO GO

The weather in Dublin is at its best from June to August. September can be warm and sunny. November to February are cold, but dry; May sees rain and sun.

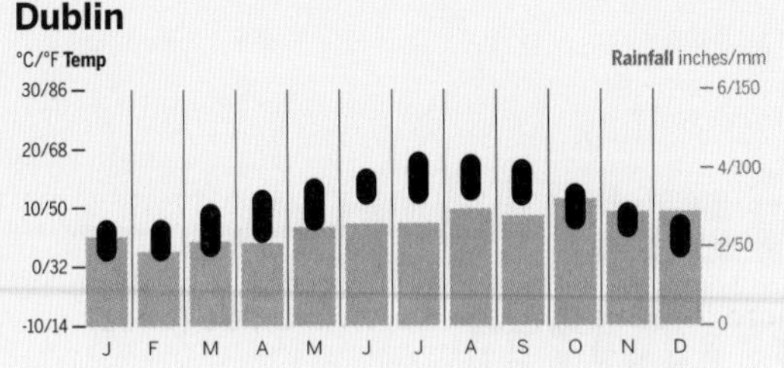

Arriving in Dublin

Dublin Airport Buses to the city centre run every 10 to 15 minutes between around 6am and 12.30am; taxis (€25) take around 45 minutes.

Dublin Port Terminal Buses (adult/child €3.50/2, 20 minutes) are timed to coincide with arrivals and departures.

Busáras All Bus Éireann services arrive at Busáras; private operators have arrival points in different parts of the city.

Heuston and Connolly Stations Main-line trains from all over Ireland arrive at Heuston or Connolly Stations. Connolly Station is a stop on the DART line into town; the Luas Red Line serves both Connolly and Heuston stations.

For much more on **arrival** see p242

Getting Around

Walking Dublin's city centre is compact, flat and eminently walkable – it's less than 2km from one end of the city centre to the other.

Bicycle The city's rent-and-ride Dublinbikes scheme is the ideal way to cover ground quickly.

Bus Useful for getting to the west side of the city and the suburbs.

Luas A two-line light-rail transport system that links the city centre with the southern suburbs.

Taxi Easily recognised by light-green-and-blue 'Taxi' signs on the doors, they can be hailed or picked up at ranks in the city centre.

DART Suburban rail network that runs along the eastern edge of the city along Dublin Bay.

For more on **getting around** see p244

Sleeping

A surge in tourist numbers and a relative lack of beds means hotel prices can skyrocket, particularly at weekends and during the high season (May to September). There are good midrange options north of the Liffey, but the biggest spread of accommodation is south of the river, from midrange Georgian townhouses to the city's top hotels. Budget travellers rely on the selection of decent hostels, many of which have private rooms as well as dorms.

For much more on **sleeping** see p198

First Time Dublin

For more information, see Survival Guide (p241)

Checklist

- ➡ Ensure your passport is valid for at least six months past your arrival date.
- ➡ Check airline baggage restrictions (for liquids and fresh products in particular).
- ➡ Arrange travel insurance and, if you're from the EU, a European Health Insurance Card.
- ➡ Inform your debit-/credit-card company of your travel plans.
- ➡ Check if you can use your mobile phone abroad.

What to Pack

- ➡ Raincoat – yes, it will most likely rain at some point
- ➡ Good walking shoes – Dublin is best explored on foot
- ➡ UK/Ireland electrical adaptor
- ➡ A few extra layers – it can get cool, even in summer
- ➡ A small day pack
- ➡ A hollow leg – that beer needs to go somewhere

Top Tips for Your Trip

- ➡ The city centre is small enough to be easily walkable, but make sure you have comfortable shoes.
- ➡ If you're going to use public transport, be sure to get a Leap card (from most convenience stores): it's cheaper and much easier than cash.
- ➡ With over 100 public bicycle-rental stations spread throughout the city, Dublinbikes is a convenient way to get around, and the first 30 minutes are free.
- ➡ Book tables at popular restaurants at least a few days in advance if you want to avoid disappointment or dodge the 5.30pm seating nobody else wants.
- ➡ Lunch deals and pre-theatre menus are the best way to enjoy fine dining, even in the very best restaurants in town.
- ➡ If you're looking for an authentic traditional-music session, get away from the pubs of Temple Bar and look for one removed from those cobbled, touristy streets.

What to Wear

You can wear pretty much whatever you want: smart casual is the most you'll need for fancy dinners, the theatre or the concert hall.

Irish summers are warm but rarely hot, so you'll want an extra layer for when the temperatures cool, especially in the evening.

Ultimately, the ever-changeable weather will determine your outfits, but a light waterproof jacket and waterproof shoes should never be beyond reach, for the almost inevitable rain.

Be Forewarned

Dublin is a safe city by any standards, except maybe those set by the Swiss. Basically, act as you would at home. See p250 for more information.

Best Blogs about Dublin

➡ **All The Food** (www.allthefood.ie) Reliable restaurant reviews and lots more, such as the best cafes to work from.

➡ **Come Here To Me!** (www.comeheretome.com) A practical guide to Dublin's history, full of fascinating detail and interesting facts about places and people.

➡ **Totally Dublin** (www.totallydublin.ie) Comprehensive listings guide for the city.

Taxes & Refunds

A standard value-added tax (VAT) rate of 23% is applied to all goods sold in Dublin excluding books, children's clothing and educational items. Non-EU residents can claim the VAT back so long as the store operates either the Cashback or Taxback refund programme. You'll get a voucher with your purchase that must be stamped at the last point of exit from the EU.

Tipping

You're not obliged to tip if the service or food was unsatisfactory.

➡ **Hotels** Only for bellhops who carry luggage, then €1 per bag.

➡ **Pubs** Not expected unless table service is provided, then €1 for a round of drinks.

➡ **Restaurants** Tip 10% for decent service, up to 15% in more expensive places.

➡ **Taxis** Tip 10% or round up to the nearest euro.

➡ **Toilet attendants** Tip €0.50.

KEITH DONEGAN/ GETTY IMAGES ©

Bicycle-rental station

Etiquette

➡ **Greetings** Shake hands with both men and women when meeting for the first time. Female friends are greeted with a single kiss on the cheek.

➡ **Queues** Dubliners can be a little lax about proper queuing etiquette, but are not shy about confronting queue-skippers who jump in front of them.

➡ **Polite requests** Dubliners often use 'Sorry' instead of 'Excuse me' when asking for something; they're not really apologising for anything.

Language

Irish (Gaeilge) is the country's official language. The Official Languages Act, introduced by the government in 2003, determines that all official documents, street signs and official titles must be either in Irish or in both Irish and English. Despite its official status, Irish is really only spoken in pockets of rural Ireland known as the Gaeltacht, the main ones being Cork (Corcaigh), Donegal (Dún na nGall), Galway (Gaillimh), Kerry (Ciarraí) and Mayo (Maigh Eo).

For more on the Irish Language and key phrases see p252.

Top Itineraries

Day One

Grafton Street & St Stephen's Green (p54)

Start with a stroll through the grounds of **Trinity College**, visiting the **Long Room** and the **Book of Kells** before ambling up **Grafton St** to **St Stephen's Green**. For more beautiful books and artefacts, drop into the **Chester Beatty Library**. On your way, you can do a spot of retailing in **Powerscourt Townhouse** shopping centre or the many boutiques west of Grafton St.

Lunch The lunch bento at Sisu Izakaya (p74) is great value and delicious.

Merrion Square & Around (p88)

Pick your heavyweight institution, or visit all three: the **National Museum of Ireland – Archaeology** (if only for the Ardagh Chalice and Tara Brooch), the **National Gallery** (be sure to check out the Jack B Yeats room) and the **Museum of Natural History**, which the kids will surely enjoy.

Dinner Etto (p101) is one of the best Italian restaurants in town.

Temple Bar (p105)

Dublin's one-time party zone still likes to have a good time, and is definitely at its most animated in the evenings, where you have the choice of a **traditional-music session**, some decent clubbing at **Mother** (Saturdays only) or just straight up drinking at any of the district's many **pubs**.

Day Two

Kilmainham & the Liberties (p121)

Begin with a little penance at either (or both) of Dublin's medieval cathedrals, **St Patrick's** and **Christ Church**, before pursuing pleasure at Dublin's most popular tourist attraction, the **Guinness Storehouse**. Along the way, you have your choice of distillery experiences, but **Teeling** is at least now selling whiskey produced on its own premises.

Lunch Fumbally (p137) has great soups, sandwiches and coffee.

Kilmainham & the Liberties (p121)

Go further west to Kilmainham, visiting first the fine collection at the **Irish Museum of Modern Art** (don't forget to visit the gardens too) before going out the back entrance and stepping into **Kilmainham Gaol**, the tour of which offers one of the most illuminating and interesting insights into Ireland's struggle for independence. If the weather is good, a stroll in the **War Memorial Gardens** is also recommended.

Dinner Super seafood at Fish Shop (p159), in Stoneybatter.

North of the Liffey (p142)

Walshs of Stoneybatter is a superb traditional bar, full of interesting locals and hipster blow-ins looking for a 'real' Dublin experience. Alternatively, you could take in a play at either the **Gate Theatre** or Ireland's national theatre, the **Abbey**. Use the Luas to get you from Stoneybatter (get on at the Museum stop) to Abbey St.

REMIZOV/SHUTTERSTOCK ©

Whiskeys at Teeling Distillery (p133)

BOULENGER XAVIER/SHUTTERSTOCK ©

Museum of Natural History (p97)

Day Three

North of the Liffey (p142)

After walking the length of **O'Connell St**, and pausing to inspect the bullet holes in the **General Post Office**, explore the collection of the **Hugh Lane Gallery, Dublin**, including Francis Bacon's reconstructed studio. At **14 Henrietta St** you'll discover the story of a Georgian townhouse; at **Jameson Distillery Bow Street** you can uncover the secrets of Irish whiskey.

Lunch Get a sandwich or healthy salad at the wonderful Fegan's 1924 (p156).

North of the Liffey (p142)

The collection of the **National Museum of Ireland – Decorative Arts & History** is excellent, but you'll be distracted by the stunning 18th-century barracks that is its home. The nearby **Arbour Hill Cemetery** is where the executed leaders of the 1916 Easter Rising are buried, while further west again is the broad expanse of **Phoenix Park**, Europe's largest city park.

Dinner Chapter One (p159) is ideal for a special occasion. Book ahead.

Grafton Street & St Stephen's Green (p54)

The biggest choice of nightlife is in the streets around **Grafton St**: there are traditional pubs, trendy new bars and music venues. You can drink, chat and dance the night away, or see a show at the **Gaiety Theatre**. Whatever you choose, everything is easily reached in what is a pretty compact district.

Day Four

North of the Liffey (p142)

You'll get a particularly interesting insight into the vagaries of Irish history with a visit to **Glasnevin Cemetery**, the final resting place of so many Irish notables – be sure to take the brilliant tour. The **National Botanic Gardens** are just around the corner, and well worth an amble. Sporting fans will enjoy the tour of **Croke Park**, Ireland's biggest stadium and the HQ of the Gaelic Athletic Association.

Lunch Oxmantown (p157) has a great range of lunch options.

Howth (p189)

Hop on a DART and head northwards to **Howth**, a nice fishing village at the foot of a bulbous headland overlooking Dublin Bay. There are great walks around the headland itself, but if you prefer something a little more sedate, there's a fine selection of pubs in the village and some excellent seafood restaurants along the pier. There's also a terrific **farmers market** at weekends.

Dinner Mr Fox (p159) is one of the best restaurants in town for Irish cuisine.

Merrion Square & Around (p88)

A visit to **O'Donoghue's** on Merrion Row is guaranteed to be memorable. This beautiful traditional bar is always full of revellers, and there's a good chance there'll be a trad-music session on.

If You Like...

Traditional Pubs

Kehoe's Beautiful traditional pub with elegant Victorian bar beloved of locals and visitors alike. (p78)

John Mulligan's This historic place has featured in films and is synonymous with the quiet, ticking-clock style of the Dublin pub. (p168)

Fallon's Great neighbourhood bar at the edge of the Liberties frequented by locals and hipsters in the know. (p138)

John Kavanagh's It's worth the trek to the north Dublin suburb of Glasnevin for this traditional classic. (p160)

Stag's Head The most picturesque of Dublin's traditional bars hasn't changed a jot since it was remodelled in 1895. (p80)

Toner's Flagstone floors and an old-style bar make this a favourite boozer for the local business crowd. (p103)

Old Royal Oak Traditional pub in the western suburb of Kilmainham beloved of aficionados of the classic pub experience. (p138)

Walshs Wonderful local pub frequented by old men in flat caps and young arty types in...flat caps. (p160)

Modern Bars

Bow Lane Late-night cocktail lounge with an industrial art deco design but the dark, moody atmosphere of a '50s Vegas bar. (p74)

Farrier & Draper Prohibition-era cool in the decadent surroundings of an 18th-century Georgian mansion. (p80)

Little Museum of Dublin (p66)

Vintage Cocktail Club A little oasis in the madness of Temple Bar, serving expert cocktails in cosy, 1920s-inspired rooms. (p114)

House A beautiful bar in a gorgeous Georgian home, with a garden in the middle of it. (p104)

Square Ball Craft beers, a vintage arcade, board games and sports – this cool bar has something for everyone. (p104)

Liquor Rooms Basement boozer with an impressive cocktail menu, lots of nooks and crannies and excellent music. (p114)

The Oak A 1920s-style bar that oozes elegance from its handsome leather booths and high-backed blue velvet chairs. (p114)

Traditional Music

Cobblestone The best pub in Dublin for hearing good traditional music, both old-style and contemporary. (p159)

O'Donoghue's Folk music's unofficial HQ during the 1960s, O'Donoghue's still hosts regular sessions of traditional music. (p104)

Ha'Penny Bridge Inn A regular session of ballads, folk and traditional music takes place on Sunday nights. (p118)

Devitt's This buzzy pub has open sessions in which anyone can play – so long as you're really good at playing traditional music. (p82)

Oliver St John Gogarty Sessions here may be strictly for tourists, but they're performed by some excellent musicians. (p115)

Irish History

Kilmainham Gaol Ireland's troubled and bloody struggle for independence is revealed in a visit to this historic jail. (p129)

Glasnevin Cemetery Almost everyone who was anyone in the last two centuries of Irish history is interred at this cemetery. (p150)

1916 Rebellion Walking Tour A detailed and informative walking tour of all the sites and stories associated with the Easter Rising. (p87)

EPIC The Irish Emigration Museum This interactive museum explores the story of emigration and the diaspora. (p166)

Irish Family History Centre The ideal place to begin – or further – your exploration of your own Irish family history. (p166)

14 Henrietta Street The history of Dublin as told through the story of one of its Georgian houses. (p149)

Jeanie Johnston An exact replica of a 19th-century Famine ship that sailed across the Atlantic. (p166)

Admiring Art

Irish Museum of Modern Art Art from the 20th and 21st centuries on its walls, amid elegant surroundings and beautiful gardens. (p131)

Hugh Lane Gallery, Dublin Impressionist masterpieces and Francis Bacon's actual studio, reconstructed piece by exacting piece. (p144)

National Gallery Home of the Irish State's art collection, including a Caravaggio and a whole room dedicated to Jack B Yeats. (p94)

Royal Hibernian Academy (RHA) Gallagher Gallery Privately run gallery where installations, sound pieces and other treats complement the contemporary paintings. (p97)

For more top Dublin spots, see the following:

- Eating (p33)
- Drinking & Nightlife (p37)
- Entertainment (p41)
- Shopping (p45)
- Sports & Activities (p47)

City Assembly House Dublin's original art gallery stages occasional exhibitions in its beautiful main room. (p68)

Museum Meanders

National Museum of Ireland – Archaeology The country's most important cultural institution, with sacred historical treasures. (p90)

Chester Beatty Library Breathtaking collection of sacred books and objets d'art from the Middle East and Asia. (p64)

Little Museum of Dublin Tells the story of Dublin in the 20th century through photographs and objects. (p66)

Museum of Natural History The Dead Zoo's collection has hardly changed since 1857. (p97)

National Print Museum May sound dull, but is anything but – if you've any interest in the printed word then it's a memorable visit. (p172)

Live Gigs

Workman's Club A great spot for left-of-centre stuff, from electronica to alt rock and beardy folk music. (p118)

Whelan's The spiritual home of the singer-songwriter, this terrifically intimate venue allows you to get up close and personal. (p82)

Vicar Street A midsized venue that generally hosts soul, folk and world music. (p140)

3 Arena The place to see your favourite touring international superstar, along with 23,000 others. (p169)

Wigwam First-class DJs do their thing in the basement bar. (p161)

Button Factory A good mix of live music and DJs at this Temple Bar venue. (p118)

Markets & Shopping

Powerscourt Townhouse The city's most elegant shopping centre, selling everything from hand-crafted leather bags to hats by Irish designers. (p84)

George's Street Arcade Beneath the arches of this Victorian arcade you'll find everything from secondhand LPs to patchouli oil. (p84)

Temple Bar Food Market The best gourmet food market in town is the place to sample all kinds of goodies. (p112)

Ulysses Rare Books Rare books, maps and first editions are found in this beautiful bookshop, which specialises in Irish titles. (p85)

Irish Design Shop Irish crafts, from jewellery to kitchenware, that make for excellent local mementos or gifts. (p83)

Article Imaginative and elegant collection of homewares and gift ideas, from egg cups to posters. (p84)

Eating Out

Chapter One Michelin-starred and beloved by its regulars, this is one of the best restaurants in town. (p159)

Banyi Japanese Dining If you want authentic Japanese cuisine, look no further than this sensational restaurant in Temple Bar. (p112)

Greenhouse One Michelin star hardly does justice to the superb Scandi-Irish cuisine of this wonderful restaurant. (p77)

Clanbrassil House A cosy neighbourhood restaurant turning out some of the city's finest food. (p138)

Etto Superb, modern interpretations of Italian fare. (p101)

Fish Shop The best seafood restaurant in town works only with the freshest catch. (p159)

Restaurant Patrick Guilbaud For the ultimate splash-out meal, this is arguably the best restaurant in Ireland. (p102)

Literary Locations

Marsh's Library Founded in 1701, Ireland's oldest library is home to more than 25,000 books and manuscripts dating back to the 1400s. (p133)

Old Library Trinity College is home to the world's most famous illuminated Gospels and the breathtaking Long Room library. (p66)

Dublin Writers Museum Dublin's literary heritage is explored through writers' personal possessions, scribblings and memorabilia. (p154)

Bloomsday Edwardian gear is de rigueur on 16 June if you want to celebrate Dublin's unique tribute to James Joyce. (p25)

James Joyce Cultural Centre A fascinating flavour of Joyce's Edwardian heyday intermingled with some excellent films on the author's life and work. (p152)

Green Spaces

St Stephen's Green The city's favourite sun trap, with every blade of its manicured lawns occupied by lounge lizards and lunchers. (p66)

Merrion Square Perfectly raked paths meander by beautifully maintained lawns and flower beds. (p96)

Phoenix Park Dublin's biggest park, it's home to deer, the zoo, the president and the US ambassador. (p146)

Iveagh Gardens Delightful, slightly dishevelled gardens hidden behind St Stephen's Green. (p68)

War Memorial Gardens The best-kept open secret in town are these magnificent gardens by the Liffey. (p134)

Herbert Park This extensive park is one of the most popular green lungs south of the Liffey. (p172)

Georgian Buildings

Leinster House Richard Cassels built this home for the Duke of Leinster; it's now the home of the Irish parliament. (p97)

Hugh Lane Gallery, Dublin Formerly Charlemont House, Lord Charlemont's city dwelling, this was one of the city's finest Georgian homes. (p144)

Powerscourt Townhouse Once home to the third Viscount Powerscourt, Robert Mack's beautiful building is now a popular shopping centre. (p84)

Four Courts The home of the highest courts in the land is the joint effort of Thomas Cooley and James Gandon. (p152)

Custom House James Gandon announced his arrival in Dublin with this architectural stunner. (p166)

(Top) Marsh's Library (p133)
(Bottom) War Memorial Gardens (p134)

OLIVIER CIRENDINI/LONELY PLANET ©

ALAN MALONE/SHUTTERSTOCK ©

Bank of Ireland Now housing a bank, this building was designed by Edward Lovett Pearce for the Irish parliament. (p69)

Free Stuff

Bank of Ireland The world's first purpose-built parliament building; free entry to the surviving House of Lords. (p69)

Irish Museum of Modern Art Contemporary Irish and international art is housed in the elegant, airy expanse of the Royal Hospital Kilmainham. (p131)

National Museum of Ireland – Archaeology The primary repository of the nation's archaeological treasures. (p90)

National Gallery Home to 15,000 paintings and sculpture, including a wonderful Caravaggio. (p94)

National Museum of Ireland – Decorative Arts & History The building, formerly the world's largest military barracks, is as impressive as the collection it houses. (p149)

Trinity College No trip to Dublin is complete without a wander through the grounds of Trinity. (p56)

Forty Foot Pool An open-air, seawater bathing pool. (p196)

Glasnevin Cemetery The final resting place for many names from Irish history. (p150)

Phoenix Park This huge park houses the president, the American ambassador, the zoo and a herd of fallow deer. (p146)

Chester Beatty Library The city's foremost small museum is a treasure trove of ancient books and other gorgeous objets d'art. (p64)

Month By Month

TOP EVENTS

St Patrick's Festival, March

Forbidden Fruit, June

Taste of Dublin, June

Culture Night, September

Dublin Fringe Festival, September

January

It's cold and often wet, and the city is slowly getting over the Christmas break.

New Year's Celebrations

Experience the birth of another year with a cheer among thousands of revellers at Dublin's iconic Christ Church Cathedral.

February

Bad weather makes February the perfect month for indoor activities. Some museums launch new exhibits.

Dublin International Film Festival

Most of Dublin's cinemas participate in the city's film festival (www.diff.ie), a two-week showcase for new films by Irish and international directors, which features local flicks, arty international films and advance releases of mainstream movies.

Six Nations Rugby

Ireland plays its three home matches at the Aviva Stadium in the southern suburb of Ballsbridge. The season runs from February to April (www.irishrugby.ie).

March

This month is all about one festival. Weather is uncertain; it is often warmer but really cold spells are also common.

St Patrick's Festival

The mother of all Irish festivals (www.stpatricksfestival.ie), where hundreds of thousands gather to 'honour' St Patrick on city streets and in venues throughout the centre over four days around 17 March.

April

The weather is getting better, the flowers are beginning to bloom and the festival season begins anew.

Irish Grand National

Dublin loves horse racing, and the race that's loved the most is the Grand National (www.fairyhouse.ie), the showcase of the national hunt season that takes place at Fairyhouse in County Meath, 25km northwest of the city centre, on Easter Monday.

May

The May bank holiday (on the first Monday) sees the first of the busy summer weekends as Dubliners take to the roads to enjoy the budding good weather.

Bloom in the Park

Ireland's largest gardening expo (www.bloominthepark.com) sees more than 90,000 visitors coming to Phoenix Park over one weekend at the beginning of the month to eat food, listen to music and, yes, test their green thumbs.

(Top) Bloomsday

(Bottom) St Patrick's Festival

CARLOS SANCHEZ PEREYRA/GETTY IMAGES ©

CEZARY ZAREBSKI PHOTOGRAPHY/GETTY IMAGES ©

International Dublin Gay Theatre Festival

A fortnight at the beginning of May (www.gaytheatre.ie) devoted exclusively to gay theatre – plays by gay writers past and present that have a gay or gay-related theme.

International Literature Festival Dublin

A 10-day literature festival (p224) held from mid-May, attracting Irish and international writers to its readings, performances and talks.

June

The bank holiday at the beginning of the month sees the city spoilt for choice as to what to do. There's a bunch of festivals to choose from in the good weather.

Forbidden Fruit

An alternative-music festival (www.forbiddenfruit.ie) on the grounds of the Irish Museum of Modern Art, on the first weekend in June.

Women's Mini-Marathon

A 10km charity run (www.vhiwomensminimarathon.ie) on the second Sunday of the month that attracts up to 50,000 participants – including some poorly disguised men.

Bloomsday

Edwardian dress and breakfast of 'the inner organs of beasts and fowls' are but two of the elements of the Dublin festival (www.jamesjoyce.ie) celebrating 16 June, the day on which James Joyce's *Ulysses* takes place; the real highlight is retracing Leopold Bloom's steps.

Taste of Dublin

The city's best restaurateurs share their secrets and dishes with each other and the public at the wonderful Taste of Dublin (https://dublin.tastefestivals.com) in the Iveagh Gardens, which takes place over a long weekend in June and features talks, demonstrations, lessons and some extraordinary grub.

July

There's something on every weekend, including the biggest music festival of the year.

Dublin Horse Show

The international horsey set trot down to the Royal Dublin Society (RDS) for the social highlight of the year (www.dublinhorseshow.com). Particularly popular is the Aga Khan Trophy, an international-class competition packed with often heart-stopping excitement in which eight nations participate.

Longitude

A mini-Glastonbury in Dublin's Marlay Park, Longitude (www.longitude.ie) packs them in over three days in mid-July for a feast of EDM, nu-folk, rock and pop.

City Spectacular

The world's best street performers (www.cityspectacular.com) – from jugglers to sword-swallowers – test their skills over a July weekend in Merrion Sq .

(Top) Fire eater performing at City Spectacular

(Bottom) Dublin City Liffey Swim

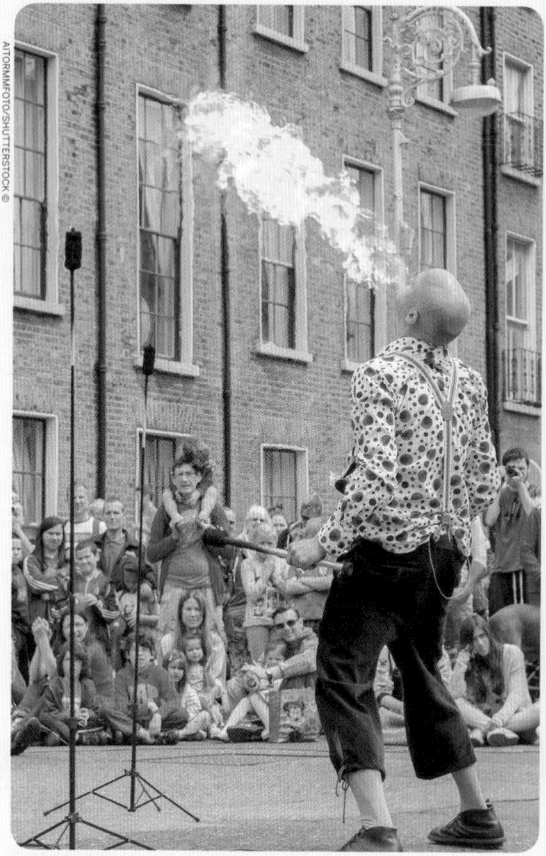

August

Schools are closed, the sun is shining (or not!) and Dublin is in a holiday mood. It's the busiest time of the year for visitors.

Dublin City Liffey Swim

Five hundred lunatics swim (www.leinsteropensea.ie/liffey-swim) 2.2km from Rory O'Moore Bridge to the Custom House – one can't but admire their steel will.

Irish Craft Beer Festival

The country's largest celebration of craft beer (www.irishcraftbeerfestival.ie) has plenty of music, cuisine and, of course, 200-plus craft beers.

Great Dublin Bike Ride

More than 5000 cyclists in shimmering lycra gather for the charity Great Dublin Bike Ride (www.greatdublinbikeride.ie), which has 60km and 100km routes around the city.

September

Summer may be over, but September weather can be surprisingly good, so you can often enjoy the dwindling crowds amid an Indian summer.

All-Ireland Finals

The climax of the year for fans of Gaelic games as the season's most successful county teams battle it out for the All-Ireland championships in hurling and football, on the first and third Sundays in September, respectively.

Culture Night

For one night in September (www.leinsteropensea.ie/liffey-swim), there's free entry to museums, churches, galleries and historic homes throughout the city, which host performances, workshops and talks.

Dublin Fringe Festival

This excellent two-week theatre showcase (p43) precedes Dublin's main theatre festival, with more than 700 performers and 100 events. It's held in the Famous Spiegeltent.

October

The weather starts to turn cold, so it's time to move the fun indoors again. The calendar is still packed with activities and distractions, especially over the last weekend of the month.

Dublin Theatre Festival

Held between the end of September and early October, this is Europe's oldest theatre festival (p43), showcasing the best of Irish and international productions at various locations around town.

Dublin City Marathon

If you fancy a 42km running tour through the streets of Dublin on the last Monday of October (www.sseairtricitydublinmarathon.ie), you'll have to register at least three months in advance. The winner crosses the finishing line on O'Connell St at around 10.30am.

Hard Working Class Heroes

The only showcase (www.hwch.net) in town for unsigned Irish acts, this three-day music festival features 100 bands and musicians playing at venues on and around Camden St on the south side of the city.

Samhain (Hallowe'en)

Tens of thousands take to the city streets on 31 October for a night-time parade, fireworks, street theatre, drinking and music in this traditional pagan festival celebrating the dead, the end of the harvest and the Celtic new year.

November

There's less going on in November. It's too cold for outdoor activities, and everyone is getting ready for Christmas.

December

Christmas in Dublin is a big deal, with everyone looking forward to at least a week's holiday.

Christmas Dip at the Forty Foot

At 11am on Christmas Day, a group of very brave swimmers jump into the icy waters at the Forty Foot, just below the Martello Tower in the southern suburb of Sandycove, for a 20m swim to the rocks and back.

Leopardstown Races

Blow your dough and your post-Christmas crankiness at this historic and hugely popular racing festival at one of Europe's loveliest courses (www.leopardstown.com). Races run from 26 to 30 December.

Travel with Kids

Kid-friendly? You bet. Dublin loves the little 'uns, and will enthusiastically 'ooh' and 'aah' at the cuteness of your progeny. But alas such admiration hasn't fully translated into child services such as widespread and accessible baby-changing facilities.

LARRYDJ/SHUTTERSTOCK ©

Orangutan in Dublin Zoo (p146)

Hands-on Museums

Ark Children's Cultural Centre

If your kids are aged between three and 14, spend an afternoon at Ark Children's Cultural Centre (p118), which runs activities aimed at stimulating participants' interests in science, the environment and the arts – but be sure to book well in advance.

Imaginosity

Only five minutes' walk from the Stillorgan stop on the Luas is **Imaginosity** (www.imaginosity.ie; The Plaza, Beacon South Quarter, Sandyford; adult/child €8/7; ⏰9.30am-5.30pm Tue-Fri, 10am-6pm Sat & Sun, 1.30-5.30pm Mon; 🚸; 🚊Sandyford), the country's only designated interactive museum for kids. Over the course of two hours they can learn, have fun and get distracted by the museum's exhibits and activities.

Dublinia: Experience Viking & Medieval Dublin

There are loads of ways to discover Dublin's Viking past, but Dublinia (p110), the city's Viking and medieval museum, has interactive exhibits that are specifically designed to appeal to younger visitors.

Dublin Zoo

Dublin Zoo

A recommended mobile option is a hop-on, hop-off open-top bus tour (p163), which helps you get your bearings and lets the kids enjoy a bit of Dublin from the top deck. You can use the bus to get to Dublin Zoo (p146), where you can hop aboard the zoo train and visit the animals. There are roughly 400 creatures from 100 different species across eight different habitats, which range from an Asian jungle to a family farm, where kids get to meet the inhabitants up close.

Make a Splash

Viking Splash Tours

Kids of all ages will love Viking Splash Tours (www.vikingsplash.com; Stephen's Green N; ☎01-707 6000; adult/child

Imaginosity

€25/13; ⏱10am-3pm, tours every 30-90min; 🚌all city centre), where you board an amphibious vehicle, put on a plastic Viking hat and roar at passers-by as you do a tour of the city before landing in the water at the Grand Canal basin.

National Aquatic Centre

The AquaZone at the National Aquatic Centre (p49) in Blanchardstown has water roller coasters, wave and surf machines, a leisure pool and all types of flumes to keep the kids happy.

Only in Ireland

National Leprechaun Museum

The National Leprechaun Museum (p154), despite its high-sounding name, is really just a romper room for kids with a little bit of Irish folklore thrown in for good measure. The optical-illusion tunnel (which makes you appear smaller to those at the other end), the room full of oversized furniture, the wishing wells and, invariably, the pot of gold are especially appealing for little ones.

Wide Open Spaces

Dublin's Parks

While it's always good to have a specific activity in mind, don't forget Dublin's parks – from St Stephen's Green (p66) to Merrion Square (p96), from Herbert Park (p172) to Phoenix Park (p146), the city has plenty of green spaces for the kids to run wild in.

NEED TO KNOW

Transport Children under five travel free on all public transport.

Pubs Unaccompanied minors are not allowed in pubs; accompanied children can remain until 9pm (until 10pm from May to September).

Resources Parents with young children should check out www.everymum.ie. An excellent site about family-friendly accommodation is www.babygoes2.com.

Like a Local

Dublin is, depending on your perspective, a small city or a very large village, which makes it at once easy to navigate but difficult to understand. Spend enough time here and you'll realise exactly what we mean.

ANDREW MONTGOMERY/LONELY PLANET ©

Pints of Guinness

'Slagging'

Dubliners are, for the most part, an informal and easy-going lot who don't stand on excessive ceremony and generally prefer not to make too much fuss. Which doesn't mean that they don't abide by certain rules, or that there isn't a preferred way of doing things in the city. But the transgressions of the unknowing are both forgiven and often enjoyed – the accidental faux pas is a great source of entertainment in a city that has made 'slagging', or teasing, a veritable art form. Indeed, slagging is a far more reliable indicator of the strength of friendship than virtually any kind of compliment: a fast, self-deprecating wit and an ability to take a joke in good spirits will win you plenty of friends. Mind you, even slagging has its hidden codes, and is only acceptable among friends: it wouldn't do at all to follow an introduction to someone by making fun of their shoes!

Dublin Accents

Even in a small city like Dublin there is a lot of variation, ranging from suburban dialects that sound faintly American to working-class 'Dublinese' that is nearly incomprehensible to outsiders.

Dartspeak

Aka the D4 accent (after the posh southside postal district). Reminiscent of Home Counties British English and American English and is distinctive for its distorted vowels ('Dort' instead of 'DART'), liberal use of 'like' (pronounced 'loike') and 'right' (pronounced 'roysh') as well as use of upspeak, where every sentence ends with an upwards inflection, like a question.

'Inner City' Accent

Synonymous with working-class Dubliners, the most impenetrable of Dublin dialects, marked by cramped vowels and words that run into each other, coupled with the liberal insertion of extra consonants ('world' pronounced 'wordled'). It is stigmatised as the uneducated accent of the city's poorer quarters, but of all the city's accents it is the closest to the earliest days of modern English and is peppered with curiously old-fashioned, high-brow phrases, such as 'I was mortified' instead of 'I was embarrassed' and 'Pardon me' instead of 'Excuse me'.

Suburban Accent

The easiest accent to understand, this is also the accent of the overwhelming majority of the city's middle-class population. It is self-consciously clear and enunciated, and has its origins in the efforts of post-independence educators to foster a well-spoken accent that was deliberately 'unBritish', instead filtering its clear diction and pronunciation through an Irish voice.

Dubliners & Sport

Dubliners can tell a lot about each other based on their preferred sport and favourite teams.

Gaelic Football

Generally the preserve of the middle-class suburbs of the north side and southwest Dublin, where most of the city's clubs are located. True fans will support not just 'the Dubs' but their local club too; the county championship is a highly competitive affair. The game is also popular in the working-class areas of the north inner city, where supporting Dublin is an expression of local pride.

Football

The most popular game in Dublin has support throughout the city, primarily in working-class and middle-class neighbourhoods, where it is known as 'football' or, simply, 'ball' (as in 'Did you watch the ball last night?'). Although the Dublin-based teams in the League of Ireland have trenchant support, your average football fan in Dublin is also a die-hard supporter of a team in the English Premier League, usually one of Manchester United, Liverpool or Arsenal, but also Aston Villa (particularly among fans born in the late 1970s and early 1980s, who came of age when Dublin legend Paul McGrath played for that team) and, latterly, Manchester City and Chelsea (mostly young fans born since the millennium). Generally speaking, Dubliners who refer to the game as 'soccer' are doing so derisively.

Rugby

The traditional game of the city's elite – love and knowledge of rugby was a telltale indicator of privilege and elevated social status. The most exclusive schools in the city favour rugby over other sports, and to be a Blackrock boy (an exclusive boys school in the southern suburb of the same name) is code for privileged youngster whose greatest ambition is to line out for Ireland while taking a law or medical degree. The advent of professionalism, Ireland's repeated successes at international level and the Celtic Tiger changed all that, however, transforming rugby from an elitist pursuit to a more general expression of national pride (flavoured by the social aspirations that accompanied the disposable wealth of the Celtic Tiger years). The girls' equivalent is hockey, which is played at the most exclusive schools. But, like most sport played by girls in Dublin, it's generally out of the limelight.

The Rounds System

The rounds system – the simple custom whereby someone buys you a drink and you buy one back – is the bedrock of Irish pub culture. It's summed up in the Irish saying: 'It's impossible for two men to go to a pub for one drink'. Nothing will hasten your fall from social grace here like the failure to uphold this pub law. The Irish are extremely generous and one thing they can't abide is tight-fistedness.

Another golden rule about the system is that the next round starts when the first person has finished (or preferably is just about to finish) their drink. It doesn't matter if you're only halfway through your pint; if it's your round, get them in.

Your greatest challenge will probably be trying to keep up with your fellow drinkers, who may keep buying you drinks in every round even when you've still got a collection of unfinished pints in front of you and you're sliding face first down the bar.

NEED TO KNOW

Dinner Time At home, Dubliners dine early, between 6pm and 7pm. When they go out, they usually eat after 7pm.

Rounds If someone buys you a drink, you always need to return the favour – or at least offer to.

Drinking Water Don't bother with bottled water in restaurants; Dublin's tap water is perfectly safe, free and generally excellent.

For Free

Dublin has a reputation for being expensive and there's no doubt you can haemorrhage cash without too much effort. But the good news is you can see and experience much of what's great about Dublin without having to spend a cent.

Museums

The nation's cultural and historical legacy is yours to enjoy at no cost.

National Museum of Ireland

All three Dublin branches of the National Museum – Archaeology (p90), Decorative Arts & History (p149) and Natural History (p97) – are free of charge, and you're welcome to wander in and explore its treasures and fascinating exhibits at your leisure.

National Gallery

The State's proud collection of art, from the Middle Ages up to the modern age, is well represented on the walls of the National Gallery (p94).

Hugh Lane Gallery, Dublin

This extraordinary collection (p144) of modern art (as well as Francis Bacon's studio) are free to peruse.

Irish Museum of Modern Art

Ireland's most important collection of contemporary art (p131) is available to all at no cost.

Chester Beatty Library

The city's foremost small museum (p64) is a treasure trove of ancient books, illuminated manuscripts, precious scrolls and other gorgeous objets d'art.

Science Gallery

Tap into your inner nerd and discover how interesting it all is…for free (p68).

Green Spaces

Dublin is blessed with green spaces, all but one of which is open to the public.

St Stephen's Green

The city's most popular park (p66) is always packed with folks looking to take advantage of the good weather.

Merrion Square

The most elegant of Dublin's free parks (p96) has beautiful lawns, delicate flower beds and a statue of Oscar Wilde (among others).

Iveagh Gardens

A little wilder and not as well known as Dublin's other parks is this bit of countryside smack in the middle of the city (p68).

Phoenix Park

The largest non-wildlife enclosed park (p146) in Europe is huge – big enough to house the Irish president, the American ambassador, the zoo, a herd of fallow deer and more green space than you could ever need.

Herbert Park

Jog, run, walk or play tennis – it's all yours to enjoy (p172).

Grand Canal

It's green in big chunks, and a walk along its banks is one of the more bucolic activities you can engage in in the city centre.

No Cost Tours

Áras an Uachtaráin

Guided tours of the presidential residence (p146) are free.

Irish Museum of Modern Art

Free tours of the artworks (p131) with an expert.

Sandeman's New Dublin Tour

The city guided tour is free (p87); all you have to do is tip.

Beef carpaccio at Chapter One (p159)

Eating

The choice of restaurants in Dublin has never been better. Every cuisine and every trend – from doughnuts on the run to kale with absolutely everything – is catered for, as the city seeks to satisfy the discerning taste buds of its diners.

NEED TO KNOW

Opening Hours

Cafes 8am to 5pm Monday to Saturday

Restaurants Noon to 10pm (or midnight); food service generally ends around 9pm. Top-end restaurants often close between 3pm and 6pm; restaurants serving brunch open around 11am.

Price Ranges

The following price ranges refer to a main course.

€ less than €15

€€ €15 to €30

€€€ more than €30

Booking Tables

You'll need to reserve a table for most city-centre restaurants Thursday to Saturday, and all week for the trendy spots. Most restaurants operate multiple sittings, which means 'Yes, you can have a table at 7pm, but we'll need it back by 9pm'. A recent trend is to adopt a no-reservations policy in favour of a get-on-the-list, get-in-line policy.

Tipping

It's standard to tip between 10% and 12% of the bill, unless the waiter has dumped the dinner in your lap and given you the finger, while the gratuity for exceptional service is only limited by your generosity and/or level of inebriation. If you're really unhappy, don't be afraid to leave absolutely nothing, though it'll rarely come to that.

Traditional Irish breakfast

Local Specialities

It's a wonder the Irish retain their good humour amid the perpetual potato-baiting they endure. But, despite the stereotyping, potatoes are still paramount here and you'll see lots of them on Dublin menus. The mashed-potato dishes colcannon and champ (with cabbage and spring onion respectively) are two of the tastiest recipes you'll find.

Most meals are meat-based, with beef, lamb and pork common options. The most Dublin of dishes is coddle, a working-class concoction of bacon rashers, sausages, onions, potato and plenty of black pepper. More easily available is the national edible icon: Irish stew, the slow-simmered one-pot wonder of lamb, potatoes, onions, parsley and thyme (note no carrots).

The most famous Irish bread, and one of the signature tastes of Ireland, is soda bread. Irish flour is soft and doesn't take well to yeast as a raising agent, so Irish bakers of the 19th century leavened their bread with bicarbonate of soda. Combined with buttermilk, it makes a superbly light-textured and tasty bread, and is often on the breakfast menus at B&Bs. Scones, tarts and biscuits are specialities too.

Irish seafood is considered to be some of the best in the world, with the waters surrounding the island fit to bursting with juicy mackerel, lobsters and oysters. Dublin Bay prawns are deliciously plump, and native oysters are best enjoyed with a pint of Guinness – the chocolate notes in the stout pair perfectly with the salinity of the oysters.

Veggie Bites

Vegetarians (and vegans) are finding it increasingly easier in Dublin, as the capital has veered away from the belief that food isn't food until your incisors have ripped flesh from bone and towards an understanding that healthy eating leads to, well, longer lives.

There's a selection of general restaurants that cater to vegetarians beyond the token dish of mixed greens and pulses – places

SELF-CATERING

Dublin's choice of artisan street and covered markets continues to improve. If you're looking to self-cater, there are some excellent options for supplies, especially south of the river, including Fallon & Byrne (p73), Dollard & Co (p112) and the Temple Bar Food Market (p112) – not to mention a fine selection of cheesemongers and bakeries. North of the river, the traditional Moore Street Market (p162) is the city's most famous, where the colour of the produce is matched by the language of the spruikers.

such as M&L (p157), Yamamori (p76) and Chameleon (p113). The Wednesday night dinner at the Fumbally (p137) always includes a tasty vegetarian option, while Assassination Custard (p136) strikes an even balance between meat and vegetarian dishes.

Solidly vegetarian places include Blazing Salads (p73), with organic breads, Californian-style salads and pizza; Cornucopia (p73), Dublin's best-known vegetarian restaurant, serving wholesome salads, sandwiches and a selection of hot main courses; and Govinda's (p73), an authentic beans-and-pulses place run by the Hare Krishna.

Dynamic Dining in Dublin

It can be hard keeping up with the restaurant scene in Dublin – each week seems to see a spate of new openings (along with another restaurant closing its doors). December 2018 saw five new restaurants open, with one shutting up shop just six weeks after its launch. The government's decision to increase VAT for hospitality services (it had been reduced from 13.5% to 9% in 2011) means that restaurants in particular are feeling the pinch, and it would be no surprise to see more bite the dust.

All of which means things can change in the blink of an eye – even the city's most popular spots can be gone in a heartbeat. On the plus side, there is always a new place to check out, whether you're in the mood for a hearty vegan salad bowl or a steaming bowl of dumplings.

When to Eat

- **Breakfast** Usually eaten before 9am, although hotels and B&Bs will serve until 11am Monday to Friday, and to noon at weekends. Many cafes serve an all-day breakfast.
- **Lunch** Usually a sandwich or a light meal between 12.30pm and 2pm. On weekends Dubliners have a big meal (called dinner) between 2pm and 4pm.
- **Tea** No, not the drink, but the evening meal – also confusingly called dinner. A Dubliner's main daily meal, usually eaten around 6.30pm.

Eating by Neighbourhood

- **Grafton Street & St Stephen's Green** (p71) The best choice of restaurants and cafes in all price brackets.
- **Merrion Square & Around** (p101) Sandwich bars and Michelin-starred gourmet experiences, but little in-between.
- **Temple Bar** (p111) A fine selection of food-as-fuel eateries and international cuisine, including the best Japanese restaurant in town.
- **Kilmainham & the Liberties** (p136) A relative latecomer to the foodie scene, but catching up with an increasing number of excellent choices.
- **North of the Liffey** (p156) A fine selection of cafes, midrange restaurants and international cuisine that's just getting better all the time.
- **Docklands** (p167) A handful of vaguely trendy restaurants.
- **Southside** (p172) Some excellent dining for weekend gourmands.

Lonely Planet's Top Choices

Chapter One (p159) Sublime cuisine, fabulous service and a wonderfully relaxed atmosphere.

Clanbrassil House (p138) Probably the most exciting cooking in Dublin.

Greenhouse (p77) Dreamily innovative – and Michelin-starred.

Pi Pizza (p73) Absolute perfection, with a legion of loyal fans.

Assassination Custard (p136) An unexpected delight.

Best by Budget

€

Fumbally (p137) Great warehouse space with filling sandwiches and good coffee.

Han Sung (p158) Authentic Korean cuisine served up canteen-style.

Coke Lane Pizza (p136) Its pizza and a pint is a (delicious) bargain.

Assassination Custard (p136) Inventive small plates in a teeny cafe.

Oxmantown (p157) Great sandwiches and breakfasts.

€€

Pi Pizza (p73) Probably the best pizza in the city, if not the country.

Clanbrassil House (p138) Family-style dining in a chic neighbourhood restaurant.

Banyi Japanese Dining (p112) The best Japanese food in town.

Fish Shop (p159) Exquisitely fresh seafood at this tiny restaurant.

€€€

Chapter One (p159) The food is sublime; the atmosphere is wonderfully relaxed.

Restaurant Patrick Guilbaud (p102) Perhaps the best restaurant in Ireland, where everything is just right.

Greenhouse (p77) Michelin-starred and marvellous: Irish meets Scandinavian.

Mr Fox (p159) A cool new take on Irish classics, in a gorgeous Georgian setting.

L'Ecrivain (p102) Impeccable French cuisine.

Best Asian

Yamamori (p76) Tasty Japanese classics north and south of the Liffey.

Musashi Noodles & Sushi Bar (p157) Lovely atmosphere, tasty food.

Banyi Japanese Dining (p112) Superb sushi and gorgeously made rolls.

Saba (p74) Thai and Vietnamese classics in a handsome darkwood room.

Sisu Izakaya (p74) Authentic Japanese bar bites.

Best Italian

Da Mimmo's (p156) It's worth heading to North Strand for this wonderfully authentic cuisine.

Pi Pizza (p73) Pizza that's practically perfect in every way.

Terra Madre (p158) A small menu of classic, proper Italian food.

Etto (p101) An ever-changing array of modern Italian dishes.

Manifesto (p172) Gorgeous pizza in a cosy little bistro.

Best Irish Cuisine

Chapter One (p159) Nobody knew Irish cuisine could taste this good!

Clanbrassil House (p138) This intimate bistro is a foodie magnet.

Legal Eagle (p158) The best Sunday roast in town.

Winding Stair (p159) Classic Irish dishes given an elegant twist.

Mr Fox (p159) Exquisite modern Irish cuisine.

Best Quick Bites

Honest to Goodness (p73) Tasty sandwiches and hot stuff to go.

Dublin Pizza Company (p71) Excellent pizza in a couple of minutes.

Soup Dragon (p157) Offers the city's best liquid lunches.

Lemon (p72) Crêpes both savoury and sweet like you'd get in France.

Oxmantown (p157) Breakfast and sandwiches to go.

Best Afternoon Tea

Merrion (p204) Decadent petit fours with an artistic flair.

Shelbourne (p204) A timeless experience.

Westbury Hotel (p203) Afternoon tea with a view of Grafton St.

Best for Lingering

Fumbally (p137) Grab a kombucha and lounge on one of the battered couches.

Third Space (p157) Perpetual refills, great music...is that the time?

L Mulligan Grocer (p158) When you're done eating, stay for the beer.

Michael's (p174) Excellent seafood in a fun, lively setting.

Musicians playing traditional Irish music at O'Donoghue's (p104)

Drinking & Nightlife

If there's one constant about life in Dublin, it's that Dubliners will always take a drink. Come hell or high water, the city's pubs will never be short of customers, and we suspect that exploring a variety of Dublin's legendary pubs and bars ranks pretty high on the list of reasons you're here.

NEED TO KNOW

Opening Hours

Last orders are at 11.30pm from Monday to Thursday, 12.30am on Friday and Saturday and 11pm on Sunday, with 30 minutes' drinking-up time each night. However, many central pubs have secured late licences to serve until 1.30am or even 2.30am (usually pubs that double as dance clubs).

Made to Measure

- When drinking beer the usual measure is a 'pint' (568mL).
- Half a pint is called a 'glass'.
- If you come to Ireland via Britain and drink spirits, watch out: the English measure is a measly 25mL, while in Dublin you get a whopping 35mL, nearly 50% more.

Tipping

The American-style gratuity is not customary in bars. If there's table service, it's polite to give your server the coins in your change (up to €1).

Pubs

The pub – or indeed anywhere people gather to have a drink and a chat – remains the heart of the city's social existence and the broadest window through which you can experience the essence of the city's culture, in all its myriad forms. There are pubs for every taste and sensibility, although the traditional haunts populated by flat-capped pensioners bursting with insightful anecdotes are about as rare as hen's teeth and most Dubliners opt for their favourite among a wide selection of trendy bars, designer boozers and hipster locales. But despair not, for it is not the spit or sawdust that makes a great Dublin pub but the patrons themselves, who provide a reassuring guarantee that Dublin's reputation as the pub capital of the world remains in perfectly safe (if occasionally unsteady!) hands.

Long Hall (p78)

Bars & Clubs

Dubliners like to throw down some dance-floor moves, but for the most part they do it in bars equipped with a late licence, a decent sound system and a space on the floor. It's all changed from even a decade ago, when clubbing was all the rage: these days fewer people pay to simply go dancing, preferring instead the option of dancing in a bar they've been in most of the evening. DJs are an increasingly rare breed, but the ones that thrive usually play it pretty safe; the handful of more creative DJs (including occasional international guests) play in an increasingly restricted number of venues.

The busiest nights are Thursday to Saturday, and most clubs are free if you arrive before 11pm. After that, you'll pay between €5 and €10.

Cafes

Dublin's coffee junkies are everywhere, looking for that perfect barista fix that will kill the cravings until the next one. You can top-up at any of the chains – including that one from Seattle (with multiple branches throughout the city centre) – but we reckon you'll get the best fix at places such as Clement & Pekoe (p82), Brother Hubbard (p157) and Wall and Keogh (p82).

Drinking & Nightlife

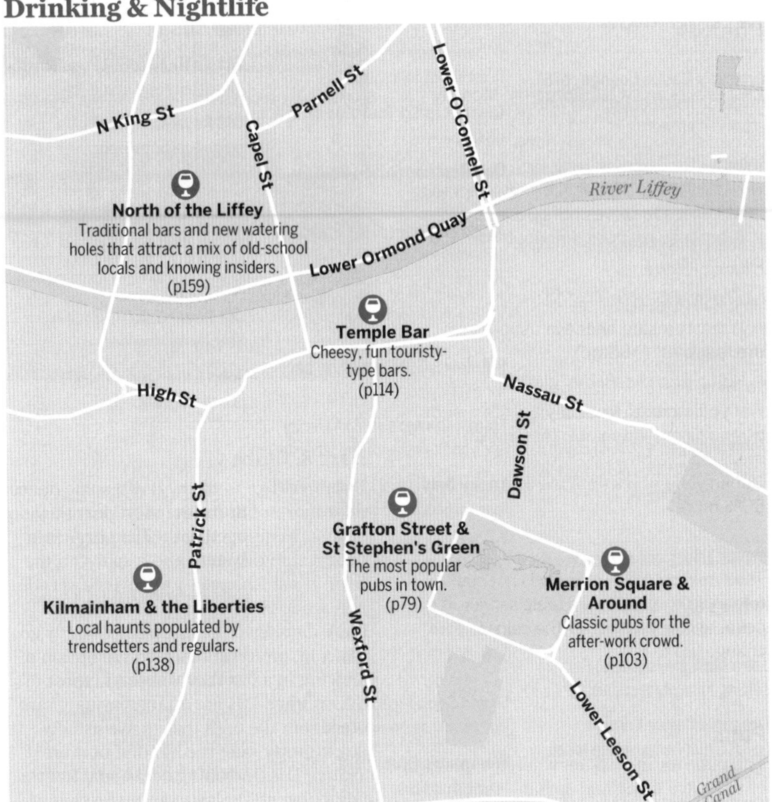

Drinking & Nightlife by Neighbourhood

➡ **Grafton Street & St Stephen's Green** (p78) Biggest choice of bars – from contemporary superpub to traditional pub.

➡ **Merrion Square & Around** (p103) Some beautiful pubs popular with the after-work crowd.

➡ **Temple Bar** (p114) Popular choice of contemporary bars and 'traditional' boozers (strangely devoid of locals but full of Spanish tourists).

➡ **Kilmainham & the Liberties** (p138) A mixture of old-fashioned boozers and trendy new bars.

➡ **North of the Liffey** (p159) Fine choice of old pubs packed with locals and a growing selection of trendy bars.

➡ **Docklands** (p168) Nice mix of older pubs and newer bars popular with sports fans.

➡ **Southside** (p174) Contemporary bars catering to affluent locals.

Lonely Planet's Top Choices

Grogan's Castle Lounge (p78) Favourite haunt of Dublin's writers and painters.

Toner's (p103) Closest thing you'll get to a country pub in the heart of the city.

Kehoe's (p78) Atmospheric pub in the city centre.

Long Hall (p78) One of the city's most beautiful and best-loved pubs.

No Name Bar (p78) Great bar in a restored Victorian townhouse.

John Mulligan's (p168) Established in 1782, this old boozer is still going strong.

Best Pint of Guinness

Kehoe's (p78) Stalwart popular with locals and tourists.

John Mulligan's (p168) Perfect setting for a perfect pint.

Grogan's Castle Lounge (p78) Great because the locals demand it!

Fallon's (p138) Centuries of experience.

Best Choice of Beer

L Mulligan Grocer (p158) A wide range of cask ales.

Porterhouse (p115) Serves its own delicious brews.

Against the Grain (p79) A dizzying selection of craft beers on tap.

P.Mac's (p80) Thirty different IPAs as well as established brews.

Best Musical Pubs

O'Donoghue's (p104) The unofficial HQ of folk music.

Devitt's (p82) Trad music most nights.

Cobblestone (p159) Best sessions in town.

Auld Dubliner (p114) Traditional sessions for tourists.

Best New Bars

9 Below (p79) Super-luxe bar for a fancy cocktail.

Fourth Corner (p138) A trendy spot on the edge of the Liberties.

Lucky Duck (p79) Modern vibes in a gorgeous old building.

Drop Dead Twice (p138) Rowdy and funky, with a BYO cocktail bar.

Best Club Nights

Grand Social (p161) Open, free jazz jam session on Monday.

Workman's Club (p118) Indie, house and disco in different rooms on Friday.

Mother (p118) Disco, electro and pop on Saturday…not for the faint-hearted.

Whelan's (p82) Electric acts on Thursday.

Best Traditional Pubs

John Mulligan's (p168) The gold standard of traditional.

Long Hall (p78) Stylishly old-fashioned.

Hartigan's (p104) The bare essentials.

Stag's Head (p80) Popular with journalists and students.

Old Royal Oak (p138) A proper neighbourhood pub.

Best Local Haunts

Fallon's (p138) The Liberties' favourite bar.

Old Royal Oak (p138) Shh. Strictly for insiders.

John Kavanagh's (p160) A poorly kept secret.

Best Terraces

Bruxelles (p82) Drink next to the statue of Thin Lizzy's Phil Lynott.

Café en Seine (p82) Elegance and heaters.

Pygmalion (p81) A long line of tables that's always lively.

Grogan's Castle Lounge (p78) On-street overspill.

Lucky's (p139) A lively suntrap.

Best DJ Bars

Whelan's (p82) Classic and contemporary rock.

Dice Bar (p161) Dive bar with an eclectic range, from rock to lounge and dance.

Bernard Shaw (p80) Great DJs playing a mix of tunes.

Workman's Club (p118) Regular line-up of excellent DJs.

Wigwam (p161) Basement bar with rockin' DJs.

Gate Theatre (p161)

Entertainment

Believe it or not, there is life beyond the pub. There are comedy clubs and classical concerts, recitals and readings, marionettes and music – lots of music. The other great Dublin treat is the theatre, where you can enjoy a light-hearted musical alongside the more serious stuff by Beckett, Yeats and O'Casey – not to mention a host of new talents.

NEED TO KNOW

Opening Hours

- Doors for most gigs open at 7pm.
- By law, gigs in bigger venues and arenas finish by 11pm.

Bookings

Theatre, comedy and classical concerts are usually booked directly through the venue. Otherwise you can buy through booking agencies such as Ticketmaster (p83), which sells tickets to every genre of big- and medium-sized show – but be aware that it levies a 12.5% service charge.

Newspaper Listings

- *The Herald* (www.herald.ie) The Thursday edition has a good listings page.
- *Hot Press* (www.hotpress.com) Fortnightly music mag; Ireland's answer to *NME* or *Rolling Stone*.
- *Irish Times* (www.irishtimes.com) Friday listings pullout called 'The Ticket'.
- *Irish Independent* (www.independent.ie) 'Night/Day' listings pullout on Friday.

Online Listings

- **Entertainment.ie** (www.entertainment.ie) For all events.
- **MCD** (www.mcd.ie) Biggest promoter in Ireland.
- **Nialler9** (www.nialler9.com) Excellent indie blog with listings.
- **Totally Dublin** (www.totallydublin.ie) Comprehensive listings and reviews.
- **What's On In** (www.whatsonin.ie) From markets to gigs and club nights.

Pre-Theatre Deals

Look out for good-value pre-theatre menus in some restaurants, which will serve dinner before opening curtain and coffee and drinks after the final act.

Live Music

POPULAR

Dubliners love their live music and are as enthusiastic about supporting local acts as they are about cheering touring international stars – even if the latter command the bigger crowds and ticket prices. You can sometimes buy tickets at the venue itself, but you're probably better off going through an agent. Prices for gigs range dramatically, from as low as €5 for a tiny local act to anywhere up to €90 for the really big international stars. The listings sections of both paper and online resources will have all the gigs.

TRADITIONAL & FOLK

The best place to hear traditional music is in the pub, where the 'session' – improvised or scheduled – is still best attended by foreign visitors who appreciate the form far more than most Dubs and will relish any opportunity to drink and toe-tap to some extraordinary virtuoso performances.

Also worth checking out is the **Temple Bar Trad Festival** (www.templebartrad.com; ⏲Jan), which takes place in the pubs of Temple Bar over the last weekend in January. For online info on sessions, check out www.dublinsessions.ie.

CLASSICAL

Classical music is constantly fighting an uphill battle in Dublin, with inadequate funding, poor management and questionable repertoire all contributing to its limited appeal. Resources are appalling, and there's neither the talent nor the funding to match their European counterparts. But before lambasting Ireland's commitment to classical forms, it's well worth bearing in mind that this country has never had a tradition of classical music or lyric opera – the musical talents round these parts naturally focused their attentions on Ireland's homegrown repertoire of traditional music. And still they managed to produce one of the great lyric tenors of the 20th century, Count John McCormack (1884–1945).

But it's not all doom and gloom. Classical music may be small fry, but it survives thanks to the efforts of a number of (subsidised) orchestras and the Opera Theatre Company, which works to keep opera alive.

Theatre

Despite Dublin's rich theatrical heritage, times are tough for the city's thespians. Once upon a time, everybody went to the theatre to see the latest offering by Synge, Yeats or O'Casey. Nowadays a night at the theatre is the preserve of the passionate few, which has resulted in the city's bigger theatres taking a conservative approach to their programming and many fringe companies having to make do with non-theatrical spaces to showcase their skills.

The theatre scene in Dublin is rarely without controversy – in 2019, more than 300 members of the theatre community signed a letter to the Minister for Culture, condemning the way in which the Abbey Theatre has been run since the appointment of new directors in 2016. Concerns were raised about the decrease in Irish-based actors employed by what is the national theatre, founded with the intent of supporting homegrown talent. As a result, it's likely future seasons will focus more on Irish productions, many of which more than hold their own on the world stage.

Theatre bookings can usually be made by quoting a credit-card number over the phone, then you can collect your tickets just before the performance. Expect to pay anything between €12 and €25 for most shows, with some costing as much as €30. Most plays begin between 8pm and 8.30pm. Check www.irishtheatreonline.com to see what's playing.

THEATRE FESTIVALS

For around three weeks between the end of September and early October most of the city's theatres participate in the **Dublin Theatre Festival** (www.dublintheatrefestival.com; ⏲Sep-Oct), originally founded in 1957 and today a glittering parade of quality productions and elaborate shows.

Initially a festival for those shows too 'out there' or insignificant to be considered for the main festival, the **Dublin Fringe Festival** (www.fringefest.com; ⏲Sep) is now a two-week extravaganza with more than 100 events and over 700 performances. The established critics may keep their reviews for the bigger festival, but we strongly recommend the Fringe for its daring and diversity.

Comedy

The Irish have a reputation for hilarity – mostly off-the-cuff, iconoclastic humour – and the funniest of them generally find their way out of Ireland and onto bigger stages. Notable among these are Dara Ó Briain, Dylan Moran and Chris O'Dowd, who's a bona fide star thanks to films such as *Bridesmaids* (2011) and *This Is 40* (2012).

Other big names to look out for include Sharon Horgan, the Irish-born, London-based creator and star of TV sitcoms *Pulling, Catastrophe* and *Divorce,* the last starring Sarah Jessica Parker. Another big talent is David O'Doherty, who's been a festival winner since the early noughties, and is now a regular on the UK comedy TV circuit. Newcomers to the scene include Kildare-born, London-based Aisling Bea, who besides comedy has also starred in crime thriller *The Fall,* and Alison Spittle, who also hosts an excellent eponymous podcast.

Film

Of the five cinemas in the city centre, two (Irish Film Institute and Lighthouse) offer a more offbeat list of foreign releases and art-house films. Save yourself the hassle of queuing and book your tickets online, especially for Sunday-evening screenings of popular first-run films. After drinking sessions on Friday and Saturday nights, most Dubliners have neither the energy nor the cash for more of the same, so it's a trip to the cinema at the end of the weekend. Admission prices are generally €9. If you have a student card, you pay only €6.

Entertainment by Neighbourhood

➡ **Grafton Street & St Stephen's Green** (p82) The entertainment heartland of Dublin has something for everyone.

➡ **Merrion Square & Georgian Dublin** (p104) Quiet at night-time except for the pubs, some of which have live music.

➡ **Temple Bar** (p115) From clubbing to live traditional music, you'll find a version of it in Temple Bar.

➡ **Kilmainham & the Liberties** (p140) The Vicar Street venue is a huge draw for homegrown and international acts.

➡ **North of the Liffey** (p161) Live gigs, traditional music and the city's two most historic theatres dominate the entertainment skyline.

➡ **Docklands** (p169) Make your way eastward along the Liffey to Dublin's biggest theatre.

➡ **Southside** (p175) Only the very biggest acts play the Aviva Stadium, which holds 50,000.

Irish alternative-rock band Delorentos perform at Whelan's (p82)

Lonely Planet's Top Choices

Cobblestone (p159) Best traditional-music sessions in town.

Dublin Fringe Festival (p43) Exciting new theatre.

Gate Theatre (p161) Masterfully presented classics.

Bord Gáis Energy Theatre (p169) Top-class show venue.

Whelan's (p82) For the intimate gig.

Workman's Club (p118) To see the best new bands.

Best Live-Music Venues

Cobblestone (p159) For traditional music.

3 Arena (p169) Big-name acts.

Whelan's (p82) Singer-songwriter HQ.

Workman's Club (p118) Who's cool, right now.

Best Theatres

Gate Theatre (p161) Wonderful old classic.

Project Arts Centre (p118) For interesting fringe plays.

Bord Gáis Energy Theatre (p169) The best indoor venue in town.

Abbey Theatre (p161) A hotbed of talent.

Best High Culture

Abbey Theatre (p161) Top names in Irish theatre.

Bloomsday (p25) Making sense of *Ulysses*.

Culture Night (p27) Art, architecture and heritage.

Best Comedy

Ha'Penny Bridge Inn (p118) Local humour hits and misses.

International Bar (p81) Rising crop of Irish talent, with a great improv night on Mondays.

Laughter Lounge (p162) Established names and visiting acts.

Best Festivals

Dublin Fringe Festival (p43) Best of contemporary theatre.

St Patrick's Festival (p24) A city goes wild.

Temple Bar Trad Festival (p42) One of the best parties of the year.

Taste of Dublin (p26) A weekend of gourmet goodness.

Forbidden Fruit (p25) Excellent alternative-music fest.

Best Busking Spots

Grafton St From hard rock to Japanese *noh*.

Temple Bar Comedy, poetry and earnest guitars.

Henry St Dublin's wannabe hip-hop artists.

Shopping

If it's made in Ireland – or pretty much anywhere else – you can find it in Dublin. Grafton St is home to a range of largely British-owned high-street chain stores; you'll find the best local boutiques in the surrounding streets. On the north side, pedestrianised Henry St has international chain stores, as well as Dublin's best department store, Arnott's.

Traditional Irish Products

Traditional Irish products such as crystal and knitwear remain popular choices, and you can increasingly find innovative modern takes on the classics. But steer clear of the mass-produced junk whose joke value isn't worth the hassle of carting it home on the plane: trust us, there's no such thing as a genuine *shillelagh* (Irish fighting stick) for sale anywhere in town.

Fashion

Men's bespoke tailoring is rather thin on the ground. Designers have tried to instil a sense of classical style in the Dublin male, but the species doesn't seem too interested – any pressed shirt and leather shoe seems to suffice.

There's a burgeoning vintage-shopping scene, with a number of shops in Temple Bar well worth a rummage, and well-curated stalls in the city's various markets, too.

At the other end of the fashion spectrum, you'll find all the knit and tweed you want at Avoca Handweavers (p83).

Markets

In recent years Dublin has gone gaga for markets, but the fluctuating rental crisis has seen many of them pushed from location to location, which means it can be hard to keep track of what's happening where. The best now happen in static businesses, such as at Lucky's (p139) or the George (p81).

Shopping Centres

Dublin offers a handful of 'under the one roof' shopping experiences. North of the Liffey, the Jervis Centre (p162) has a handful of high-street shops, as does the St Stephen's Green Shopping Centre (p86) south of the Liffey. The beautiful Powerscourt Townhouse (p84) is home to a selection of independent boutiques, but by far the biggest centre of them all is the **Dundrum Town Centre** (01-299 1700; www.dundrum.ie; Sandyford Rd; 9am-9pm Mon-Fri, to 7pm Sat, 10am-7pm Sun; 17, 44C, 48A, 75 from city centre, Dundrum, Balally) in the southern suburb of Dundrum, home to more than 100 stores.

Opening Hours

Opening hours are generally 9.30am to 6pm Monday to Wednesday, Friday and Saturday, 9.30am to 8pm Thursday and noon to 6pm Sunday.

Duty-Free

Non-EU residents are entitled to claim VAT (value-added tax) on goods (except books, children's clothing or educational items) purchased in stores operating the Cashback or Taxback return programme. Fill in a voucher at your last point of exit from the EU to arrange refund of duty paid.

Shopping by Neighbourhood

➡ **Grafton Street & St Stephen's Green** (p83) International chains and big stores on main street, and boutiques in the warren of surrounding streets (the Creative Quarter).

➡ **Temple Bar** (p118) Tourist-only tat retailers, weird and wonderful individual boutiques, as well as weekend markets.

➡ **North of the Liffey** (p162) High-street chain stores and easy-access shopping centres.

Cheeses for sale at Sheridan's Cheesemongers (p83)

Lonely Planet's Top Choices

Avoca Handweavers (p83) Irish knits and handicrafts.

Irish Design Shop (p83) Beautifully crafted jewellery, kitchenware and more.

Ulysses Rare Books (p85) For that rare first edition.

Article (p84) Homewares and gift ideas.

Sheridan's Cheesemongers (p83) A proper cheese shop.

Best Markets

Temple Bar Book Market (p120) Rummage through secondhand books.

Cow's Lane Designer Mart (p119) A real market for hipsters: more than 60 of the best clothing, accessory and craft stalls.

Temple Bar Food Market (p112) The city's best open-air food market.

Moore Street Market (p162) Open-air, steadfastly 'Old Dublin' market, with fruit, fish and flowers.

Best Fashion

Louis Copeland (p85) Fabulous suits made to measure, as well as ready-to-wear suits by international designers.

Costume (p85) Exclusive contracts with some of Europe's most innovative designers.

Nowhere (p84) The very latest fashions for young men.

Scout (p119) Stylish, modern basics.

Best Guaranteed Irish

Avoca Handweavers (p83) Our favourite department store in the city has myriad homemade gift ideas.

Irish Design Shop (p83) Wonderful handicrafts carefully sourced.

Barry Doyle Design Jewellers (p84) Exquisite handcrafted jewellery with unique contemporary designs.

Ulysses Rare Books (p85) For that priceless first edition or a beautiful, leather-bound copy of Joyce's *Dubliners*.

Louis Copeland (p85) Dublin's very own top tailor, with made-to-measure suits.

Best Homewares

April and the Bear (p175) Quirky home decor in Rathmines.

Industry (p85) Scandi-style homewares with an Irish touch.

Article (p84) Beautiful tableware and decorative home accessories made by Irish designers.

Avoca Handweavers (p83) Stylish but homey brand of modern Irish life.

RAMSEY CARDY/SPORTSFILE VIA GETTY IMAGES ©

Leinster players in a rugby match against the Glasgow Warriors at RDS Arena

Sports & Activities

To many Dubliners, sport is a religion. For an ever-increasing number, it's all about faith through good works such as jogging, amateur football, cycling and yoga; for everyone else, observance is enough, especially from the living-room chair or the pub stool.

Spectator Sports

Sport has a special place in the Irish psyche, probably because it's one of the few occasions when an overwhelming expression of emotion won't cause those around you to wince or shuffle in discomfort. Sit in a pub while a match is on and watch the punters foam at the mouth as they yell pleasantries at the players on the screen, such as, 'They should pay me for watching you!'

GAELIC FOOTBALL & HURLING

Gaelic games are at the core of Irishness; they are enmeshed in the fabric of Irish life and hold a unique place in the heart of the culture. Of the two main games, gaelic football is by far the most popular – and Dublin (www.dublingaa.ie) is the most dominant team in Ireland at the time of writing, winner of four consecutive All-Ireland Senior Championship titles between 2015 and 2018.

NEED TO KNOW

Sporting Seasons

Football April to November

Gaelic sports April to September

Rugby internationals February to April

Planning Ahead

Two months Tickets for rugby internationals or the latter stages of the Gaelic championship.

One month Leinster rugby matches in the Champions Cup.

One week Local football matches and Gaelic league games.

Online Resources

Gaelic Athletic Association (www.gaa.ie)

Football Association of Ireland (www.fai.ie)

Irish Rugby Football Union (www.irishrugby.ie)

Horse Racing Ireland (www.goracing.ie)

Golf Union of Ireland (www.gui.ie)

Ladies Gaelic Football Association (www.ladiesgaelic.ie)

The big event in both sports is the All-Ireland championship, a knockout contest that begins in April and ends on the first (for hurling) and third (for football) Sunday in September with the All-Ireland Final, played at a jam-packed **Croke Park** (☎01-819 2300; www.crokepark.ie; Clonliffe Rd; 🚌3, 11, 11A, 16, 16A, 123 from O'Connell St), which is also where the Dubs play all of their championship matches. The All-Ireland's poorer cousin is the National Football League (there's also a National Hurling League), which runs from February to mid-April. Dublin plays its league matches at **Parnell Park** (www.dublingaa.ie; Clantarkey Rd, Donnycarney; adult/child €15/5; 🚌20A, 20B, 27, 27A, 42, 42B, 43, 103 from Lower Abbey St or Beresford Pl), which is smaller and infinitely less impressive than Croke Park, though a great place to see games up close. Tickets for league games can be easily bought at the ground; tickets for All-Ireland matches are tougher to get the further on the competition is, but those that are available can be bought online (https://gaa.tickets.ie) or at most Centra and SuperValu convenience stores throughout the city centre.

FOOTBALL

Although Dubliners are football (soccer) mad, the five Dublin teams that play in the League of Ireland (www.leagueofireland.com) are semi-pro, as the best players are all drawn to the glamour of the English Premier League. The season runs from April to November; tickets are available at all grounds.

The national side plays its home games at the Aviva Stadium (p175); a relatively high pricing structure and the general mediocrity of the team means that home matches don't always sell out. You can buy tickets (€30 to €60) from the **Football Association of Ireland** (FAI; ☎01-676 6864; www.fai.ie).

RUGBY

Rugby is a big deal in certain parts of Dublin – generally the more affluent neighbourhoods of south Dublin – and the successes of both provincial side Leinster and the national team have catapulted rugby to the forefront of sporting obsessions. Three-time European champions Leinster play home games at the Royal Dublin Society Showground (p175). Tickets for both competitions are available at the Spar opposite the Donnybrook Rugby Ground or online from Leinster Rugby (www.leinsterrugby.ie).

The premier competition is the yearly Six Nations championship, played between February and April by Ireland, England, Wales, Scotland, France and Italy. Home matches are played at the Aviva Stadium (p175); tickets are available from the IRFU (www.irishrugby.ie).

HORSE & GREYHOUND RACING

Horse racing is a big deal in Dublin, especially when you consider that Irish trainers are among the best in the world and Irish jockeys dominate the field in British racing. There are several racecourses within driving distance of the city centre that host good-quality meetings throughout the year. These include the **Curragh Racecourse** (☎045-441 205; www.curragh.ie; R413, Newbridge; tickets €20; ⏰mid-Apr–Oct), which hosts five classic flat races between May and September; **Fairyhouse** (☎01-825 6167; www.fairyhouse.ie; Fairyhouse Rd, Ratoath; €15-25), home of the Grand National on Easter Monday; and **Leopardstown Racecourse** (☎01-289 0500; www.leopardstown.com; Foxrock, Dublin 18; tickets from €12.75; 🚌special from Eden Quay, 🚊Sandyford), where the big event is February's Hennessy Gold Cup. The flat-racing season runs from March to November, while the National Hunt season – when horses jump over things – is October to April. There are also events in summer.

Greyhound racing has its aficionados, but 2019 revelations about the killing of dogs considered too slow have cast a dark pall over what was traditionally known as the poor-man's punt. Dublin's dog track is Shelbourne Park Greyhound Stadium (p169) in the Docklands.

Golf

A round of golf is a highlight of many an Irish visit. Dublin's suburban courses are almost all private clubs, but many of them allow visitors on a pay-to-play basis. Tough times mean reduced green fees, especially if you book online beforehand. You'll generally need your own transport if you wish to head to any of the major courses.

One of Ireland's best courses is Portmarnock Golf Club (p197), by the sea in North County Dublin; otherwise, there's wonderful golf to be played at **Killeen Castle** (www.killeencastle.com; green fees from €55) in Dunsany, County Meath; **Carton House** (☎01-651 7727; www.cartonhouse.com; green fees from €60), just outside Maynooth in County Kildare; and **Druid's Glen Resort** (☎01-287 0812; www.druidsglenresort.com; Newtownmountkennedy; green fees from €60), 45km south of the city in County Wicklow.

Swimming & Water Sports

Dublin might have miles of beachy coastline, but swimming and water sports aren't as big a deal as they might be in, say, a destination where the climate is more conducive to being wet and outdoors. There are boating aficionados (and designated clubs) in the seaside suburbs of Dun Laoghaire, Howth and Malahide, but when it comes to regular old swimming, there's relatively little choice, although one option is the international-standard **National Aquatic Centre** (☎01-646 4300; www.nationalaquaticcentre.ie; Snugborough Rd; adult/child & student €7.50/5.50, incl AquaZone €16/14; 6am-10pm Mon-Fri, 9am-8pm Sat & Sun; 38 & 38A from O'Connell St). The relatively new sport of cable wakeboarding (waterskiing by holding on to a fixed overhead cable instead of a motorboat) is also available in the Docklands with Wakedock (p169).

Sports & Activities by Neighbourhood

- **Kilmainham & the Liberties** (p141) Jogging and walking in the War Memorial Gardens.
- **North of the Liffey** (p163) Running, football and cycling in Phoenix Park, as well as cricket and polo.
- **Docklands** (p169) Wakeboarding in the Grand Canal Dock, jogging along the canal.

Lonely Planet's Top Choices

- **Fab Food Trails** (p86) Unearthing the best of Dublin's food producers on tasting walks.
- **Green Mile** (p86) A brilliant guided tour of St Stephen's Green.
- **Dublin Musical Pub Crawl** (p120) Pubs, beer and music...the winning trifecta.
- **Howth Summit Walk** (p191) A gorgeous walk with stunning views.
- **Portmarnock Golf Club** (p197) The best golf course in County Dublin.

WOMEN'S FOOTBALL IN DUBLIN

The men's football team might get most of the attention, but the Dublin women's team won All-Ireland finals in 2017 and 2018, with the 2018 final – against a historically brilliant Cork team – attracting 50,141 spectators, the first women's game to break the 50,000 barrier and the most attended women's sport final in the world for that year.

Women's football – or Ladies Gaelic Football, to give it its proper name – is one of the fastest-growing participation sports in Europe. There are over 1000 clubs nationwide, a remarkable achievement given the sport was only properly established in 1974 (curiously, women's football is governed by the Ladies Gaelic Football Association, not the GAA, even though they play by the same rules in the same grounds). The game's growth has accelerated apace in recent years, thanks in part to a cash injection and big promotional push by primary sponsor Lidl, the German supermarket group.

Explore Dublin

Grafton Street & St Stephen's Green . . . 54
Top Sights 56
Sights 66
Eating 71
Drinking & Nightlife 78
Entertainment 82
Shopping. 83
Sports & Activities 86

Merrion Square & Georgian Dublin 88
Top Sights 90
Sights 97
Eating 101
Drinking & Nightlife 103
Entertainment 104
Shopping. 104
Sports & Activities 104

Temple Bar 105
Top Sights 107
Sights 110
Eating 111
Drinking & Nightlife 114
Entertainment 115
Shopping. 118
Sports & Activities 120

Kilmainham & the Liberties 121
Top Sights 123
Sights 133
Eating 136
Drinking & Nightlife 138
Entertainment 140
Shopping. 140
Sports & Activities 141

North of the Liffey 142
Top Sights 144
Sights 149
Eating 156
Drinking & Nightlife 159
Entertainment 161
Shopping. 162
Sports & Activities 163

Docklands 164
Sights 166
Eating 167
Drinking & Nightlife 168
Entertainment 169
Shopping. 169
Sports & Activities 169

The Southside. 170
Sights 172
Eating 172
Drinking & Nightlife 174
Entertainment 175
Shopping. 175

Day Trips from Dublin. 178
Top Sights 179
Howth 189
Enniskerry & Powerscourt Estate 192
Castletown House & Around 193
Dalkey 194
Malahide 196

Sleeping 198

DUBLIN'S TOP SIGHTS

Trinity College 56

Dublin Castle 61

Chester Beatty Library.... 64

National Museum of Ireland – Archaeology 90

National Gallery 94

Merrion Square 96

Christ Church Cathedral 107

Guinness Storehouse & St James's Gate..........123

St Patrick's Cathedral 126

Kilmainham Gaol 129

Irish Museum of Modern Art 131

Hugh Lane Gallery, Dublin 144

Phoenix Park 146

Brú na Bóinne.................179

Glendalough 184

Neighbourhoods at a Glance

1 Grafton Street & St Stephen's Green p54

Busy, pedestrianised Grafton St is both the city's most famous street and its unofficial centre. You'll find the biggest range of pubs, shops and restaurants in the bustling hive that surrounds it. Many of the city's most important sights and museums are here, as is Dublin's best-loved city park, St Stephen's Green (p66).

2 Merrion Square & Around p88

Georgian Dublin's apotheosis occurred in the exquisite architecture and elegant spaces of Merrion and Fitzwilliam Sqs. Here you'll find the perfect mix of imposing public buildings, museums, and private offices and residences. It is round these parts that much of moneyed Dublin works and plays, amid the neoclassical beauties thrown up during Dublin's 18th-

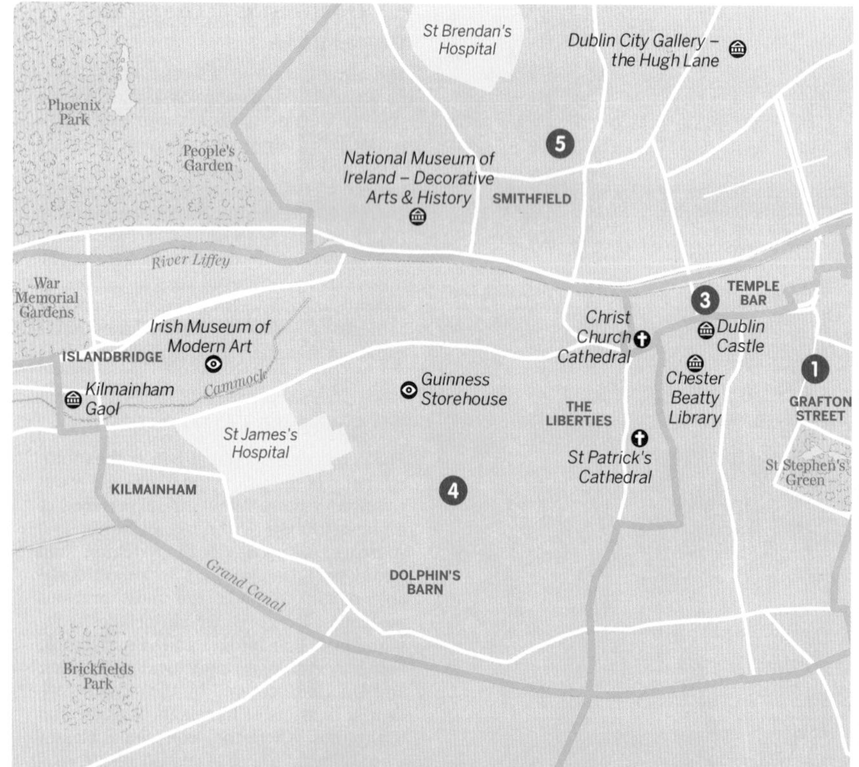

century prime. These include the home of the Irish parliament at Leinster House and, the National Gallery, the main branch of the National Museum of Ireland and the Museum of Natural History.

3 Temple Bar p105

Dublin's best-known district is the cobbled playpen of Temple Bar, where mayhem and merriment is standard fare, especially on summer weekends when the pubs are full and the party spills out onto the streets. During daylight hours there are shops and galleries to discover, which at least lend some truth to the area's much-mocked title of 'cultural quarter'.

4 Kilmainham & the Liberties p121

Dublin's oldest and most traditional neighbourhoods, immediately west of the south city centre, have a handful of tourist big hitters, not least the Guinness Storehouse, Dublin's most-visited museum. Keeping watch over the ancient Liberties is St Patrick's Cathedral, the most important of Dublin's three (!) cathedrals, while further west is the country's premier modern-art museum and a Victorian prison that played a central role in Irish history.

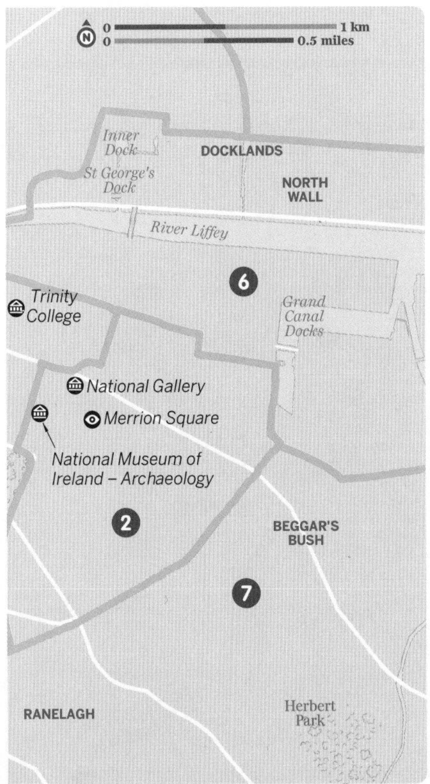

5 North of the Liffey p142

Grittier than its more genteel southside counterpart, the area immediately north of the River Liffey offers a fascinating mix of 18th-century grandeur, traditional city life and the multicultural melting pot that is contemporary Dublin. Beyond its widest, most elegant boulevard you'll find art museums and whiskey museums, bustling markets and some of the best ethnic eateries in town. Oh, and Europe's largest enclosed park (p146) – home to the president, the US ambassador and the zoo.

6 Docklands & the Grand Canal p164

The gleaming modern blocks of the Docklands were first laid during the Celtic Tiger years of the late 1990s and came to a stuttering halt following the crash but have continued apace since then. Home to digital tech giants including Google, Facebook, Twitter and LinkedIn, the stretch from the Irish Financial Services Centre (IFSC) down to Grand Canal Dock on both sides of the Liffey has been dubbed the Silicon Docks. A couple of architectural beauties – notably a theatre designed by Daniel Libeskind – stand out among the modern buildings.

7 Southside p170

The neighbourhoods that border the southern bank of the Grand Canal are less about sights and more about the experience of affluent Dublin – dining, drinking and sporting occasions, both watching and taking part. Here are the city's most desirable neighbourhoods and most precious postcodes: Dublin 4, which includes fancy schmancy Ballsbridge and Donnybrook, home to embassies and local potentates; and Dublin 6, covered by the elegant residential districts of Ranelagh, Rathgar and Rathmines, where the professional classes who still want a slice of city life reside.

Grafton Street & St Stephen's Green

Neighbourhood Top Five

❶ **Chester Beatty Library** (p64) Basking quietly in the aesthetic glow of the magnificent collection at one of the finest museums in Ireland.

❷ **Old Library & Book of Kells** (p66) Staring in wonderment at the colourful pages of the *Book of Kells,* the world's most famous illuminated gospel, before visiting the majestic Long Room.

❸ **St Stephen's Green** (p66) Enjoying a sunny, summer afternoon on the grass, where Dubliners come to rest, romance and remind themselves of what makes life worth living.

❹ **Little Museum of Dublin** (p66) Exploring the marvellous collection of donated historical objects.

❺ **A Night Out** (p78) Eating dinner in one of the area's fabulous restaurants followed by a pint or more in a pub, such as Kehoe's.

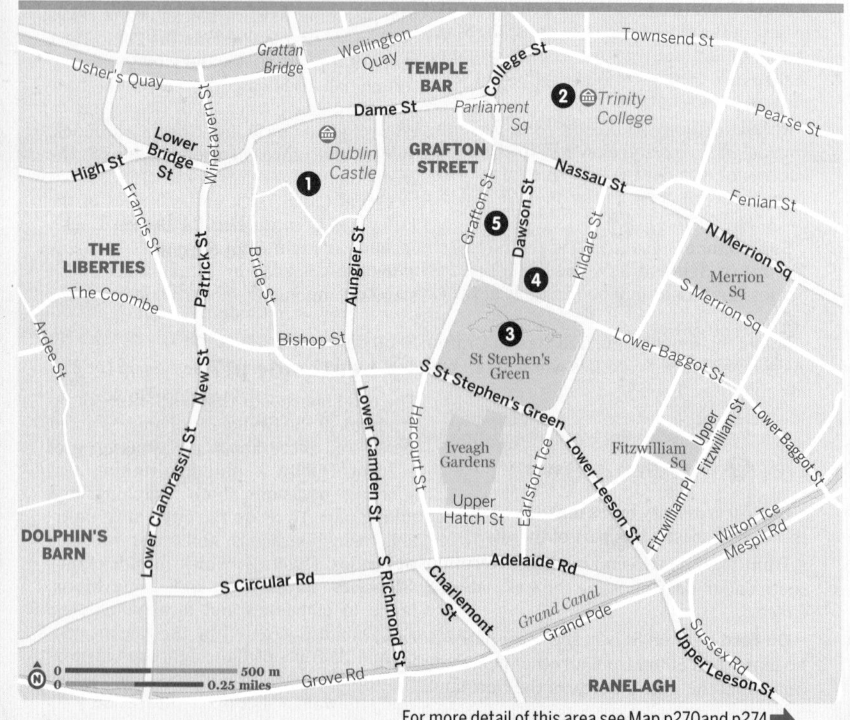

For more detail of this area see Map p270and p274

Explore Grafton Street & St Stephen's Green

Grafton St and its surrounding precinct are something of a flexible feast of activities and sights, but it'll take you two days to even begin to do them justice – and much longer if you really want to get to the heart of what this part of the city is all about. The main attraction is Trinity College (p56), whose pleasures and treasures can be explored in no more than a couple of hours; right on its doorstep is Grafton St itself, always worth an amble for a little retail experience or just to take in the sound of one of its many buskers.

Just south of Grafton St is the centrepiece of Georgian Dublin, St Stephen's Green (p66), beautifully landscaped and dotted with statuary that provides a veritable who's who of Irish history. But to really get the most out of the neighbourhood, you'll need to get off Grafton St and into the warren of narrow lanes and streets to the west of it – here you'll find a great mix of funky shops and boutiques, some of our favourite restaurants, and a handful of the best bars in the city. Further west again are Dublin Castle (p61) and the Chester Beatty Library (p64), both of which can be explored in half a day.

Local Life

- **Hang-Outs** Grogan's Castle Lounge (p78) is the artiest of the city's bohemian pubs; the Stag's Head (p80) is a Victorian classic; sit at the window in fashionable Clement & Pekoe (p82) and watch the fashion parade outside.
- **Retail** Costume (p85) is the place for high-end women's fashions and Nowhere (p84) the men's equivalent; wander the boutiques of the Powerscourt Townhouse (p84) for quirky one-offs and local fashions, like Chupi (p83).
- **Sustenance** Bunsen (p72) is great for a burger, and Pi Pizza (p73) might serve the tastiest pizzas in town, but for sumptuous fare book a table at the Greenhouse (p77).
- **Music** Buskers provide free gigs on Grafton St all day every day; Whelan's (p82) is where those buskers would like to graduate to.

Getting There & Away

- **Bus** All cross-city buses make their way to – or through, at least – this part of the city.
- **Tram** The Luas Green Line has its terminus at the south end of Grafton St, on the west side of St Stephen's Green.
- **On Foot** Grafton St is in the heart of the city and no more than 500m from all other neighbourhoods (including the western edge of the Docklands).

Lonely Planet's Top Tip

The most interesting shops in town are in the warren of streets between Grafton and South Great George's Sts; here you'll also find some of the best lunch deals.

- Pi Pizza (p73)
- Featherblade (p74)
- Greenhouse (p77)
- Richmond (p74)
- Pichet (p76)

For reviews, see p71

- Grogan's Castle Lounge (p78)
- No Name Bar (p78)
- Long Hall (p78)
- Lucky Duck (p79)
- Kehoe's (p78)
- Farrier & Draper (p80)

For reviews, see p78

- Article (p84)
- Costume (p85)
- Chupi (p83)
- Irish Design Shop (p83)
- Ulysses Rare Books (p85)

For reviews, see p83

TOP SIGHT
TRINITY COLLEGE

This calm and cordial retreat from the bustle of contemporary Dublin is Ireland's most prestigious university, a collection of elegant Georgian and Victorian buildings, cobbled squares and manicured lawns that is among the most delightful places to wander.

DON'T MISS

- Long Room
- *Book of Kells*
- Science Gallery
- Walking Tour

PRACTICALITIES

- Map p270, F2
- ☎01-896 1000
- www.tcd.ie
- College Green
- admission free
- ⏲8am-10pm
- 🚌all city centre, 🚊Westmoreland or Trinity

History

The college was established by Elizabeth I in 1592 on land confiscated from an Augustinian priory in an effort to stop the brain drain of young Protestant Dubliners, who were skipping across to continental Europe for an education and becoming 'infected with popery'. Trinity went on to become one of Europe's most outstanding universities, producing a host of notable graduates – how about Jonathan Swift, Oscar Wilde and Samuel Beckett at the same alumni dinner?

Front Square & Parliament Square

The elegant **Regent House entrance** on College Green is guarded by statues of the writer **Oliver Goldsmith** (1728–74) and the orator **Edmund Burke** (1729–97). The railings outside are a popular meeting spot.

Through the entrance, past the Students Union, are Front Sq and Parliament Sq, the latter dominated by the 30m-high **Campanile,** designed by Edward Lanyon and erected from 1852 to 1853 on what was believed to be the centre of the monastery that preceded the college. According to superstition, students who pass beneath it when the bells toll will fail their exams. To the north of the Campanile is a statue of **George Salmon**, the college provost from 1886 to 1904, who fought bitterly to keep women out of the college. He carried out his threat to permit them in 'over his dead body' by dropping dead when the worst happened. To the south of the Campanile is a statue of historian **WEH Lecky** (1838–1903).

Chapel & Dining Hall

North of Parliament Sq is the 1798 **Chapel** (☎01-896 1260; ⌚8.30am-5pm, admission by special permission only), designed by William Chambers and featuring fine plasterwork by Michael Stapleton, Ionic columns and painted-glass windows. It has been open to all denominations since 1972 and is only accessible by organised tour. Next is the **Dining Hall** (⌚closed to public), originally built by Richard Cassels in the mid-18th century. The great architect must have had an off day because the vault collapsed twice and the entire structure was dismantled 15 years later. The replacement was completed in 1761 and extensively restored after a fire in 1984.

Library Square

On the far east of Library Sq, the red-brick **Rubrics Building** (⌚closed to public) dates from around 1690, making it the oldest building in the college. Extensively altered in an 1894 restoration, it underwent serious structural modification in the 1970s.

If you are following the less-studious-looking throng, you'll find yourself drawn south of Library Sq to the Old Library (p66), home to Trinity's prize possession and biggest crowd-puller, the astonishingly beautiful *Book of Kells*.

Upstairs is the highlight of Thomas Burgh's building, the magnificent 65m Long Room with its barrel-vaulted ceiling. It's lined with shelves containing 200,000 of the library's oldest manuscripts, busts of scholars, a 14th-century harp and an original copy of the Proclamation of the Irish Republic.

Fellows' Square

West of the brutalist, brilliant **Berkeley Library** (Fellows' Sq; ⌚closed to public;), designed by Paul Koralek in 1967, the **Arts & Social Science Building** (closed to public) is home to the Douglas Hyde Gallery of Modern Art (p68), one of the country's leading contemporary galleries. It hosts regularly rotating shows presenting the works of top-class Irish and international artists across a range of media.

Examination Hall

On the way back towards the main entrance, past the Reading Room, is the late 18th-century Palladian **Examination Hall** (⌚9am-6pm during exams only), which closely resembles the chapel opposite because it too was the work of William Chambers. It

A CATHOLIC BAN

Trinity was exclusively Protestant until 1793, but even when the university relented and began to admit Catholics, the Catholic Church forbade it; until 1970 any Catholic who enrolled here could consider themselves excommunicated.

A great way to see the grounds is on a walking tour (p87), departing from the College Green entrance.

SWORD & GUNS

For nearly two centuries students weren't allowed through the grounds without a sword – and duels with pistols were not uncommon in the 17th and 18th centuries.

Book a fast-track ticket online to get cheaper and speedier access to the Book of Kells and the Long Room.

Trinity College, Dublin

STEP INTO THE PAST

Ireland's most prestigious university, founded by Queen Elizabeth I in 1592, is an architectural masterpiece, mostly of the 18th and 19th centuries, and a cordial retreat from the bustle of modern life in the middle of the city. Step through its main entrance and you step back in time, the cobbled stones transporting you to another era, when the elite discussed philosophy and argued passionately in favour of empire.

Standing in Front Square, the 30m-high ❶ **Campanile** is directly in front of you with the ❷ **Dining Hall** to your left. On the far side of the square is the Old Library building, the centrepiece of which is the magnificent ❸ **Long Room**, which was the inspiration for the computer-generated imagery of the Jedi Archive in *Star Wars Episode II: Attack of the Clones*. Here you'll find the university's greatest treasure, the ❹ **Book of Kells**. You'll probably have to queue to see this masterpiece, and then only for a brief visit, but it's very much worth it.

Just beyond the Old Library is the very modern ❺ **Berkeley Library**, which nevertheless fits perfectly into the campus' overall aesthetic. Directly in front of it is the distinctive ❻ **Sphere Within a Sphere**, the most elegant of the university's sculptures.

DON'T MISS

- ➡ Douglas Hyde Gallery, the campus' designated modern-art museum.
- ➡ A cricket match on the pitch, the most elegant of pastimes.
- ➡ A pint in the Pavilion Bar, preferably while watching the cricket.
- ➡ A visit to the Science Gallery, where science is made completely relevant.

Campanile
Trinity College's most iconic bit of masonry was designed in the mid-19th century by Sir Charles Lanyon; the attached sculptures were created by Thomas Kirk.

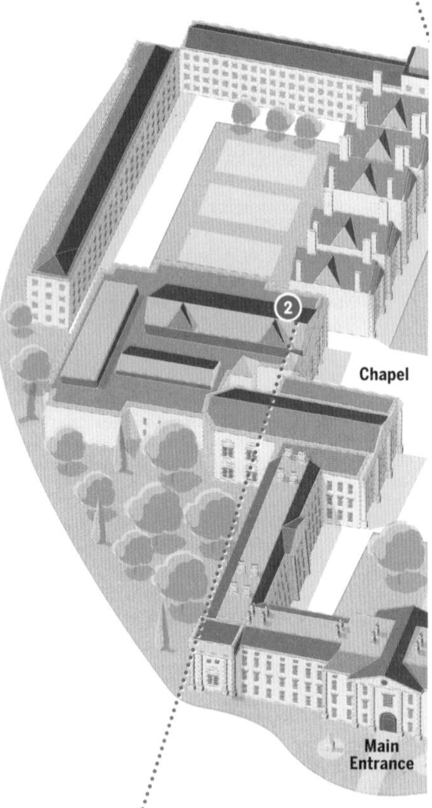

Dining Hall
Richard Cassels' original building was designed to mirror the Examination Hall directly opposite on Front Square: the hall collapsed twice and was rebuilt from scratch in 1761.

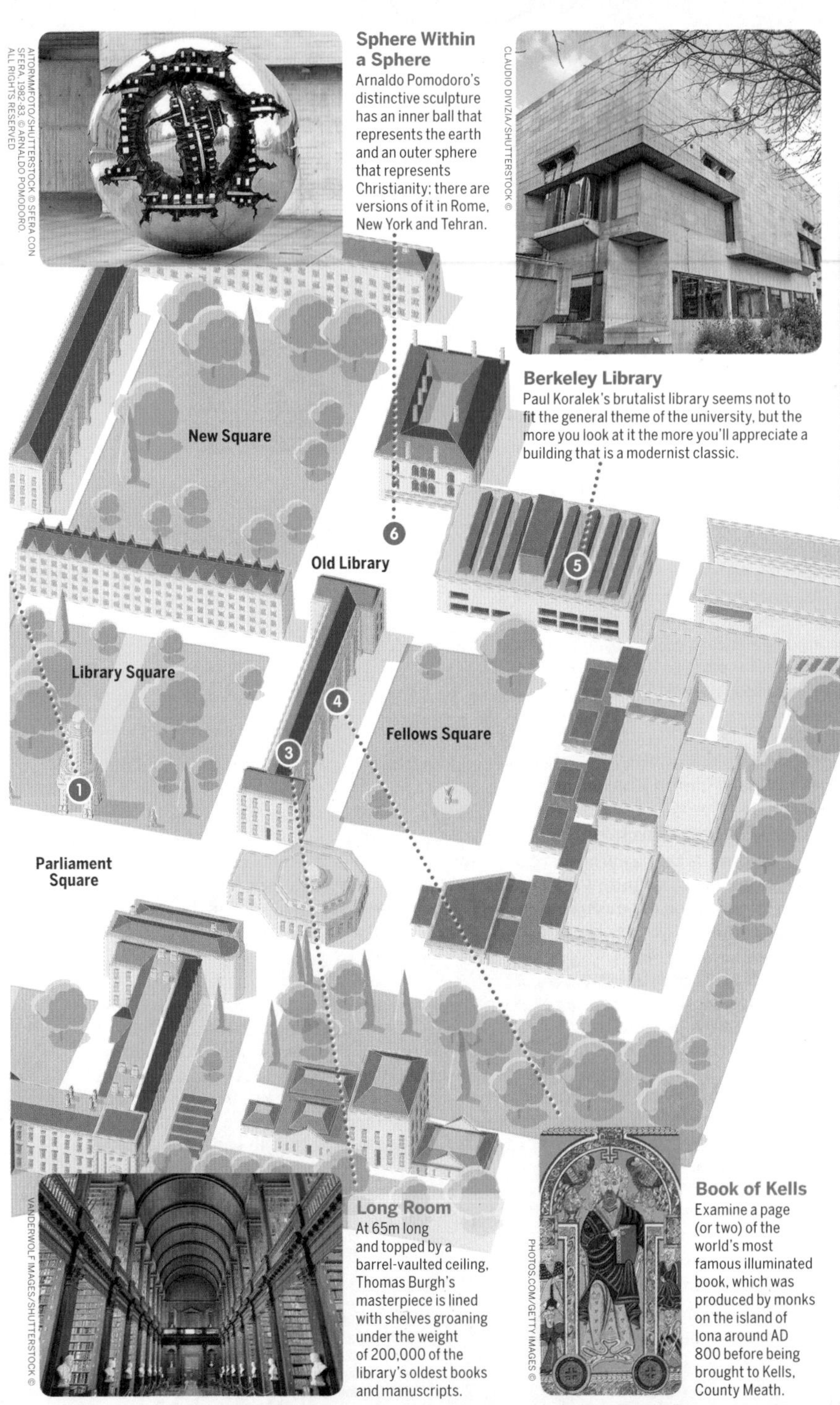

Sphere Within a Sphere
Arnaldo Pomodoro's distinctive sculpture has an inner ball that represents the earth and an outer sphere that represents Christianity; there are versions of it in Rome, New York and Tehran.

Berkeley Library
Paul Koralek's brutalist library seems not to fit the general theme of the university, but the more you look at it the more you'll appreciate a building that is a modernist classic.

Long Room
At 65m long and topped by a barrel-vaulted ceiling, Thomas Burgh's masterpiece is lined with shelves groaning under the weight of 200,000 of the library's oldest books and manuscripts.

Book of Kells
Examine a page (or two) of the world's most famous illuminated book, which was produced by monks on the island of Iona around AD 800 before being brought to Kells, County Meath.

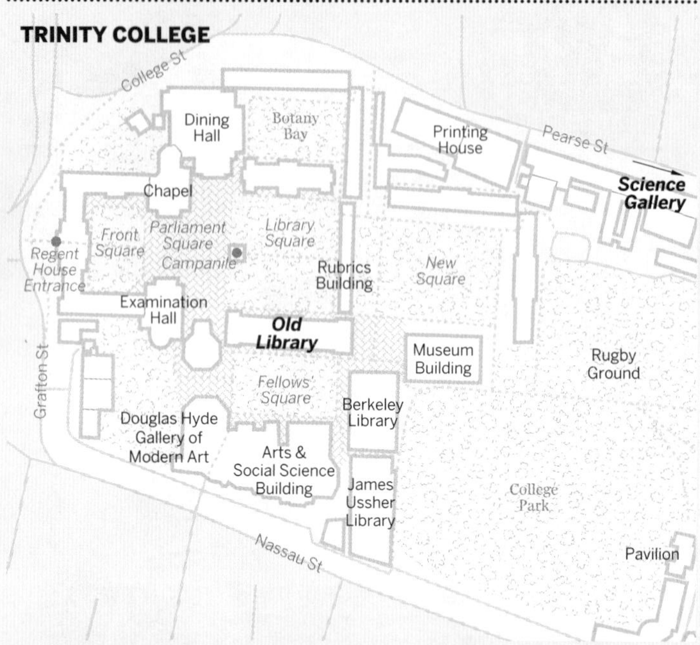

contains an oak chandelier rescued from the original Irish parliament building (now the Bank of Ireland).

College Park

Towards the eastern end of the complex, College Park is a lovely place to lounge around on a sunny day and occasionally you'll catch a game of cricket, a bizarre sight in Ireland. Keep in mind that **Lincoln Place Gate** is located in the southeast corner of the grounds, providing a handy shortcut to Merrion Sq.

Science Gallery

Although it's part of the campus, you'll have to walk along Pearse St to get into Trinity's newest attraction, the Science Gallery (p68). Since opening in 2008, it has proven immensely popular with everyone for its refreshingly lively and informative exploration of the relationship between science, art and the world we live in. Exhibits have touched on a range of fascinating topics including the science of desire and an exploration of the relationship between music and the human body. The ground-floor cafe (p68), bathed in floor-to-ceiling light, is a pretty good spot to take a load off.

SERGEY-73/SHUTTERSTOCK ©

TOP SIGHT
DUBLIN CASTLE

If you're looking for a medieval castle straight out of central casting you'll be disappointed; the stronghold of British power here for 700 years is principally an 18th-century creation that is more hotchpotch palace than turreted castle.

DON'T MISS

- Chapel Royal
- State Apartments
- Upper Yard

PRACTICALITIES

- Map p274, A2
- 01-645 8813
- www.dublincastle.ie
- Dame St
- guided tours adult/child €12/6, self-guided tours €8/4
- 9.45am-5.45pm, last admission 5.15pm
- all city centre

History

Only the Record Tower survives from the original Anglo-Norman fortress, which was built in the early 13th century and served as the centre of English colonial administration until 1922.

When Henry VIII's firm-handed representative in Ireland, Lord Deputy Henry Sidney, took charge in 1565, he declared the castle to be 'ruinous, foul, filthy and great decayed' – and he wasn't far wrong. Until then most of the king's deputies in Ireland had been Anglo-Irish lords who preferred living in their own castles than taking up residence at Dublin Castle, and so it fell into disrepair. Sidney oversaw a 13-year building program that saw the construction of 'a verie faire house for the Lord Deputie or Chief Governor to reside in' as well as a new chapel and the Clock Tower.

Sidney's new castle became the permanent residence of the monarch's chief representative – known at different times as the Justiciar, Chief Lieutenant, Lord Lieutenant or Viceroy – until the construction of the vice-regal lodge in Phoenix Park in 1781 (now Áras an Uachtaráin, the residence of the president).

The new castle reflected the changing status of English power in Ireland – Henry's conquest of the whole island ('beyond the Pale') and his demolition of the old Anglo-Irish hegemony resulted in the castle no longer being a colonial outpost but the seat of English

CASTLE CATHOLICS

Until independence, Catholic Dubliners who were deemed to be too friendly with or sympathetic to the British crown were derisively termed 'Castle Catholics'.

The only way you'll get to see the castle's most interesting bits is by guided tour. The castle is occasionally used for government functions, so parts may be closed to the public.

HIGH SOCIETY

During British rule the castle's social calendar was busiest for the six weeks leading up to St Patrick's Day, with a series of lavish dinners, receptions and balls for the city's aristocratic residents – even during the Famine years.

power and the administrative centre for all of Ireland – a new role that brought with it a huge civil service.

The Irish parliament met in the Great Hall, which burnt down (along with most of the rest of the castle) in the great fire of 1684 – the parliament eventually moved in 1731 to what is now the Bank of Ireland building in College Green.

Below ground, the castle dungeons were home to the state's most notorious prisoners, including – most famously – 'Silken' Thomas Fitzgerald, whose defeated challenge to Henry VIII in 1534 kicked off Henry's invasion of Ireland in the first place. Needless to say, the native Irish came to view the castle as the most menacing symbol of their oppressed state.

When it was officially handed over to Michael Collins on behalf of the Irish Free State in 1922, the British viceroy is reported to have rebuked Collins for being seven minutes late. Collins replied, 'We've been waiting 700 years, you can have the seven minutes'. The castle is now used by the Irish government for meetings and functions, and can only be visited on a guided tour.

Chapel Royal

As you walk into the grounds from the main Dame St entrance, there's a good example of extravagant 19th-century Irish architecture: on your left is the Victorian Chapel Royal (occasionally part of the Dublin Castle tours), decorated with more than 90 heads of various Irish personages and saints carved out of Tullamore limestone. The interior is wildly exuberant, with fan vaulting alongside quadripartite vaulting, wooden galleries, stained glass and lots of lively looking sculpted angels.

Upper Yard

The Upper Yard enclosure roughly corresponds with the dimensions of the original medieval castle. On your right is a Figure of Justice with her back turned to the city, reckoned by Dubliners to be an appropriate symbol for British justice. Next to it is the **Bedford Tower**, built in 1761 on the site of the original Norman gate. The Irish Crown Jewels were stolen from the tower in 1907 and never recovered.

Guided Tours

The 70-minute **guided tours** (departing every 20 to 30 minutes, depending on numbers) are pretty dry, seemingly pitched at tourists more likely to ooh and aah over period furniture than historical anecdotes, but they're included in the entry fee. You get to visit

DUBLIN CASTLE

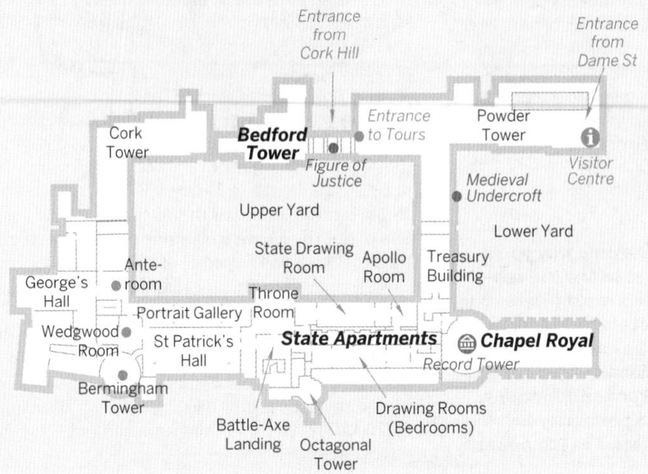

the **State Apartments**, many of which are decorated in dubious taste. There are beautiful chandeliers (ooh!), plush Irish carpets (aah!), splendid rococo ceilings, a Van Dyck portrait and the throne of King George V. You also get to see **St Patrick's Hall**, where Irish presidents are inaugurated and foreign dignitaries toasted, and the room in which the wounded James Connolly was tied to a chair while convalescing after the 1916 Easter Rising – brought back to health to be executed by firing squad.

The highlight is a visit to the **medieval undercroft** of the old castle, discovered by accident in 1986. It includes foundations built by the Vikings (whose long-lasting mortar was made of ox blood, eggshells and horsehair), the hand-polished exterior of the castle walls that prevented attackers from climbing them, the steps leading down to the moat and the trickle of the historic River Poddle, which once filled the moat on its way to join the Liffey.

The Rest of the Castle

Beside the Victorian Chapel Royal is the Norman **Record Tower**, the last intact medieval tower in Dublin. On your right is the Georgian **Treasury Building**, the oldest office block in Dublin, and behind you, yikes, is the uglier-than-sin **Revenue Commissioners Building** of 1960.

TOP SIGHT
CHESTER BEATTY LIBRARY

The world-famous Chester Beatty Library, housed in the Clock Tower at the back of Dublin Castle (p61), is not just Ireland's best small museum, but one of the best you'll find anywhere in Europe.

This extraordinary collection, so lovingly and expertly gathered by New York mining magnate Alfred Chester Beatty, is breathtakingly beautiful and virtually guaranteed to impress.

Alfred Chester Beatty

An avid traveller and collector, Alfred Chester Beatty (1875–1968) was fascinated by different cultures and amassed more than 20,000 manuscripts, rare books, miniature paintings, clay tablets, costumes and any other objets d'art that caught his fancy and could tell him something about the world. Fortunately for Dublin, he also happened to take quite a shine to the city and made it his adopted home. In return, the Irish made him their first honorary citizen in 1957.

Arts of the Book

The collection is spread over two levels. On the ground floor you'll find *Arts of the Book,* a compact but stunning collection of artworks from the Western, Islamic and East Asian worlds. Highlights include the finest collection of Chinese jade books in the world and illuminated European texts featuring exquisite calligraphy that stand up in comparison with the *Book of Kells.* Audiovisual displays explain the process of bookbinding, paper-making and printing.

DON'T MISS

- Nara e-hon scrolls (East Asian Collection, Sacred Traditions)
- Ibn al-Bawwab Qu'ran (Qu'ran Collection, Sacred Traditions)
- New Testament papyri (Western Collection, Sacred Traditions)

PRACTICALITIES

- Map p274, A2
- 01-407 0750
- www.cbl.ie
- Dublin Castle
- admission free
- 10am-5pm Mon-Fri, from 11am Sat & Sun Mar-Oct, 10am-5pm Tue-Fri, from 11am Sat & Sun Nov-Feb
- all city centre

Sacred Traditions

The 2nd floor is home to *Sacred Traditions,* a wonderful exploration of the world's major religions through decorative and religious art, enlightening text and a cool cultural-pastiche video at the entrance. The collection of Qu'rans dating from the ninth to the 19th centuries (the library has more than 270 of them; see example pictured) is considered by experts to be the best example of illuminated Islamic texts in the world. There are also outstanding examples of ancient papyri, including renowned Egyptian love poems from the 12th century, and some of the earliest illuminated gospels in the world, dating from around AD 200. The collection is rounded off with some exquisite scrolls and artwork from China, Japan, Tibet and Southeast Asia, including the two-volume Japanese *Chogonka Scroll,* painted in the 17th century by Kano Sansetu.

The Building

As if all of this wasn't enough for one visit, the library also hosts temporary exhibits that are usually too good to be missed. Not only are the contents of the museum outstanding, but the layout, design and location are also unparalleled, from the marvellous **Silk Road Café** (www.silkroadkitchen.ie; mains €12; ⏲10am-4.45pm Mon-Fri, from 11am Sat, from 1pm Sun May-Oct, closed Mon Nov-Apr) and **gift shop** (☎01-407 0753; www.chesterbeatty.ie; ⏲10am-5pm Mon-Fri, from 11am Sat, from 1pm Sun, closed Mon Nov-Feb) to the Zen rooftop terrace and the beautiful landscaped garden out the front. These features alone would make this an absolute Dublin must-do.

THE YOUNG PHILATELIST

Beatty's main collecting activity began in Denver between 1898 and 1905, where he amassed an impressive, prize-winning collection of stamps that chronicled the early postal history of the United States.

There are free public tours of the museum on Wednesday at 1pm,Saturday at 2pm and Sunday at 3pm. The museum hosts a series of free lunchtime talks; check the website for details.

INSIDE JOB

Between 1983 and 1989 the library's Islamic curator, Dr David James (1941–2012), stole manuscripts from the collection valued at nearly £500,000. Most of them were recovered with his help, however. He was nevertheless convicted of theft and served time in prison for the crime.

The garden atop the building is a slice of serenity in the middle of the city.

SIGHTS

If you were to limit your sightseeing to only one neighbourhood, this would be it. Not that we'd recommend anything of the sort, of course, but there's enough to see in the Grafton St area to give you more than a decent flavour of Dublin. From leafy Trinity College and the unmissable *Book of Kells* to St Stephen's Green and the exquisite Little Museum of Dublin, there's enough to keep you in wonder for much of your Dublin visit.

TRINITY COLLEGE — HISTORIC BUILDING

See p56.

DUBLIN CASTLE — HISTORIC BUILDING

See p61.

CHESTER BEATTY LIBRARY — MUSEUM

See p64.

★OLD LIBRARY & BOOK OF KELLS — LIBRARY

Map p270 (www.tcd.ie; Library Sq; adult/student/family €11/11/28, fast-track €14/11/28; 8.30am-5pm Mon-Sat, from 9.30am Sun May-Sep, 9.30am-5pm Mon-Sat, noon-4.30pm Sun Oct-Apr; all city centre, Westmoreland or Trinity) Trinity's greatest treasures are found within the Old Library, built by Thomas Burgh between 1712 and 1732. The star of the show is the Book of Kells (p69), a breathtaking, illuminated manuscript of the four Gospels of the New Testament, created around AD 800 by monks on the Scottish island of Iona, but more stunning still is the 65m **Long Room**, the library's main chamber, which houses around 200,000 of the library's oldest volumes.

Other displays include a rare copy of the **Proclamation of the Irish Republic**, read out by Pádraig Pearse at the beginning of the Easter Rising in 1916, as well as the so-called **harp of Brian Ború**, which was definitely not in use when the army of this early Irish hero defeated the Danes at the Battle of Clontarf in 1014. It does, however, date from around 1400, making it one of the oldest harps in Ireland.

Your entry ticket also includes admission to temporary exhibitions on display in the East Pavilion. The Old Library gets very busy during the summer months, so it's recommended to go online and buy a **fast-track ticket**, which gives timed admission to the exhibition and allows visitors to skip the queue. You'll still get only a fleeting moment with the *Book of Kells,* as the constant flow of viewers is hurried past.

ST STEPHEN'S GREEN — PARK

Map p274 (dawn-dusk; all city centre, St Stephen's Green) As you watch the assorted groups of friends, lovers and individuals splaying themselves across the nine elegantly landscaped hectares of Dublin's most popular green lung, St Stephen's Green, consider that those same hectares once formed a common for public whippings, burnings and hangings. These days, the harshest treatment you'll get is the warden chucking you out if you disturb the carefully tended flower beds.

The buildings around the square date mainly from the mid-18th century, when the green was landscaped and became the centrepiece of Georgian Dublin. The northern side was known as the Beaux Walk and it's still one of Dublin's most esteemed stretches, home to Dublin's original society hotel, the Shelbourne (p204). Nearby is the tiny Huguenot Cemetery (p98), established in 1693 by French Protestant refugees.

Railings and locked gates were erected in 1814, when an annual fee of one guinea was charged to use the green. This private use continued until 1877 when Sir Arthur Edward Guinness pushed an act through parliament opening the green to the public once again. He also financed the central park's gardens and ponds, which date from 1880.

The main entrance to the green today is beneath **Fusiliers' Arch**, at the top of Grafton St. Modelled to look like a smaller version of the Arch of Titus in Rome, the arch commemorates the 212 soldiers of the Royal Dublin Fusiliers who were killed fighting for the British in the Boer War (1899–1902).

Spread across the green's lawns and walkways are some notable artworks; the most imposing of these is a **monument to Wolfe Tone**, the leader of the abortive 1798 Rising. Occupying the northeastern corner of the green, the vertical slabs serving as a backdrop to the statue have been dubbed 'Tonehenge'. At this entrance is a **memorial** to all those who died in the Potato Famine (1845–51).

On the eastern side of the green is a children's playground (p87) and to the south there's a fine old **bandstand**, erected to celebrate Queen Victoria's jubilee in 1887. Musical performances often take place here in summer. Near the bandstand is a **bust of James Joyce**.

LITTLE MUSEUM OF DUBLIN — MUSEUM

Map p270 (01-661 1000; www.littlemuseum.ie; 15 St Stephen's Green N; adult/student €10/8;

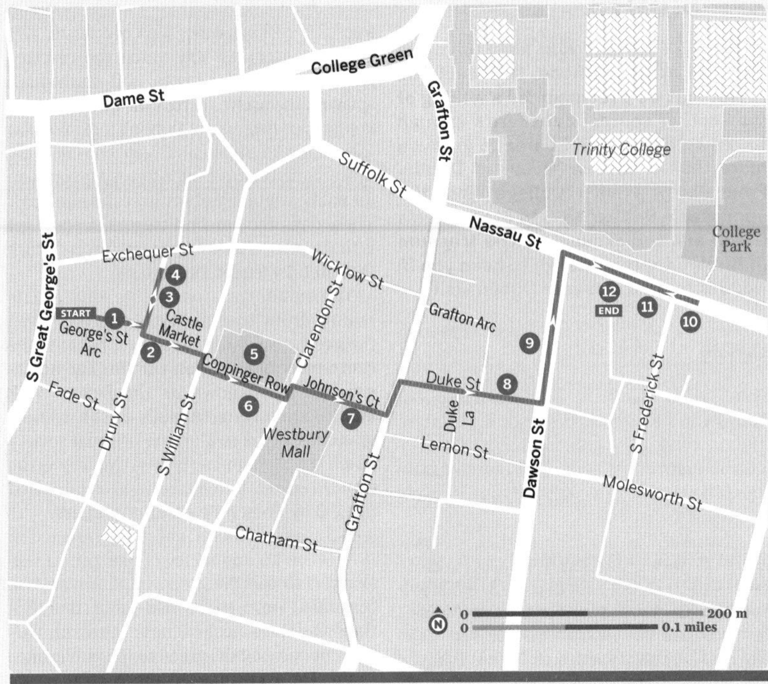

Neighbourhood Walk
A Retail Stroll

START GEORGE'S ST ARCADE
END KNOBS & KNOCKERS
LENGTH 1.1KM; TWO HOURS

Start your retail adventure in the ❶**George's Street Arcade** (p84), with its range of interesting stalls selling all kinds of alternative wares. Exit at the Drury St side and cross onto Castle Market, stopping to browse the high-end women's fashions in ❷**Costume** (p85) or, if you prefer, go north on Drury St to the gorgeous homewares and handicrafts in ❸**Industry** (p85) or, directly next door, the excellent ❹**Irish Design Shop** (p83).

From Castle Market, cross S William St and enter the ❺**Powerscourt Townhouse Shopping Centre** (p84), the city's most elegant retail space – inside you'll find cafes and a host of wonderful shops.

Exit the centre on S William St and walk south, taking the first left onto Coppinger Row. The eponymous ❻**restaurant** (p76) is a great spot for a little lunch refuelling. Continue east and cross Clarendon St. On Johnson's Ct, the southern side is lined with jewellery shops, including ❼**Appleby** (Map 270; ☎01-679 9572; www.appleby.ie; ⌚9.45am-6pm Mon-Wed, Fri & Sat, to 6.30pm Thu); you'll surely find something sparkly worth coveting in the elegant window displays.

Take a left on Grafton St and turn right onto Duke St: on your left is ❽**Ulysses Rare Books** (p85), the city's most illustrious seller of rare books. The biggest bookshop in town is ❾**Hodges Figgis** (p86), around the corner on Dawson St.

From here walk down to Nassau St and take a right to ❿**Kilkenny Shop** (p85), which has all kinds of locally produced handicrafts, knits, glassware and silverware.

If you still need to pick up some typically Irish gifts, retrace your steps back along Nassau St, stopping at ⓫**House of Names** (p85), where you can get coasters with your family's coat of arms, and ⓬**Knobs & Knockers** (p85), for that replica Georgian door handle that will go perfectly with your city-centre apartment!

9.30am-5pm, to 8pm Thu, last admission 7pm; all city centre, St Stephen's Green) This award-winning museum tells the story of Dublin over the last century via memorabilia, photographs and artefacts donated by the general public. The impressive collection, spread over the rooms of a handsome Georgian house, includes a lectern used by JFK on his 1963 visit to Ireland and an original copy of the fateful letter given to the Irish envoys to the treaty negotiations of 1921, whose contradictory instructions were at the heart of the split that resulted in the Civil War.

There's a whole room on the 2nd floor devoted to the history of U2, as well as the personal archive of Alfred 'Alfie' Byrne (1882–1956), mayor of Dublin a record 10 times and known as the 'Shaking Hand of Dublin'. Visit is by guided tour, which goes on the hour every hour. The museum also runs the Green Mile walking tour (p86) of St Stephen's Green.

IRISH WHISKEY MUSEUM MUSEUM

Map p270 (01-525 0970; www.irishwhiskeymuseum.ie; 119 Grafton St; adult/child classic tours €20/€10, premium tours €23, blending experiences €30; 10am-6pm; all city centre) If you'd like to learn a little more about one of Ireland's most famous tipples, spend an hour here. You'll find out why the Irish call it *uisce beatha* (water of life), how Dublin's whiskey trade collapsed and why it's on the rise again. The tour every half hour from 10.30am to 5.30pm also gives you a chance to taste at least three different types of whiskey.

BANK OF IRELAND CULTURAL & HERITAGE CENTRE MUSEUM

Map p270 (01-670 6153; College Green; 10am-4pm Mon-Sat, last entry 3.30pm; all city centre, Westmoreland) FREE Housed within the College Green complex of the Bank of Ireland is this 2018-opened cultural centre, which until 2021 is hosting Seamus Heaney: *Listen Now Again*, an exhibition dedicated to the poet and featuring manuscripts, letters, unpublished works, diaries, photographs and personal items, including the desk at which he wrote in the family home in Sandymount, a lamp that belonged to WB Yeats and a portrait by artist Louis le Brocquy. The exhibition is organised in tandem with the National Library.

CITY ASSEMBLY HOUSE HISTORIC BUILDING

Map p270 (www.igs.ie; 58 S William St; 10am-6pm Mon-Sat; all city centre) FREE This Georgian townhouse was built between 1766 and 1771 by the Society of Artists as the first purpose-built public exhibition room in the British Isles. During the 19th century it served as an unofficial city hall – Daniel O'Connell delivered one of his most famous speeches here in 1843 – but it is now the headquarters of the Irish Georgian Society, which is restoring it to its original purpose. It hosts occasional exhibitions.

DOUGLAS HYDE GALLERY OF MODERN ART GALLERY

Map p270 (www.douglashydegallery.com; Trinity College; 11am-6pm Mon-Wed & Fri, to 7pm Thu, to 5.30pm Sat; all city centre) FREE One of Dublin's best contemporary art galleries, the Douglas Hyde is tucked away in the Arts & Social Science Building of the Trinity College campus. Its ambitious contemporary program stays firmly in the cutting-edge camp; exhibitions here are often 'enhanced' with film, live music or performance-driven sideshows.

IVEAGH GARDENS GARDENS

Map p274 (dawn-dusk; all city centre, St Stephen's Green) FREE These beautiful gardens may not have the sculpted elegance of the other city parks, but they never get too crowded and the warden won't bark at you if you walk on the grass. They were designed by Ninian Niven in 1863 as the private grounds of **Iveagh House** (www.dfa.ie; 80 St Stephen's Green S; closed to public) and include a rustic grotto, a cascade, a fountain, a maze and a rosarium. Enter the gardens from Clonmel St, off Harcourt St.

SCIENCE GALLERY MUSEUM

Map p276 (www.sciencegallery.ie; Naughton Gallery, Pearse St; exhibitions usually 11-7pm Tue-Fri, to 6pm Sat & Sun; all city centre) FREE Demonstrating that science is fun, engaging and relevant to our everyday lives in more ways than we could even imagine is the mission statement of this immensely popular gallery, which hosts an ever-changing mix of compelling exhibits. Recent shows included an examination of design and violence and a study of the world of secrets. The ground-floor **cafe** (www.dublin.sciencegallery.com/cafe; Pearse St; sandwiches €8-9; 8am-4pm Mon-Fri; all city centre) is lovely.

MUSEUM OF LITERATURE IRELAND MUSEUM

Map p274 (MoLI; 01-477 9810; www.moli.ie; 85-86 St Stephen's Green S; adult/child under 3/conces-

THE PAGE OF KELLS

The history of the *Book of Kells* is almost as fascinating as its illuminations. It is thought to have been created around AD 800 by the monks at St Colmcille's Monastery on Iona, a remote island off the coast of Scotland; repeated looting by marauding Vikings forced the monks to flee to Kells, County Meath, along with their masterpiece. It was stolen in 1007, then rediscovered three months later buried underground. The *Book of Kells* was brought to Trinity College for safekeeping in 1654, and is now housed in the Old Library (p66), with over half a million visitors queueing up to see it annually. The 680-page (340-folio) book was rebound in four calfskin volumes in 1953.

And here the problems begin. Of the 680 pages, only two are on display – one showing an illumination, the other showing text – hence the 'page of Kells' moniker. No getting around that one, though: you can hardly expect the right to thumb through a priceless treasure at random. No, the real problem is its immense popularity, which makes viewing it a rather unsatisfactory pleasure. Punters are herded through the specially constructed viewing room at near lightning pace, making for a quick-look-and-move-along kind of experience.

To really appreciate the book, you can get your own reproduction copy for a mere €22,000. Failing that, the Old Library bookshop stocks a plethora of souvenirs and other memorabilia, including Bernard Meehan's *The Book of Kells* (€17), which includes plenty of reproductions plus excellent accompanying text.

sion/family €8/free/6/17, guided tour €12; ⌚10am-6pm; 🚌all city centre, 🚋St Stephen's Green) Reopened in 2019, the Museum of Literature Ireland is a digital, interactive exploration of Ireland's deep literary heritage, from the Middle Ages to the present day. Highlights include Joyce's *Ulysses* notebooks as well as the very first print of the novel. The museum is in two stunning Georgian townhouses collectively known as Newman House, which in 1865 saw the establishment of the Catholic University of Ireland, the alma mater of Joyce, Pádraig Pearse and Eamon de Valera.

CITY HALL — MUSEUM

Map p274 (www.dublincity.ie/dublincityhall; Dame St; adult/student/child €4/2/1.50; ⌚10am-5.15pm Mon-Sat; 🚌all city centre) This beautiful Georgian structure was originally built by Thomas Cooley as the Royal Exchange between 1769 and 1779, and botched in the mid-19th century when it became the offices of the local government (hence its name). Thankfully, a renovation in 2000 has restored it to its gleaming Georgian best. The basement has an exhibit on the city's history.

The rotunda and its ambulatory form a breathtaking interior, bathed in natural light from enormous windows to the east. A vast marble statue of former mayor and Catholic emancipator Daniel O'Connell stands here as a reminder of the building's links with Irish nationalism (the funerals of both Charles Stewart Parnell and Michael Collins were held here). Dublin City Council still meets here on the first Monday of the month, gathering to discuss the city's business in the Council Chamber, which was the original building's coffee room.

There was a sordid precursor to City Hall on this spot in the shape of the Lucas Coffee House and the adjoining Eagle Tavern, in which the notorious Hellfire Club was founded by Richard Parsons, Earl of Rosse, in 1735. Although the city abounded with gentlemen's clubs, this particular one gained a reputation for messing about in the arenas of sex and Satan, two topics that were guaranteed to fire the lurid imaginings of the city's gossip mongers.

Located in the striking vaulted basement, **The Story of the Capital** is a multimedia exhibition that traces the history of the city from its earliest beginnings to its hoped-for future – with ne'er a mention of sex and Satan. More's the pity, as the info is quite overwhelming and the exhibits are a little text-heavy. Still, it's a pretty slick museum with informative audiovisual displays.

BANK OF IRELAND — NOTABLE BUILDING

Map p270 (☎01-6711488; College Green; ⌚10am-4pm Mon-Wed & Fri, to 5pm Thu; 🚌all city centre, 🚋Westmoreland) A sweeping Palladian pile occupying one side of College Green, this magnificent building was the Irish Parliament House until 1801 and was the first purpose-built parliament building in the world. The original building – the central colonnaded section that distinguishes the present-day structure – was designed by Sir Edward Lovett Pearce in 1729 and completed by James Gandon in 1733.

When the parliament voted itself out of existence through the 1801 Act of Union, the building was sold under the condition that the interior would be altered to prevent it ever again being used as a debating chamber. It was a spiteful strike at Irish parliamentary aspirations, but while the central House of Commons was remodelled and offers little hint of its former role, the smaller **House of Lords** (admission free) survived and is much more interesting. It has Irish oak woodwork, a mahogany longcase parliament clock and a late-18th-century Dublin crystal chandelier. Its design was copied for the construction of the original House of Representatives in Washington, DC, now the National Statuary Hall. The House of Lords is open to visitors during banking hours.

IRISH-JEWISH MUSEUM MUSEUM

Map p274 (☎01-453 1797; www.jewishmuseum.ie; 3 Walworth Rd; €5; ⏰11am-3pm Sun, Tue & Thu May-Sep, 10.30am-2.30pm Sun Oct-Apr; 🚊Harcourt) Housed in an old synagogue, this jam-packed museum tells the story of Ireland's Jewish community over the last 150 years. Amid the old photos and artefacts is memorabilia from WWII, including a Star of David arm patch and the marriage certificate of Ester Steinberg, the only known Irish victim of the Holocaust.

The museum is in the (now) trendy neighbourhood of Portobello, which once had a 5000-strong Jewish community and was known as Little Jerusalem. It was opened in 1985 by the Belfast-born, then-Israeli president, Chaim Herzog.

MANSION HOUSE NOTABLE BUILDING

Map p270 (Dawson St; ⏰closed to public; 🚌all city centre, 🚊Dawson) Built in 1710 by Joshua Dawson –after whom the street is named – this has been the official residence of Dublin's mayor since 1715, and was the site of the 1919 Declaration of Independence and the meeting of the first parliament. The building's original brick Queen Anne style has all but disappeared behind a stucco facade added in the Victorian era.

NEWMAN UNIVERSITY CHURCH CHURCH

Map p274 (☎01-475 9674; www.universitychurch.ie; 87A St Stephen's Green S; ⏰8am-6pm; 🚌all city centre, 🚊St Stephen's Green) Cardinal Newman didn't care too much for the Gothic style of his day, so the 1856 church attached to his Catholic University of Ireland at Newman House (p68) is a neo-Byzantine charmer. Its richly decorated interior was mocked at first but has since become the preferred surroundings for fashionable weddings.

LUKE KELLY STATUE STATUE

Map p270 (S King St; 🚌all city centre, 🚊St Stephen's Green) A bronze figure of legendary Dublin folk singer Luke Kelly (1940–84). It was a gift to the city by Irish cartoonist Gerry Hunt (1936–2018), who had privately commissioned sculptor John Coll.

PHIL LYNOTT STATUE STATUE

Map p270 (Harry St; 🚌all city centre) Thin Lizzy frontman Phil Lynott (1949–86) was one of the most beloved of all Dubliners – the epitome of the fun-loving rocker. This bust (2005) of the singer by Paul Daly was deliberately placed outside Bruxelles pub on Harry St as this has long been the unofficial Dublin HQ of rock music. Perhaps his fans have loved not wisely but too well, as the bust has been damaged twice already, prompting a couple of restorations.

ST WERBURGH'S CHURCH CHURCH

Map p274 (☎01-478 3710; Werburgh St; ⏰closed to public; 🚌50, 50A, 56A from Aston Quay, 54, 54A from Burgh Quay) West of Dublin Castle, St Werburgh's Church stands upon ancient foundations (probably from the 12th centu-

THE TWO LUKES

In 2018 Dublin's legendary folk singer Luke Kelly (1940–84) was immortalised in sculpture not once, but twice – on the same day. The first figure (p70) to be erected was a traditional bronze sculpture on South King St by John Coll, capturing Kelly mid-song while playing the banjo. The second figure (p166) is a 2m marble head with eyes closed and featuring 3000 strands of copper hair. It's on Sheriff St, where Kelly was born, and like all bold pieces of art has generated much comment, with some wits declaring that the artist did a great job capturing Kelly mid-orgasm.

ry), but was rebuilt several times during the 17th and 18th centuries. The church's tall spire was dismantled after Robert Emmet's rising in 1803, for fear that future rebels might use it as a vantage point for snipers. It is closed for a long-running restoration.

Interred in the vault is Lord Edward Fitzgerald, who turned against Britain, joined the United Irishmen and was a leader of the 1798 Rising. In what was a frequent theme of Irish uprisings, compatriots gave him away and his death resulted from the wounds he received when captured. Coincidentally, Major Henry Sirr, the man who captured him, is buried out in the graveyard. On the porch you will notice two fire pumps that date from the time when Dublin's fire department was composed of church volunteers. The interior is rather more cheerful than the exterior, although the church is rarely used. Phone, or see the caretaker at 8 Castle St, to see inside. Donations welcome.

WHITEFRIARS STREET CARMELITE CHURCH — CHURCH

Map p270 (01-475 8821; 56 Aungier St; 8am-6.30pm Mon & Wed-Fri, to 9.30pm Tue, to 7pm Sat, to 7.30pm Sun; 16, 19, 19A, 83, 122 from Trinity College) Inside this nondescript church (more properly known as the Church of Our Lady of Mt Carmel) are some fascinating relics, not least the relics of St Valentine, donated to the Carmelites by Pope Gregory XVI in 1836. A spiral-bound notebook below the shrine is there so anyone struck (or missed) by Cupid's arrow can express their gratitude or hope.

The Carmelites have been here since 1827, when they re-established their former church that had been seized by Henry VIII in the 16th century. In the northeastern corner is a 16th-century Flemish oak statue of the Virgin and Child, believed to be the only wooden statue in Ireland to have escaped the Reformation unscathed.

EATING

While the options on Grafton St itself are minimal, the streets around it are packed with food joints to suit every taste and craving. Camden and Wexford Sts are a particular delight, with everything from funky cafes to swish restaurants attracting Dublin's foodie connoisseurs.

PANG — VIETNAMESE €

Map p274 (01-563 8702; www.lovepang.ie; 6-11 Lower Kevin St; rolls €4, pho €9; noon-8pm Mon-Sat; all city centre) Fresh and zingy Vietnamese rice paper rolls, banh mi and pho are the name of the game here, all of which are as delicious as they are well priced. There are only six stools in the window, so you won't be lingering.

LOOSE CANON — CHEESE €

Map p270 (www.loosecanon.ie; 29 Drury St; toasties €7.50-8; 10.30am-10pm Mon & Wed-Sat, to 5.30pm Tue, noon-10pm Sun; all city centre) Ostensibly a cheese shop with a few stools, at Loose Canon you can prop yourself up at the counter for a platter of cheese or Irish charcuterie, with a glass of vino chosen from the shelves of natural wines. The buttery toasties (toasted sandwiches) are generous, rich and filled with gooey Irish cheeses like smoked mozzarella or Corleggy goat's cheese.

CAKE CAFÉ — CAFE €

Map p274 (01-478 9394; www.thecakecafe.ie; 8 Pleasants Pl; mains €6-11; 9am-5pm Mon-Sat; all city centre) Sure, the cakes are dreamy – fluffy espresso walnut sponges and pretty cupcakes – but the savoury brunch options are just as fabulous. The homemade baked beans are a particular highlight, served atop sourdough toast with fried chorizo, smoked Gubbeen cheese and a perfectly poached egg. There is outdoor seating for sunnier days.

MASA — MEXICAN €

Map p270 (01-430 2841; www.masadublin.com; 2 Drury St; tacos €5-7; noon-9.30pm Mon-Wed, to 10pm Thu, to 10.30pm Fri, 1-10.30pm Sat, 2-9pm Sun; all city centre) A quick and easy taco joint serving authentic soft corn tortillas filled with pulled pork, crispy fish and fried chicken. The *elotes* (corn on the cob slathered in cheese and chilli) are fantastic.

CAMDEN ROTISSERIE — CHICKEN €

Map p274(01-538 1022; www.camdenrotisserie.ie; 37 Lower Camden St; mains €7-10; noon-10pm Mon-Thu, to 11pm Fri, 12.30-11pm Sat, 1-10pm Sun; all city centre) Things are kept simple at this cosy little spot – succulent rotisserie chicken, wings and burgers are served with skin-on fries or mash (€3.25), at long communal tables. Cheap, cheerful and delicious.

DUBLIN PIZZA COMPANY — PIZZA €

Map p270 (01-561 1714; www.dublinpizzacompany.ie; 32 Aungier St; pizzas €9-13; noon-midnight

Mon-Thu, to 3am Fri, 4pm-3am Sat, 4.30pm-midnight Sun; all city centre) A great place to grab a bite and go. Served from a wooden hatch, this is some of the best pizza in the city, helped by its woodfire oven and organic ingredients. If you'd rather sit down, you can take your pizza into the Swan (p80) pub just up the road, or get it delivered to Fourth Corner (p138).

MEET ME IN THE MORNING CAFE €

Map p274 (www.mmim.ie; 50 Pleasants St; mains €9-14; 8am-4pm Mon-Fri, 9am-4pm Sat & Sun; 14, 15, 65, 83) Scrummy all-day breakfasts (think kale with perfectly poached eggs and zingy garlic yoghurt) and gorgeous treats like sea buckthorn glazed doughnuts make this light-filled cafe an Instagrammer's dream. It's named after a Dylan song.

WOW BURGER BURGERS €

Map p270 (www.wowburger.ie; 8 Wicklow St; burgers €6-7; noon-10pm Sun-Thu, to 11pm Fri & Sat; all city centre) The basement of Mary's Bar (p80) is home to a reliable burger joint: hamburgers, cheeseburgers and a sinful bacon cheeseburger come in two sizes (double or single) and with a side of choice – the garlic-butter fries are terrific. Order at the bar, pick up at the counter and eat in the 1950s diner-styled room.

MURPHY'S ICE CREAM ICE CREAM €

Map p270 (www.murphysicecream.ie; 27 Wicklow St; scoops €5; noon-11pm; all city centre) Get your sugar hit on with a visit to what might be the best ice-cream shop in the country. Everything is handmade with fresh ingredients from Dingle, home to the first **branch** (Strand St; 1/2/3 scoops €4.50/6.50/8.50; 11.30am-10pm May-Oct, to 8pm Nov-Apr;) of this mini-chain. Flavours rotate but the Dingle Gin ice cream is always popular and the sorbets use distilled Kerry rain.

EATYARD MARKET €

Map p274 (www.the-eatyard.com; 9-10 S Richmond St; free admission; noon-10pm Thu-Sat, to 8pm Sun Mar-Dec; 14, 15, 44, 65, 140, 142 from city centre, Harcourt) Spend an hour or two eating and drinking your way through a dozen or so of the city's best food vendors. There's always seasonal produce, and plenty of veggie/vegan options, as well as craft beer. The vendors rotate every few months and the market can close for a short time to accommodate this – confirm opening times online.

BUNSEN BURGERS €

Map p270 (01-652 1022; www.bunsen.ie; 3 S Anne St; burgers €7-10; noon-9.30pm Mon-Wed, to 10.30pm Thu-Sat, 1-9.30pm Sun; all city centre, St Stephen's Green) Artisanal burgers that are so popular, the queues go out the door. There's also a branch on 36 Wexford St (burgers €7-10).

NEON ASIAN €

Map p274 (01-405 2222; www.neon17.ie; 17 Lower Camden St; mains €12-13; noon-10pm; 14, 15, 65, 83) A brilliant spot that specialises in authentic Thai and Vietnamese street food, served in takeaway boxes, which you can eat at home or in the canteen-style dining room. Hardened palates can jump right into the super-spicy *pad ki mow* noodles; more delicate taste buds can live with a delicious massaman curry. Takeaway is available until 11pm, and Neon also delivers (from 5pm).

PEPPER POT CAFE €

Map p270 (www.thepepperpot.ie; Powerscourt Townhouse, S William St; mains €6-10; 10am-6pm Mon-Fri, from 9am Sat, noon-6pm Sun; all city centre) Everything is baked and made daily at the lovely cafe on the 1st-floor balcony of the Powerscourt Townhouse (p84). The salads with homemade brown bread are delicious but the real treat is the soup of the day (€6) – the ideal liquid lunch.

LEMON CRÊPES €

Map p270 (www.lemonco.com; 66 S William St; pancakes from €4.70; 7.30am-7.30pm Mon-Wed & Fri, to 8.30pm Thu, 8.30am-7.30pm Sat, 9.40am-6.30pm Sun; ; all city centre) Dublin's best pancake joint serves a wide range of sweet and savoury crêpes – those paper-thin ones stuffed with a variety of goodies and smothered in toppings – along with super coffee in a buzzy atmosphere.

LISTONS SANDWICHES €

Map p274 (www.listonsfoodstore.ie; 25 Lower Camden St; lunch €5-12; 9am-6.30pm Mon-Fri, 10am-6pm Sat; all city centre) They've been making gourmet sandwiches for so long here that it's hard to imagine them getting any better. Besides the delicacies you put between slices of bread, this excellent spot also does roasted-vegetable quiches, rosemary potato cakes and sublime salads. The menu changes daily. On fine days, take your gourmet picnic to the nearby Iveagh Gardens (p68).

FALLON & BYRNE

DELI €

Map p270 (www.fallonandbyrne.com; Exchequer St; mains €5-10; ⏰8am-9pm Mon-Fri, from 9am Sat, 11am-7pm Sun; 🚌all city centre) Dublin's answer to the American Dean & DeLuca chain is this upmarket food hall and wine cellar, which is where discerning Dubliners come to buy their favourite cheeses and imported delicacies, as well as to get a superb takeaway lunch from the deli counter. Upstairs is an elegant **brasserie** (☎01-472 1000; mains €19-34; ⏰noon-3pm & 5.30-9pm Sun-Tue, to 10pm Wed & Thu, to 11pm Fri & Sat) that serves Irish-influenced Mediterranean cuisine.

CORNUCOPIA

VEGETARIAN €

Map p270 (www.cornucopia.ie; 19-20 Wicklow St; salads €6-10, mains €13-15; ⏰8.30am-9pm Mon, to 10pm Tue-Sat, noon-9pm Sun; 🌱; 🚌all city centre) Dublin's best-known vegetarian restaurant is a terrific eatery that serves wholesome salads, sandwiches, and a selection of hot main courses from a daily changing menu. There's live musical accompaniment Thursday and Friday evenings. The 2nd-floor dining-room windows overlooking the street below are a good spot for people-watching.

AZTECA

MEXICAN €

Map p274 (☎01-670 9476; www.azteca.ie; 19 Lord Edward St; burritos €8-9; ⏰noon-8pm Mon-Wed, to 9pm Thu-Sat, to 6pm Sun; 🚌all city centre) This spot near Dublin Castle has been around for a few years but rarely features on anyone's 'must-eat' list. It's their loss, because the burritos here are excellent.

SIMON'S PLACE

CAFE €

Map p270 (www.facebook.com/SimonsPlaceCoffeeshop; George's St Arcade, S Great George's St; sandwiches €5-6; ⏰8.30am-5pm Mon-Sat; 🌱; 🚌all city centre) Simon's soup-and-sandwich joint is a city stalwart, impervious to the fluctuating fortunes of the world around it, mostly because its doorstep sandwiches and wholesome vegetarian soups are delicious and affordable. As trustworthy cafes go, this is the real deal.

BLAZING SALADS

VEGETARIAN €

Map p270 (☎01-671 9552; www.blazingsalads.com; 42 Drury St; salads €5-10; ⏰9am-6pm Mon-Sat; 🌱; 🚌all city centre) Organic breads (including many special diet varieties), Californian-style salads from a serve-yourself salad bar, smoothies and pizza slices can all be taken away from this delicious, vegetarian deli. It also runs wildly popular cooking classes for which you would be wise to book well in advance.

COLLEGE GREEN STATUARY

The imposing grey sculptures adorning College Green are monuments to two of Ireland's most notable patriots. In front of the bank is Henry Grattan (1746–1820), a distinguished parliamentary orator, while nearby is a modern memorial to the patriot Thomas Davis (1814–45). Where College St meets Pearse St, another traffic island is topped by a 1986 sculpted copy of the *Steyne* (the Viking word for 'stone'), which was erected on the riverbank in the 9th century to stop ships from grounding and was removed in 1720.

HONEST TO GOODNESS

PIZZA €

Map p270 (www.honesttogoodness.ie; 12 Dame Ct; sandwiches €7, pizzas €10-16; ⏰8am-9pm Mon, to 10pm Tue-Thu, to 11pm Fri, 9am-11pm Sat, 10am-4pm Sun; 🚌all city centre) By day, the downstairs cafe serves wholesome sandwiches, tasty soups and a near-legendary sloppy joe hamburger. By night, the upstairs restaurant serves great pizza in a buzzy setting. Terrific staff, wonderful atmosphere.

LITTLE BIRD

CAFE €

Map p278 (☎085-161 0222; www.little-bird.ie; 82 S Circular Rd; mains €5-8; ⏰8am-7pm Mon-Fri, 10am-4pm Sat & Sun; 🚌9, 16, 68, 68A, 122) This cafe started life as an adjunct to the yoga studio upstairs and has since grown into one of Portobello's most desirable coffee spots, which in this neighbourhood of mindful affluence means artisanal Badger & Dodo coffee and a largely vegetarian and organic menu with a particular emphasis on avoiding gluten. Sounds a mite precious but is actually delicious, friendly and welcoming.

GOVINDA'S

VEGETARIAN €

Map p270 (www.govindas.ie; 4 Aungier St; mains €10.45; ⏰noon-9pm Mon-Sat; 🌱; 🚌all city centre) An authentic beans-and-pulses place run by the Hare Krishna, with two branches in the city centre. Its cheap, wholesome mix of salads and Indian-influenced hot daily specials is filling and tasty.

★PI PIZZA

PIZZA €€

Map p270 (www.pipizzas.ie; 73-83 S Great George's St; pizzas €9-16; ⏰noon-10pm Sun-Wed, to 10.30pm Thu-Sat; 🚌all city centre) Reg White cut his pie-making teeth at Flour + Water in San Francisco before opening this fabulous restaurant in 2018, and it's already a contender for best pizzeria in town. The smallish menu has just eight pizzas, each an inspired interpretation of a Neapolitan classic. Highly recommended are the *funghi* (mushroom) or *broccolini,* 'white' pizzas made without the tomato layer.

RICHMOND MODERN IRISH €€

Map p274 (☎01-478 8783; www.richmondrestaurant.ie; 43 S Richmond St; mains €18-27; ⏲5.30-9.30pm Wed-Sat, to 9pm Sun, 11am-2.30pm Sat & Sun; 🚌14, 15, 65, 83) At first glance the menu offers nothing particularly novel, just a nice selection of favourites from a burger to a roasted breast of duck. But it's the way it's prepared and presented that makes this place one of the best in town, and proof that expertise in the kitchen trumps everything else. Brunch is particularly recommended.

FEATHERBLADE STEAK €€

Map p270 (☎01-679 8814; www.featherblade.ie; 51B Dawson St; steaks €14-15; ⏲noon-3pm & 5-10.30pm Mon-Fri, noon-late Sat, 1-10pm Sun; 🚌all city centre) With an emphasis on more unusual cuts of beef – think *picanha* (sirloin cap) not fillet – this steakhouse offers amazing value for money. If you spot the West Cork Wagyu on the menu, snap it up – you couldn't ask for a more flavourful cut of beef. The wine menu is well priced too, with a number available on tap.

SISU IZAKAYA JAPANESE €€

Map p270 (☎01-475 7777; http://sisuizakaya.ie; 23-27 Lower Stephen St; mains €15-17.50; ⏲noon-10pm Sun-Wed, to 11pm Thu-Sat; 🚌all city centre) Japanese casual dining at its Dublin best is the order of the day at this wonderful new spot whose name translates as 'Sisu's Tavern'. Within its wood-panelled, low-lit interior you'll get a broad range of dishes, from rolls to ramen. The €10 lunch bento was, at the time of writing, the best in town.

BOW LANE INTERNATIONAL €€

Map p270 (☎01-478 9489; www.bowlane.ie; 17 Aungier St; bar food €7-16, mains €19-25; ⏲5pm-midnight Mon-Thu, to 2am Fri, 10.30am-2am Sat, 10.30am-midnight Sun; 🚌all city centre) It's a 1950s-style cocktail bar, but with a standout menu. Main dishes are hearty - think West Cork Wagyu beef burgers or meltingly soft lamb shanks, and the bar bites are divine - the truffle fries are smothered in Parmesan and bacon. Things get a little raucous at the weekend, when it serves bottomless booze at brunch for €25 per person.

SABA ASIAN €€

Map p270 (☎01-679 2000; www.sabadublin.com; 26-28 Clarendon St; mains €18-28; ⏲noon-9.30pm Sun-Wed, to 10pm Thu, to 10.30pm Fri & Sat; 🚌all city centre) The name means 'happy meeting place' and this Thai-Vietnamese fusion restaurant is just that. The buzzy atmosphere is all designer cool, the Southeast Asian fare a tad shy of being truly authentic (but still very tasty), and it's a good night out.

LUCKY TORTOISE DIM SUM €€

Map p270 (www.luckytortoise.co; 8 Aungier St; dim sum €6-7; ⏲noon-10pm; 🚌all city centre) It's always lively at this funky little joint, where the music is loud and the dim sum just keeps coming. Order from the ever-rotating menu or keep things simple by selecting the whole lot – the 'all in' option (€20 per person) will get you everything in the kitchen, served family style. There's a good selection of wines on tap, too.

BALFES IRISH €€

Map p270 (☎01-646 3353; www.balfes.ie; 2 Balfe St; mains €19-25; ⏲8am-10pm Mon-Thu, to 10.30pm Fri, 9am-10.30pm Sat, 9am-10pm Sun; 🚌all city centre) This all-day brasserie has a chic New York vibe, with leather banquettes and a small heated terrace luring a perpetually stylish crowd. While the menu focuses on hearty bistro dishes like duck liver pâté and steaks cooked on the Josper grill, it caters well to the healthier diner – think protein pancakes and superfood salads.

UNO MAS SPANISH €€

Map p270 (☎01-475 8538; www.unomas.ie; 6 Aungier St; tapas €4-15, mains €20-34; ⏲5.30-9.30pm Mon, noon-2.30pm & 5.30-9.30pm Tue-Sat; 🚌all city centre) Sister restaurant to Dublin favourite Etto (p101), Uno Mas quickly rose in the popularity stakes following its launch in late 2018. Expect to see dishes like octopus with kale, potato and violet garlic, alongside a tapas menu of *jamon croquetas* (ham croquettes) and *Padrón peppers.* Booking is essential, with more availability at lunch (two/three-courses €24/28).

BONSAI BAR JAPANESE €€

Map p270 (☎01-526 7701; www.thebonsaibar.com; 17 S Great George's St; bento €18; ⏲5-10.30pm Sun-Thu, to 11pm Fri & Sat; 🚌all city centre) This sultry bar from culinary superstar

Dylan McGrath serves cocktails with a Japanese twist (the Sakura Blossom blends gin, pink grapefruit and sparkling rose sake) alongside delicate bar bites like crispy artichoke skin with miso and sesame dust. The bento (served Wednesday to Saturday) is heartier, with options for meat, fish or veg.

THE IVY IRISH €€

Map p270 (☎01-695 0744; www.theivydublin.com; 13-17 Dawson St; mains €16-34; ⏱7am-12.30am Mon-Thu, to 1.30am Fri, 9am-1.30am Sat, 9am-12.30am Sun; 🚌all city centre) The first Irish outpost of The Ivy brasserie brand, this restaurant hits the mark in the style stakes (but some say this dedication isn't matched on the plate). Still, the menu of all-day classics is solid, and its well-loved shepherd's pie recipe is deeply satisfying.

JERUSALEM RESTAURANT MIDDLE EASTERN €€

Map p274 (☎01-424 4001; www.jerusalemrestaurant.ie; 77 Lower Camden St; mains €15-20; ⏱noon-10pm Mon-Wed, to 10.30pm Thu, to midnight Fri, 1pm-midnight Sat, 1-10pm Sun; 📶; 🚌14, 15, 65, 83) A candidate for best ethnic cuisine in town, this friendly spot serves a mix of Lebanese and Palestinian dishes that range from the familiar (hummus, felafel, lamb shwarma) to the exotic – how about *dajaj musahab* (deboned chicken with Palestinian spices)? The extensive menu requires repeat visits. It's strictly BYOB (€5 corkage).

HANG DAI CHINESE €€

Map p274 (☎01-545 8888; www.hangdaichinese.com; 20 Lower Camden St; mains €17-29; ⏱5pm-midnight Tue-Sat, to 9.30pm Sun; 🚌14, 15, 65, 83) You'll need a reservation to get a seat at the bar or in one of the carriage booths of this super-trendy spot, designed to look like the inside of a railway carriage. The low red lighting and soulful tunes give off the ambience of a '70s porn theatre. The food, however – contemporary versions of Chinese classics – is excellent.

CAMDEN KITCHEN BISTRO €€

Map p274 (☎01-476 0125; www.camdenkitchen.ie; 3 Camden Market, Grantham St; mains €17-24; ⏱noon-2.30pm & 5.30-10pm Wed-Fri, 5.30-10pm Tue & Sat; 🚌14, 15, 65, 83) Tucked away off busy Camden St, this inviting little bistro prides itself on its fresh, seasonal menu of changing and beautifully presented dishes, like handmade gnocchi with spring greens and wild mushrooms topped with a free-range egg; or slow-cooked duck leg with fresh sweetcorn and Morteaux sausage. The somewhat expensive wine menu complements the reasonably priced food.

SOPHIE'S @ THE DEAN ITALIAN €€

Map p274 (☎01-607 8100; www.sophies.ie; 33 Harcourt St; mains €14-34; ⏱7am-10.30pm Mon-Wed, to 1.30am Thu-Fri, 8am-1.30am Sat, 8am-10.30pm Sun; 🚌10, 11, 13, 14, 15A, 🚊Harcourt) There's perhaps no better setting in all of Dublin – a top-floor glasshouse restaurant with superb views of the city – in which to enjoy this quirky take on Italian cuisine. Delicious pizzas come with nontraditional toppings (smoked brisket with barbecue mustard?) and the 8oz fillet steak is done to perfection. A good spot for breakfast too.

PITT BROS BBQ BARBECUE €€

Map p270 (www.pittbrosbbq.com; Unit 1, Wicklow House, S Great George's St; mains €15-17; ⏱noon-late Mon-Fri, from 12.30pm Sat & Sun; 🚌all city centre) Delicious, Southern-style barbecue – you have a choice of pulled pork, brisket, ribs, sausage or half a chicken – served amid loud music and a hipster-fuelled atmosphere that says Brooklyn, New York, rather than Birmingham, Alabama. For dessert, there's a DIY ice-cream dispenser.

FADE STREET SOCIAL MODERN IRISH €€

Map p270 (☎01-604 0066; www.fadestreetsocial.com; 4-6 Fade St; mains €20-36, tapas €6-17; ⏱5-10.30pm Mon-Wed, 12.30-3pm & 5-10.30pm Thu, to 11pm Fri & Sat, to 10.30pm Sun; 📶; 🚌all city centre) 🌿 Two restaurants in one, courtesy of renowned chef Dylan McGrath. At the front, the buzzy tapas bar, which serves gourmet bites from a beautiful open kitchen; at the back, the more muted restaurant specialises in Irish cuts of meat – from veal to rabbit – served with home-grown organic vegetables. There's a bar upstairs too. Reservations recommended.

777 MEXICAN €€

Map p270 (☎01-425 4052; www.777.ie; 7 Castle House, S Great George's St; mains €16-21, tapas €11-16; ⏱5.30-10pm Mon-Wed, to 11pm Thu, to midnight Fri & Sat, 2-10pm Sun; 🚌all city centre) You won't eat better, more authentic Mexican cuisine in Dublin – the tostadas (crispy corn tortillas with various toppings) and taquitos (filled, soft corn tortillas) are great nibbles, and the perfect accompaniment for a tequila fest. All dishes for €7.77 on Sunday is one of the best deals in town.

PIG'S EAR MODERN IRISH €€

Map p270 (01-670 3865; www.thepigsear.com; 4 Nassau St; mains €19-30; noon-2.45pm & 5.30-10pm Mon-Sat; all city centre) Looking over the playing fields of Trinity College (p56) – which counts as a view in Dublin – this fashionably formal restaurant is spread over two floors and is renowned for its exquisite and innovative Irish cuisine, including dishes such as barbecued pork belly, short rib of Irish beef and a superb slow-cooked shepherd's pie.

PICHET FRENCH €€

Map p270 (01-677 1060; www.pichetrestaurant.ie; 15 Trinity St; mains €20-28; noon-3pm & 5-9.30pm Mon-Wed, to 10pm Thu-Sat, 2-8pm Sun; all city centre) Head chef Stephen Gibson (formerly of L'Ecrivain) delivers his version of modern French cuisine to this newly refurbished dining room, whose elegance matches the fabulous food and service. Load up on an expertly made cocktail before feasting on as good a meal as you'll find at this price anywhere in the city centre.

L'GUEULETON FRENCH €€

Map p270 (01-675 3708; www.lgueuleton.com; 1 Fade St; mains €20-31; 12.30-4pm & 5.30-10pm Mon-Wed, to 10.30pm Thu-Sat, noon-4pm & 5.30-9pm Sun; all city centre) Despite the tongue-twister name (it means 'gluttonous feast' in French), L'Gueuleton is a firm favourite with locals for its robust (meaty, filling) take on French rustic cuisine – it does a mean onion soup and the steak frites is a big crowd pleaser.

COPPINGER ROW MEDITERRANEAN €€

Map p270 (01-672 9884; www.coppingerrow.com; Coppinger Row; mains €21-29; noon-11pm; all city centre) Virtually all of the Mediterranean basin is represented on the ever-changing, imaginative menu here. Choices include pan-fried hake with mussels, baby potato and curried broth; or crispy pork belly with mustard mash, caramelised apple and black pudding. A nice touch are the filtered still and sparkling waters (€1): 50% goes to the Movember men's health charity.

DUNNE & CRESCENZI ITALIAN €€

Map p270 (www.dunneandcrescenzi.com; 14-16 S Frederick St; mains €14-26; 8am-11pm Mon-Sat, from 9.30am Sun; all city centre) This exceptional Italian joint delights its regulars with a basic menu of rustic pleasures, such as venison bresaola, classic pasta dishes and a superb plate of mixed antipasto drizzled in olive oil. It's always full, and the tables are just that little bit too close to one another, but the coffee is perfect and the desserts are sinfully good.

AVOCA CAFE €€

Map p270 (01-677 4215; www.avoca.ie; 11-13 Suffolk St; mains €7-18; 9.30am-4.30pm Mon-Fri, to 5.30pm Sat, 10am-5pm Sun; all city centre) This top-floor cafe, part of the marvellous Avoca group, is very popular with discerning shoppers who enjoy a gourmet lunch: how about a Toonsbridge halloumi salad with kale, sweet potato, baba ganoush and dukkah, or falafel with bulgar pilaf, caramelised onion hummus, beetroot tzatziki and pitta? There's also a takeaway salad bar and hot-food counter in the basement.

GOOD WORLD CHINESE €€

Map p270 (01-677 5373; 18 S Great George's St; dim sum €4-6, mains €12-20; noon-12am; all city centre) To truly appreciate the quality of the southside's best Chinese restaurant, ignore the green Western-style menu and stick to the black-covered one, which is packed with dishes and delicacies that have made it a favourite with Dublin's Chinese community for two decades. It's a great option for a late-night, post-pub bite if you're looking to avoid fast food.

YAMAMORI JAPANESE €€

Map p270 (01-475 5001; www.yamamori.ie; 71 S Great George's St; mains €19-24, lunch bentos €10; noon-10.30pm Sun-Thu, to 11.30pm Fri & Sat; ; all city centre) Yamamori rarely disappoints with its bubbly service and vivacious cooking that swoops from sushi and sashimi to whopping great plates of noodles, with plenty in-between. The lunch bento is a perennial favourite. There's another branch (p159) north of the river.

PORT HOUSE TAPAS €€

Map p270 (01-677 0298; www.porthouse.ie; 64A South William St; tapas €5-9; 11am-midnight; all city centre) This dark cavern restaurant is full of flickering candlelight. The extensive, delicious Spanish tapas menu is best enjoyed with the impressive Iberian wines (which the friendly staff can help you navigate). It doesn't take bookings, so if you go at the weekend prepare to wait for a table.

DRURY BUILDINGS ITALIAN €€

Map p270 (01-960 2095; www.drurybuildings.com; 52-55 Drury St; mains €21-34; noon-

11.30pm Sun-Thu, to 1.30am Fri & Sat; all city centre) An elegant restaurant in a converted rag-trade warehouse…sounds like New York's SoHo, and that's exactly what it's trying to emulate. The food – Italian dishes made with local produce and infused with an international twist – is excellent. The cocktail bar (p80) has an Italian lunch menu of sandwiches, salads and other titbits, and there's a garden to enjoy it all in.

TROCADERO INTERNATIONAL €€

Map p270 (01-677 5545; www.trocadero.ie; 3 St Andrew's St; mains €19-32; 5-11.45pm Mon-Fri, from 4pm Sat; all city centre) As old school as a Dublin restaurant gets, this art deco classic has been the social hub of the city's theatrical world for 50 years, a favourite of thespians and other luminaries. It's more of a nostalgia trip now, but the food remains uniformly good – a bunch of classics, solidly made – as does the terrific atmosphere.

OPIUM ASIAN €€

Map p274 (01-475 8555; www.opium.ie; 26 Wexford St; mains €18-25; noon-10pm Mon-Wed, to 2.30am Thu & Fri, 1pm-2.30am Sat, 1-10pm Sun; 14, 15, 65, 83) Modelled on Hakkasan in London, Opium is a late-night restaurant and bar that serves tasty pan-Asian cuisine with a soundtrack. When you're done dining you can retire to the cocktail bar or the late-night **club** (noon-11pm Mon-Thu, to 2.30am Fri & Sat, noon-11.30pm Sun). The Botanical Garden is a great outdoor space, too.

CHEZ MAX FRENCH €€

(01-633 7215; www.chezmax.ie; 1 Palace St; mains €16-25; noon-3.30pm & 5.30-10pm Mon-Thu, noon-3.30pm & 5.30-11pm Fri, noon-4pm & 5.30-11pm Sat, noon-4pm & 5.30-10pm Sun; all city centre) Guarding the main gate to Dublin Castle is a French cafe that is Gallic through and through, from the fixtures imported from gay Paree to the beautiful, sultry staff who ignore you until they're ready, and then turn the sexy pout into a killer smile. The food is worth the snub, however.

WAGAMAMA JAPANESE €€

Map p270 (www.wagamama.ie; S King St; mains €12-19; noon-10pm; all city centre, St Stephen's Green) This popular chain serves terrific Japanese grub – just no sushi. Production-line rice and noodle dishes delivered pronto at canteen-style tables mightn't seem like the most inviting way to dine, but boy this food is good, and the basement it's served in is surprisingly light and airy – for a place with absolutely no natural light.

★**GREENHOUSE** SCANDINAVIAN €€€

Map p270 (01-676 7015; www.thegreenhouserestaurant.ie; Dawson St; 2-/3-course lunch menu €45/55, 4-/6-course dinner menu €110/129; noon-2pm & 6-9.30pm Tue-Sat; all city centre, St Stephen's Green) Chef Mickael Viljanen might just be the one of the most exciting chefs working in Ireland today thanks to his Scandi-influenced tasting menus, which have made this arguably Dublin's best restaurant. The lunchtime set menu is one of the best bargains in town – a Michelin-starred meal for under fifty bucks. Reservations necessary.

GLOVERS ALLEY IRISH €€€

Map p270 (01-244 0733; www.gloversalley.ie; 128 St Stephen's Green; 3-course dinner €80, 2-course lunch €35; 6-9.30pm Tue-Sat & 12.30-2.15pm Thu-Sat; all city centre) Superstar chef Andy McFadden returned to Dublin to head up this fine-dining restaurant, where you'll find exceptional dishes served with style and panache. The menu changes regularly but you can expect dishes like Dublin Bay prawns with carrot, tarragon and lardo, and Sika deer with beetroot, endive and watercress. A fabulous addition to the Dublin dining scene.

WILDE IRISH €€€

Map p270 (01-646 3352; www.wilde.ie; Westbury Hotel, Grafton St; mains €19-38; 12.30-9.30pm; all city centre) The Westbury's (p203) restaurant is one of the finest spaces in the city, with an indoor terrace dripping with greenery and flooded with light. The art deco vibe is chic but the food is just as impressive – think whole Dover sole meunière and juicy steaks topped with lobster tails.

CLIFF TOWNHOUSE IRISH €€€

Map p270 (01-638 3939; www.thecliffTownhouse.com; 22 St Stephen's Green N; mains €20-34; noon-2.30pm & 5pm-late Mon-Sat, noon-4pm & 6-9.30pm Sun; all city centre, St Stephen's Green) Located in a beautiful townhouse on St Stephen's Green, Cliff Townhouse is a confident expression of the very best of Irish cuisine. The emphasis is on native seafood – think Kilkeel monkfish and Irish lobster – with a sleek oyster and champagne bar at the back. The dining room is supremely elegant – lots of white linen, striking artwork and deep-blue leather booths.

TRINITY COLLEGE'S FIRST FEMALE STUDENT

Despite being founded by a charter issued by a queen in 1592, Trinity College forbade women from attending until 1904 – and even dissuaded them from entering the college grounds at all. But a letter from King Edward VII in January 1904, authorising them to admit women to the degrees of Trinity College put an end to the board's resistance, even though the then-provost George Salmon was said to have declared that women would be admitted 'over his dead body'. He got his wish as he died a few days after the receipt of the king's letter, and only a few days before Isabel Marion Weir Johnston was officially enrolled as a student. She was forbidden from attending lectures and using the dining hall, and had to be off campus by 6pm. She was also prohibited from joining any of the major societies – so she started her own, the Elizabethan Society. Despite her pioneering efforts, most of the rules limiting women's activities were in place until the 1960s. Half a century later, women make up the majority of the student body.

SHANAHAN'S ON THE GREEN STEAK €€€

Map p274 (☎01-407 0939; www.shanahans.ie; 119 St Stephen's Green W; mains €42-54; ⊙5.30-10pm Mon-Thu, noon-2.30pm & 5.30-10pm Fri, 6-10pm Sat; 🚌all city centre, 🚋St Stephen's Green) You could order seafood or a plate of vegetables, but you'd be missing the point of this supremely elegant steakhouse: the finest cuts of juicy and tender Irish Angus beef you'll find anywhere. The ambience is upscale Americana – the bar downstairs is called the Oval Office and pride of place goes to a rocking chair owned by JFK.

MARCO PIERRE WHITE STEAKHOUSE & GRILL STEAK €€€

Map p270 (www.marcopierrewhite.ie; 51 Dawson St; mains €25-36; ⊙noon-10.30pm Mon-Thu, to 11pm Fri & Sat, 1-10pm Sun; 🚌all city centre) Bad-boy chef Marco Pierre White (he who once made Gordon Ramsay cry) is the inspiration behind this bustling restaurant where steaks, grilled meats and chunks of fish are the fare, presented with minimal fuss but with plenty of taste.

DRINKING & NIGHTLIFE

Amid the designer shops and trendy restaurants of the Grafton St area, a few top-notch Victorian pubs combine elegance and traditional style to pull in punters from far and near. Dawson St is popular with straight professional types; the area immediately west of Grafton St has something for everyone; and trendy Wexford and Camden Sts tick the arty, alternative box.

★NO NAME BAR BAR

Map p270 (www.nonamebardublin.com; 3 Fade St; ⊙1.30-11.30pm Mon-Wed, to 1am Thu, 12.30-2.30am Fri & Sat, noon-11pm Sun; 🚌all city centre) A low-key entrance next to the trendy French restaurant L'Gueuleton (p76) leads upstairs to one of the nicest bar spaces in town, consisting of three huge rooms in a restored Victorian townhouse plus a sizeable heated patio area for smokers. There's no sign or a name – folks just refer to it as the No Name Bar.

★KEHOE'S PUB

Map p270 (9 S Anne St; ⊙11am-11.30pm Mon-Thu, to 12.30am Fri & Sat, 12.30-11pm Sun; 🚌all city centre) This classic bar is the very exemplar of a traditional Dublin pub. The beautiful Victorian bar, wonderful snug and side room have been popular with Dubliners and visitors for generations, so much so that the publican's living quarters upstairs have since been converted into an extension – simply by taking out the furniture and adding a bar.

★GROGAN'S CASTLE LOUNGE PUB

Map p270 (www.facebook.com/groganscastlelounge; 15 S William St; ⊙10.30am-11.30pm Mon-Thu, to 12.30am Fri & Sat, 12.30-11pm Sun; 🚌all city centre) Known simply as Grogan's (after the original owner), this is a city-centre institution. It has long been a favourite haunt of Dublin's writers and painters, as well as others from the alternative bohemian set, who enjoy a fine Guinness while they wait for that inevitable moment when they're discovered.

★LONG HALL PUB

Map p270 (51 S Great George's St; ⊙noon-11.30pm Mon-Thu, to 12.30am Fri & Sat, 12.30-

11pm Sun; all city centre) A Victorian classic that is one of the city's most beautiful and best-loved pubs. Check out the ornate carvings in the woodwork behind the bar and the elegant chandeliers. The bartenders are experts at their craft, an increasingly rare attribute in Dublin these days.

AGAINST THE GRAIN — CRAFT BEER

Map p274 (www.galwaybaybrewery.com/againstthegrain; 11 Wexford St; noon-midnight Mon-Thu, to 2am Fri & Sat, 12.30pm-midnight Sun; all city centre) An excellent pub for the craft-beer fans, which is no surprise considering it's owned by the Galway Bay Brewery. There's a dizzying selection of ales and beers on tap, and the barkeeps are generous when it comes to offering tasters to help in your decision-making. Order some chicken wings for soakage if you plan on staying a while...

9 BELOW — BAR

Map p270 (01-905 9990; www.9below.ie; 9 St Stephen's Green; 5-11.30pm Tue-Thu, to 12.30am Fri & Sat; all city centre) This lavish bar is tucked into a basement on St Stephen's Green, with weathered alcoves and cosy corners in which you can hide away with a cocktail. The whiskey menu is extensive, but keep an eye on what you're ordering – a glass of the most expensive blend, Midleton Pearl 30th Anniversary, will set you back an eye-watering €1200. Booking recommended.

PERUKE & PERIWIG — COCKTAIL BAR

Map p270 (01-672 7190; www.peruke.ie; 31 Dawson St; noon-midnight Sun-Thu, to 2.30am Fri & Sat; all city centre) This teeny little Tardis of a bar has an eccentric apothecary vibe, with mixologists decked out in bow ties and a cocktail menu that reads like a novella. If the thought of trawling through pages of options seems exhausting, just tell the bar staff what you're into - their concoctions are always bang on the money.

SIDECAR — COCKTAIL BAR

Map p270 (www.doylecollection.com; Balfe St; 4pm-midnight Mon-Fri, from noon Sat & Sun; all city centre) This sleek and rather saucy cocktail bar is the place to take someone you want to impress – snifters of Prosecco are served while you browse the menu, or you can keep things simple with a martini, shaken (or stirred) right next to your table by a bow-tied waiter.

LUCKY DUCK — PUB

Map p274 (01-405 4824; www.theluckyduck.ie; 43 Aungier St; 11am-12.30am Mon-Thu, to 1am Fri & Sat, 11.30am-12.30am Sun; all city centre) This handsome building has lain dormant for decades, but a recent refurb has created the Lucky Duck, a warm and stylish bar with three floors of cosy nooks and crannies in which you can snuggle up with a drink. The cocktails are exceptional.

J. O'CONNELL — PUB

Map p274 (01-475 3704; 29 S Richmond St; 4-11.30pm Mon-Thu, to 12.30am Fri & Sat, to 11pm Sun; 14, 15, 44, 65, 140, 142 from city centre) Probably as close to a country boozer as you could find in the city, O'Connell's is the kind of place that draws in a solid crowd of locals and regulars. There is a good selection of beers on tap as well.

CAMDEN EXCHANGE — BAR

Map p274 (01-559 9028; www.camdenexchangedublin.com; 72-73 Lower Camden St; 3.30pm-midnight Mon-Thu, noon-1.30am Fri & Sat, noon-midnight Sun; all city centre) Always buzzing when the evening draws in, the Camden Exchange does a roaring trade in simple cocktails (the Gin Garden Mojito goes down a treat) and bottles of wine.

BESTSELLER — WINE BAR

Map p270 (01-671 5125; www.bestsellerdublin.com; 41 Dawson St; 9am-6pm Mon-Wed, to 11pm Thu-Sat, 10am-4pm Sun; all city centre, St Stephen's Green) A daytime cafe and evening wine bar, this relaxing bohemian spot is surrounded by an eclectic mix of books and art. Housed in the previous headquarters of the National Bible Society, you'll still find its name above the door as well as a small selection of biblically inspired cocktails. There's reasonably priced hot food during the day or sharing platters at night.

CHELSEA DRUG STORE — BAR

Map p270 (01-613 9093; www.thechelseadrugstore.ie; 25 S Great George's St; 4pm-midnight Mon-Wed, to 2.30am Thu-Sun; all city centre) It doesn't matter that its name seems plucked out of a trendy focus group and the decor carefully curated to reflect current trends (art deco elements, old looking like new), this is actually a beautiful bar that serves top-notch cocktails. Be warned, the small space means it can get very busy in the evenings.

P.MAC'S BAR

Map p270 (www.facebook.com/pmacspub; 30 Lower Stephen St; ⏲noon-midnight Sun-Thu, to 1am Fri & Sat; 🚌all city centre) This Brooklyn-style bohemian hang-out is full of mismatched vintage furniture, American-style pint glasses and an alternative soundtrack veering towards the '90s. It also has 30-odd taps serving a huge variety of craft beers.

MARY'S BAR PUB

Map p270 (www.marysbar.ie; 8 Wicklow St; ⏲11am-11.30pm Mon-Wed, to 12.30am Thu-Sat, noon-11pm Sun; 🚌all city centre) In a twist of irony, the home of the authentic pub has seen the arrival of a classic McPub, complete with pseudo-old hardware shop at the front and oak-barrel tables at the back. Utterly artificial but a popular venue; downstairs is the even more popular Wow Burger (p72).

DRURY BUILDINGS COCKTAIL BAR COCKTAIL BAR

Map p270 (☎01-960 2095; www.drurybuildings.com; 52-55 Drury St; ⏲noon-11.30pm Sun-Thu, to 12.30am Fri & Sat; 🚌all city centre) The ground-floor cocktail bar at the Drury Buildings (p76) is popular for pre-dinner drinks. It also has an Italian lunch menu of sandwiches, salads and other titbits, consumed at the bar or the high tables spread throughout (mains €10 to €12), plus a nice beer garden out the back.

FARRIER & DRAPER CLUB

Map p270 (☎01-677 1220; www.farrieranddraper.ie; Powerscourt Townhouse, S William St; ⏲4pm-midnight Mon-Wed, to 1am Thu, noon-3pm Fri & Sat, noon-midnight Sun; 🚌all city centre) This opulent bar in the 18th-century Powerscourt complex (p84) combines Prohibition-era cool (staff in *Peaky Blinders* hats and sleeve garters) and Georgian decadence (high-vaulted ceilings, lots of paintings on the walls). Upstairs, in what was once Lady Powerscourt's private quarters, is a late-night bar and a club; downstairs is the beautiful Epic Bar; and in the basement is an Italian restaurant, La Cucina.

BERNARD SHAW BAR

Map p274 (www.thebernardshaw.com; 11-12 S Richmond St; ⏲noon-midnight Mon-Thu, to 12.30am Fri & Sat; 🚌14, 15, 65, 83) This deliberately ramshackle boozer is probably the coolest bar in town for its marvellous mix of music (courtesy of its owners, the Bodytonic production crew) and diverse menu of events, such as afternoon car-boot sales, storytelling nights and fun competitions like having a 'tag-off' between a bunch of graffiti artists. It also runs the excellent Eatyard (p72).

ANSEO BAR

Map p274 (18 Lower Camden St; ⏲4-11.30pm Mon-Thu, to 12.30am Fri & Sat, to 11pm Sun; 🚌14, 15, 65, 83) Unpretentious, unaffected and incredibly popular, this cosy alternative bar – which is pronounced 'an-*shuh*', the Irish for 'here' – is a favourite with those who live by the credo that to try too hard is far worse than not trying at all. The pub's soundtrack is an eclectic mix; you're as likely to hear Peggy Lee as Lee Perry.

MCDAID'S PUB

Map p270 (☎01-679 4395; www.mcdaidspub.com; 3 Harry St; ⏲10.30am-11.30pm Mon-Thu, to 12.30am Fri & Sat, 12.30-11pm Sun; 🚌all city centre) One of Dublin's best-known literary pubs, this classic boozer was popular with the likes of Patrick Kavanagh and Brendan Behan (both of whom were eventually barred) and it still oozes character. The pints are perfect, and best appreciated during the day when it's less busy. Thankfully, there's no music – just conversation and raucous laughter.

SWAN PUB

Map p270 (☎01-647 5272; www.theswanbar.com; 70 Aungier St; ⏲11am-11.30pm Mon-Thu, to 12.30am Fri & Sat, noon-11pm Sun; 🚌all city centre) Ex-rugby international John Lynch's pub is home to two kinds of punter: the in-for-a-pint-and-a-chat tippler who doesn't venture far from the Victorian front bar; and the more animated younger person, who finds solace and music in the side bar. It's a beautiful marriage that works because neither troubles the other.

STAG'S HEAD PUB

Map p270 (www.stagshead.ie; 1 Dame Ct; ⏲10am-11pm Sun-Thu, to 1am Fri & Sat; 🚌all city centre) The Stag's Head was built in 1770, remodelled in 1895 and thankfully not changed a bit since then. It's a superb pub: so picturesque that it often appears in films and also featured in a postage-stamp series on Irish bars. A bloody great pub, no doubt.

HOGAN'S BAR

Map p270 (35 S Great George's St; ⏲1.30pm-11.30am Mon-Wed, to 1am Thu, to 2.30am Fri & Sat, 2-11pm Sun; 🚌all city centre) Midweek this big contemporary bar is a relaxing hang-out for young professionals, and restaurant and bar workers on a night off. But come the weekend the sweat bin downstairs pulls them in for some serious music courtesy of the usually excellent DJs.

IDLEWILD BAR

Map p270 (☎01-253 0593; www.idlewilddublin.com; 14 Fade St; ⊙4-11.30pm Mon-Wed, to 2.30am Thu, 3pm-1.30am Fri & Sat, 3-11.30pm Sun; 🚌all city centre) The blink-and-you'll-miss-it entrance opens up to a spacious bar with elegant 1940s-style decor, adding a touch of ageless cool to a buzzing neighbourhood. It specialises in 'Boilermakers' – a pint of beer or cider paired with a shot – and most of the pairings are proudly Irish concoctions.

SAM'S BAR BAR

Map p270 (www.samsbar.ie; 36 Dawson St; ⊙4pm-12.30am Mon-Wed, to 2.30am Fri & Sat, 4pm-12.30am Sun; 🚌all city centre, 🚊St Stephen's Green) A posh Dawson St drinking spot, Sam's has decor that is Middle Eastern (a hangover of its previous incarnation as an Asian-themed bar) meets art-college graffiti. An odd mix, but it doesn't bother the young professional clientele, who come to share tales of success over fancy cocktails.

DICEY'S GARDEN BAR

Map p274 (☎01-478 4066; Russell Court Hotel, 21-25 Harcourt St; ⊙4pm-2.30am; 🚌all city centre, 🚊Harcourt) This massive place is better known as Dicey Reilly's (or just Dicey's) and is one of Dublin's most popular bars, spread across a couple of levels with about three different styles, including old-school pub, modern superbar and European beer garden. Charty music and a fun-lovin' crowd keep it going till the small hours.

PYGMALION BAR

Map p270 (☎01-674 6712; www.facebook.com/PygmalionDublin; Powerscourt Townhouse, 59 S William St; ⊙noon-2.30am Mon-Thu, to 3.30am Fri & Sat, noon-2am Sun; 🚌all city centre) The 'Pyg', with its craft beers, flavoured cocktails, excellent, pounding music and myriad nooks and crannies, is hugely popular with younger drinkers and partygoers. By day, those same revellers work out the previous night's shenanigans over coffee at the covered outside tables.

INTERNATIONAL BAR PUB

Map p270 (www.international-bar.com; 23 Wicklow St; ⊙10.30am-11.30pm Mon-Thu, to 12.30am Fri & Sat, 12.30-11pm Sun; 🚌all city centre) This smallish pub with a huge personality is a top spot for an afternoon pint. It has a long bar, stained-glass windows, red-velour seating and a convivial atmosphere. Some of Ireland's most celebrated comedians stuttered through their first set in the **Comedy Cellar**, which is, of course, upstairs.

COPPER FACE JACKS CLUB

Map p274 (www.copperfacejacks.ie; Jackson Court Hotel, 29-30 Harcourt St; free-€10; ⊙11pm-3am Sun-Thu, from 10pm Fri & Sat; 🚌10, 11, 13, 14, 15A, 🚊St Stephen's Green) In rural Ireland you don't go clubbing; you go to 'the disco' for a drink, a dance and – hopefully – 'the shift', a particularly Irish way of describing making out. Coppers (Twitter: @CopperFaceJacks) is a slice of country clubbing in the middle of the capital, and it's all the more popular for it.

GEORGE GAY

Map p270 (www.thegeorge.ie; 89 S Great George's St; weekends after 10pm €5-10, other times free; ⊙2pm-2.30am Mon-Fri, from 12.30pm Sat, 12.30pm-1am Sun; 🚌all city centre) The purple mother of Dublin's gay bars is a long-standing institution, having lived through the years when it was the only place in town where the gay crowd could, well, be gay. Shirley's legendary Sunday-night bingo is as popular as ever, while Wednesday's Space N Veda is a terrific night of cabaret and drag.

37 DAWSON STREET BAR

Map p270 (☎01-902 2908; www.37dawsonstreet.ie; 37 Dawson St; ⊙noon-2.30am Tue-Sun, to 11.30pm Mon; 🚌all city centre) Antiques, eye-catching art and elegant bric-a-brac adorn this bar that quickly established itself as a favourite with the trendy crowd. At the back is Whiskey Bar, a 1950s-style bar in which Don Draper and Co would feel comfortable sipping a fine Scotch; upstairs is an elegant restaurant that serves a terrific brunch.

RÍ RÁ CLUB

Map p270 (www.theglobe.ie; Dame Ct; ⊙4pm-2.30am Mon-Thu, from 2pm Fri-Sun; 🚌all city centre) A true veteran of the city's club scene, Rí Rá – one half of the Irish expression *rí rá agus ruaile buaile* ('ree raw aw-gus roola boola'), which translates roughly as 'devilment and good fun' – has been keeping the dance floor full with funky beats for a quarter of a century.

CAFÉ EN SEINE BAR

Map p270 (☎01-677 4369; www.cafeenseine.ie; 40 Dawson St; ⏰noon-11.30pm Sun-Thu, to 3am Fri & Sat; 🚌all city centre) The wildly extravagant art nouveau style of this huge bar is very popular with suburbanites, the after-work crowd and out-of-towners. Maybe it's the glass panelling, or the real 12m-high trees, but most likely it's the beautiful people propping up the wood-and-marble bar.

DAWSON LOUNGE PUB

Map p270 (25 Dawson St; ⏰12.30-11.30pm Mon-Thu, to 12.30am Fri & Sat, to 11pm Sun; 🚌all city centre, 🚊St Stephen's Green) To experience *the* smallest bar in Dublin, go through a little doorway, down a narrow flight of steps and into two tiny rooms that always seem to be filled with a couple of bedraggled drunks who look like they're hiding.

GLOBE BAR

Map p270 (☎01-671 1220; www.theglobe.ie; 11 S Great George's St; ⏰4pm-2.30am Mon-Thu, from 2pm Fri-Sun; 📶; 🚌all city centre) The grandaddy of the city's contemporary bars has steadfastly stuck to the formula that made it cool in the first place: wooden floors, plain brick walls and a no-attitude atmosphere that you just can't fake. And some pretty good music.

BRUXELLES PUB

Map p270 (www.bruxelles.ie; 7-8 Harry St; ⏰9.30am-1.30am Sun-Thu, to 2.30am Fri & Sat; 🚌all city centre) Bruxelles is a raucous music bar split across different areas. It's comparatively trendy on the ground floor, while downstairs is a great, loud and dingy rock bar with live music each weekend.

CLEMENT & PEKOE CAFE

Map p270 (www.clementandpekoe.com; 50 S William St; ⏰8am-7pm Mon-Fri, 9am-6.30pm Sat, 11am-6pm Sun; 🚌all city centre) Our favourite cafe in town is this contemporary version of an Edwardian tearoom. Walnut floors, art deco chandeliers and wall-to-wall displays of handsome tea jars are the perfect setting in which to enjoy the huge range of loose-leaf teas and carefully made coffees, along with a selection of cakes.

NETWORK COFFEE

Map p274 (www.networkcafe.ie; 39 Aungier St; ⏰7.30am-6pm Mon-Fri, from 9am Sat, 10am-5pm Sun; 🚌all city centre) If you're a fan of latte art, you'll be swooning at the creations that come out of this cool little cafe on Aungier St. But, thankfully, it's not all Instagram-luring bluster – the coffee itself is exquisite.

WALL AND KEOGH CAFE

Map p274 (www.wallandkeogh.ie; 45 S Richmond St; ⏰7.30am-7.30pm Mon-Fri, 9.30am-6.30pm Sat & Sun; 🚌all city centre) The Irish love their tea, and this marvellous cafe is the place to enjoy your choice of 150 different types, served in ceramic Japanese teapots with all the care of a traditional tea ceremony. It also serves a fabulous coffee and, for the peckish, sandwiches, baked goods and even sushi.

KAPH CAFE

Map p270 (www.kaph.ie; 31 Drury St; ⏰8am-7pm Mon-Sat, 11am-6pm Sun; 🚌all city centre) One of the newer breed of cafes where the barista's creations are considered caffeinated art. Order a flat white and use it to dunk one of the (homemade) madeleines.

☆ ENTERTAINMENT

★WHELAN'S LIVE MUSIC

Map p274 (☎01-478 0766; www.whelanslive.com; 25 Wexford St; 🚌16, 122 from city centre) Perhaps the city's most beloved live-music venue is this midsized room attached to a traditional bar. This is the singer-songwriter's spiritual home: when they're done pouring out the contents of their hearts on stage, you can find them filling up in the bar along with their fans.

★DEVITT'S LIVE MUSIC

Map p274 (☎01-475 3414; www.devittspub.ie; 78 Lower Camden St; ⏰from 9pm Mon & Tue, 9.30pm Wed & Thu, 7.45pm Fri & Sat, 6.30pm Sun; 🚌14, 15, 65, 83) Devitt's – aka the Cusack Stand – is one of the favourite places for the city's talented musicians to display their wares, with sessions as good as any you'll hear in the city centre. Highly recommended.

NATIONAL CONCERT HALL LIVE MUSIC

Map p274 (☎01-417 0000; www.nch.ie; Earlsfort Tce; 🚌all city centre) Ireland's premier orchestral hall hosts a variety of concerts year-round, with an increasingly diverse roster of performances including author interviews and spoken-word events.

UKIYO KARAOKE

Map p270 (☎01-633 4071; www.ukiyobar.com; 7-9 Exchequer St; per hour €40-80; ⏰noon-

2.30am Mon-Sat, to 1.30am Sun; all city centre) The basement rooms of this trendy sake bar can fit up to 20 people each for a night of singalong fun from the 30,000-odd songs on the menu (in a variety of languages). If you eat lunch here, the rooms are free until 5pm. Bookings recommended, especially for weekend nights.

SAMUEL BECKETT THEATRE THEATRE

Map p270 (01-896 2461; www.tcd.ie/beckett-theatre; Regent House, Pearse St; all city centre) The Trinity College Players' Theatre hosts student productions throughout the academic year, as well as the most prestigious plays from the Dublin Theatre Festival (p43).

TICKETMASTER BOOKING SERVICE

Map p270 (0818 719 300; www.ticketmaster.ie; St Stephen's Green Shopping Centre; all city centre, St Stephen's Green) Sells tickets to every genre of big- and medium-sized show – but be aware that it charges a 12.5% service charge *per ticket*.

GAIETY THEATRE THEATRE

Map p270 (0818 719 388; www.gaietytheatre.com; S King St; 7-10pm; all city centre) The 'Grand Old Lady of South King St' is over 150 years old and has for much of that time thrived on a diet of fun-for-all-the-family fare: West End hits, musicals, Christmas pantos and classic Irish plays keep the more serious-minded away, leaving more room for those simply looking to be entertained.

SHOPPING

Pedestrianised Grafton St was traditionally the shopping street, but the preponderance of the major chain stores has resulted in few surprises. To make the most of the area's excellent retail opportunities, head into the grid of streets surrounding it, especially to the west, where you'll find some of Dublin's most interesting outlets, from bookshops to boutiques, as well as two extraordinary shopping centres. As well as being accessible by all city-centre buses, most places around Grafton St can be accessed from the St Stephen's Luas stop.

★CHUPI JEWELLERY

Map p270 (01-551 0352; www.chupi.com; Powerscourt Townhouse, S William St; 10am-6pm Mon-Wed, Fri & Sat, to 7pm Thu, noon-5pm Sun; all city centre) Exceptional modern jewellery inspired by the Irish landscape and worn by all the city's style fiends. The pretty shop also stocks Irish-designed clothing and accessories.

★IRISH DESIGN SHOP ARTS & CRAFTS

Map p270 (01-679 8871; www.irishdesignshop.com; 41 Drury St; 10am-6pm Mon-Sat, 1-5pm Sun; all city centre) Beautiful, imaginatively crafted items – from jewellery to kitchenware – carefully curated by owners Clare Grennan and Laura Caffrey. If you're looking for a stylish Irish-made memento or gift, you'll surely find it here.

★AVOCA HANDWEAVERS ARTS & CRAFTS

Map p270 (01-677 4215; www.avoca.ie; 11-13 Suffolk St; 9.30am-6pm Mon-Wed & Sat, to 7pm Thu & Fri, 11am-6pm Sun; all city centre) Combining clothing, homewares, a basement food hall and an excellent top-floor cafe (p76), Avoca promotes a stylish but homey brand of modern Irish life – and is one of the best places to find an original present. Many of the garments are woven, knitted and naturally dyed at its Wicklow factory. There's a terrific kids' section.

★SHERIDAN'S CHEESEMONGERS FOOD

Map p270 (01-679 3143; www.sheridanscheesemongers.com; 11 S Anne St; 10am-6pm Mon-Fri, from 9.30am Sat; all city centre) If heaven were a cheese shop, this would be it. Wooden shelves are laden with rounds of farmhouse cheeses, sourced from around the country by Kevin and Seamus Sheridan, who have almost single-handedly revived cheese-making in Ireland.

OM DIVA VINTAGE

Map p270 (01-679 1211; www.omdivaboutique.com; 27 Drury St; 10am-6.30pm Mon-Wed, Fri & Sat, to 7.30pm Thu, noon-6pm Sun; all city centre) There are three floors of funky fashion in this cosy spot on Drury St – well-curated vintage in the basement, cutting-edge Irish design upstairs and contemporary style when you walk in. A one-stop shop for cool Dublin style.

PARFUMARIJA PERFUME

Map p270 (01-671 0255; www.parfumarija.com; 25 Westbury Mall; 10am-6pm Mon-Wed, Fri & Sat, to 7pm Thu; all city centre) The charming and passionate staff at Parfumarija won't rest until you've found a scent you love, but they are surprisingly non-pushy. They specialise in niche and rare scents from around the world, sourced by the founder, Marija Aslimoska.

SIOPAELLA FASHION & ACCESSORIES

Map p270 (☎01-558 1389; www.siopaella.com; 29 Wicklow St; ⏰10am-6pm Mon-Wed, to 7pm Thu-Sat, noon-6pm Sun; 🚌all city centre) Specialising in luxury secondhand clothing and accessories, Siopaella is the place to nab pre-loved designer goods at a reasonable price—think Hermés Birkin bags and vintage Versace.

LOULERIE JEWELLERY

Map p270 (☎01-672 4024; www.loulerie.com; 14B Chatham St; ⏰10.30am-5.30pm Mon & Tue, 10am-6pm Wed, Fri & Sat, to 7pm Thu; 🚌all city centre) Owner Louise Stokes learned her craft in New York, and has since returned with an unerring eye for finding that individual piece of jewellery – rings, necklaces, earrings etc – to suit every mood and occasion.

MOMUSE JEWELLERY

Map p270 (☎01-707 1763; www.momuse.ie; Powerscourt Townhouse, S William St; ⏰10.30am-6.30pm Mon-Wed, Fri & Sat, to 7pm Thu, 1-5pm Sun; 🚌all city centre) Exquisite modern jewellery by designer Margaret O'Rourke, with many of the pieces finished in this lovely boutique on the ground floor of Powerscourt Townhouse.

NOWHERE FASHION & ACCESSORIES

Map p270 (☎01-607 8983; www.nowhere.ie; 65 Aungier St; ⏰11am-6pm Mon-Sat; 🚌all city centre) Men's clothing and accessories with a streetwear and sports vibe. It operates an extensive online shop, too.

ARTICLE HOMEWARES

Map p270 (☎01-679 9268; www.articledublin.com; 1st fl, Powerscourt Townhouse, S William St; ⏰10.30am-6pm Mon-Wed, Fri & Sat, to 7pm Thu, 1-5pm Sun; 🚌all city centre) Beautiful tableware and decorative home accessories all made by Irish designers. Ideal for unique, tasteful gifts that you won't find elsewhere.

POWERSCOURT TOWNHOUSE SHOPPING CENTRE

Map p270 (☎01-679 4144; www.powerscourtcentre.ie; 59 S William St; ⏰10am-6pm Mon-Wed & Fri, to 8pm Thu, 9am-6pm Sat, noon-6pm Sun; 🚌all city centre) This absolutely gorgeous and stylish centre is in a carefully refurbished Georgian townhouse, built between 1741 and 1744. These days it's best known for its cafes and restaurants but it also does a top-end, selective trade in high fashion, art, exquisite handicrafts and other chi-chi sundries.

GEORGE'S STREET ARCADE MARKET

Map p270 (www.georgesstreetarcade.ie; btwn S Great George's & Drury Sts; ⏰9am-6.30pm Mon-Wed, to 7pm Thu-Sat, noon-6pm Sun; 🚌all city centre) Dublin's best nonfood market is sheltered within an elegant Victorian Gothic arcade. Apart from shops and stalls selling new and old clothes, secondhand books, hats, posters, jewellery and records, there's a fortune teller, some gourmet nibbles, and a fish and chipper that does a roaring trade.

DESIGN CENTRE CLOTHING

Map p270 (☎01-679 5718; www.designcentre.ie; Powerscourt Townhouse, S William St; ⏰10am-6pm Mon-Wed, Fri & Sat, to 8pm Thu; 🚌all city centre) Mostly dedicated to Irish designer womenswear, featuring well-made classic suits, evening wear and knitwear. Irish labels include Jill De Burca, Philip Treacy, Aoife Harrison and Erickson Beamon – a favourite with Michelle Obama.

BROWN THOMAS DEPARTMENT STORE

Map p270 (☎01-605 6666; www.brownthomas.com; 92 Grafton St; ⏰11am-7pm Mon & Sun, 10am-8pm Tue, 9.30am-8pm Wed, 9.30am-9pm Thu & Fri, 9am-8pm Sat; 🚌all city centre) Soak up the Jo Malone–laden rarefied atmosphere of Dublin's most exclusive shop, where presentation is virtually artistic. Here you'll find fantastic cosmetics, shoes to die for, exotic homewares and a host of Irish and international fashion labels, such as Balenciaga, Lainey Keogh and Philip Treacy. The 3rd-floor Bottom Drawer outlet stocks the finest Irish linen you'll find anywhere.

WEIR & SON'S JEWELLERY

Map p270 (☎01-677 9678; www.weirandsons.ie; 96-99 Grafton St; ⏰9.30am-6pm Mon-Wed, Fri & Sat, to 8pm Thu; 🚌all city centre) The largest jeweller in Ireland, this huge shop on Grafton St first opened in 1869 and still has its original wooden cabinets and a workshop on the premises. There's new and antique Irish jewellery (including Celtic designs) and a huge selection of watches, Irish crystal, porcelain, leather and travel goods.

BARRY DOYLE DESIGN JEWELLERS JEWELLERY

Map p270 (☎01-671 2838; www.barrydoyledesign.com; 30 George's St Arcade; ⏰10am-6pm

Mon-Sat; all city centre) Goldsmith Barry Doyle's upstairs shop is one of the best of its kind in Dublin. The handmade jewellery – using white gold, silver, and some truly gorgeous precious and semiprecious stones – is exceptional in its beauty and simplicity. Most of the pieces have Afro-Celtic influences.

ULYSSES RARE BOOKS BOOKS

Map p270 (01-671 8676; www.rarebooks.ie; 10 Duke St; 9.30am-5.45pm Mon-Sat; all city centre) Our favourite bookshop in the city stocks a rich and remarkable collection of Irish-interest books, with a particular emphasis on 20th-century literature and a large selection of first editions, including rare ones by the big guns: Joyce, Yeats, Beckett and Wilde.

KILKENNY SHOP ARTS & CRAFTS

Map p270 (01-677 7066; www.kilkennyshop.com; 6 Nassau St; 8.30am-7pm Mon-Wed, Fri & Sat, to 8pm Thu, 10am-6.30pm Sun; all city centre) A large, long-running repository for contemporary, innovative Irish crafts, including multicoloured modern Irish knits, designer clothing and lovely silver jewellery. The glassware and pottery is beautiful and sourced from workshops around the country. A great source for traditional presents.

LOUIS COPELAND CLOTHING

Map p270 (01-872 1600; www.louiscopeland.com; 18-19 Wicklow St; 9am-6pm Mon-Wed, Fri & Sat, to 8pm Thu, noon-5pm Sun; all city centre) Dublin's answer to the famed tailors of London's Savile Row, this shop makes fabulous suits to measure, and stocks plenty of ready-to-wear suits by international designers. There's another outlet on Capel St (p162).

COSTUME CLOTHING

Map p270 (01-679 5200; www.costumedublin.ie; 10 Castle Market; 10am-6pm Mon-Wed, Fri & Sat, to 7pm Thu, 2-5pm Sun; all city centre) Costume is considered a genuine pacesetter by Dublin's fashionistas; it has exclusive contracts with innovative designers such as Vivetta, Isabel Marant, Cedric Charlier and Zadig & Voltaire.

STOKES BOOKS BOOKS

Map p270 (01-671 3584; 19 George's St Arcade; 10.30am-6pm Mon-Sat; all city centre) A small bookshop specialising in Irish history books, both old and new. Other titles, covering a range of subjects, include a number of beautiful old, leather-bound editions.

KNOBS & KNOCKERS ARTS & CRAFTS

Map p270 (01-671 0288; www.knobsandknockers.ie; 19 Nassau St; 9.30am-5.30pm Mon-Sat; all city centre) Replica Georgian door knockers are a great souvenir of your Dublin visit, and there are plenty of other souvenir door adornments to look at here too.

ARAN SWEATER MARKET FASHION & ACCESSORIES

Map p270 (064-662 3102; www.aransweatermarket.com; 115 Grafton St; 9.30am-9pm; all city centre) If your trip isn't bringing you west, this is the best place in Dublin to pick up a timeless icon of Irish craft. All items are handknitted (although not necessarily on the Aran Islands) using traditional patterns and come with an explanation of the stitches' symbols. If you don't have room in your suitcase, it can ship your souvenirs home.

RHINESTONES JEWELLERY

Map p270 (01-679 0759; 18 St Andrew's St; 9.30am-6.30pm Mon-Wed, Fri & Sat, to 9pm Thu, noon-6pm Sun; all city centre) Exceptionally fine antique and quirky costume jewellery from the 1920s to 1970s, with pieces priced from €25 to €2000. Victorian jet, 1950s enamel, art deco turquoise, 1930s mother-of-pearl, cut-glass and rhinestone necklaces, bracelets, brooches and rings are displayed in old-fashioned cabinets.

INDUSTRY HOMEWARES

Map p270 (01-613 9111; www.industryandco.com; 41 Drury St; 8am-6pm Mon-Wed, to 7pm Thu, to 6.30pm Fri, 9am-6.30pm Sat, 10am-6pm Sun; all city centre) High-end homewares and accessories are the stock at this supercool independently owned design shop, where you can pick up everything from kids' booties to a birch veneer desk. It also has an excellent cafe.

DANKER ANTIQUES ARTS & CRAFTS

Map p270 (01-677 4009; www.dankerantiques.com; 4-5 Royal Hibernian Way; by appointment only; all city centre) Chock-full of exquisite treasures, this shop specialises in Irish and English antique silver, jewellery and objets d'art. You can find period suites of antique cutlery, candlesticks and candelabra as well as unusual items like potato rings – dish rings to insulate tables from hot bowls.

HOUSE OF NAMES ARTS & CRAFTS

Map p270 (01-679 7287; www.houseofnames.ie; 26 Nassau St; 10am-6pm Mon-Wed, Fri & Sat, to 8pm Thu, 11am-6pm Sun; all city centre) Impress your friends by serving them drinks on coasters emblazoned with your family's coat of arms, matching the sweatshirt you're wearing and, of course, the glasses or mugs the drinks are served in. All this and more can be yours from the House of Names, so long as you have a surname with Irish roots.

DUBRAY BOOKS BOOKS

Map p270 (01-677 5568; www.dubraybooks.ie; 36 Grafton St; 9am-7pm Mon-Wed & Sat, to 9pm Thu & Fri, 10am-6pm Sun; all city centre) Three floors devoted to bestsellers, recent releases, coffee-table books and a huge travel section make this one of the better bookshops in town. It can't compete with its larger, British-owned rivals on price, but it holds its own with helpful staff and a lovely atmosphere that encourages you to linger.

HODGES FIGGIS BOOKS

Map p270 (01-677 4754; www.waterstones.com; 56-58 Dawson St; 9am-7pm Mon-Wed & Fri, to 8pm Thu, to 6pm Sat, noon-6pm Sun; all city centre) The mother of all Dublin bookshops has books on every conceivable subject for every kind of reader spread across four huge floors, including a substantial Irish section on the ground floor. Keep an eye out for author signings and book launches, which are held fairly regularly.

ST STEPHEN'S GREEN SHOPPING CENTRE SHOPPING CENTRE

Map p270 (01-478 0888; www.stephensgreen.com; St Stephen's Green W; 9am-7pm Mon-Wed, Fri & Sat, 9am-9pm Thu, 11am-6pm Sun; all city centre) A 1980s version of a 19th-century shopping arcade; the dramatic, balconied interior and central courtyard are a bit too grand for the nondescript chain stores within. There's Boots, Benetton and a large Dunnes Store with a supermarket, as well as last-season designer warehouse TK Maxx.

DESIGNYARD ARTS & CRAFTS

Map p270 (01-474 1011; www.designyard.ie; 25 S Frederick St; 10am-5.30pm Mon-Wed & Fri, to 6pm Thu & Sat; all city centre) A high-end, craft-as-art shop where everything you see – glass, batik, sculpture, painting – is one-off and handmade in Ireland. It also showcases contemporary jewellery stock from young international designers. Perfect for that bespoke engagement ring or a very special present.

JENNY VANDER CLOTHING

Map p270 (01-677 0406; 50 Drury St; 10am-5.30pm Mon-Sat, 1-6pm Sun; all city centre) This secondhand shop oozes elegance and sophistication. Discerning fashionistas and film stylists snap up the exquisite beaded handbags, fur-trimmed coats, richly patterned dresses and costume jewellery priced as if it were the real thing.

HARLEQUIN VINTAGE

Map p270 (01-671 0202; 13 Castle Market; 11am-6pm Mon-Wed & Fri, to 7pm Thu, 10.30am-6pm Sat; all city centre) A fantastically cluttered shop, jam-packed with authentic vintage clothing gems from the 1920s onwards, as well as satin gloves, top hats, snakeskin bags and jet-beaded chokers.

SPORTS & ACTIVITIES

★GREEN MILE WALKING

Map p270 (01-661 1000; www.littlemuseum.ie; Little Museum of Dublin, 15 St Stephen's Green N; adult/student €15/13; 11am Sat & Sun; all city centre, St Stephen's Green) Excellent one-hour tour of St Stephen's Green led by local historian Donal Fallon. Along the way you'll hear tales of James Joyce, the park's history and the drafting of the Irish Constitution. Book ahead as tours fill up pretty quickly. The tour also includes admission to and a guided tour of the Little Museum of Dublin (p66).

★FAB FOOD TRAILS WALKING

(www.fabfoodtrails.ie; tours €60; 10am Sat) Highly recommended 2½- or three-hour tasting walks through the city centre's choicest independent producers. You'll visit up to eight bakeries, cheesemongers, markets and delis, learning about the food culture of each neighbourhood you explore. There is also a Food & Fashion walk. You meet in the city centre.

★HISTORICAL WALKING TOUR WALKING

Map p270 (01-878 0227; www.historicaltours.ie; Trinity College Gate; adult/student/child €14/12/free; 11am & 3pm May-Sep, 11am Apr & Oct, 11am Fri-Sun Nov-Mar; all city centre) Trinity College history graduates lead this 'seminar on the street' that explores the Potato Famine, Easter Rising, Civil War and Partition. Sights include Trinity, City Hall, Dublin Castle and the Four Courts. In summer, themed tours on architecture, women in Irish history and the birth of the Irish state are also held. Tours depart from the College Green entrance.

LITTLE BIRD YOGA

Map p278 (www.little-bird.ie; 82 S Circular Rd; 1hr classes €15; classes from 6.30am; 9, 16, 68, 68A, 122) A range of walk-in classes in a number of styles, including hatha, Iyengar, yin and vinyasa for all levels. Also hosts Pilates classes. Mats are provided free of charge. See the website for times and booking info.

CHILDREN'S PLAYGROUND PLAYGROUND

Map p274 (St Stephen's Green; dawn-dusk; all city centre, St Stephen's Green) On the eastern side of St Stephen's Green (p66) is a children's playground.

1916 REBELLION WALKING TOUR WALKING

Map p270 (086 858 3847; www.1916rising.com; 23 Wicklow St; adult/child €15/9; 11.30am Mon-Sat, 1pm Sun Mar-Oct, 11.30am Fri & Sat & 1pm Sun Nov-Feb; all city centre) Superb two-hour tour starting in the International Bar (p81), Wicklow St. Lots of information, humour and irreverence to boot. The guides – all Trinity graduates – are uniformly excellent and will not say no to the offer of a pint back at tour's end. They also have a tour based around Michael Collins, hero of the War of Independence.

SEE DUBLIN BY BIKE CYCLING

Map p270 (01-280 1899; www.seedublinbybike.ie; Drury St Car Park; tours €30; all city centre) Three-hour themed tours that start outside the Daintree Building on Pleasants Pl and take in the city's highlights and not-so-obvious sights. The Taste of Dublin is the main tour, but you can also take a U2's Dublin tour and a Literary Dublin tour. Bikes, helmets and hi-vis vests included. They're based in the bike storage area on the ground floor of the car park on Drury St.

PAT LIDDY WALKING TOURS WALKING

Map p270(01-831 1109; www.walkingtours.ie; Visit Dublin Centre, 25 Suffolk St; tours €10-15; all city centre) A variety of guided walks on a host of themes, from literary Dublin to U2. You can also get a whiskey or a Guinness tour and travel out to Howth for a tour of the lovely fishing village. The company's founder and tour guide trainer, Pat Liddy, is one of the city's best-known local historians. Check the website for timings.

DUBLIN LITERARY PUB CRAWL WALKING

Map p270 (01-670 5602; www.dublinpubcrawl.com; 9 Duke St; adult/student €14/12; 7.30pm daily Apr-Oct, 7.30pm Thu-Sun Nov-Mar; all city centre) A tour of pubs associated with famous Dublin writers is a sure-fire recipe for success, and this 2½-hour tour-performance by two actors is a riotous laugh. There's plenty of drink taken, which makes it all the more popular. It leaves from the Duke on Duke St; get there by 7pm to reserve a spot for the evening tour.

VIKING SPLASH TOURS TOURS

Map p270 (01-707 6000; www.vikingsplash.com; St Stephen's Green N; adult/child €25/13; every 30-90min 10am-3pm; all city centre, St Stephen's Green) Go on, what's the big deal? You stick a plastic Viking's helmet on your head and yell 'yay' at the urging of your guide, but the upshot is you'll get a 1¼-hour semi-amphibious tour that ends up in the Grand Canal Dock. 'Strictly for tourists' seems so... superfluous.

TRINITY COLLEGE WALKING TOUR WALKING

(Authenticity Tours; www.tcd.ie/visitors/tours; Trinity College; tours €6, incl Book of Kells €15; 9.30am-3.40pm Mon-Sat, to 3.15pm Sun May-Sep, fewer midweek tours Oct & Feb-Apr; all city centre, College Green) A great way to see Trinity's grounds is on a student-led walking tour. They depart from the College Green entrance every 20 to 40 minutes.

CARRIAGE TOURS TOURS

Map p270 (30min/1hr €50/85; Apr-Oct; all city centre, St Stephen's Green) Horse-drawn carriage tours of Dublin. They congregate by St Stephen's Green, and also by the entrance to the Guinness Storehouse (the only spots they're licensed to pick up passengers).

SANDEMAN'S NEW DUBLIN TOUR WALKING

Map p274 (01-878 8547; www.newdublintours.com; City Hall, Castle St; free-€30; hourly 10am-2pm; all city centre) A high-energy and thoroughly enjoyable three-hour walking tour of the city's greatest hits for free: tip only if you enjoyed the tour (guides make sure you do). There's does a Howth day tour (€30), a tour of haunted Dublin (€12; 5pm Tuesday to Saturday) and a pub crawl (€12; 7.30pm Friday).

Merrion Square & Around

Neighbourhood Top Five

1 National Gallery (p94) Perusing the collection at Ireland's pre-eminent gallery, packed with art from eight centuries of European tradition.

2 Museum of Natural History (p97) Visiting this antiquated museum, which has changed little since it was opened in the middle of the 19th century.

3 National Museum of Ireland – Archaeology (p90) Uncovering the fascinating treasures of the most important repository of Irish culture, from finely worked gold to prehistoric bodies.

4 O'Donoghue's (p104) Enjoying a night of music and beer in the very epitome of an Irish traditional pub.

5 Fine Dining (p102) Feasting on the superb cuisine offered by some of Dublin's very best restaurants, including Restaurant Patrick Guilbaud, Ireland's only Michelin two-star.

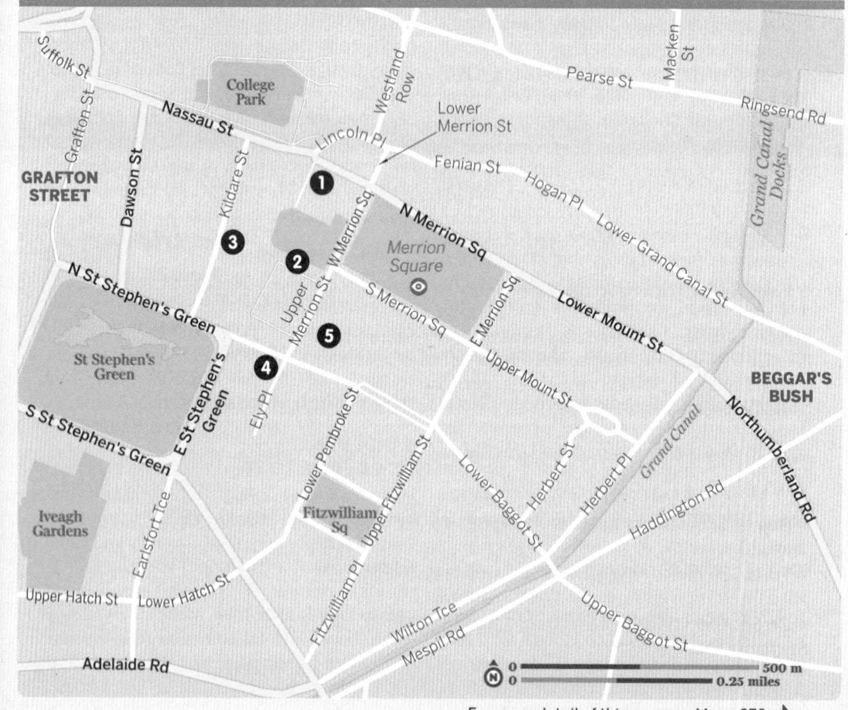

For more detail of this area see Map p276

Explore Merrion Square & Around

Ireland's national collections of art, history and natural history are to be found in the imposing neoclassical buildings that line the elegant Georgian streets and parks of the city's best-maintained 18th-century neighbourhood. Depending on your level of interest you'll need to devote as much as half a day to each, or just an hour or two if all you want is an overview.

You'll also want to spend some time looking at the private residences that line Merrion (p96) and Fitzwilliam Sqs (p98) – the many plaques on these Georgian buildings remind us that it was behind these brightly coloured doors that the likes of Oscar Wilde and William Butler Yeats hung their hats.

These streets also house the offices of some of the country's most important businesses, so when there's even a hint of sunshine, workers pour out into the various parks, or lounge along the banks of the Grand Canal. After work they head to the wonderfully atmospheric and historical pubs of Baggot St and Merrion Row for a couple of scoops of chips and some unwinding banter. There are also some smart restaurants, including several of Dublin's best.

Local Life

➡ **High Art** The Jack B Yeats collection in the National Gallery (p94) soothes a Dubliner's troubled soul, while the Royal Hibernian Academy (p97) is an excellent showcase of contemporary art. For something a little more affordable, the weekend art market (p101) along the railings of Merrion Sq displays surprisingly good-quality work.

➡ **Beer Power** Follow the power brokers, politicians and business crowd as they unwind in some of the city's best traditional boozers: Toner's (p103) and Doheny & Nesbitt's (p104) are established favourites, but O'Donoghue's (p104) of Merrion Row is in a league of its own.

➡ **Fine Dining** The critics regularly praise Restaurant Patrick Guilbaud (p102) as the best in the country; whatever debate there is exists as a result of restaurants like L'Ecrivain (p102), but there's also a bunch of less-exalted spots worth checking out, such as Etto (p101) and Coburg Brasserie (p101).

Getting There & Away

➡ **Bus** Most cross-city buses will get you here (or near enough).

➡ **Train** The most convenient DART stop is Pearse St, with the station entrance on Westland Row.

➡ **On Foot** Merrion Sq is less than 500m from St Stephen's Green (and Grafton St).

Lonely Planet's Top Tip

The Vaughan Collection of watercolours by JMW Turner at the National Gallery (p94) is only displayed during the month of January, when the light is just right to appreciate the delicacy and beauty of these masterpieces.

Best Places to Eat

➡ Restaurant Patrick Guilbaud (p102)

➡ L'Ecrivain (p102)

➡ Coburg Brasserie (p101)

➡ Etto (p101)

For reviews, see p101 ➡

Best Places to Drink

➡ Toner's (p103)

➡ O'Donoghue's (p104)

➡ Doheny & Nesbitt's (p104)

➡ House (p104)

➡ Square Ball (p104)

For reviews, see p103 ➡

Best Irish Art

➡ Yeats Room, National Gallery (p94)

➡ Treasury, National Museum of Ireland – Archaeology (p90)

➡ Royal Hibernian Academy (RHA) Gallagher Gallery (p97)

For reviews, see p90 

ANTON_IVANOV/SHUTTERSTOCK ©

TOP SIGHT
NATIONAL MUSEUM OF IRELAND – ARCHAEOLOGY

This is the mother of all Irish museums and the country's foremost cultural institution. One of four branches, this is the most important, home to Europe's finest selection of Bronze and Iron Age gold artefacts, the most complete collection of medieval Celtic metalwork in the world, and fascinating prehistoric and Viking relics.

DON'T MISS

- Tara Brooch
- Ardagh Chalice
- Loughnashade Horn
- *Kingship and Sacrifice* exhibition

PRACTICALITIES

- Map p276, A3
- www.museum.ie
- Kildare St
- admission free
- 10am-5pm Tue-Sat, from 1pm Sun
- all city centre

Treasury

The Treasury is the most famous part of the collection, and its centrepieces are Ireland's best-known crafted artefacts, the **Ardagh Chalice** and the **Tara Brooch**. The 12th-century Ardagh Chalice is made of gold, silver, bronze, brass, copper and lead; it measures 17.8cm high and 24.2cm in diameter and, put simply, is the finest example of Celtic art ever found. The equally renowned Tara Brooch was crafted around AD 700, primarily in white bronze, but with traces of gold, silver, glass, copper, enamel and wire beading, and was used as a clasp for a cloak. It was discovered on a beach in Bettystown, County Meath, in 1850, but later came into the hands of an art dealer who named it after the hill of Tara, the historic seat of the ancient high kings. It doesn't have quite the same ring to it, but it was the Bettystown Brooch that sparked a revival of interest in Celtic jewellery that hasn't let up to this day. There are many other pieces that testify to Ireland's history as the land of saints and scholars.

Ór – Ireland's Gold

Elsewhere in the Treasury is the *Ór – Ireland's Gold* exhibition, featuring stunning jewellery and decorative objects created by Celtic artisans in the Bronze and Iron Ages. Among them are the **Broighter Hoard**, which includes a 1st-century-BC large gold collar, unsurpassed anywhere in Europe, and an extraordinarily delicate gold boat. There's also the wonderful **Loughnashade Horn,** a bronze war trumpet, which also dates from the 1st century BC. It is 1.86m long and made of sheets of bronze, riveted together, with an intricately designed disc at the mouth. It produces a sound similar to the Australian didgeridoo, though you'll have to take our word for it. Running alongside the wall is a **15m log boat**, which was dropped into the water to soften, abandoned and then pulled out 4000 years later, almost perfectly preserved in the peat bog.

Kingship & Sacrifice

One of the museum's biggest showstoppers is the collection of Iron Age 'bog bodies' in the *Kingship and Sacrifice* exhibit – four figures in varying states of preservation dug out of the midland bogs. The bodies' various eerily preserved details – a distinctive tangle of hair, sinewy legs and fingers with fingernails intact – are memorable, but it's the accompanying detail that will make you pause: scholars now believe that all of these bodies were victims of the most horrendous ritualistic torture and sacrifice – the cost of being notable figures in the Celtic world.

Other Exhibits

If you can cope with any more history, upstairs are **Medieval Ireland 1150–1550**, **Viking Age Ireland** – which features exhibits from the excavations at Wood Quay, the area between Christ Church Cathedral and the river – and our own favourite, the aptly named **Clothes from Bogs in Ireland**, a collection of 16th- and 17th-century woollen garments recovered from the bog. Enthralling stuff!

WHAT'S IN A NAME?

Virtually all of the treasures held here are named after the location in which they were found. It's interesting to note that most of them were discovered not by archaeologists' trowels but by bemused farmers out ploughing their fields, cutting peat or, in the case of the Ardagh Chalice, digging for spuds.

If you don't mind groups, the themed guided tours will help you wade through the myriad exhibits. If you want to avoid crowds, the best time to visit is weekday afternoons, when school groups have gone, and never during Irish school holidays.

DID YOU KNOW?

The museum was founded by an Act of (British) Parliament on 14 August 1877 as the Museum of Science and Art, Dublin. Its original purview was to house the expanding collection of the Royal Dublin Society, which was duly transferred to state ownership along with important collections owned by Trinity College and the Royal Irish Academy.

National Museum of Ireland

NATIONAL TREASURES

Ireland's most important cultural institution is the National Museum, and its most important branch is the original one, housed in this fine neoclassical (or Victorian Palladian) building designed by Sir Thomas Newenham Deane and finished in 1890. Squeezed in between the rear entrance of Leinster House – the Irish parliament – and a nondescript building from the 1960s, it's easy to pass by the museum. But within its fairly cramped confines you'll find the most extensive collection of Bronze and Iron Age gold artefacts in Europe and the extraordinary collection of the Treasury. This includes the stunning ❶**Ardagh Chalice** and the delicately crafted ❷**Tara Brooch**. Amid all the lustre, look out for the ❸**Broighter Gold Collar** then pay a visit to the exquisite ❹**Cross of Cong**, which was created after the other pieces but is just as beautiful. Finally, on the other side of the building is the unforgettable ❺ **Kingship & Sacrifice** exhibit, where you'll find 'bog bodies' - actual Celts preserved to an uncanny level of detail.

As you visit these treasures – all created after the arrival of Christianity in the 5th century – bear in mind that they were produced with the most rudimentary of instruments.

VIKING DUBLIN

Archaeological excavations in Dublin between 1961 and 1981 unearthed evidence of a Viking town and cemeteries along the banks of the River Liffey. The graves contained weapons such as swords and spears, together with jewellery and personal items. Craftsmen's tools, weights and scales, silver ingots and coins show that the Vikings, as well as marauding and raiding, were also engaged in commercial activities. The Viking artefacts are now part of the National Museum's collection.

LUNCH BREAK

The museum's own cafe, Brambles, is an excellent choice for lunch; for something a little more gourmet, Etto (18 Merrion Row) is an exceptional Italian restaurant.

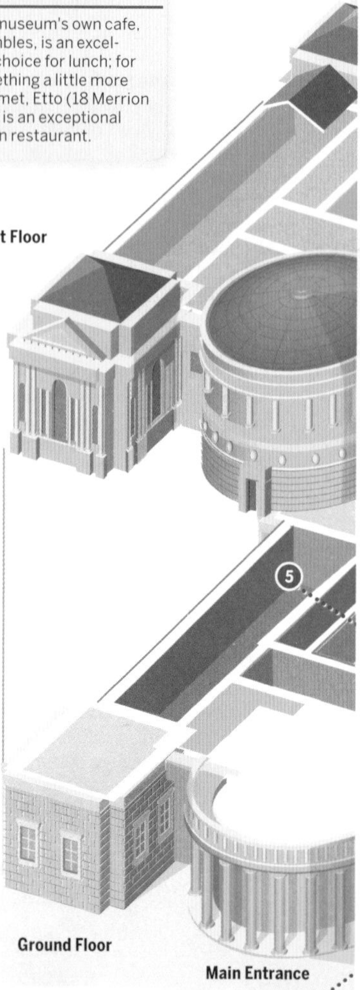

Cross of Cong
Made in 1123 to encase a fragment of the True Cross that was touring the country at the time, it was kept by the Augustinian monks at their friary in Cong, County Galway. The exquisite gold filigree on both the front and back are testament to the important role the cross was designed to have.

1
2
3
4

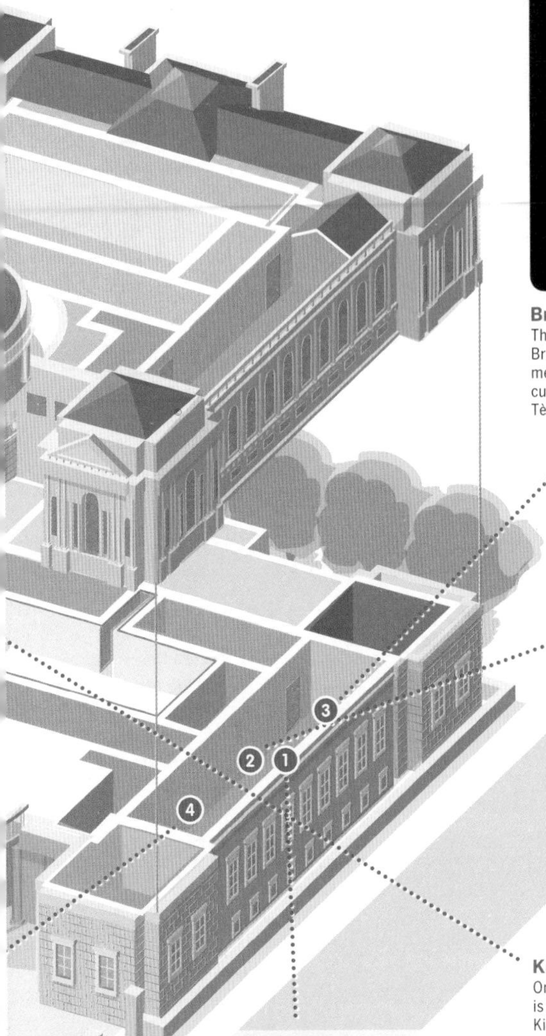

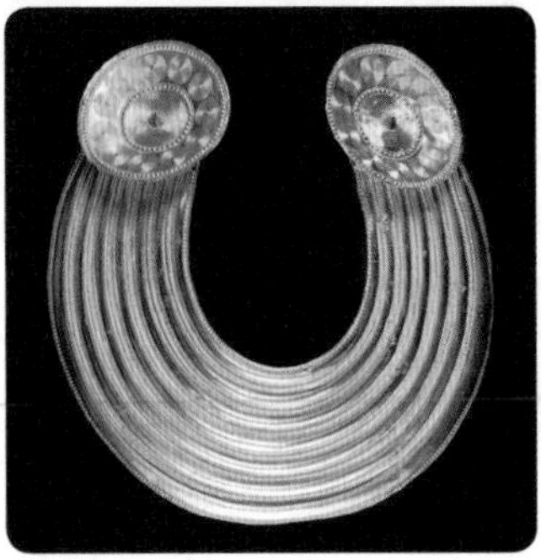

Broighter Gold Collar
The most exquisite element of the larger Broighter Hoard, this beautiful gold neck ornament (called a torc) is decorated in the elaborate curved patterns of high Celtic art, called La Tène style.

Tara Brooch
Designed around AD 700 as a clasp for a cloak, this is the second superstar of the collection – its delicate craftsmanship has become a symbol of the excellence of Irish art.

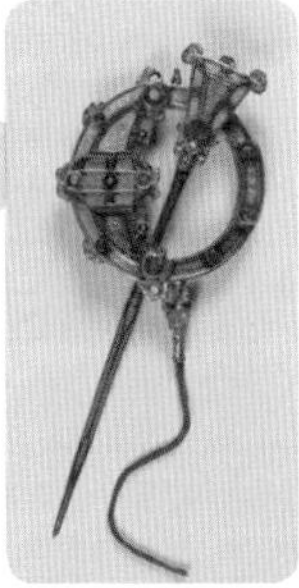

Kingship & Sacrifice
One of the museum's biggest showstoppers is the collection of Iron Age 'bog bodies' in the Kingship and Sacrifice exhibit – four figures in varying states of preservation dug out of the midland bogs.

Ardagh Chalice
Made of gold, silver, bronze, brass, copper and lead, the 12th-century Ardagh Chalice is the finest example of Celtic art ever found.

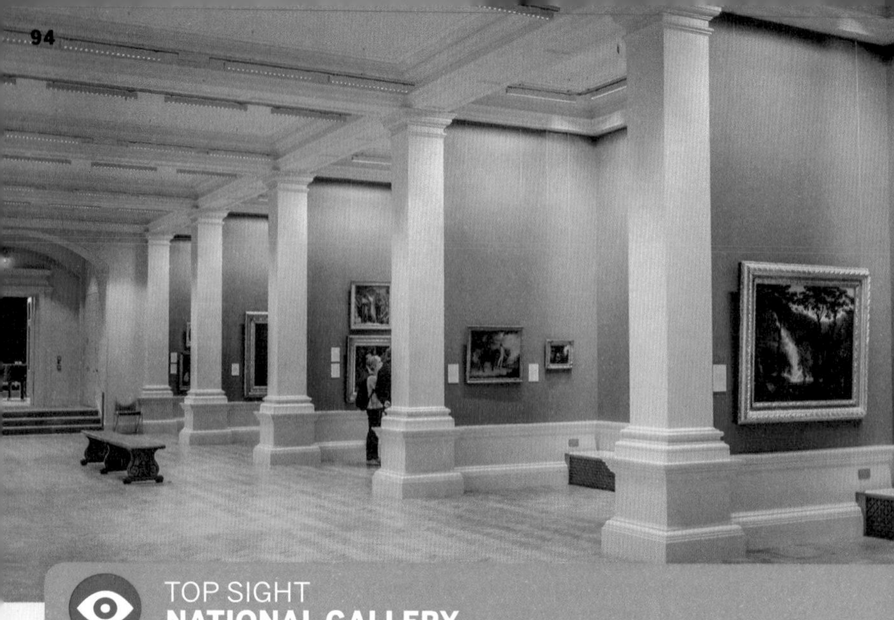

BENOIT DAOUST/SHUTTERSTOCK ©

TOP SIGHT
NATIONAL GALLERY

A stunning Caravaggio and a room full of the work of Ireland's pre-eminent artist, Jack B Yeats, are just a couple of highlights from this fine collection.

Its original assortment of 125 paintings has grown, mainly through bequests, to more than 13,000 artworks, including oils, watercolours, sketches, prints and sculptures.

The Building

The building itself was designed by Francis Fowke (1823–65), whose architectural credits also include London's Victoria & Albert Museum. The entire building comprises 54 galleries; works are divided by history, school, geography and theme. There are four wings: the original Dargan Wing, the Milltown Wing (1899–1903), the Beit Wing (1964–68) and the Millennium Wing (2002). A major refurbishment was completed in 2016.

The Collection

The collection spans works from the 14th to the 20th centuries and includes all the major continental schools.

There is an emphasis on Irish art, and among the works to look out for are William Orpen's *Sunlight,* Roderic O'Conor's *Reclining Nude* and *Young Breton Girl,* and Paul Henry's *The Potato Diggers*. But the highlight, and one you should definitely take time to explore, is the **Yeats Room**, devoted to and containing more than 30 paintings by Jack B Yeats, a uniquely Irish impressionist and arguably the country's greatest artist. Some of his finest moments are *The Liffey Swim, Men of Destiny* and *Above the Fair.*

DON'T MISS

- The Yeats Room
- *The Taking of Christ* (Caravaggio)
- *A Lady Writing a Letter* (Vermeer)
- Vaughan Collection

PRACTICALITIES

- Map p276, B2
- www.nationalgallery.ie
- Merrion Sq W
- admission free
- 9.15am-5.30pm Tue-Wed, Fri & Sat, to 8.30pm Thu, 11am-5.30pm Sun-Mon
- 4, 7, 8, 39A, 46A from city centre

Caravaggio's The Taking of Christ

The absolute star exhibit from a pupil of the European schools is Caravaggio's sublime *The Taking of Christ,* in which the troubled Italian genius attempts to light the scene figuratively and metaphorically (the artist himself is portrayed holding the lantern on the far right). Fra Angelico, Titian and Tintoretto are all in this neighbourhood. Facing Caravaggio, way down the opposite end of the gallery, is *A Genovese Boy Standing on a Terrace* by Van Dyck. Old Dutch and Flemish masters line up in between, but all defer to Vermeer's *A Lady Writing a Letter,* which is lucky to be here at all, having been stolen by Dublin gangster Martin Cahill in 1992, as featured in the film *The General.*

French Collection

The French section contains Jules Breton's famous 19th-century *The Gleaners,* along with works by Monet, Degas, Pissarro and Delacroix, while Spain chips in with an unusually scruffy *Still Life with Mandolin* by Picasso, as well as paintings by El Greco and Goya, and an early Velázquez. There is a small British collection with works by Reynolds, Hogarth and Gainsborough (*The Cottage Girl* is especially beautiful).

Vaughan Collection

One of the most popular exhibitions occurs only in January, when the gallery hosts its annual display of the Vaughan Collection, featuring watercolours by Joseph Mallord William Turner (1775–1851). The 35 works in the collection are best viewed at this time due to the particular quality of the winter light.

MONET RESTORED

Take a close look at Monet's *Argenteuil Basin with a Single Sail Boat* (1874). Notice anything? Probably not, but in 2012 the painting was slashed and seriously damaged; however, the restoration has been virtually flawless. The consequences were far greater for the individual who caused the damage – he was given a six-year jail term in 2014.

The best time to visit the gallery is Thursday evening, when it's open late and there are fewer visitors.

A MASTERPIECE IN THE CELLAR

Caravaggio's *The Taking of Christ* lay undiscovered for more than 60 years in a Jesuit house in nearby Leeson St, and was found accidentally by the chief curator of the gallery, Sergio Benedetti, in 1992.

There are family workshops for kids to try their hand at art throughout the year, usually on Saturdays; check the gallery website for details.

TOP SIGHT MERRION SQUARE

Elegant Merrion Sq was laid out in 1762 and is to this day the most prestigious of Dublin's squares. Its well-kept lawns and beautifully tended flower beds are flanked on three sides by gorgeous Georgian houses with colourful doors and peacock fanlights, and on the remaining side by the National Gallery, Leinster House and the Museum of Natural History.

DON'T MISS

- Oscar Wilde statue
- Georgian doorways
- Peacock fanlights

PRACTICALITIES

- Map p276, C3
- dawn-dusk
- all city centre

Oscar Wilde Statue

Just inside the northwestern corner of the square is a flamboyant **statue of Oscar Wilde**, who grew up across the street at **No 1**. This was the first residence built on the square (1762) and during the Wilde tenancy was renowned for the literary salon hosted by his mother, Lady 'Speranza' Wilde. Alas, you can't visit the restored house (used exclusively by students of the American College Dublin) so you'll have to make do with the statue of Wilde, wearing his customary smoking jacket and reclining on a rock. Wilde may well be sneering at Dublin and his old home, although the expression may have more to do with the artist's attempt to depict the deeply divided nature of the man: from one side he looks to be smiling and happy; from the other, gloomy and preoccupied. Atop one of the plinths, daubed with witty one-liners and Wildean throwaways, is a small green statue of Oscar's pregnant mother.

Other Statuary

Just inside the western side of the square is the **National Memorial** (Merrion Sq W; 24hr; all city centre), a pyramid-shaped sculpture by Brian King. Inside are four bronze figures, representing all elements of the Irish Defence Forces, standing guard over an eternal flame. The middle of the park has the sculpture of a **Jester's Chair**, commissioned in memory of Dermot Morgan, aka Father Ted.

Troubled Times

Despite the air of affluent calm, life around here hasn't always been a well-pruned bed of roses. During the Famine (1845–51), the lawns of the square teemed with destitute rural refugees who lived off the soup kitchen organised here. After independence, the new Irish Free State government considered it an unwelcome symbol of British rule in Ireland and developed plans to demolish and redevelop the square, but the plans were put aside during WWII and thankfully never pursued. After the killing of 13 civilians on Bloody Sunday in Derry in 1972, an angry crowd of about 20,000 gathered outside the British embassy at 39 Merrion Sq East and burnt the building out (the embassy then moved to Ballsbridge).

Damage to fine Dublin buildings hasn't always been the prerogative of vandals, terrorists or protesters. East Merrion Sq once continued into Lower Fitzwilliam St in the longest unbroken series of Georgian houses in Europe. Despite this, in 1961 the Electricity Supply Board (ESB) knocked down 16 of them to build an office block – just another in a long list of crimes against architectural aesthetics that plagued the city in the latter half of the 20th century. The Royal Institute of the Architects of Ireland is rather more respectful of its Georgian address and hosts regular exhibitions.

SIGHTS

The Merrion Sq area is where the big guns of Dublin's sights are gathered: separated by the back entrance of the Irish parliament are the National Gallery and the Museum of Natural History, while not far away on Kildare St (by the front entrance of the parliament) is the National Museum of Ireland.

NATIONAL MUSEUM OF IRELAND – ARCHAEOLOGY MUSEUM

See p90.

NATIONAL GALLERY MUSEUM

See p94.

MERRION SQUARE PARK

See p96.

★MUSEUM OF NATURAL HISTORY MUSEUM

Map p276 (National Museum of Ireland – Natural History; www.museum.ie; Upper Merrion St; ⏲10am-5pm Tue-Sat, from 1pm Sun; 🚌7, 44 from city centre) FREE Affectionately known as the 'Dead Zoo', this dusty, weird and utterly compelling museum is a fine example of the scientific wonderment of the Victorian age. Its enormous collection of stuffed beasts and carefully annotated specimens has barely changed since Scottish explorer Dr David Livingstone opened it in 1857 – before disappearing into the African jungle for a meeting with Henry Stanley.

The **Irish Room** on the ground floor is filled with mammals, sea creatures, birds and some butterflies all found in Ireland at some point, including the skeletons of three 10,000-year-old Irish elk that greet you as you enter. The **World Animals Collection**, spread across three levels, has as its centrepiece the skeleton of a 20m-long fin whale found beached in County Sligo. Evolutionists will love the line-up of orang-utan, chimpanzee, gorilla and human skeletons on the 1st floor.

A newer addition is the **Discovery Zone**, where visitors can do some firsthand exploring of their own, handling taxidermy specimens and opening drawers. Other notables include a Tasmanian tiger (an extinct Australian marsupial, mislabelled as a Tasmanian wolf), a giant panda from China, and several African and Asian rhinoceros. The wonderful **Blaschka Collection** comprises finely detailed glass models of marine creatures whose zoological accuracy is incomparable.

THE NEARLY CATHEDRAL

In the early 20th century Merrion Square was owned by the church, who as late as 1938 still had plans to build a cathedral on it. One former resident of the square was WB Yeats (1865–1939), who was less than impressed by the square and described the architecture as 'grey 18th century'. There's just no pleasing some people.

LEINSTER HOUSE NOTABLE BUILDING

Map p276 (Oireachtas Éireann; ☎01-618 3271; www.oireachtas.ie; Kildare St; ⏲observation galleries 2.30-8.30pm Tue, from 10.30am Wed, 10.30am-5.30pm Thu Nov-May; 🚌all city centre) All the big decisions are made at the Oireachtas (Parliament). This Palladian mansion was built as a city residence for James Fitzgerald, the Duke of Leinster and Earl of Kildare, by Richard Cassels between 1745 and 1748. Pre-arranged free guided tours (p104) are available when parliament is in session (but not sitting); entry tickets to the observation galleries are available.

The Kildare St facade looks like a townhouse (which inspired Irish architect James Hoban's design for the US White House), whereas the Merrion Sq frontage resembles a country mansion. The obelisk in front of the building is dedicated to Arthur Griffith, Michael Collins and Kevin O'Higgins, the architects of independent Ireland.

The first government of the Irish Free State moved in from 1922, and both the Dáil (lower house) and Seanad (senate, or upper house) still meet here to discuss the affairs of the nation and gossip at the exclusive members bar. The 60-member Seanad meets for fairly low-key sessions in the north-wing saloon, while there are usually more sparks and tantrums when the 166-member Dáil bangs heads in a less-interesting room, formerly a lecture theatre, which was added to the original building in 1897. Parliament sits for 90 days a year.

ROYAL HIBERNIAN ACADEMY (RHA) GALLAGHER GALLERY GALLERY

Map p276 (☎01-661 2558; www.rhagallery.ie; 15 Ely Pl; ⏲11am-5pm Mon-Tue & Thu-Sat, to 8pm Wed, noon-5pm Sun; 🚌10, 11, 13B, 51X from city centre) FREE This large, well-lit gallery at the end of a serene Georgian cul-de-sac has a grand name to fit its exalted reputation as one of the most prestigious exhibition spaces for modern and contemporary art in Ireland. Its exhibitions are usually of a very high quality, and well worth a visit.

The big event is the Annual Exhibition, held in May, which shows the work of those artists deemed worthy enough by the selection committee that is made up of members of the academy (easily identified amid the huge throng that attends the opening by their scholars' gowns). The show is a mix of technically proficient artists, Sunday painters and the odd outstanding talent.

FITZWILLIAM SQUARE — PARK

Map p276 (closed to public; 10, 11, 13B, 46A from city centre) The smallest of Dublin's great Georgian squares was completed in 1825. William Dargan (1799–1867), the railway pioneer and founder of the National Gallery, lived at No 2, and the artist Jack B Yeats (1871–1957) lived at No 18. In 2017 it began hosting a summer market of more than a dozen vendors.

It's the only one left where the central garden is still the private domain of the square's residents. Look out for the attractive 18th- and 19th-century metal coal-hole covers. The square is now a centre for the medical profession.

PATRICK KAVANAGH STATUE — STATUE

Map p276 (37 from city centre) A bronze sculpture of Patrick Kavanagh (1904–67), erected in 1968, shows the poet with arms and legs crossed in one of his favourite spots. It is inspired by his poem 'Lines written on a Seat on the Grand Canal, Dublin'.

HUGUENOT CEMETERY — CEMETERY

Map p276 (St Stephen's Green; closed to public; all city centre) This tiny cemetery was established in 1693 by French Protestant refugees. The cemetery is closed but you can see graves through the railings; of the 239 surnames one is Becquett, a relation of the writer Samuel Beckett.

NATIONAL LIBRARY OF IRELAND — HISTORIC BUILDING

Map p276 (www.nli.ie; Kildare St; 9.30am-7.45pm Mon-Wed, to 4.45pm Thu & Fri, 9.30am-12.45pm Sat; all city centre) FREE The domed reading room of this august establishment is the main visitor highlight, and it was here that Stephen Dedalus expounded his views

Neighbourhood Walk
A Georgian Block

START KILDARE ST
END NATIONAL GALLERY
LENGTH 1.7KM; ONE HOUR

Although Dublin is rightfully known as a Georgian city and many of its buildings were built between 1720 and 1814, the style cast such a tall shadow over Dublin design that for more than a century afterwards it was still being copied.

Begin your amble at the bottom (northern) end of ❶ **Kildare St**, opposite the walls of Trinity College Dublin. This street is named after James Fitzgerald, the Duke of Leinster and Earl of Kildare, who broke with 18th-century convention and opted to build his city mansion on the south side of the Liffey, away from the elegant neighbourhoods of the north side where most of his aristocratic peers lived. 'Where I go,' he confidently predicted, 'society will follow.'

He was right, and over the following century the street was lined with impressive buildings. On the left-hand side as you begin is the old Kildare Street Lords Club, a members' club famous for 'aristocracy, claret and whist' that was founded in 1782. In 1860 the original building was replaced by this Byzantine-style construction, designed by Thomas Newenham Deane, where the club remained until 1976. It is now the home of the Alliance Française.

On the same side a little further up is the ❷ **National Library of Ireland**, another one of Deane's designs; immediately after the library, the imposing black gates and police presence protect ❸ **Leinster House** (p97), the Palladian city pile that Fitzgerald commissioned Richard Cassels to build for him between 1745 and 1748. It is now the seat of both houses of the Irish Parliament. From this side American visitors might think the building looks oddly familiar: the townhouse look is what inspired James Hoban to submit a design that won the competition to build the White House in 1792.

The next building along the street is the ❹ **National Museum of Ireland – Archaeology** (p90), another Deane

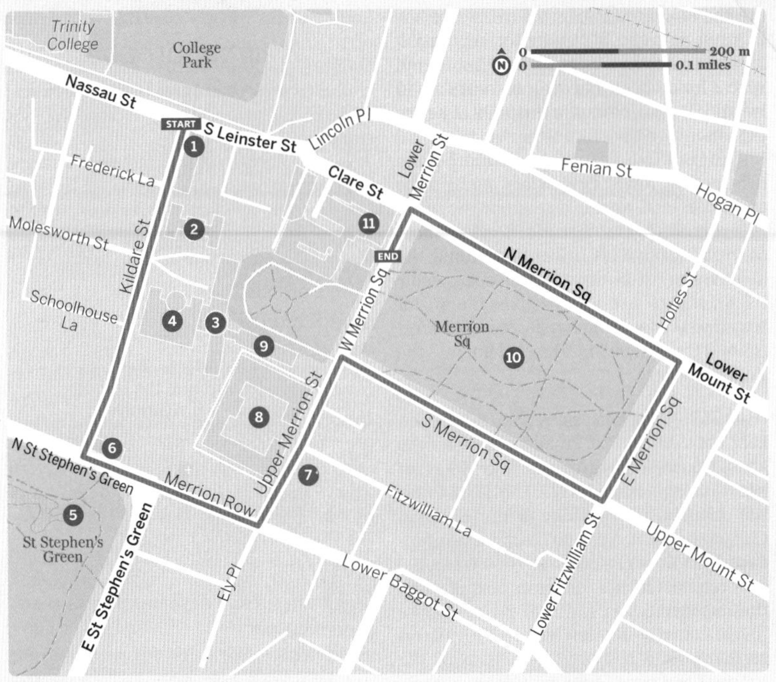

building, which opened in 1890 and has since been the repository of the state's most valuable cultural treasures. As you reach the top of the street, the greenery in front of you is that of **5 St Stephen's Green** (p66), the city's best-loved public square. Once a common used for punishments and hangings, the green was landscaped with Guinness money in the mid-18th century and quickly became the aristocracy's favourite spot to take a walk.

Turn left onto Merrion Row and walk along the green. You'll pass the **6 Shelbourne** (p204), Dublin's most historic hotel. During the Easter Rising of 1916 it treated the injured from both rebel and British sides, and the Irish Constitution of 1922 was framed in Room 112. The hotel even has a tenuous link to Hitler: his half-brother Alois worked as a waiter here. Take another left onto Merrion St. On your right, No 24 in the row of elegant Georgian houses is reputed to be the birthplace of Arthur Wellesley, the Duke of Wellington, who dealt with jibes about being born in Ireland by snippily responding that 'being born in a stable does not make one a horse'. That 'stable' is now part of the city's most elegant hotel, the **7 Merrion** (p204).

On your left-hand side you'll pass the **8 Government Buildings** (p100), where the current government runs its day-to-day affairs, and just past it, the rear entrance to Leinster House; from here it looks more like a country mansion. The smaller building wedged in between the Government Buildings and Leinster House is the **9 Museum of Natural History** (p97), opened in 1857.

On your right is **10 Merrion Square** (p96), the most elegant of Dublin's public spaces. The park itself is gorgeous, while the houses that surround it are magnificent: their doorways and peacock fanlights are the most photographed of the city's Georgian heritage and a disproportionate number of Dublin's most famous residents lived on it at one point or another.

Walk around or through Merrion Sq, making your way back to West Merrion Sq and the **11 National Gallery** (p94), which opened in 1864 and was built by Francis Fowke after a design by Charles Lanyon. For the sake of symmetry, the facade is a copy of that of the Museum of Natural History.

on Shakespeare in James Joyce's *Ulysses*. For everyone else, it's an important repository of early manuscripts, first editions and maps. It was built between 1884 and 1890 by Sir Thomas Newenham Deane to echo the design of the facade of the National Museum of Ireland – Archaeology. There's a Genealogy Advisory Service (p102) on the 2nd floor.

For those prints that are worth a thousand words, you'll have to head down to Temple Bar to the National Photographic Archive (p111) extension of the library, for which you'll need to pick up a reader's ticket (look for the Readers Ticket Office in the main building).

NUMBER 29 LOWER FITZWILLIAM STREET — HISTORIC BUILDING

Map p276 (www.numbertwentynine.ie; 29 Lower Fitzwilliam St; closed until 2020; 7, 44 from city centre) This carefully restored Georgian home, owned by the Electricity Supply Board (ESB), is closed until 2020 while the ESB rebuilds its headquarters next door. In the meantime, you can still get a glimpse inside courtesy of a virtual tour, available on the website.

What you won't hear is the terrible tale of how the ESB came to own this house in the first place: in order to build its original headquarters in the 1960s, the government granted it permission to tear down 16 Georgian houses, breaking up Europe's most perfect Georgian row.

ST STEPHEN'S 'PEPPER CANISTER' CHURCH — CHURCH

Map p276 (01-288 0663; www.peppercanister.ie; Upper Mount St; open for services and concerts only; 4, 7, 8, 120 from city centre) Built in 1825 in Greek Revival style and commonly known as the 'pepper canister' on account of its appearance, St Stephen's is one of Dublin's most attractive and distinctive churches, and looks particularly fetching at twilight when its exterior lights have just come on.

It occasionally hosts classical concerts, but don't go out of your way to see the interior. It's only open during services, usually held at 11am Sunday and 11.30am Wednesday, with an extra one at 11am on Friday in July and August.

ORIGIN GALLERY — GALLERY

Map p276 (01-478 5159; https://theorigingallery.com; 37 Upper Fitzwilliam St; 10am-5.30pm Mon-Fri; 14, 15, 16, 19 from city centre, Harcourt) FREE A relaxed space on the 1st floor of a Georgian terrace, Origin functions primarily as a showcase for artists who've stayed at the gallery's County Kerry retreat, Cill Rialaig, and emerging artists putting on their first show. In a similarly encouraging spirit, buyers can pay for artworks in instalments.

GOVERNMENT BUILDINGS — NOTABLE BUILDING

Map p276 (www.taoiseach.gov.ie; Upper Merrion St; tours hourly 10.30am-1.30pm Sat; 7, 44 from city centre) FREE This gleaming Edwardian pile opened as the Royal College of Science in 1911 before being transformed into government offices in 1989. Free 40-minute tours include the Taoiseach's (Prime Minister's) office, the Cabinet Room and the ceremonial staircase with a stunning stained-glass window – designed by Evie Hone (1894–1955) for the 1939 New York Trade Fair. Pick up tickets from 9.30am on the day of the tour at the Clare St entrance of the National Gallery.

LITERARY ADDRESSES

Merrion Square has long been the favoured address of Dublin's affluent intelligentsia. **Oscar Wilde** spent much of his youth at 1 North Merrion Sq, now the campus of the American College Dublin. Grumpy **WB Yeats** (1865–1939) lived at 52 East Merrion Sq and later, from 1922 to 1928, at 82 South Merrion Sq. **George (AE) Russell** (1867–1935), the self-described 'poet, mystic, painter and cooperator', worked at No 84. The great Liberator **Daniel O'Connell** (1775–1847) was a resident of No 58 in his later years. Austrian **Erwin Schrödinger** (1887–1961), he of the alive, dead or simultaneously both cat paradox and co-winner of the 1933 Nobel Prize for Physics, lived at No 65 from 1940 to 1956. Dublin seems to attract writers of horror stories and **Joseph Sheridan Le Fanu** (1814–73), who penned the vampire classic *Camilla*, was a resident of No 70.

EATING

The area around Merrion Row is a culinary hotbed, whether it's casual lunches for the business trade or upmarket dining at restaurants that hold most of the city's Michelin stars. Sandwich bars and nondescript cafes make up the rest of the dining landscape.

BRAMBLES CAFE €

Map p276 (National Museum of Ireland Cafe; National Museum of Ireland, Kildare St; mains around €11; ⏲10am-5pm Tue-Sat, 1-5pm Sun & Mon; 🚌all city centre) The award-winning cafe of this branch of the National Museum of Ireland serves excellent salads, sandwiches and hearty hot dishes such as braised beef and Guinness pie. It also serves Fairtrade teas and coffees.

MUSASHI HOGAN PLACE JAPANESE €

Map p276 (☎01-441 0106; www.musashidublin.com; 48 Hogan Pl; sushi €3-4, maki rolls €7-8, mains €14-15; ⏲noon-10pm Sun-Thu, to 11pm Fri & Sat; 🚌4, 7 from city centre) A branch of the expanding Musashi empire, serving the same excellent and authentic sushi, sashimi and maki as the original restaurant (p157) on the north side of the Liffey.

★ETTO ITALIAN €€

Map p276 (☎01-678 8872; www.etto.ie; 18 Merrion Row; mains €18-24; ⏲noon-9.30pm Mon-Wed, to 10pm Thu-Fri, 12.30-10pm Sat; 🚌all city centre) Award-winning restaurant and wine bar that does contemporary versions of classic Italian cuisine. All the ingredients are fresh, the presentation is exquisite and the service is just right. Portions are small, but the food is so rich you won't leave hungry. The only downside is the relatively quick turnover; lingering over the excellent wine would be nice. Book ahead.

★COBURG BRASSERIE FRENCH €€

Map p276 (☎01-602 8900; www.thecoburgdublin.com; Conrad Dublin, Earlsfort Tce; mains €17-26; ⏲6.30am-11pm; 🚌all city centre) The French-inspired, seafood-leaning cuisine at this revamped hotel brasserie puts the emphasis on shellfish: the all-day menu offers oysters, mussels and a range of 'casual' lobster dishes, from lobster rolls to lobster cocktail. The bouillabaisse is chock-full of sea flavours, and you can also get a crab and shrimp burger and an excellent yellowfin tuna Niçoise salad. Top-notch.

LOCAL KNOWLEDGE

STREET ART

On Sunday, the wrought-iron fences of Merrion Sq convert to gallery walls for the traditional open-air **art market** (Map p276; www.merrionart.com; Merrion Sq; ⏲10am-5pm Sun; 🚌all city centre). At any given time you'll find the work of 150 artists, mostly Sunday-painter types with a penchant for landscapes and still lifes, some of whom are very talented indeed.

HOUSE MEDITERRANEAN €€

Map p276 (☎01-905 9090; www.housedublin.ie; 27 Lower Leeson St; small plates €9-12, mains €15-26; ⏲8am-midnight Mon-Wed, to 3am Thu & Fri, 4pm-3am Sat; 🚌11, 46, 118, 145 from city centre) This gorgeous bar does a limited selection of main courses, but the real treats are the tapas-style sharing plates, which cover the full Mediterranean spread, from wild mushroom risotto and pulled pork to grilled halloumi and salt-and-pepper calamari.

XICO MEXICAN €€

Map p276 (☎01-661 8829; www.xico.ie; 143 Lower Baggot St; mains €12-22; ⏲5pm-midnight Mon-Sat; 🚌all city centre) It's quite the scene at this underground Mexican restaurant, where the music is loud and the food – tacos, tostadas and main courses such as salmon ceviche and a fine chilli bowl – is washed down with margaritas. Yes, it's a restaurant, but you'd better be in the mood for a fiesta.

ELY WINE BAR IRISH €€

Map p276 (☎01-676 8986; www.elywinebar.ie; 22 Ely Pl; mains €22-38; ⏲noon-11.30pm Mon-Fri, 5pm-12.30am Sat; 🚌all city centre) 🍃 Scrummy organic burgers, nine-hour braised beef cheek and perfectly charred steaks are all on the menu in this basement restaurant. Meals are prepared with organic and free-range produce from the owner's family farm in County Clare, so you can rest assured of the quality. There's another branch (p167) in the Docklands.

LA PENICHE EUROPEAN €€

Map p276 (☎087 790 0077; www.lapeniche.ie; Grand Canal, Mespil Rd; 2-/3-course menu €24.50/29.50, plus €5 per person cruise contribution fee; ⏲7-10pm Wed & Thu, 5.30pm-midnight Fri & Sat, 7.30-9.30pm Sun; 🚌38,

LOCAL KNOWLEDGE

TRACING YOUR ANCESTORS

Go on, you're dying to see if you've got a bit of Irish in you, and maybe tracking down your roots is the main reason for your visit. It will make things much easier if you've done some preliminary research in your home country – particularly finding out the precise date and point of entry of your ancestors – but you might still be able to plot your family tree even if you're acting on impulse.

Accredited Genealogists Ireland (AGI; www.accreditedgenealogists.ie; c/o the Genealogy Advisory Service, Kildare St; all city centre) The regulating board governing all professional genealogists in Ireland. To engage the service of a genealogist, you'll have to contact them directly; the website has details of all members who will undertake a commission.

Genealogical Office (01-603 0200; 2nd fl, National Library of Ireland, Kildare St; 9.30am-5pm Mon-Fri, to 1pm Sat; all city centre) Obtain information on how best to trace your Irish roots. A genealogist can do the trace for you (at a fee dependent on research) or simply point you in the right direction (for free).

Genealogy Advisory Service (01-603 0256; www.nli.ie; National Library of Ireland, Kildare St; 9.30am-5pm Mon-Wed, to 4.45pm Thu & Fri; all city centre) You don't need an appointment to avail yourself of this free genealogy service run by the National Library of Ireland. Besides offering advice on where to start your search it also offers on-site access to a number of subscription websites including newspaper archives and ancestry searches.

39 from city centre) One of the most atmospheric ways to experience the Grand Canal – and enjoy a fine dinner – is on an evening barge trip. Board *La Peniche,* sit on the deck and enjoy fine wine and Belgian food while your skipper navigates the locks.

★ RESTAURANT
PATRICK GUILBAUD — FRENCH €€€

Map p276 (01-676 4192; www.restaurantpatrickguilbaud.ie; 21 Upper Merrion St; 2-/3-course set lunch €52/62, dinner menus €135-203; 12.30-2.30pm & 7-10.30pm Tue-Fri, 1-2.30pm & 7-10.30pm Sat; 7, 46 from city centre) Ireland's only Michelin two-star is understandably considered the best in the country by its devotees, who proclaim Guillaume Lebrun's French haute cuisine the most exalted expression of the culinary arts. If you like formal dining, this is as good as it gets: the lunch menu is an absolute steal, at least in this stratosphere. Innovative and beautifully presented.

The room itself is all contemporary elegance and the service expertly formal yet surprisingly friendly – the staff are meticulously trained and as skilled at answering queries and addressing individual requests as they are at making sure not one breadcrumb lingers too long on the immaculate tablecloths. Owner Patrick Guilbaud usually does the rounds of the tables himself in the evening to salute regular customers and charm first-timers into returning. Reservations are absolutely necessary.

L'ECRIVAIN — FRENCH €€€

Map p276 (01-661 1919; www.lecrivain.com; 109A Lower Baggot St; 3-course lunch menus €47.50, 8-course tasting menus €115, mains €38-46; 12.30-3.30pm Fri, 6.30-10.30pm Mon-Sat; 38, 39 from city centre) Head chef Derry Clarke is considered a gourmet god for the exquisite simplicity of his creations, which put the emphasis on flavour and the best local ingredients – all given the French once-over and turned into something that approaches divine dining. The Michelin people like it too and awarded it one of their stars.

UNICORN — ITALIAN €€€

Map p276 (01-662 4757; www.theunicorn.restaurant; 12B Merrion Ct, Merrion Row; mains €23-38; 12.30-3pm & 5.30-10pm Mon-Wed, 12.30-10.30pm Thu-Sat; all city centre) Saturday lunch at this Italian restaurant in a laneway off Merrion Row is a tradition for Dublin's media types, socialites, politicos and their cronies who guffaw and clink glasses in conspiratorial rapture. The

Oscar Wilde statue at Merrion Square (p96)

extensive lunchtime antipasto bar is popular, but we still prefer the meaty à la carte menu. There are pasta and fish dishes to cater to all palates.

DAX FRENCH €€€

Map p276 (01-676 1494; www.dax.ie; 23 Upper Pembroke St; mains €28-35; 12.30-2pm & 6.30-9.30pm Tue-Thu, to 10pm Fri, 6-10pm Sat; all city centre) Olivier Meisonnave's posh-rustic basement restaurant, named after his hometown north of Biarritz, is popular with serious foodies. They come for the expertly made dishes such as braised Comeragh lamb with aubergine and miso; or the roasted wild duck, with chervil root purée, braised barley and Madeira.

BANG CAFÉ EUROPEAN €€€

Map p276 (01-400 4229; www.bangrestaurant.com; 11 Merrion Row; mains €24-36; 5.30-10pm Mon, noon-3pm & 5.30-10pm Tue-Fri, 12:30-3pm & 5.30-11pm Sat; all city centre) Fashionistas and foodies have long been aficionados of this stylish spot, which turns out top-notch contemporary Irish fare, including Wicklow venison and Salt Marsh duck. The two-course pre-theatre menu (€29.95) is a good deal and is available until 6.30pm Monday to Friday (until 6pm Saturday).

DRINKING & NIGHTLIFE

Away from the city centre there are some fine pubs that are worthy of the trek. Many fill up with office workers straight after (or just before) clocking-off time and then get quieter as the night progresses.

★TONER'S PUB

Map p276 (01-676 3090; www.tonerspub.ie; 139 Lower Baggot St; 10.30am-11.30pm Mon-Thu, to 12.30am Fri & Sat, 11.30am-11.30pm Sun; 7, 46 from city centre) Toner's, with its stone floors and antique snugs, has changed little over the years and is the closest thing you'll get to a country pub in the heart of the city. Next door, Toner's Yard is a comfortable outside space. The shelves and drawers are reminders that it once doubled as a grocery shop.

The writer Oliver St John Gogarty once brought WB Yeats here, after the upper-class poet – who lived just around the corner – decided he wanted to visit a pub. After a silent sherry in the noisy bar, Yeats turned to his friend and said, 'I have seen the pub, now please take me home'. He would probably be horrified by the good-natured business crowd making the racket these days too. His loss.

★**O'DONOGHUE'S** PUB

Map p276 (www.odonoghues.ie; 15 Merrion Row; ⏲10am-midnight Mon-Thu, to 1am Fri & Sat, 11am-midnight Sun; 🚌all city centre) The pub where traditional music stalwarts The Dubliners made their name in the 1960s still hosts live music nightly, but the crowds would gather anyway – for the excellent pints and superb ambience, in the old bar or the covered coach yard next to it.

SQUARE BALL BAR

Map p276 (☎01-662 4473; www.the-square-ball.com; 45 Hogan Pl; ⏲noon-11.30pm Tue-Thu, to 12.30am Fri & Sat, noon-11pm Sun; 🚌4, 7 from city centre) This bar is many things to many people: craft beer and cocktail bar at the front, sports lounge and barbecue pit at the back and an awesome vintage arcade upstairs. There are also plenty of board games, so bring your competitive spirit.

HOUSE BAR

Map p276 (☎01-905 9090; www.housedublin.ie; 27 Lower Leeson St; ⏲8am-midnight Mon, to 2am Tue & Wed, to 3am Thu & Fri, noon-3am Sat, noon-11pm Sun; 🚌11, 46, 118, 145) Spread across two Georgian townhouses, this could be Dublin's most beautiful modern bar, with gorgeous wood-floored rooms, comfortable couches and even log fires in winter to amp up the cosiness. In the middle there's a lovely glassed-in outdoor space that on a nice day bathes the rest of the bar with natural light. There's also an excellent menu.

HARTIGAN'S PUB

Map p276 (100 Lower Leeson St; ⏲2.30-11.30pm Mon-Thu, 1.30pm-12.30am Fri & Sat, 12.30pm-midnight Sun; 🚌all city centre) This is about as spartan a bar as you'll find in the city, and the daytime home of some serious drinkers, who appreciate the quiet, no-frills surroundings. In the evening it's popular with students from the medical faculty of University College Dublin (UCD).

DOHENY & NESBITT'S PUB

Map p276 (☎01-676 2945; www.dohenyandnesbitts.ie; 5 Lower Baggot St; ⏲9am-12.30am Mon & Tue, to 1am Wed & Thu, to 2am Fri, 9.30am-2am Sat, 10.30am-midnight Sun; 🚌all city centre) A standout, even in a city of wonderful pubs, Nesbitt's is equipped with antique snugs and is a favourite place for the high-powered gossip of politicians and journalists; Leinster House is only a short stroll away.

ENTERTAINMENT

Beyond the restaurants and pubs of the area, there's only a handful of other options for a good night out.

O'DONOGHUE'S TRADITIONAL MUSIC

Map p276 (☎01-660 7194; www.odonoghues.ie; 15 Merrion Row; ⏲from 7pm; 🚌all city centre) There's traditional music nightly in the old bar of this famous boozer. Regular performers include local names such as Tom Foley, Joe McHugh, Joe Foley and Maria O'Connell.

SUGAR CLUB LIVE MUSIC

Map p276 (☎01-678 7188; www.thesugarclub.com; 8 Lower Leeson St; €7-20; ⏲7pm-late; 🚌7, 46 from city centre) There are a huge variety of gigs, party nights and movie screenings in this intimate theatre-style venue on the corner of St Stephen's Green.

SHOPPING

Retail opportunities are few and far between in this neighbourhood, as most available retail space here is taken up with restaurants and cafes.

HERALDIC ARTISTS BOOKS

Map p270 (☎01-679 7020; www.heraldicartists.com; 3 Nassau St; ⏲1-5.30pm Mon-Wed, to 6pm Thu-Sat; 🚌all city centre) Hand-painted heraldic plaques and scrolls, as well as an extensive research facility on genealogy, with plenty of books to aid both professional and amateur researchers.

SPORTS & ACTIVITIES

GUIDED TOUR OF OIREACHTAS TOURS

Map p276 (☎01-618 3271; www.oireachtas.ie; Kildare St; ⏲10.30am, 11.30am, 2.30pm & 3.30pm Mon-Fri; 🚌all city centre) FREE Pre-arranged guided tours of the Oireachtas (Houses of Parliament) are available when parliament is in session (but not sitting). Book in advance or show up at the visitors' entrance 15 minutes before the tour.

Temple Bar

Neighbourhood Top Five

❶ **Temple Bar Food Market** (p112) Feasting on organic and exotic nibbles from all over, at Dublin's most exciting food market.

❷ **Claddagh Records** (p119) Shopping for all kinds of Irish traditional and folk music – as well as sounds from around the globe – in this wonderful record shop.

❸ **Christ Church Cathedral** (p107) Visiting the most impressive – from the outside at least – of Dublin's three cathedrals.

❹ **Dublin Musical Pub Crawl** (p120) Exploring the pubs of the area to a wonderful traditional soundtrack – sure, isn't this why you came?

❺ **Gutter Bookshop** (p119) Browsing the shelves of this locally owned bookshop, one of the best in town because it's the kind of place that encourages you to linger.

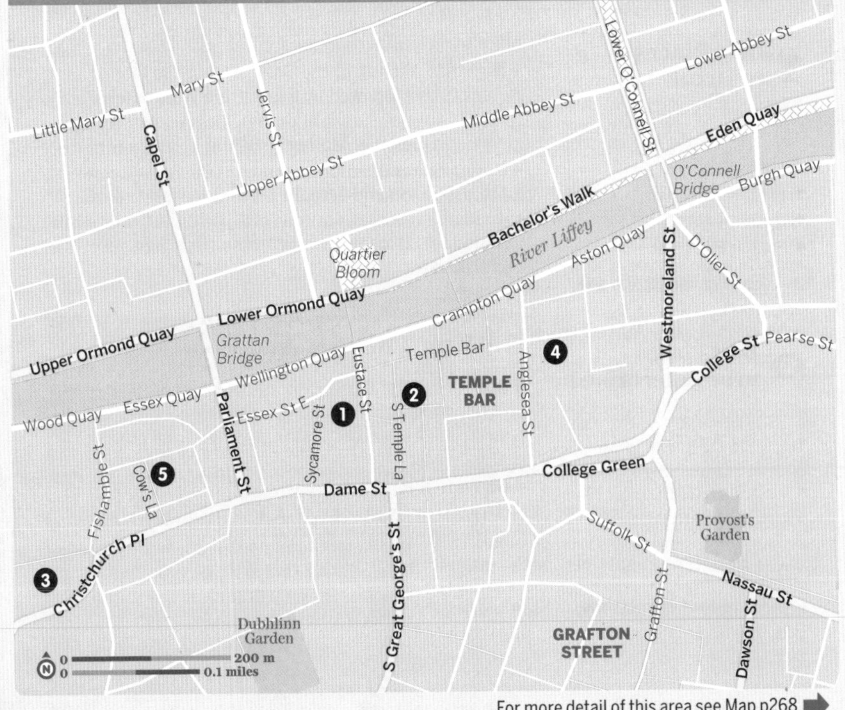

For more detail of this area see Map p268

Lonely Planet's Top Tip

Unless you're in for a no-holds-barred, knees-up weekend and don't care too much about sleeping, don't overnight in Temple Bar – hotel rooms are generally more cramped and noisier here than elsewhere. Temple Bar's central location and the city's size mean you can get in and out of here with relative ease.

Best Places to Eat

- Bunsen (p112)
- Banyi Japanese Dining (p112)
- Sano Pizza (p111)
- Seafood Cafe (p112)
- Temple Bar Food Market (p112)

For reviews, see p111.

Best Places to Drink

- Vintage Cocktail Club (p114)
- The Oak (p114)
- Temple Bar (p114)
- Liquor Rooms (p114)
- Palace Bar (p114)

For reviews, see p114.

Best Places to be Entertained

- Workman's Club (p118)
- Project Arts Centre (p118)
- Irish Film Institute (p118)
- Mother (p118)
- Smock Alley Theatre (p115)

For reviews, see p115.

Explore Temple Bar

You can visit all of Temple Bar's attractions in less than half a day, but that's not really the point: this cobbled neighbourhood, for so long the city's most infamous party zone, is really more about ambience than attractions. If you visit during the day, the district's bohemian bent is on display. You can browse for vintage clothes, get your nipples pierced, nibble on Mongolian barbecue, buy organic food, pick up the latest musical releases and buy books on every conceivable subject. You can check out the latest art installations or join in a pulsating drum circle.

By night – or at the weekend – it's a different story altogether, as the area's bars are packed to the rafters with revellers looking to tap into their inner Bacchus: it's loud, raucous and usually a lot of fun. Temple Bar is also Dublin's official 'cultural quarter', so you shouldn't ignore its more high-minded offerings like the progressive Project Arts Centre (p118), Temple Bar Gallery & Studios (p110) and the Irish Film Institute (p118).

Local Life

- **Markets** The Temple Bar Food Market (p112) is all about gourmet goodies and organic foodstuffs; the Cow's Lane Designer Mart (p119) is a showcase of local art and clothing; while the Book Market (p120) is the place to pick up secondhand novels and CDs.
- **Nightlife** A drink in the Oak (p114) or the Liquor Rooms (p114), followed by a gig at the Workman's Club (p118), is always a great night out, and you can really get your grind on at Mother (p118) on a Saturday night.
- **Dining** Soaking up the excesses of the night before is a favourite weekend activity, and we recommend the succulent burgers at Bunsen (p112) or the sublime sushi at Banyi (p112), a favourite with the city's Japanese population.

Getting There & Away

- **Bus** As Temple Bar is right in the heart of the city, all cross-city buses will deposit you by the cobbled, largely pedestrianised streets, making access – and escape – that bit easier.
- **On Foot** Temple Bar is easily accessible on foot from Grafton St to the southeast, Kilmainham to the west and the north side of the river to the north.

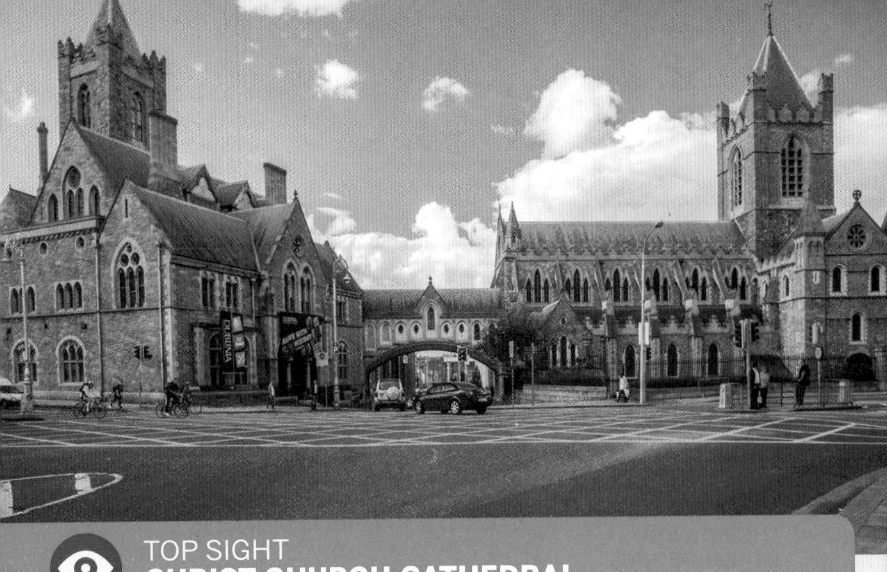

DAVID SOANES PHOTOGRAPHY/GETTY IMAGES ©

TOP SIGHT
CHRIST CHURCH CATHEDRAL

Its hilltop location and eye-catching flying buttresses make this the most photogenic of Dublin's three cathedrals as well as one of the capital's most recognisable symbols.

Early Beginnings

A wooden church was first erected here by Dunán, the first bishop of Dublin, and Sitric, the Viking king, around 1030, at the southern edge of Dublin's Viking settlement. In 1163, however, the secular clergy was replaced by a group of Augustinian monks installed by the patron saint of Dublin, Archbishop Laurence O'Toole. Six years later, the Normans of Richard de Clare, Earl of Pembroke (better known as Strongbow), blew into town and got themselves into the church-building business, arranging with O'Toole (and his successor John Cumin) for the construction of a new stone cathedral that would symbolise Anglo-Norman glory. The new cathedral opened its doors late in the 12th century, by which time Strongbow, O'Toole and Cumin were long dead.

Above ground, the north wall, the transepts and the western part of the choir are almost all that remain from the original. It has been restored several times over the centuries and, despite its apparent uniformity, is a hotchpotch of different styles, ranging from Romanesque to English Gothic.

DON'T MISS

- Mummified cat and rat in the crypt
- The Treasury
- Strongbow monument

PRACTICALITIES

- Church of the Holy Trinity
- Map p268, A5
- www.christchurchcathedral.ie
- Christ Church Pl
- adult/student/child €7/5.50/2.50, with Dublinia €15/12.50/7.50
- 9.30am-5pm Mon-Sat, from 12.30pm Sun year-round, longer hours Mar-Oct
- 50, 50A, 56A from Aston Quay, 54, 54A from Burgh Quay

DID YOU KNOW?

In March 2012 the heart of St Laurence O'Toole, which had been kept in the church for 890 years, was stolen by a gang linked to the international trade in rhino horns.

The combination ticket that includes Dublinia is good value if you're visiting with kids.

THE BOY WHO WOULD BE KING

As part of an elaborate attempt to overthrow the Lancastrian Henry VII with a Yorkist, the Earl of Kildare crowned a baker's son called Lambert Simnel as King Edward VI in Christ Church Cathedral on 24 May 1487, to the cheers of gathered Dubliners. The Yorkists were defeated at the Battle of Stoke Field later that year but Simnel was spared and given a job in Henry's kitchens.

The cathedral has a weekly schedule of sung Masses, which can be very beautiful; check the website for details.

Hard Times

From its inception, Christ Church was the State Church of Ireland, and when Henry VIII dissolved the monasteries in the 16th century, the Augustinian priory that managed the church was replaced with a new Anglican clergy, which still runs the church today.

Until the disestablishment of the Church of Ireland in 1869, senior representatives of the Crown all swore their allegiance here. The church's fortunes, however, were not guaranteed. By the turn of the 18th century its popularity waned along with the district itself as the upper echelons of Dublin society fled north, where they attended a new favourite, St Mary's Abbey.

Through much of its history, Christ Church vied for supremacy with nearby St Patrick's Cathedral, but both fell on hard times in the 18th and 19th centuries. Christ Church was virtually derelict – the nave had been used as a market and the crypt had earlier housed taverns – by the time restoration took place. Whiskey distiller Henry Roe donated the equivalent of €30 million to save the church, which was substantially rebuilt from 1871 to 1878. Ironically, both of the great Church of Ireland cathedrals are essentially outsiders in a Catholic nation today, dependent on tourist donations for their very survival.

Chapter House & Northern Wall

From the southeastern entrance to the churchyard you walk past ruins of the **chapter house**, which dates from 1230. The **main entrance** to the cathedral is at the southwestern corner, and as you enter, you face the ancient **northern wall**. This survived the collapse of its southern counterpart but has also suffered from subsiding foundations (much of the church was built on a peat bog) and, from its eastern end, it leans visibly.

Strongbow Monument

The southern aisle has a **monument to the legendary Strongbow**. The armoured figure on the tomb is unlikely to be of Strongbow (it's more probably the Earl of Drogheda), but his internal organs may have been buried here. A popular legend relates an especially visceral version of the daddy-didn't-love-me tale: the half-figure beside the tomb is supposed to be Strongbow's son, who was cut in two by his father when his bravery in battle was suspect – an act that surely would have saved the kid a fortune in therapist's bills.

CHRIST CHURCH CATHEDRAL

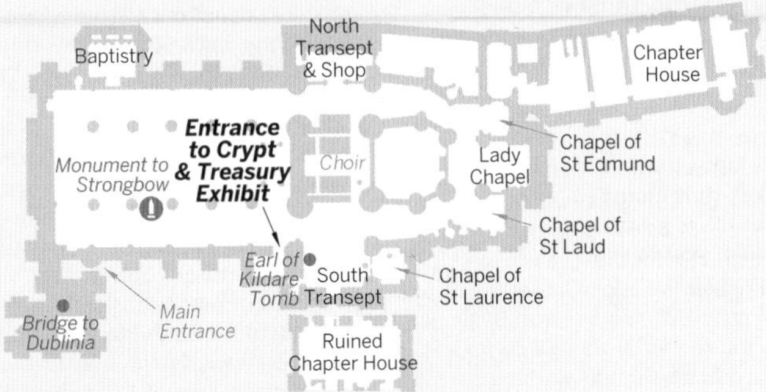

South Transept

The south transept contains the super baroque **tomb of the 19th Earl of Kildare**, who died in 1734. His grandson, Lord Edward Fitzgerald, was a member of the United Irishmen and died in the abortive 1798 Rising. The entrance to the **Chapel of St Laurence** is off the south transept and contains two effigies, one of them reputed to be of either Strongbow's wife or sister.

Crypt

An entrance by the south transept descends to the unusually large arched **crypt**, which dates back to the original Viking church. Curiosities in the crypt include a glass display case housing a mummified cat in the act of chasing a mummified rat (aka Tom and Jerry), frozen mid-pursuit inside an organ pipe in the 1860s. Also on display are the stocks from the old 'liberty' of Christ Church, used when church authorities meted out civil punishments to wrongdoers. The **Treasury** exhibit includes rare coins, the Stuart coat of arms and gold given to the church by William of Orange after the Battle of the Boyne. From the main entrance, a **bridge**, part of the 1871 to 1878 restoration, leads to Dublinia (p110).

SIGHTS

Temple Bar is less about sights and more about experiences, but still there's a handful of museums and galleries to explore within its cobbled confines. The biggest sight of all is on its western edge: the eye-catching flying buttresses and early English Gothic of Christ Church Cathedral (p107), Dublin's oldest.

CHRIST CHURCH CATHEDRAL — CHURCH

See p107.

DUBLINIA: EXPERIENCE VIKING & MEDIEVAL DUBLIN — MUSEUM

Map p268 (01-679 4611; www.dublinia.ie; Christ Church Pl; adult/student/child €10/9/6.50, with Christchurch Cathedral €15/12.50/7.50; 10am-5.30pm Mar-Sep, to 4.30pm Oct-Feb; 50, 50A, 56A from Aston Quay, 54, 54A from Burgh Quay) A must for the kids, the old Synod Hall, added to Christ Church Cathedral (p107) during its late-19th-century restoration, is home to the seemingly perennial Dublinia, a lively and kitschy attempt to bring Viking and medieval Dublin to life. Models, streetscapes and somewhat old-fashioned interactive displays do a fairly decent job of it, at least for kids.

The model of a medieval quayside and a cobbler's shop in **Medieval Dublin** are both excellent, as is the scale model of the medieval city. Up one floor is **Viking Dublin**, which has a large selection of objects recovered from Wood Quay, the world's largest Viking archaeological site. Interactive exhibits tell the story of Dublin's 9th- and 10th-century Scandinavian invaders, but the real treat is exploring life aboard the recreated longboat. You can also climb neighbouring **St Michael's Tower** and peek through its grubby windows for views over the city to the Dublin hills. There is also a pleasant cafe and the inevitable souvenir shop.

HA'PENNY BRIDGE — BRIDGE

Map p268 (all city centre) Dublin's most famous bridge is the Ha'penny Bridge, built in 1816. One of the world's oldest cast-iron bridges, it was built to replace the seven ferries that plied a busy route between the two banks of the river. Officially known as the Liffey Bridge, it gets its name from the ha'penny (half penny) toll that was charged until 1919 (for a time the toll was one-and-a-half pence, and so it was called the Penny Ha'penny Bridge).

TEMPLE BAR GALLERY & STUDIOS — GALLERY

Map p268 (01-671 0073; www.templebargallery.com; 5 Temple Bar; 11am-6pm Tue-Sat; all city centre) FREE This multistorey gallery showcases the works of dozens of up-and-coming Irish artists at any one time, and is a great spot to see cutting-edge Irish art across a range of media. The gallery runs occasional open days where you can explore the work of artists working in the studios that are part of the complex.

ICON FACTORY — ARTS CENTRE

Map p268 (086 202 4533; www.iconfactorydublin.ie; 3 Aston Pl; 11am-6pm; all city centre) FREE This artists' collective in the heart of Temple Bar hosts exhibitions on Ireland's cultural heritage. You'll find colourful, unique souvenirs celebrating the very best in Irish music and literature, and every sale goes towards the artists themselves. Take a stroll around their **Icon Walk** outside and get better acquainted with Irish playwrights, rock stars, sporting heroes and actors.

GALLERY OF PHOTOGRAPHY — GALLERY

Map p268 (www.galleryofphotography.ie; Meeting House Sq; 11am-6pm Mon-Sat, 1-6pm Sun; all city centre) FREE This small gallery devoted to the photograph is set in an airy three-level space overlooking Meeting House Sq. It features a constantly changing menu of local and international work, as well as photography classes. The downstairs shop is well stocked with all manner of photographic tomes and manuals.

MOSAIC — HISTORIC SITE

Map p268 (Winetavern St; all city centre) Fishamble St, Dublin's oldest street, dates back to Viking times. Brass symbols in the pavement direct you towards a mosaic, just northeast of the overpass between Christ Church Cathedral and Dublinia, laid out to show the ground plan of the sort of Viking dwelling excavated here in the early 1980s.

NATIONAL WAX MUSEUM PLUS — MUSEUM

Map p268 (www.waxmuseumplus.ie; 22-25 Westmoreland St; adult/child/concession €15/10/13; 10am-10pm; all city centre) More a mini history museum in wax than Dublin's version of Madame Tussauds. The quality of the waxworks remains inconsistent – some look like the result of a hastily conceived school project. Still, the Chamber of Horrors (Dracula has a starring role) is pretty good. The 'plus' in the name refers to the interactive use of video and music. Buy tickets online for a 10% discount.

NATIONAL PHOTOGRAPHIC ARCHIVE MUSEUM

Map p268 (www.nli.ie; Meeting House Sq; ⏲10am-1pm Tue-Thu, plus 2.30-4.30pm Wed; 🚌all city centre) FREE The archive of photographs taken from the mid-19th century onwards are part of the collection of the National Library, and so are open by appointment and only with a reader's ticket, which can be obtained from the main branch (p98).

HANDEL'S HOTEL (SITE OF NEAL'S NEW MUSICK HALL) HISTORIC SITE

Map p268 (16-18 Fishamble St; 🚌all city centre) The clue is the name: on the site of this hotel was once Neal's New Musick Hall, where, on 13 April 1742, the nearly broke GF Handel conducted the very first performance of his epic work *Messiah*. All that's left now is the original arch, restored to something like its elegant original. Every year the *Messiah* is performed in an open-air concert on Fishamble St – Dublin's oldest street – to commemorate the event.

Ironically, Jonathan Swift – author of *Gulliver's Travels* and dean of St Patrick's Cathedral – suggested the choirs of St Patrick's and Christ Church participate in the original performance, but then he revoked his invitation, vowing to punish vicars who took part for their 'disobedience, rebellion, perfidy and ingratitude'. The concert went ahead nonetheless, in front of an appreciative crowd of roughly 700.

SUNLIGHT CHAMBERS NOTABLE BUILDING

Map p268 (Parliament St; ⏲closed to the public; 🚌all city centre) On the southern banks of the Liffey, Sunlight Chambers, designed by Liverpool architect Edward Ould (designer of Port Sunlight in the Wirral, in England), stands out among the Georgian and modern architecture for its romantic Italianate style and beautiful art nouveau frieze work by German sculptor Conrad Dressler. Sunlight was a brand of soap made by Lever Brothers and the frieze shows the Lever Brothers' view of the world: men make clothes dirty, women wash them.

LOCAL KNOWLEDGE

A SAUCY PAST

Purists may cry foul that Temple Bar never lived up to its cultural quarter moniker, but in many ways it's just staying true to its heritage. Imagine yourself back in 1742, for instance, when Handel was conducting the first-ever performance of his *Messiah* in Fishamble St, while just down the road on Bagnio Slip – now Lower Fownes St – gentlemen were lining up for an altogether different kind of distraction. Bagnio, from the Italian for bath house, had by then become the term for a brothel, and Temple Bar had plenty of them. It seems that pleasures of the flesh and of the mind have never been that far apart!

CONTEMPORARY MUSIC CENTRE ARTS CENTRE

Map p268 (☎01-490 1857; www.cmc.ie; 19 Fishamble St; ⏲10am-5.30pm Mon-Fri; 🚌all city centre) FREE Anyone with an interest in Irish contemporary music must visit the CMC's national archive where you can hear (and play around with, on an electronic organ) 10,000 samples from composers of this and the last century. There's also a good reference library where you can attend courses and meet composers.

EATING

Scattered among the panoply of overpriced and underwhelming eateries in Temple Bar are some excellent spots to get a bite that will suit a variety of tastes and pocket depths.

SANO PIZZA PIZZA €

Map p268, C5 (☎01-445 3344; www.sano.pizza; 2 Upper Exchange St; pizzas €6-12; ⏲noon-10pm Sun-Wed, to 11pm Thu-Sat; 🚌all city centre) The authentic Neapolitan pizza served here is fantastic, with a chewy, charred crust and a sparse smattering of toppings — we love the *Sapori del Sud,* with spicy *nduja* pork, fennel sausage, broccoli and mozzarella. And it's a bargain to boot.

TEMPLE BAR FOOD MARKET MARKET €

Map p268 (www.facebook.com/TempleBarFoodMarket; Meeting House Sq; ⏲10am-5pm Sat; all city centre) Every Saturday this small square is taken over by food trucks, filling the air with the scent of pastries, artisan hot dogs, vegan curries and crêpes. The oyster bar is a highlight – grab half a dozen with a glass of chilled white wine and people-watch the afternoon away.

KLAW SEAFOOD €

Map p268 (www.klaw.ie; 5a Crown Alley; mains €8-15; ⏲noon-10pm Mon-Wed & Sun, to 11pm Thu-Sat; all city centre) There's nothing sophisticated about this crab-shack-style place except the food: Irish oysters served naked, dressed or torched; Lambay Island crab claws served with a yuzu aioli; or half a lobster. Whatever you go for it's delicious; the 'shucknsuck' oyster happy hour is a terrific deal with all oysters €1.50.

BUNSEN BURGERS €

Map p268 (www.bunsen.ie; 22 Essex St E; burgers €7-10; ⏲noon-9.30pm Mon-Wed, to 10.30pm Thu-Sat, 1-9.30pm Sun; all city centre) The tag line says Straight Up Burgers, but Bunsen serves only the tastiest, most succulent lumps of prime beef cooked to perfection and served between two halves of a homemade bap. Want fries? You've a choice between skinny, chunky or sweet potato. Order the double at your peril. There are two other branches: on Wexford St and S Anne St (p72).

BISON BAR & BBQ BARBECUE €

Map p268 (☎01-533 7561; www.bisonbar.ie; 11 Wellington Quay; mains €14-22; ⏲noon-9pm; all city centre) Beer, whiskey sours and finger-lickingly good Texas-style barbecue – served with tasty sides such as slaw or mac 'n' cheese – is the fare at this boisterous restaurant. The cowboy theme is taken to the limit with the saddle chairs (yes, actual saddles); this is a place to eat, drink and be merry.

QUEEN OF TARTS CAFE €

Map p268 (☎01-670 7499; www.queenoftarts.ie; 4 Cork Hill; mains €5-13; ⏲8am-7pm Mon-Fri, from 9am Sat & Sun; all city centre) This cute little cake shop does a fine line in tarts, meringues, crumbles, cookies and brownies, not to mention a decent breakfast: the smoked bacon and leek potato cakes with eggs and cherry tomatoes are excellent. There's another, bigger, branch around the corner on **Cow's Lane** (www.queenoftarts.ie; 3-4 Cow's Lane; mains €5-13; ⏲8am-7pm Mon-Fri, 9am-7pm Sat & Sun; all city centre).

DOLLARD & CO FOOD HALL €

Map p268 (☎01-616 9606; www.dollardandco.ie; 2-5 Wellington Quay; pizza slice €4.50, mains €8-15; ⏲8am-9pm Mon-Thu, to 10pm Fri, 9am-10pm Sat, 10am-8pm Sun, pizzas until 4am; all city centre) This sleek food hall is housed in the oldest steel-frame structure in Ireland, and serves as a foodie emporium – pick up high-end groceries (including refillable wines on tap) or settle into the deli for a bite. You'll find all-day flat breads, burgers and pastas on the menu, but the pizza, available by the slice from a hatch until 4am, is a winner.

MUSIC CAFE DUBLIN CAFE €

Map p268 (www.facebook.com/djmusiccafe; 1 Wellington Quay; cakes €2-4; ⏲8am-10pm Mon, to 11.30pm Tue-Sat, 9am-11.30pm Sun; all city centre) A friendly coffee shop with a view, the Music Cafe Dublin serves excellent coffee, expertly made – not always the case in Temple Bar – in a lovely glass-encased room. The cakes are all lovely, too. The tiny stage upstairs hosts regular gigs, including weekly blues and jazz nights.

ZAYTOON MIDDLE EASTERN €

Map p268 (www.zaytoon.ie; 14-15 Parliament St; meals €8.50-15; ⏲noon-4am Sun-Thu, to 5am Fri & Sat; all city centre) It's the end of the night and you've got a desperate case of the munchies. Head straight for this terrific kebab joint and gobble the house speciality, the chicken shish-kebab meal, complete with chips and a soft drink. You'll feel all the better for it.

★**BANYI JAPANESE DINING** JAPANESE €€

Map p268 (☎01-675 0669; www.banyijapanesedining.com; 3-4 Bedford Row; lunch bento €11, small/large sushi platter €19/32; ⏲noon-10.30pm; all city centre) This compact restaurant in the heart of Temple Bar has arguably the best Japanese cuisine in Dublin. The rolls are divine, and the sushi as good as any you'll eat at twice the price. If you don't fancy raw fish, the classic Japanese main courses are excellent, as are the lunchtime bento boxes. Dinner reservations are advised, particularly at weekends.

SEAFOOD CAFE SEAFOOD €€

Map p268 (☎01-515 3717; www.facebook.com/klawcafe; 11 Sprangers Yard; mains €17-24;

Banyi Japanese Dining

⌚8am-9pm Mon-Thu, to 10pm Fri, 11am-10pm Sat, 11am-9pm Sun; 🚌all city centre) Sister restaurant to the seafood shack Klaw, the Seafood Cafe is a more spacious outpost where you can enjoy native lobster dripping in garlic butter, roasted bone-in monkfish or Lambay Island crab with buttered sourdough toast. Delightful.

ROBERTA'S INTERNATIONAL **€€**

Map p268 (☎01-616 9612; www.robertas.ie; 1 Essex St E; mains €20-31; ⌚5-10pm Mon-Wed, to 10.30pm Thu & Fri, 11am-2.30pm & 5-10.30pm Sat, 11am-2.30pm & 5-10pm Sun; 🚌all city centre) Inside this austere-looking protected building lies a beautiful red-brick restaurant with some of the most atmospheric views you can get in Dublin while dining, taking in both the River Liffey and the cobblestones of Temple Bar. The range of budget options makes it suitable for groups, and the cocktails are excellent.

ELEPHANT & CASTLE AMERICAN **€€**

Map p268 (☎01-679 3121; www.elephantandcastle.ie; 18 Temple Bar; mains €12-26; ⌚8am-11.30pm Mon-Fri, from 10.30am Sat & Sun; 🚌all city centre) If it's massive New York–style sandwiches or sticky chicken wings you're after, this bustling upmarket diner – a long-time presence in Temple Bar – is just the joint. Be prepared to queue, though, especially at weekends when the place heaves with the hassled parents of wandering toddlers and 20-somethings looking for a carb cure for the night before.

CHAMELEON INDONESIAN **€€**

Map p268 (☎01-671 0362; www.chameleonrestaurant.com; 1 Lower Fownes St; set menus €29-40, tapas €8-11; ⌚4-11pm Wed-Sun; 🌱; 🚌all city centre) Friendly and full of character, Chameleon is draped in exotic fabrics and serves renditions of Indonesian classics such as satay, gado gado and nasi goreng. Choose from four rijsttafel set menus – Java, Sumatra, Bali or Vegan – or from the selection of smaller tapas-style dishes. The top floor has low seating on cushions, which is perfect for intimate group get-togethers.

CLEAVER EAST IRISH **€€**

Map p268 (☎01-531 3500; www.cleavereast.ie; Clarence, 6-8 Wellington Quay; mains €21-32; ⌚12.30-3pm Fri, from 10.30am Sat & Sun & 5.30-10.30pm daily; 🚌all city centre) Michelin-starred chef Oliver Dunne has brought his cooking chops to bear in Cleaver East, where the decor (think New York brasserie but with cleavers everywhere) is as macho as some of the mains – feast on a succulent 'pornburger' or monster mac 'n' cheese ball. The bottomless Bellinis and mimosas at weekend brunch costs €18.95.

AL VESUVIO ITALIAN **€€**

Map p268 (☎01-671 4597; www.alvesuviodublin.com; Meeting House Sq; pizzas €11-16; ⌚4-10.30pm Mon-Thu, noon-11pm Fri-Sun; 🚌all city centre) Pizzas – with *(rosse)* or without *(bianche)* cheese – and pastas are the speciality at this vaulted basement restaurant that is like a rustic piece of the Old Boot. Everything is authentic, from the bruschetta starter to the superb tiramisu on the dessert menu, and the Italian wines are *buonissimi*.

BEEF AND LOBSTER SEAFOOD **€€**

Map p268 (☎01-531 3810; www.beefandlobster.ie; 40 Parliament St; mains €19-39; ⌚noon-3pm & 5-10.30pm; 🚌all city centre) With a simple menu focusing on beef and seafood, this is an excellent example of a small menu done well. Everything is succulent and fresh and service quick and attentive, but the portions are small and sides are extra so don't come with a light wallet and a big appetite.

F.X. BUCKLEY STEAK €€€

Map p268 (☎01-671 1248; www.fxbuckley.ie; 2 Crow St; steaks €27-55; ⏲5-11pm Mon-Wed, from 12.30pm Thu & Fri, 12.30-10pm Sat; 🚌all city centre) Specialising in grass-fed, 28-day aged steak from its very own butchers, this is beef at its best. The steak may be the star of the show but don't leave without trying the beef dripping chips. Book ahead in high season.

DRINKING & NIGHTLIFE

Temple Bar's loud and busy pubs are a far cry from authentic, but they're undoubtedly fun – that is, if your idea of fun is mixing it with a bunch of lads and lasses from the north of England, egging each other on to show off their family jewels and daring one another to drain 10 Fat Frogs in a row, in front of a bemused audience of Spanish and Italian tourists, sharing one glass of Guinness per group. You've been warned!

★VINTAGE COCKTAIL CLUB BAR

Map p268 (☎01-675 3547; www.vintagecocktailclub.com; Crown Alley; ⏲5pm-1.30am Mon-Fri, from 12.30pm Sat & Sun; 🚌all city centre) The atmosphere behind this inconspicuous, unlit doorway initialled with the letters 'VCC' is that of a Vegas rat pack hang-out or a '60s-style London members' club. It's so popular you'll probably need to book for one of the 2½-hour evening sittings, which is plenty of time to sample some of the excellent cocktails and finger food.

★PALACE BAR PUB

Map p268 (www.thepalacebardublin.com; 21 Fleet St; ⏲10.30am-11.30pm Mon-Thu, to 12.30am Fri & Sat, 12.30-11.30pm Sun; 🚌all city centre) With its mirrors and wooden niches, the Palace (established in 1823) is one of Dublin's great 19th-century pubs, still stubbornly resisting any modernising influences from the last half-century or so. Literary figures Patrick Kavanagh and Flann O'Brien were once regulars and it was for a long time the unofficial head office of the *Irish Times*.

LIQUOR ROOMS COCKTAIL BAR

Map p268 (☎087 339 3688; www.theliquorrooms.com; 5 Wellington Quay; ⏲5pm-2am Sun-Tue, to 2.30am Wed, to 3am Thu-Sat; 🚌all city centre) A subterranean cocktail bar decorated in the manner of a Prohibition-era speakeasy. There's lots of rooms – and room – for hip lounge cats to sprawl and imbibe both atmosphere and a well-made cocktail. There's dancing in the Boom Room, classy cocktails in the Blind Tiger Room and art deco elegance in the Mayflower Room.

THE OAK BAR

Map p268 (☎01-671 8267; www.theoak.ie; 1 Parliament St; ⏲11am-midnight Sun-Thu, to 1.30am Fri & Sat; 🚌all city centre) Blue-velvet chairs, handsome leather booths and walls adorned with prints of Georgian Dublin set a sophisticated tone for this bar, which has a whole shelf devoted to negronis and a cocktail menu straight out of the roaring '20s. A touch of class.

STREET 66 BAR

Map p268 (www.street66.bar; 33 Parliament St; ⏲12.30pm-midnight Mon-Thu, to 2.30am Fri & Sat, noon-midnight Sun; 🚌all city centre) In late 2016 this place replaced the very popular LGBT Front Lounge and promised to be all things to all people: a dog-friendly coffee shop and bar dressed in upcycled chic that is LGBTQ-friendly. The front is the Dive Bar, the back the Disco Lounge. Better than most Temple Bar joints.

TEMPLE BAR BAR

Map p268 (☎01-677 3807; www.thetemplebarpub.com; 48 Temple Bar; ⏲10.30am-1.30am Mon-Wed, 10am-2.30am Thu-Sat, 11.30am-1am Sun; 🚌all city centre) The most photographed pub facade in Dublin, perhaps the world, the Temple Bar (aka Flannery's) is smack bang in the middle of the tourist precinct and is usually chock-a-block with visitors. It's good craic, though, and presses all the right buttons, with traditional musicians, a buzzy atmosphere and even a beer garden.

AULD DUBLINER PUB

Map p268 (☎01-677 0527; www.aulddubliner.ie; 24-25 Temple Bar; ⏲10.30am-11.30pm Mon & Tue, to 2.30am Wed-Sat, 12.30-11pm Sun; 🚌all city centre) Predominantly patronised by tourists, 'the Auld Foreigner', as locals have dubbed it, has a carefully manicured 'old world' charm that has been preserved – or refined – after a couple of renovations. It's a reliable place for a singsong and a laugh, as long as you don't mind taking 15 minutes to get to and from the jax (toilets).

DARKEY KELLY'S BAR & RESTAURANT IRISH PUB

Map p268 (☎01-679 6500; www.darkeykellys.ie; 19 Fishamble St; ⊙10.30am-11.30pm Mon-Thu, to 12.30am Fri & Sat, 12.30-11pm Sun; 🚌all city centre) Once the home of Ireland's first female serial killer, Darkey's now boasts a killer whiskey selection instead. It has a decent range of craft beer, and is a compromise between the tourist bars of Temple Bar and more local boozers. The pint prices are on the steep side, but there's a great buzz and traditional music is guaranteed.

This pub is built on the site of Darkey Kelly's 18th-century brothel. For years she was believed to have been burned at the stake in 1746 for the crime of witchcraft. In fact, papers discovered in 2010 showed she was executed after the bodies of five men were found in her vaults. Her motives are lost to history, but at her wake prostitutes from her brothel had a minor riot in Temple Bar, leading to 13 arrests.

FITZSIMONS BAR

Map p268 (☎01-677 9315; www.fitzsimonshotel.com; 21-22 Wellington Quay; ⊙10.30am-3am Mon-Sat, noon-2am Sun; 🚌all city centre) The epitome of Temple Bar's commitment to a kind of loud and wonderfully unsophisticated nightlife is this sprawling hotel bar (four bars on five floors), which serves booze, sports and cheesy music to a crowd of pumped revellers. At weekends it gets so busy the bouncers don't even try to keep the crowd from spilling out onto the cobbled streets.

OLIVER ST JOHN GOGARTY PUB

Map p268 (www.gogartys.ie; 58-59 Fleet St; ⊙10.30am-2.30am Mon-Sat, noon-11.30pm Sun; 🚌all city centre) You won't see too many Dubs ordering drinks in this bar, which is almost entirely given over to tourists who come for the carefully manufactured slice of authentic traditionalism...and the knee-slappin', toe-tappin' sessions that run throughout the day. The kitchen serves Irish cuisine of questionable quality.

TURK'S HEAD BAR

Map p268 (☎01-679 9701; www.facebook.com/TurksHeadChopHouse; 27-30 Parliament St; ⊙4pm-1am Mon & Tue, to 3am Wed-Sat, 1pm-1am Sun; 🚌all city centre) This super-pub is decorated in two completely different styles – one really gaudy, the other a recreation of LA c 1930 – and is one of the oddest and most interesting in Temple Bar. It pulsates nightly with a young pumped-up crowd of mainly tourists, out to boogie to chart hits. Be mindful of hidden steps all over the place.

OCTAGON BAR BAR

Map p268 (☎01-670 9000; www.theclarence.ie; Clarence Hotel, 6-8 Wellington Quay; ⊙noon-11.30pm Mon-Thu, to 2am Fri & Sat, 12.30-11pm Sun; 🚌all city centre) Gone are the days when this was the bar to be seen in – preferably within proximity of a celeb or two – but this handsome room decked out in art deco elegance is still a lovely spot in which to enjoy an expertly made cocktail.

PORTERHOUSE BAR

Map p268 (www.theporterhouse.ie; 16-18 Parliament St; ⊙11.30am-midnight Mon-Wed, to 1am Thu, to 2am Fri & Sat, noon-midnight Sun; 🚌all city centre) The Porterhouse looks like a cross between a Wild West bar and a Hieronymus Bosch painting. It has lots of its own delicious brews, including its Plain Porter (some say it's the best stout in town), as well as unfamiliar imported beers.

BROGAN'S PUB

Map p268 (☎01-679 9570; 75 Dame St; ⊙4-11.30pm Mon-Thu, 2pm-12.30am Fri & Sat, 2-11pm Sun; 🚌all city centre) Only a couple of doors down from the Olympia Theatre (p118), this is a wonderful old-style bar where conversation – not loud music – is king. The beer is also pretty good.

☆ ENTERTAINMENT

Looking for an alternative to a pub? Temple Bar has two terrific live-music venues, a handful of theatres and a couple of comedy clubs.

SMOCK ALLEY THEATRE THEATRE

Map p268 (☎01-677 0014; www.smockalley.com; 6-7 Exchange St; 🚌all city centre) One of the city's most diverse theatres is hidden in this beautifully restored 17th-century building. It boasts a broad program of events (expect anything from opera to murder mystery nights, puppet shows and Shakespeare) and many events also come with a dinner option.

The theatre was built in 1622 and was the only Theatre Royal ever built outside London. It was reinvented as a warehouse and a Catholic church, and was lovingly restored in 2012 to become a creative hub once again.

SEMMICK PHOTO/SHUTTERSTOCK ©

1. Temple Bar Food Market (p112)
Dublin's most exciting food market has organic and gourmet goodies aplenty.

2. Sunlight Chambers (p111)
This romantic Italianate-style building stands out with its beautiful art nouveau frieze work.

3. Ha'penny Bridge (p110)
Dublin's most famous bridge gets its name from the toll that was charged until 1919 for crossing it.

4. Temple Bar (p114)
With traditional musicians and a great atmosphere, Temple Bar is usually full of customers.

3

WORKMAN'S CLUB LIVE MUSIC

Map p268 (☎01-670 6692; www.theworkmansclub.com; 10 Wellington Quay; free-€20; ⏰5pm-3am; 🚌all city centre) A 300-capacity venue and bar in the former working-men's club of Dublin. The emphasis is on away from the mainstream, which means everything from singer-songwriters to electronic cabaret. When the live music at the Workman's Club is over, DJs take to the stage, playing rockabilly, hip-hop, indie, house and more.

MOTHER CLUB

Map p268 (www.motherclub.ie; Copper Alley, Exchange St; €10; ⏰11pm-3.30am Sat; 🚌all city centre) The best club night in the city is ostensibly a gay night, but it does not discriminate: clubbers of every sexual orientation come for the sensational DJs – mostly local but occasionally brought in from abroad – who throw down a mixed bag of disco, modern synth-pop and other danceable styles.

ARK CHILDREN'S CULTURAL CENTRE ARTS CENTRE

Map p268 (www.ark.ie; 11A Eustace St; 🚌all city centre) Aimed at youngsters between the ages of three and 14, the Ark runs a range of age-specific programs, talks and interactive experiences designed to stimulate participants' interest in science, the environment and the arts. The centre also has an open-air stage for summer events.

PROJECT ARTS CENTRE THEATRE

Map p268 (☎01-881 9613; www.projectartscentre.ie; 39 Essex St E; ⏰45min before showtime; 🚌all city centre) The city's most interesting venue for challenging new work – be it drama, dance, live art or film. Three separate spaces allow for maximum versatility. You never know what to expect, which makes it all that more fun: we've seen some awful rubbish here, but we've also seen some of the best shows in town.

OLYMPIA THEATRE THEATRE

Map p268 (☎0818 719 330; www.olympia.ie; 72 Dame St; tickets €22.50-60; ⏰shows from 7pm; 🚌all city centre) This lovely Victorian-era theatre specialises in light plays and, at Christmastime, pantomimes. It also hosts some terrific live gigs.

CHAPLINS COMEDY CLUB COMEDY

Map p268 (www.chaplinscomedy.com; Chaplin's Bar, 2 Hawkins St; €10; ⏰8-11pm Sat & select other days; 🚌all city centre) A regularly changing line-up of up-and-coming and local talent look for laughs at this all-seater club; failing that, there's always pizza and craft beer to guarantee a decent night out. Shows start at 9pm.

BUTTON FACTORY LIVE MUSIC

Map p268 (☎01-670 0533; www.buttonfactory.ie; Curved St; €10-20; ⏰7.30-11.30pm Mon-Thu, to 2.30am Fri-Sun; 🚌all city centre) A multi-purpose venue where one night you might be shaking your glow light to a thumping live set by a top DJ, and the next you'll be shifting from foot to foot as members of an esoteric Finnish band drag their violin bows over their electric guitar strings. Live gigs are usually followed by club nights.

HA'PENNY BRIDGE INN COMEDY

Map p268 (☎01-677 2515; www.hapennybridgeinn.com; 42 Wellington Quay; €6; ⏰10.30am-12.30am; 🚌all city centre) A traditional old bar that features local comics on the rise upstairs at the Unhinged Comedy Club on Sundays and Wednesdays, and Irish music downstairs.

NEW THEATRE THEATRE

Map p268 (☎01-670 3361; www.thenewtheatre.com; 43 Essex St E; adult/concession €17/14; ⏰shows 7.30pm Mon-Fri, 2.30pm & 7.30pm Sat; 🚌all city centre) This small theatre's location above a left-wing bookshop should be a guide to the kind of thinking that informs most of the performances taking place on its small stage. It's all about having a social conscience, whether by promoting new work by emerging playwrights or by putting on established works that highlight society's injustices.

IRISH FILM INSTITUTE CINEMA

Map p268 (IFI; ☎01-679 5744; www.ifi.ie; 6 Eustace St; ⏰11am-11pm; 🚌all city centre) The IFI has a couple of screens and shows classics and new art-house films. The complex also has a bar, a cafe and a bookshop.

SHOPPING

This is Dublin's most touristy neighbourhood, so of course you'll find 'Kiss Me I'm Irish' T-shirts and all kinds of other tat, but between the shillelaghs and the singing leprechauns you'll find some of the city's most interesting boutiques, where you can get everything from a Celtic-design wall hanging to

a handcrafted bong. In recent years Temple Bar has seen the arrival of a new generation of retailers, from vintage secondhand sellers to purveyors of new Irish design. A couple of Dublin's best markets take place in this area on Saturdays.

★GUTTER BOOKSHOP BOOKS

Map p268 (☎01-679 9206; www.gutterbookshop.com; Cow's Lane; ⏰10am-6.30pm Mon-Wed, Fri & Sat, to 7pm Thu, 11am-6pm Sun; 🚇all city centre) Taking its name from Oscar Wilde's famous line from *Lady Windermere's Fan* – 'We are all in the gutter, but some of us are looking at the stars' – this fabulous place is flying the flag for the downtrodden independent bookshop, stocking a mix of new novels, children's books, travel literature and other assorted titles.

★CLADDAGH RECORDS MUSIC

Map p268 (☎01-677 0262; www.claddaghrecords.com;2 Cecilia St; ⏰10am-6pm Mon-Sat, from noon Sun; 🚇all city centre) An excellent collection of good-quality traditional and folk music is the mainstay at this centrally located record shop. The profoundly knowledgable staff should be able to locate even the most elusive recording for you. There's also a decent selection of world music. There's another **branch** (☎01-888 3600; www.claddaghrecords.com; 5 Westmoreland St; ⏰10am-6pm Mon-Sat, from noon Sun; 🚇all city centre) on Westmoreland St; you can also shop online.

FIND HOMEWARES

Map p268 (☎086 607 8667; www.findonline.ie; Cow's Lane; ⏰11.30am-5.30pm Mon-Sat, noon-5pm Sun; 🚇all city centre) A cute little hodgepodge of Irish-designed homewares, scented candles and vintage furniture.

LUCY'S LOUNGE VINTAGE

Map p268 (☎01-677 4779; www.lucysloungevintage.com; 11 Lower Fownes St; ⏰noon-6pm Thu-Sat, from 2pm Sun; 🚇all city centre) Go through the upstairs boutique and you'll find a staircase to an Aladdin's basement of vintage goodies. You can easily while away an hour or two here before re-emerging triumphant with something unique to brighten up your wardrobe. Looking for something specific? The super-friendly staff know where everything is hiding.

SIOPAELLA DESIGN EXCHANGE VINTAGE

Map p268 (☎01-532 1477; www.siopaella.com; 8A Crow St; ⏰noon-6pm Mon-Wed, Fri & Sat, to 7pm Thu; 🚇all city centre) A secondhand shop like no other in Dublin, with racks upon racks of excellent vintage clothing. There's another branch on Wicklow St (p84), which specialises more in designer pieces.

JAM ART FACTORY DESIGN

Map p268 (☎01-616 5671; www.jamartfactory.com; 14 Crown Alley; ⏰11am-8pm Mon, from 10am Tue-Sat, 11am-8pm Sun; 🚇all city centre) This quirky little shop is a good bet for souvenirs. ICrammed full of Irish art and design, you can expect everything. Look for nostalgic gifts from Irish childhoods, hilarious comics or colourful renditions of the icons of the Dublin landscape.

SCOUT CLOTHING

Map p268 (☎01-677 8846; www.scoutdublin.com; 5 Smock Alley Ct, Essex St W; ⏰10.30am-6pm Mon-Wed, Fri & Sat, to 6.30pm Thu, noon-5pm Sun; 🚇all city centre) Owner Wendy carefully selects every item of clothing from Irish and international labels including Armor Lux and Manley, plus accessories by Baggu and footwear by Grenson.

FLIP, SHARPSVILLE & HELTER SKELTER FASHION & ACCESSORIES

Map p268 (☎01-671 4299; 4 Upper Fownes St; ⏰10.30am-6pm; 🚇all city centre) Three shops in one all selling the same vintage male fashion moods of the 1950s, from *Rebel Without a Cause*–style leathers to Hawaiian shirts. Downstairs it's newer stuff; upstairs it's really good-quality secondhand clothing.

COW'S LANE DESIGNER MART MARKET

Map p268 (Cow's Lane; ⏰10am-5pm Sat Jun-Sep; 🚇all city centre) A real market for hipsters, on the steps of Cow's Lane, this market brings together over 60 of the best clothing, accessory and craft stalls in town. It's open from June to September; the rest of the year it moves indoors to **St Michael's and St John's Banquet Hall** (⏰10am-5pm Oct-May), just around the corner.

Buy cutting-edge designer duds from the likes of Drunk Monk, punky T-shirts, retro handbags, costume jewellery by Kink Bijoux and even clubby babywear.

FOLKSTER CLOTHING

Map p268 (☎01-675 0917; www.folkster.com; 9 Eustace St; ⏰10.30am-6.30pm Mon-Wed, to 8pm

Thu, to 7pm Fri, 10am-6.30pm Sat, noon-6pm Sun; all city centre) This surprisingly affordable independent boutique stocks a blend of cool clothing and funky homewares. The clothes here are mainly smart casual with sleek lines and minimalist prints selected by owner stylist Blanaid Hennessy.

ALL CITY RECORDS MUSIC

Map p268 (01-677 2994; www.allcitygraffiti.com; 4 Crow St; 10am-7pm Mon-Wed & Fri, to 8pm Thu, to 6pm Sat, noon-6pm Sun; all city centre) Vinyl in all genres, especially EDM, hip-hop and alternative beats. It also sells spray paint for graffiti artists.

TAMP & STITCH FASHION & ACCESSORIES

Map p268 (http://tampandstitch.blogspot.com; Unit 3, Scarlet Row, Essex St W; 10am-6pm Mon-Wed & Fri, to 7pm Thu, 11am-6pm Sat, 1-6pm Sun; all city centre) The latest midrange fashions and a trendy little cafe doing nearly perfect coffee.

LIBRARY PROJECT BOOKS

Map p268 (http://tlp.photoireland.org; 4 Temple Bar; 11am-6pm Tue-Fri, from noon Sat & Sun; all city centre) A bookshop and library of contemporary images from all over the world.

URBAN OUTFITTERS FASHION & ACCESSORIES

Map p268 (01-670 6202; www.urbanoutfitters.com; 4 Cec-ilia St; 10am-7pm Mon-Wed & Sat, to 8pm Thu & Fri, noon-6pm Sun; all city centre) With a blaring techno soundtrack, the Temple Bar branch of this American chain sells ridiculously cool clothes to discerning young buyers. Besides clothing, the shop stocks all kinds of interesting gadgets, accessories and furniture. On the 2nd floor you'll find a hyper-trendy record shop (hence the techno).

CONNOLLY BOOKS BOOKS

Map p268 (01-670 8707; www.connollybooks.org; 43 Essex St E; 10am-5.30pm Tue-Sat; all city centre) Left-wing bookshop beloved of Marxists and radicals.

TEMPLE BAR BOOK MARKET MARKET

Map p268 (Temple Bar Sq; 11am-5pm Sat & Sun; all city centre) Bad secondhand potboilers, sci-fi, picture books and other assorted titles invite you to rummage about on weekend afternoons. If you look hard enough, you're bound to find something worthwhile.

RORY'S FISHING TACKLE SPORTS & OUTDOORS

Map p268 (01-677 2351; www.rorys.ie; 17A Temple Bar; 9.30am-6pm Mon-Sat, 11am-5pm Sun; all city centre) Temple Bar's most famous shop is also its most incongruous: there's not a huge demand in these parts for tackle and fishing equipment.

SPORTS & ACTIVITIES

CHRIST CHURCH GUIDED TOURS TOURS

Map p268 (www.christchurchcathedral.ie; Christ Church Pl; tour €11; hourly 11am-noon & 2-4pm Mon-Fri, 2-4pm Sat; 50, 50A, 56A from Aston Quay, 54, 54A from Burgh Quay) With its hilltop location and eye-catching flying buttresses, Christ Church Cathedral (p107) is the most photogenic of Dublin's cathedrals. Guided tours include the belfry, where you get to hear the campanologist explain the art of bell-ringing and have a go yourself. Under 12s are not allowed access to the belfry.

DUBLIN MUSICAL PUB CRAWL WALKING

Map p268 (01-475 8345; www.musicalpubcrawl.com; Anglesea St; adult/student €16/14; 7.30pm daily Apr-Oct, 7.30pm Thu-Sat Nov-Mar; all city centre) The story of Irish traditional music and its influence on contemporary styles is explained and demonstrated by two expert musicians in a number of Temple Bar pubs over 2½ hours. Tours meet upstairs in the Oliver St John Gogarty (p115) pub.

MELT HEALTH & FITNESS

Map p268 (01-679 8786; www.meltonline.com; 2 Temple Lane; full body massages 30/60min €45/60; 9am-7pm Mon-Sat; all city centre) A full range of massage techniques – from Swedish to shiatsu and many more in-between – are doled out by expert practitioners at Melt, aka the Temple Bar Healing Centre. Also available are a host of other left-of-centre healing techniques, including acupuncture, reiki and polarity therapy. Melt has also set up shop in the Westin (p203).

Kilmainham & the Liberties

Neighbourhood Top Five

❶ **Kilmainham Gaol** (p129) Taking a trip through Ireland's troubled history at this foreboding 18th-century prison, which housed many an Irish rebel.

❷ **Guinness Storehouse** (p123) Sampling a pint of the black stuff at the factory where it all began in 1759 – and continues to this day.

❸ **Teeling Distillery** (p133) Getting familiar with Irish whiskey at the first distillery to open in Dublin for more than a century.

❹ **St Patrick's Cathedral** (p126) Visiting Jonathan Swift's tomb in the cathedral where he served as dean for more than 30 years.

❺ **Irish Museum of Modern Art** (p131) Admiring modern art in exquisite surroundings at a former hospital for wounded soldiers.

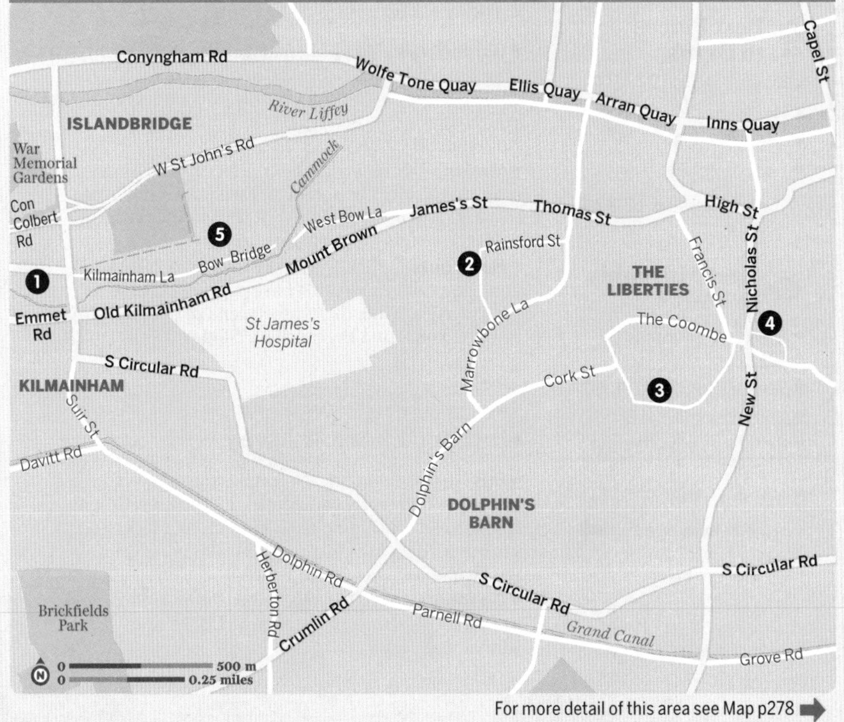

For more detail of this area see Map p278

Lonely Planet's Top Tip

The most convenient way to explore the area is as part of a hop-on, hop-off bus tour, all of which stop at the Guinness Storehouse, the Irish Museum of Modern Art and Kilmainham Gaol. This way, you're also free to take a load off in a cafe or a restaurant. When your visit is done you can hop back on and return to the city centre without hassle.

Best Places to Eat

- Fumbally (p137)
- Clanbrassil House (p138)
- Assassination Custard (p136)
- Two Pups Coffee (p137)

For reviews, see p136.

Best Places to Drink

- Fallon's (p138)
- Old Royal Oak (p138)
- Arthur's (p139)
- Lucky's (p139)

For reviews, see p138.

Best Museums to Visit

- Guinness Storehouse (p123)
- Teeling Distillery (p133)
- Kilmainham Gaol (p129)
- Irish Museum of Modern Art (p131)
- Marsh's Library (p133)

For reviews, see p123.

Explore Kilmainham & the Liberties

Stretching westward along the Liffey from the city centre, you'll need a little planning to get the most out of these two historic neighbourhoods. Coming from the heart of the city centre, you'll first stumble into the Liberties, on the edge of which is St Patrick's Cathedral (p126) and, behind the cathedral, the wonderful Marsh's Library (p133). This traditionally working-class enclave is the latest neighbourhood to be transformed by gentrification, with new cafes and restaurants, a trendy new hotel and a handful of distilleries – modern echoes of its 18th-century past when the Liberties was a hub of whiskey making.

The Liberties' western edge is where you'll find the Guinness brewery at St James's Gate, now the city's most-visited museum. Further west again, in the riverside burg of Kilmainham, you'll come across the country's greatest modern-art museum (p131) and Kilmainham Gaol (p129), which has played a key role in the tormented history of a country's slow struggle to gain its freedom. Both are well worth the westward trek (which can be made easier by bus). This is strictly day-trip territory – there's almost nothing in the way of accommodation and just a couple of decent eating options.

Local Life

- **Garden walks** The Italianate garden at the Irish Museum of Modern Art (p131) is beautiful for a gentle amble, but one of the city's best-kept open secrets is the War Memorial Gardens (p134) in Kilmainham, which runs along the Liffey.
- **Markets** Dublin Food Co-op (p141) in Kilmainham is one of the city's best, and an excellent example of socially responsible retailing; it thrives thanks to the dedication of its many customers.
- **Hang-outs** Fumbally (p137), Two Pups Coffee (p137) and Legit Coffee Co (p137) have brought cafe life to the Liberties, while the southern end of Clanbrassil St is where you'll find the excellent Gaillot et Gray (p137) pizzeria.

Getting There & Away

- **Bus** Nos 50, 50A and 56A from Aston Quay and the 55 and 54A serve the cathedrals and the Liberties; for Kilmainham (including Irish Museum of Modern Art) use bus 51, 51D, 51X, 69, 78 or 79 from Aston Quay or the Luas to Heuston, from which it's a short walk.
- **On foot** It's a 1.5km walk to the Guinness Storehouse from the city centre; about 3km to IMMA and Kilmainham Gaol.

TOP SIGHT

GUINNESS STOREHOUSE & ST JAMES'S GATE

COURTESY DIAGEO ©

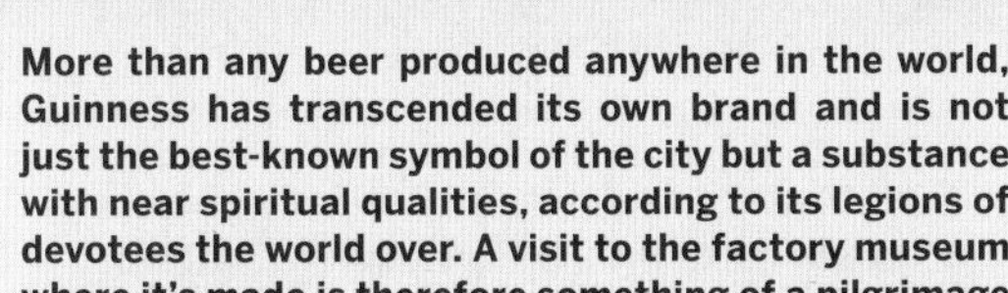

More than any beer produced anywhere in the world, Guinness has transcended its own brand and is not just the best-known symbol of the city but a substance with near spiritual qualities, according to its legions of devotees the world over. A visit to the factory museum where it's made is therefore something of a pilgrimage for many of its fans.

Mythology

The mythology around Guinness is remarkably durable: it doesn't travel well; its distinctive flavour comes from Liffey water; it is good for you – not to mention the generally held belief that you will never understand the Irish until you develop a taste for the black stuff. All absolutely true, of course, so it should be no surprise that the Guinness Storehouse, in the heart of the St James's Gate Brewery, is the city's most-visited tourist attraction, an all-singing, all-dancing extravaganza that combines sophisticated exhibits, spectacular design and a thick, creamy head of marketing hype.

The Beginnings of World Domination

In the 1770s, while other Dublin brewers fretted about the popularity of a new English beer known as porter – which was first created when a London brewer accidentally burnt his hops – Arthur Guinness started making his own version. By 1799 he decided to concentrate all his efforts on this single brew. He died four years later, aged 83, but the foundations for world domination were already in place.

DON'T MISS

- A drink of Guinness
- Gravity Bar view
- 1837 Bar & Brasserie
- Advertising exhibit
- Connoisseur Experience

PRACTICALITIES

- Map p278, E2
- www.guinness-storehouse.com
- St James's Gate, S Market St
- adult/child from €18.50/16, Connoisseur Experience €55
- 9.30am-7pm Sep-Jun, 9am to 8pm Jul & Aug
- 13, 21A, 40, 51B, 78, 78A, 123 from Fleet St, jJames's

BEST DEAL IN TOWN

When Arthur started brewing in Dublin in 1759, he couldn't have had any idea that his name would become synonymous with Dublin around the world. Or could he? Showing extraordinary foresight, he had just signed a lease for a small disused brewery under the terms that he would pay just £45 annually for the next 9000 years, with the additional condition that he'd never have to pay for the water used.

Aficionados can opt for the Connoisseur Experience, where you sample the four different kinds of Guinness while hearing their story from your designated bartender.

DID YOU KNOW?

St Patrick's Tower, the large smock windmill on the extensive factory grounds, was originally built as part of the Roe Distillery, which once occupied 7 hectares on the north side of James's St and was Europe's largest producer of whiskey. Arthur Guinness didn't much care for whiskey, branding it the 'curse of the nation' (and his own brew the 'nurse of the nation').

At one time a Grand Canal tributary was cut into the brewery to enable special Guinness barges to carry consignments out onto the Irish canal system or to the Dublin port. When the brewery extensions reached the Liffey in 1872, the fleet of Guinness barges became a familiar sight. Pretty soon Guinness was being exported as far afield as Africa and the West Indies. As the barges chugged their way along the Liffey towards the port, boys used to lean over the wall and shout, 'Bring us back a parrot'. Old-school Dubliners still say the same thing to each other when they're going off on holiday.

The Essential Ingredients

One link with the past that hasn't been broken is the yeast used to make Guinness, essentially the same living organism that has been used since 1770. Another vital ingredient is a hop by the name of fuggles, which used to be grown exclusively around Dublin but is now imported from Britain, the USA and Australia (everyone take a bow).

Guinness Storehouse Museum

The brewery is far more than just a place where beer is manufactured. It is an intrinsic part of Dublin's history and a key element of the city's identity. Accordingly, the quasi-mythical stature of Guinness is the central theme of the brewery's museum, the Guinness Storehouse, which is the only part of the brewery open to visitors.

It occupies the old Fermentation House, built in 1904. As it's a listed building, the designers could only adapt and add to the structure without taking anything away. The result is a stunning central atrium that rises seven storeys and takes the shape of a pint of Guinness. The head is represented by the glassed Gravity Bar, which provides panoramic views of Dublin to savour with your complimentary half-pint.

Before you race up to the top, however, you might want to check out the museum for which you've paid so handsomely. Actually, it's designed as more of an 'experience' than a museum. It has nearly 1.5 hectares of floor space, featuring a dazzling array of audiovisual and interactive exhibits, which cover most aspects of the brewery's story and explain the brewing process in overwhelming detail.

On the ground floor, a copy of Arthur Guinness' original lease lies embedded beneath a pane of glass in the floor. Wandering up through the various exhibits, including 70-odd years of advertising, you can't help feeling that the now wholly foreign-owned

COURTESY DIAGEO ©

company has hijacked the mythology Dubliners attached to the drink, and it has all become more about marketing and manipulation than mingling and magic.

Gravity Bar

Whatever reservations you may have about the marketing and hype of today's Guinness can be more than dispelled at the top of the building in the circular Gravity Bar, where you get a complimentary glass of Guinness. The views from the bar are superb, but the Guinness itself is as near-perfect as a beer can be.

1837 Bar & Brasserie

Sitting one floor below the Gravity Bar and blessed with the same views of the city is this surprisingly good lunchtime spot (p137) that would be worth checking out as a stand-alone restaurant, never mind one in a museum. The menu is fairly straightforward – chicken, burgers etc – but everything is exquisitely made.

TOP SIGHT
ST PATRICK'S CATHEDRAL

Situated on the very spot that St Paddy reputably rolled up his sleeves and dunked the heathen Irish into a well and thereby gave them a fair to middling shot at salvation, St Patrick's Cathedral is one of Dublin's earliest Christian sites and a most hallowed chunk of real estate.

History

Although a church has stood here since the 5th century, this building dates from the turn of the 12th century and has been altered several times, most notably in 1864 when it was saved from ruin and, some might say, over-enthusiastically restored. The interior is as calm and soothing as the exterior is sombre. The picturesque St Patrick's Park, adjoining, was a crowded slum until it was cleared in the early 20th century.

It's likely that St Patrick's was intended to replace Christ Church as the city's cathedral, but the older church's stubborn refusal to be usurped resulted in the two cathedrals being virtually a stone's throw from one another. Separated only by the city walls (with St Patrick's outside), each possessed the rights of cathedral of the diocese. While St Pat's isn't as photogenic as its neighbour, it probably surpasses its more attractive rival in historical terms.

Political Interference

Following Henry VIII's 16th-century dissolution of the monasteries, St Patrick's was ordered to hand over all of its estates, revenues and possessions. The chapter (bureaucratic head of the church) was imprisoned until he 'agreed' to the handover, the cathedral's privileges were revoked

DON'T MISS

- Swift's Tomb
- Stained-glass windows
- Boyle Monument

PRACTICALITIES

- Map p278, H3
- ☎01-453 9472
- www.stpatrickscathedral.ie
- St Patrick's Close
- adult/student €8/7
- 9.30am-5pm Mon-Fri, 9am-6pm Sat, 9-10.30am, 12.30-2.30pm & 4.30-6pm Sun Mar-Oct, 9.30am-5pm Mon-Fri, from 9am Sat, 9-10.30am & 12.30-2.30pm Sun Nov-Feb
- 50, 50A, 56A from Aston Quay, 54, 54A from Burgh Quay

and it was demoted to the rank of parish church. It was not restored to its previous position until 1560.

Further indignity followed at the hands of Oliver Cromwell in 1649, when the nave was used as a stable for his horses. In 1666 the Lady Chapel was given to the newly arrived Huguenots and became known as the French Church of St Patrick. It remained in Huguenot hands until 1816. The northern transept was known as the parish church of St Nicholas Without (meaning outside the city), essentially dividing the cathedral into two distinct churches.

Such confusion led to the building falling into disrepair as the influence of the deanery and chapter waned. Although the church's most famous dean, Jonathan Swift (author of *Gulliver's Travels,* who served here from 1713 to 1745), did his utmost to preserve the integrity of the building, by the end of the 18th century it was close to collapse. It was just standing when the benevolent Guinness family stepped in to begin a massive restoration in 1864.

Baptistry & Swift's Tomb

Fittingly, the first Guinness to show an interest in preserving the church, Benjamin, is commemorated with a **statue** at the main entrance. Inside to your left is the oldest part of the building, the **baptistry**, which was probably the entrance to the original building. It contains the original **12th-century floor tiles** and **medieval stone font**, which is still in use. Inside the cathedral proper, you come almost immediately to the **tombs of Jonathan Swift and Esther Johnson**, his long-term companion, better known as Stella. The Latin epitaphs are both written by Swift, and assorted Swift memorabilia lies all over the cathedral, including a pulpit and a death mask.

Boyle Monument

You can't miss the huge Boyle Monument, erected in 1632 by Richard Boyle, Earl of Cork. It stood briefly beside the altar until, in 1633, Dublin's viceroy, Thomas Wentworth, Earl of Strafford, had it shifted from its prominent position because he felt he shouldn't have to kneel to a Corkman. Boyle took his revenge in later years by orchestrating Wentworth's impeachment and execution. A figure in a niche at the bottom left of the monument is the earl's son Robert, the noted scientist who discovered Boyle's Law, which determined that the pressure and volume of a gas have an inverse relationship at a constant temperature.

St Patrick's Well

In the opposite corner, there is a cross on a stone slab that once marked the position of St Patrick's original well, where, according to legend, the patron saint of Ireland rolled up his sleeves and got to baptising the natives.

NATURAL DISASTERS

The cathedral had been built twice by 1254 but succumbed to a series of natural disasters over the following century. Its spire was taken out in a 1316 storm, while the original tower and part of the nave were destroyed by fire in 1362.

Attend a sung Mass for the best atmosphere – at 11.15am on Sundays throughout the year, or at 9am Monday to Friday during school term only.

VISITING

Advance tickets are not valid on Sundays between 10.45am and 12.30pm and between 2.45pm and 4.30pm.

Last admission is 30 minutes before closing time.

LIVING STONES

On your way around the church, you will also take in the four sections of the permanent exhibition, Living Stones, which explores the cathedral's history and the contribution it has made to the culture of Dublin.

South Transept & South Aisle

Passing through the south transept, which was once the chapterhouse where the Earl of Kildare chanced his arm, you'll see magnificent **stained-glass windows** above the funerary monuments. The south aisle is lined with memorials to prominent 20th-century Irish Protestants, including Erskine Childers, who was president of Ireland from 1973 to 1974, and whose father was executed by the Free State during the Civil War. The son never spoke of the struggle for Irish independence because, on the eve of his death, his father made him promise never to do anything that might promote bitterness among the Irish people.

North Transept

The north transept contains various military memorials to Royal Irish Regiments, while the northern choir aisle has a tablet marking the **grave of the Duke of Schomberg**, a prominent casualty of the Battle of the Boyne in 1690. Swift provided the duke's epitaph, caustically noting on it that the duke's own relatives couldn't be bothered to provide a suitable memorial. On the opposite side of the choir is a chair used by William of Orange when he came to give thanks to God for his victory over the Catholic James II during the same battle.

Feature: Door of Reconciliation

Towards the north transept is a door that has become a symbol of peace and reconciliation since it helped resolve a scrap between the Earls of Kildare and Ormond in 1492. After a feud, supporters of the squabbling nobles ended up in a pitched battle inside the cathedral, during which Ormond's nephew – one Black James – barricaded himself in the chapterhouse. Kildare, having calmed down, cut a hole in the door between them and stuck his arm through it to either shake his opponent's hand, or lose a limb in his attempt to smooth things over. James chose mediation over amputation and took his hand. The term 'to chance your arm' entered the English lexicon and everyone lived happily ever after – except Black James, who was murdered by Kildare's son-in-law four years later.

ST PATRICK'S CATHEDRAL

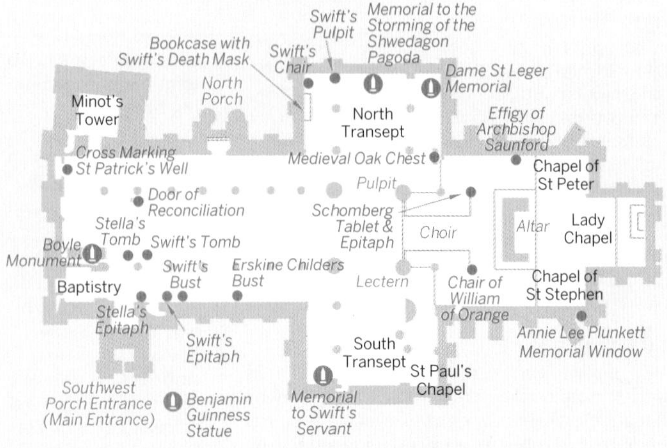

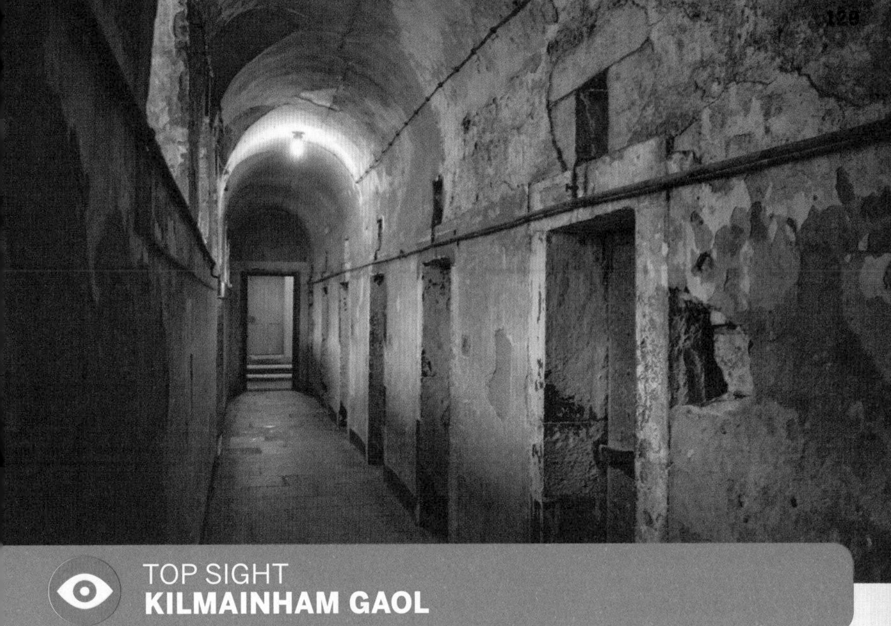

TOP SIGHT
KILMAINHAM GAOL

If you have *any* interest in Irish history, you must visit this infamous prison. It was the stage for many of the most tragic and heroic episodes in Ireland's recent past, and its list of inmates reads like a who's who of Irish nationalism. Solid and sombre, its walls absorbed the hardship of British occupation and recount it in whispers to visitors.

DON'T MISS

- Prison Museum
- Stone Breakers' Yard
- Prison cells

PRACTICALITIES

- Map p278, A3
- 01-453 5984
- www.kilmainhamgaolmuseum.ie
- Inchicore Rd
- adult/child €9/5
- 9am-7pm Jun-Aug, 9.30am-5.30pm Oct-Mar, 9am-6pm Apr, May & Sep
- 69, 79 from Aston Quay, 13, 40 from O'Connell St

History

It took four years to build, and the prison opened – or rather closed – its doors in 1796. The Irish were locked up for all sorts of misdemeanours, some more serious than others. A six-year-old boy spent a month here in 1839 because his father couldn't pay his train fare, and during the Famine (1845–51) it was crammed with the destitute imprisoned for stealing food and begging. But it is most famous for 120 years of incarcerating Irish nationalists, from Robert Emmet in 1803 to Éamon de Valera in 1923. All of Ireland's botched uprisings ended with the leaders' confinement here, usually before their execution.

It was the treatment of the leaders of the 1916 Easter Rising that most deeply etched the jail into the Irish consciousness. Fourteen of the rebel commanders were executed in the Stone Breakers' Yard, including James Connolly, who was so badly injured at the time of his execution that he was strapped to a chair at the opposite end of the yard, just inside the gate. The places where they were shot are marked by two simple black crosses. The executions set a previously apathetic nation on a course towards violent rebellion.

The jail's final function was as a prison for the newly formed Irish Free State, an irony best summed up by the story of Ernie O'Malley, who escaped from the jailin 1921 when

GALLOWS HILL

The prison was built on a site known as Gallows Hill, where criminals would meet their fate at the end of a rope strung from a tree. The grim ritual continued after the prison's construction, with public executions taking place every couple of months just by the prison entrance.

Arrive early to avoid the usually long queues; try to get on the first tour of the day (tours can't be booked in advance).

PRISON LOVE

Joseph Plunkett, one of the leaders of the 1916 Easter Rising, was given permission to marry his fiancée Grace Gifford. The ceremony took place in Kilmainham Chapel. Seven hours later, Plunkett was executed by firing squad.

incarcerated by the British but was locked up again by his erstwhile comrades during the Civil War. This chapter is played down on the tour, and even the passing comment that Kilmainham's final prisoner was the future president, Éamon de Valera, doesn't reveal that he had been imprisoned by his fellow Irish citizens. The jail was decommissioned in 1924.

Guided Tour

Visits are by guided tour and start with a stirring audiovisual introduction, screened in the chapel where 1916 leader Joseph Plunkett was wed to his beloved just hours before his execution. The thought-provoking (but too crowded) tour takes you through the old and new wings of the prison, where you can see former cells of famous inmates, read graffiti on the walls and immerse yourself in the atmosphere of the execution yards.

Asgard & Museum

Incongruously sitting outside in the yard is the *Asgard,* the ship that successfully ran the British blockade to deliver arms to nationalist forces in 1914. It belonged to, and was skippered by, Erskine Childers, father of the future president of Ireland. He was executed by Michael Collins' Free State army in 1922 for carrying a revolver, which had been a gift from Collins himself. There is also an outstanding museum dedicated to Irish nationalism and prison life. On a lighter note, U2 fans will recognise the prison as the setting for the video to their 1982 single 'A Celebration'.

TOP SIGHT

IRISH MUSEUM OF MODERN ART

The Irish Museum of Modern Art is the country's foremost gallery for contemporary Irish art, although it takes second billing to the majestic building in which it is housed: the Royal Hospital Kilmainham. The hospital (built from 1680 to 1684) served as a retirement home for veteran soldiers until 1928.

Royal Hospital Kilmainham

The inspiration for the design came from James Butler, Duke of Ormonde and Charles II's viceroy, who had been so impressed by Les Invalides on a trip to Paris that he commissioned William Robinson to knock up a Dublin version. What the architect designed was Dublin's finest 17th-century building and the high point of the Anglo-Dutch style of the day. It consists of an unbroken range enclosing a vast, peaceful courtyard with arcaded walks. A chapel in the centre of the northern flank has an elegant clock tower and spire. This was the first truly classical building in Dublin and was a precursor for the grand Georgian constructions of the 18th century. Christopher Wren began building London's Chelsea Royal Hospital two years after work commenced here.

After closing in 1928 the Royal Hospital languished for half a century but was spectacularly restored in the 1980s, and reopened in 1984, on the 300th anniversary of its construction. The next year it received the prestigious Europa Nostra award, which recognises efforts in preservation of Europe's architectural heritage. Another refurb between 2012 and 2013 saw the upgrade of the museum's lighting and fire-safety systems.

DON'T MISS

- The Madden Arnholz Collection
- Formal gardens

PRACTICALITIES

- Map p278, C2
- IMMA
- www.imma.ie
- Military Rd
- admission free
- 11.30am-5.30pm Tue-Fri, from 10am Sat, from noon Sun, tours 1.15pm Wed, 2.30pm Sat & Sun
- 51, 51D, 51X, 69, 78, 79 from Aston Quay, Heuston

POTENTIAL GOVERNMENT

The Royal Hospital Kilmainham was considered a possible site for the newly established Irish Parliament after the formation of the Irish Free State in 1922.

The formal gardens are a gorgeous spot for a nice leisurely walk.

LONDON TWIN

Sir Christopher Wren's Royal Hospital Chelsea in London opened in 1692 and both its design and function were hugely influenced by the Royal Hospital Kilmainham, which opened a couple of years earlier.

You can exit the museum by the back entrance, which abuts Kilmainham Gaol.

Guided Tours

There are free guided tours of the museum's exhibits at 2.30pm on Wednesday, Friday and Sunday throughout the year. They show off some of the building's treasures, including the **Banqueting Hall**, with 22 specially commissioned portraits, and the stunning **baroque chapel**, with papier-mâché ceilings and a set of exquisite Queen Anne gates. Also worth seeing are the fully restored formal gardens.

Artworks

In 1991 the hospital became home to IMMA and the best of modern and contemporary Irish art. The blend of old and new is wonderful, and you'll find Irish artists such as Louis le Brocquy, Sean Scully, Kathy Prendergast and Dorothy Cross featured here, as well as a film installation by Neil Jordan. The permanent exhibition also features paintings from heavy-hitters Pablo Picasso and Joan Miró, and is topped up by regular temporary exhibitions. There's a good cafe (p137) and a bookshop (p141) on the grounds.

Madden Arnholz Collection

A museum highlight is the collection of roughly 2000 prints by Old Masters including Dürer, Rembrandt, Goya and others, donated in 1998 by Clare Madden, who had been left the collection upon the death of her daughter Etain and son-in-law Fritz Arnholz. The prints date from the 15th to the late 19th centuries and is especially strong in work by William Hogarth, who was renowned for his satirical prints and drawings – included are complete sets including *Marriage-á-la-Mode, A Rake's Progress* and *A Harlot's Progress.*

Formal Gardens

Below the north terrace (formerly the Master's Garden) are the formal gardens, which are a late-20th-century addition, but done in the style of a late-17th- or early-18th-century garden. The main axes radiate from the focal points created by the garden house, central fountain and modern statuary, which establish a wonderful juxtaposition between modern forms and classical formality: the eight limestone monoliths by Ulrich Rückriem echo the yew topiary they overlook.

SIGHTS

Moving westward, the main sights start with St Patrick's Cathedral – which borders the eastern boundary of the Liberties, home to a slew of new distilleries. The western edge of that neighbourhood is where you'll find the Guinness Storehouse. Kilmainham Gaol and the Irish Museum of Modern Art are west again, in the old neighbourhood of Kilmainham, which you can walk to, although you're better off getting a bus.

GUINNESS STOREHOUSE — BREWERY
See p123.

ST PATRICK'S CATHEDRAL — CATHEDRAL
See p126.

KILMAINHAM GAOL — MUSEUM
See p129.

IRISH MUSEUM OF MODERN ART — MUSEUM
See p131.

★MARSH'S LIBRARY — LIBRARY
Map p278 (www.marshlibrary.ie; St Patrick's Close; adult/child €5/free; ⌚9.30am-5pm Mon & Wed-Fri, from 10am Sat; 🚌50, 50A, 56A from Aston Quay, 54, 54A from Burgh Quay) This magnificently preserved scholars' library, virtually unchanged in three centuries, is one of Dublin's most beautiful open secrets and an absolute highlight of any visit. Atop its ancient stairs are beautiful dark-oak bookcases, each topped with elaborately carved and gilded gables, and crammed with 25,000 books, manuscripts and maps dating back to the 15th century.

Founded in 1701 by Archbishop Narcissus Marsh (1638–1713) and opened in 1707, the library was designed by Sir William Robinson, the man also responsible for the Royal Hospital Kilmainham (p131). It's the oldest public library in the country, and contains 25,000 books dating from the 16th to the early 18th century, as well as maps, manuscripts (including one in Latin dating back to 1400) and a collection of incunabula (books printed before 1500).

TEELING DISTILLERY — DISTILLERY
Map p278 (www.teelingwhiskey.com; 13-17 Newmarket; tours €15-30; ⌚10am-5.40pm; 🚌27, 77A & 151 from city centre) FREE The first new distillery in Dublin for 125 years, Teeling only began production in 2015 and it will be several years before any of the distillate can be called whiskey. In the meantime, you can explore the visitor centre and taste (and buy) whiskeys from the family's other distillery on the Cooley Peninsula.

You'll get a taste of whiskey at the end of the tour, but to try the really good stuff you'll have to upgrade to one of the organised tastings, which range from the Teeling Tasting (€15) to the Single Malt Reserve Tasting (€30), where you'll indulge in three special whiskeys, including the exceptional 21-year-old award-winning Reserve Single Malt. There's also an excellent cafe on the premises.

ROE & CO DISTILLERY — DISTILLERY
Map p278 (www.roeandcowhiskey.com; 91 James's St; €19-25; ⌚11am-7pm, last admission 5pm; 🚌123 from city centre) The newest kid in Dublin's distillery district, Roe & Co took up residence in 2019 in the old Guinness Power Station, a cool brick building opposite the main brewery entrance. The emphasis here is on cocktails – after a traditional tasting you learn about flavour profiles in a mixology workshop, before heading to the bar to sample the bartender's wares. Book ahead.

DUBLIN LIBERTIES DISTILLERY — DISTILLERY
Map p278 (https://thedld.com; 33 Mill St; adult/child €16/14; ⌚9.30am-6pm Mon-Thu, to 7pm Fri & Sat, 11am-7pm Sun Apr-Aug, 10am-5.30pm Mon-Sat, from 11am Sun Sep-Mar; 🚌49, 54A from city centre) Housed in a 400-year-old building is Dublin's newest distillery venture, which opened in 2019 and cements the Liberties' newly established rep as a centre for whiskey production. There's a standard tour, where you learn about the distilling process and finish with a tasting of three whiskies – the Dubliner, the Dublin Liberties and the Dead Rabbit – although these have all been distilled elsewhere as it'll be at least three years before any of the distillate can be called whiskey.

There's also an Experience tour (€32) where you get to taste six whiskies, and plans are afoot for a Master Blender experience (€100).

PEARSE LYONS DISTILLERY — DISTILLERY
Map p278(☎01-825 2244; www.pearselyonsdistillery.com; 121-122 James's St; guided tours €20-30; 🚌21A, 51B, 78, 78A, 123 from Fleet St) This boutique distillery opened in the former St James' Church in the summer of 2017, distilling small-batch, craft Irish whiskey.

You have a choice of three tours: the Trilogy tour, which includes a distillery visit, a tour of St James' graveyard and a three-whiskey tasting; the Signature Tour, which has four tastings; and the Legacy Tour, where you get to sample five whiskies, including a five-year-old single malt.

The guided tour also includes a history of distilling in the Liberties, as well as the local history of owner Pearse Lyons' family.

WAR MEMORIAL GARDENS PARK

Map p278 (www.heritageireland.ie; S Circular Rd, Islandbridge; ⏲8am-dusk Mon-Fri, from 10am Sat & Sun; 🚌69, 79 from Aston Quay, 13, 40 from O'Connell St) FREE Hardly anyone ever ventures this far west, but they're missing a lovely bit of landscaping in the shape of the War Memorial Gardens – by our reckoning as pleasant a patch of greenery as any you'll find in the heart of the Georgian centre. Designed by Sir Edwin Lutyens, the memorial commemorates the 49,400 Irish soldiers who died during WWI – their names are inscribed in the two huge granite bookrooms that stand at one end.

ST AUDOEN'S CHURCH OF IRELAND CHURCH

Map p278 (☎01-677 0088; www.heritageireland.ie; Cornmarket, High St; ⏲9.30am-4.45pm May-Oct; 🚌50, 50A, 56A from Aston Quay, 54, 54A from Burgh Quay) Two churches, side by side, each bearing the same name, a tribute to St Audoen, the 7th-century bishop of Rouen (aka Ouen) and patron saint of the Normans. They built the older of the two, the Church of Ireland, between 1181 and 1212, and today it is the only medieval church in Dublin still in use. A free 30-minute guided tour departs every 30 minutes from 9.30am to 4.45pm. Attached to it is the newer, bigger, 19th-century Catholic St Audoen's (p136).

Through the Norman church's heavily moulded Romanesque Norman door, you can touch the 9th-century 'lucky stone' that was believed to bring good luck to business, and check out the 9th-century slab in the porch that suggests it was built on an even older church. As part of the tour you can explore the ruins as well as the present church, which has funerary monuments that were beheaded by Cromwell's purists. Its tower and door date from the 12th century and the aisle from the 15th century, but the church today is mainly a product of a 19th-century restoration.

Neighbourhood Walk
Viking & Medieval Dublin

START ESSEX GATE, PARLIAMENT ST
END DUBLIN CASTLE
LENGTH 2.5KM; TWO HOURS

Begin your walk in Temple Bar, at the corner of Parliament St and Essex Gate, once a main entrance gate to the city. A **1 bronze plaque** on a pillar marks the spot where the gate once stood. Further along, you can see the original foundations of the 13th-century **2 Isolde's Tower**, once part of the city walls, through a grill in the pavement in front of the pub of the same name. It is thought the original tower was between 12m and 15m high, but it was demolished in the 17th century to make way for Georgian houses (also now demolished!).

Head west down Essex Gate and West Essex St until you reach Fishamble St; turn right towards the quays and left into Wood Quay. Cross Winetavern St and proceed along Merchant's Quay. To your left you'll see the **3 Church of the Immaculate Conception**, otherwise known as Adam & Eve's, after a tavern through which worshippers gained access to a secret chapel during Penal Law times during the 17th and 18th centuries. To make matters even more confusing, it is also known as the Church of St Francis (to whom it was originally dedicated).

Further down Merchant's Quay you'll spot the **4 Father Mathew Bridge**, built in 1818 on the spot of the fordable crossing that gave Dublin its Irish name, Baile Átha Cliath (Town of the Hurdle Ford) and named after temperance reformer Theobold Mathew (1790–1856), whose singular contribution to Irish life is 'the Pledge', a commitment to abstain from alcohol that most Irish Catholics took when they were confirmed (around age 12) and then abandoned when they were of age to drink (or earlier). Take a left into Bridge St and stop for said indulgence at Dublin's oldest pub, the **5 Brazen Head** (p139), dating from 1198 (although the present building dates from a positively youthful 1668).

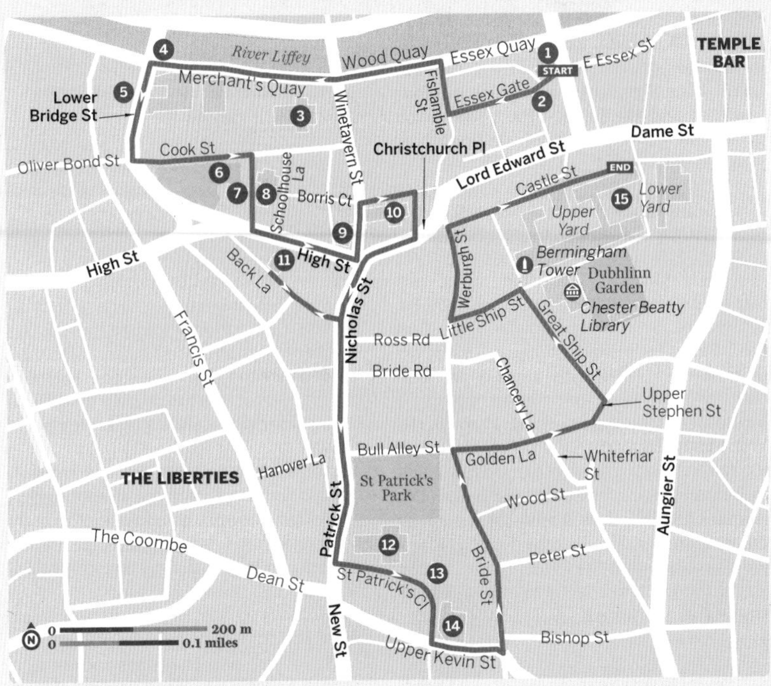

Take the next left onto Cook St, where you'll find **6 St Audoen's Arch**, one of the only remaining gates of the 32 that were built into the medieval city walls, dating from 1240. Climb through the arch up to the ramparts to see one of the city's oldest existing churches, **7 St Audoen's Church of Ireland** (p134). It was built around 1190, and is the only medieval church in the city that is still in use. Next door is the much newer (and larger) **8 St Audoen's Catholic Church** (p136), which was known for the speedy sermons of Father 'Flash' Kavanagh, keen to ensure that he and his parishioners were out in time for the Sunday game of Gaelic football.

Leave the little park, join High St and head east until you reach the first corner. Here on your left is the former Synod Hall, now **9 Dublinia** (p110), where medieval Dublin has been interactively recreated. Turn left and walk under the Synod Hall Bridge, which links Dublinia to one of the city's most important landmarks – **10 Christ Church Cathedral** (p1107) – and, in medieval times, the most important church inside the city walls.

Exit the cathedral onto Christ Church Pl, cross over onto Nicholas St and turn right onto Back Lane. Proceed to **11 Tailors' Hall**, Dublin's oldest surviving guild hall, built between 1703 and 1707 (though it says 1770 on the plaque) for the Tailors Guild. It's now the headquarters of An Taisce, the National Trust for Ireland.

Do an about-turn, head back along the lane and turn right into Nicholas St, which becomes Patrick St. To your left you'll see **12 St Patrick's** (p126), Dublin's most important cathedral, which stood outside the city walls. Along St Patrick's Close, beyond the bend on the left, is the stunningly beautiful **13 Marsh's Library** (p133), named after Archbishop Narcissus Marsh, dean of St Patrick's. Further along again on your left is the **14 Dublin Metropolitan Police** building, once the Episcopal Palace of St Sepulchre.

Finally, follow our route up Bride St, Golden Lane and Great Ship St, and finish up with a long wander around **15 Dublin Castle** (p61). Be sure not to miss the striking powder-blue Bermingham Tower and the nearby Chester Beatty Library, which houses one of the city's most fascinating collections of rare books and manuscripts, and is well worth a visit.

EVENSONG AT THE CATHEDRALS

In a rare coming together, the choirs of St Patrick's Cathedral and Christ Church Cathedral both participated in the first-ever performance of Handel's *Messiah* in nearby Fishamble St in 1742, conducted by the great composer himself. Both houses of worship carry on their proud choral traditions, and visits to the cathedrals during evensong will provide enchanting and atmospheric memories. The choir performs evensong in St Patrick's at 5.30pm Monday to Friday and 3.15pm Sundays, while the Christ Church choir performs at 6pm on Wednesday and Thursday and 5pm Saturday (times may vary, so check ahead at www.christchurchcathedral.ie). If you're going to be in Dublin around Christmas, do not miss the carols at St Patrick's; call ahead for the hard-to-get tickets on 01-453 9472.

St Anne's Chapel, the visitor centre, houses a number of tombstones of leading members of Dublin society from the 16th to 18th centuries. At the top of the chapel is the tower, which holds the three oldest bells in Ireland, dating from 1423. Although the church's exhibits are hardly spectacular, the building itself is beautiful and a genuine slice of medieval Dublin.

The church is entered from the south off High St through **St Audoen's Arch**, which was built in 1240 and is the only surviving reminder of the city gates. The adjoining park is pretty but attracts many unsavoury characters, particularly at night.

ST AUDOEN'S CATHOLIC CHURCH — CHURCH

Map p278 (Cornmarket, High St; Mass 1.15 & 7pm Mon-Fri, 6pm Sat, 9.30am, 11am, 12.30 & 6pm Sun; 50, 50A, 56A from Aston Quay, 54, 54A from Burgh Quay) FREE Attached to the medieval St Audoen's Church of Ireland (p134) is the bigger, 19th-century Catholic St Audoen's, which since 2006 has been home to the Polish chaplaincy in Ireland. It opens just before its scheduled Mass times.

ST PATRICK'S TOWER — TOWER

Map p278 (Thomas St; closed to public; 69 from Aston Quay) St Patrick's Tower is Europe's tallest smock windmill (with a revolving top). It was built in 1757 to power the Roe Distillery, which by 1887 covered 7 hectares and produced more than two million gallons of whiskey annually, making it Europe's largest distillery. By the mid-1920s, however, the global whiskey market was in decline and the distillery was eventually sold in 1949 to its neighbours, Guinness.

KILMAINHAM GATE — LANDMARK

Map p278 (69, 79 from Aston Quay, 13, 40 from O'Connell St) Francis Johnston's impressive Georgian gate was designed in 1812 as the Richmond Tower and located on the quays, near the Guinness Brewery. It was moved here in 1846 as it obstructed the increasingly heavy traffic to the new Kingsbridge Station (Heuston Station), which opened in 1844.

EATING

Cheaper rents have lured restaurateurs out to the neighbourhoods in Dublin 8, which means there has been a (much-lauded) culinary explosion in the area. You'll now find some of the city's most exciting cooking in and around the Liberties, with inventive, funky dishes enchanting gaggles of hipsters and locals alike.

★ASSASSINATION CUSTARD — CAFE €

Map p278 (087 997 1513; www.facebook.com/assassinationcustard; 19 Kevin St; mains €7-9; noon-3pm Tue-Fri; all city centre) It doesn't look like much, but this is one of the tastiest treats in town. The small menu changes daily – think roasted cauliflower with toasted dukkah, or broccoli with spicy Italian 'nduja pork sausage and Toonsbridge ricotta. If you're feeling really adventurous, try the tripe sandwich. The name comes from a phrase coined by Samuel Beckett.

COKE LANE PIZZA — PIZZA €

Map p278 (www.cokelanepizza.com; 78 Meath St; pizzas €10-13; 5-11pm Sun-Fri, from 2pm Sat; 13, 40, 123 from city centre) Excellent sourdough pizzas served fresh from the hatch on the terrace of Luckys (p139) pub. Visit before 7pm and you can get pizza and a pint (or a glass of wine) for €13 – possibly the best bargain in town.

FUMBALLY CAFE €

Map p278 (☎01-529 8732; www.thefumbally.ie; Fumbally Lane; mains €7-12; ⊙8am-5pm Tue-Fri, from 10am Sat, plus 7-9.30pm Wed; 🚌49, 54A from city centre) A bright, airy warehouse cafe that serves healthy breakfasts, salads and sandwiches – while the occasional guitarist strums away in the corner. Its Wednesday dinner (tapas from €6) is an organic, locally sourced exploration of the cuisines of the world that is insanely popular with locals; advance bookings suggested.

CLANBRASSIL COFFEE SHOP CAFE €

Map p278 (www.clanbrassilhouse.com; 6 Upper Clanbrassil St; mains €6-12; ⊙8am-3pm Mon-Fri, 9am-3.30pm Sat; 🚌9, 16, 49, 54A from city centre) The daytime incarnation of Clanbrassil House (p138) next door, this cafe has a small but solid menu of sandwiches, bagels and pastries, made fresh each day.

TWO PUPS COFFEE VEGETARIAN €

Map p278 (www.facebook.com/twopupscoffee; 74 Francis St; mains €7-10; ⊙8am-5pm Mon-Fri, 9.30am-4pm Sat & Sun; 🌶; 🚌51B, 123, 206 from city centre) A gem of a local cafe serving fresh, inventive food. The decor may be somewhat hipster but the food is wholesome, tasty and unpretentious, with excellent coffee too. Always busy at lunchtime so it's worth arriving early to grab a table.

LEGIT COFFEE CO CAFE €

Map p278 (www.legitcoffeeco.com; 1 Meath Mart, Meath St; mains €5-12; ⊙8am-4pm Mon-Fri, from 9.30am Sat; 🚊James's) A rare trendy spot in the middle of one of Dublin's most traditional streets, Legit is full of stripped-down wood, speciality teas and strong espressos. A great spot to enjoy a toasted brioche or a filling sandwich.

GAILLOT ET GRAY PIZZA €

Map p278 (☎01-454 7781; www.facebook.com/GaillotGrayP; 59 Lower Clanbrassil St; pizzas €10-15; ⊙8am-10pm Tue-Sat; 🚌49, 54A from city centre) *Mon dieu,* a French pizzeria? Gilles Gaillot and his wife Emma Gray have combined the forces of Emmental cheese and pizza (biscuit-thin sourdough bases) to create this delicious hybrid. It doesn't taste like classic Italian pizza, which is precisely the point. And it works. It also operates as a bakery during the day.

1837 BAR & BRASSERIE BRASSERIE €

Map p278 (☎01-471 4602; www.guinness-storehouse.com; Guinness Storehouse, St James's Gate; mains €14-18; ⊙noon-3pm; 🚌21A, 51B, 78, 78A, 123 from Fleet St, 🚊James's) This lunchtime brasserie serves tasty dishes, from really fresh oysters to an insanely good Guinness burger, with skin-on fries and red-onion chutney. The drinks menu features a range of Guinness variants such as West Indian porter and Golden Ale. Highly recommended for lunch if you're visiting the museum.

TASTY 8 CAFE €

Map p278 (☎01-691 7609; www.tasty8.ie; 67-68 Meath St; ⊙8am-5pm Mon-Sat, 9.30am-3pm Sun; 🚌13, 40, 123 from city centre) A friendly local cafe, its menu caters for every palate, while keeping the 'old Dublin' atmosphere the Liberties is famous for. If you're in the mood for a big feed, this has one of the most reasonably priced full Irish breakfasts in the city.

CONTAINER COFFEE CAFE €

Map p278 (www.containercoffee.ie; 161 Thomas St; mains €5; ⊙7.30am-4pm Mon-Fri, from 9am Sat, from 10am Sun; 🚌13, 40, 123 from city centre) With strong coffee, ready-to-go gourmet sandwiches, pastries and hearty sausage rolls, this makes for a good pit stop to quickly refuel. Seating is limited inside but on a fine day there are plenty of picnic tables out the back. Compostable takeaway cups gives it an ecofriendly boost.

DUBLIN COOKIE COMPANY BAKERY €

Map p278 (☎01-473 6566; www.thedublincookieco.com; 29 Thomas St; cookies from €1; ⊙8am-4.30pm Mon-Wed, to 5pm Thu-Fri, 10am-5pm Sat, 10am-4pm Sun; 🚌13, 69 from city centre) Artisanal cookies by Jenny and Elaine, made fresh all day right in front of you. It's always experimenting with new and exciting flavours, and offers strong, aromatic coffee and chocolate or cookie-flavoured milk.

ITSA@IMMA CAFE €

Map p278 (www.imma.ie; Irish Museum of Modern Art, Military Rd; mains €7-10; ⊙10am-3pm Mon, to 5pm Tue-Sat, noon-5pm Sun; 🚌51, 51D, 51X, 69, 78, 79 from Aston Quay, 🚊Heuston) Freshly made gourmet sandwiches and bagels as well as healthy salads and soups are the mainstay of the museum cafe at the Irish Museum of Modern Art. There's wine available too, and coffee comes from the Dublin roastery Cloudpicker.

LEO BURDOCK'S
FISH & CHIPS €

Map p278 (www.leoburdock.com; 2 Werburgh St; cod & chips €10.25; ⌚11.30am-midnight Sun-Thu, to 1am Fri & Sat; 🚌all city centre) The fresh cod and chips served these days in Dublin's most famous fish and chip shop is no better than that found in most other chippers, but the deep-fried fumes of Burdock's reputation still count for something, judging by the longish queues for a 'Dubliner's caviar'.

★CLANBRASSIL HOUSE
IRISH €€

Map p278 (☎01-453 9786; www.clanbrassilhouse.com; 6 Upper Clanbrassil St; mains €19-28; ⌚5-10pm Tue-Fri, 11.30am-2.30pm & 5-10pm Sat; 🚌9, 16, 49, 54A from city centre) With an emphasis on family-style sharing plates, this intimate restaurant consistently turns out exquisite dishes, cooked on a charcoal grill. Think rib-eye with bone marrow and anchovy, or ray wing with capers and brown shrimp butter. The hash brown chips are a thing of glory, too. Order the full feast menu (€50) for the chef's choice.

VARIETY JONES
IRISH €€

Map p278 (☎01-454 4976; www.varietyjones.ie; 78 Thomas St; mains €14-30; ⌚5.30-10pm Tue-Sat; 🚌13, 40, 123 from city centre) With a simple menu of stellar dishes, Variety Jones is offering some of the most exciting cooking in Dublin. Dishes are cooked on a hearth for a hearty, smoky flavour, and there's an emphasis on sharing dishes. Booking essential.

UNION8
MODERN IRISH €€

Map p278 (☎01-677 8707; www.union8.ie; 740 S Circular Rd; mains €19-28; ⌚10am-3pm & 5-9.30pm Mon-Wed, to 9.30pm Thu-Fri, 10.30am-3.30pm & 5-9.30pm Sat, 10.30am-3.30pm & 5-8pm Sun; 🚌69, 79 from Aston Quay, 13, 40 from O'Connell St) A hub for the local community of Dublin 8 (hence the name), this terrific spot serves tasty breakfasts and contemporary Irish cuisine (beautifully presented fish dishes, succulent lamb, tasty pork belly and the like) for lunch and dinner. Highly recommended if you're in this part of town.

57 THE HEADLINE
PUB FOOD €€

Map p278 (☎01-532 0279; www.57theheadline.com; 56/57 Lower Clanbrassil St; mains €15-22; ⌚4-11pm Mon, 3-11.30pm Tue-Thu, 3pm-12.30am Fri & Sat, 1-11pm Sun; 🚌49, 54A from city centre) A neighbourhood pub with an excellent menu of bar food and snacks. The Sunday roast is consistently good, with fluffy Yorkshire puddings, tender beef and crispy roast potatoes. Be warned – the roasts tend to sell out by around 5pm.

DRINKING & NIGHTLIFE

It shouldn't come as a surprise that Dublin's oldest neighbourhoods are also where you'll find some of its most authentic pubs. But there are an increasing number of cool bars popping up on the scene, too.

★OLD ROYAL OAK
PUB

Map p278 (11 Kilmainham Lane; ⌚5pm-midnight Mon-Thu, 3pm-1am Fri, 12.30pm-1am Sat, 12.30-11pm Sun; 🚌68, 79 from city centre) Locals are fiercely protective of this gorgeous traditional pub, which opened in 1845 to serve the patrons and staff of the Royal Hospital (now the Irish Museum of Modern Art). The clientele has changed, but everything else remains the same, which makes this one of the nicest pubs in the city in which to enjoy a few pints.

FALLON'S
PUB

Map p278 (☎01-454 2801; 129 The Coombe; ⌚10.30am-11.30pm Mon-Thu, to 12.30am Fri & Sat, 12.30-11pm Sun; 🚌51B, 123, 206 from city centre) A fabulously old-fashioned bar that has been serving a great pint of Guinness since the end of the 17th century. Prizefighter Dan Donnelly, the only boxer ever to be knighted, was head bartender here in 1818. A local's local.

DROP DEAD TWICE
BAR

Map p278 (www.dropdeadtwice.com; 18/19 Francis St; ⌚5-11.30pm Tue-Thu, to 12.30am Fri, noon-12.30am Sat, noon-11pm Sun; 🚌51B, 51C, 78A, 123 from city centre) The taproom downstairs is a great little boozer, but upstairs things are a bit jazzier with the BYO cocktail lounge. Bring a bottle of your favourite spirit, pay for a sitting of two/three hours (€25/35) and the bartenders will whizz you up cocktails using their extensive ingredients. We've seen cocktails infused with peat smoke, homemade bitters and even bacon.

FOURTH CORNER
BAR

Map p278 (www.fourthcorner.ie; 50 Patrick St; ⌚4-11.30pm Mon-Thu, 1pm-12.30am Fri, 2pm-12.30am Sat & Sun; 🚌49, 54A from city centre) Back in the day, this little intersection in the Liberties was known as the Four Corners of Hell, with a rowdy pub on each corner (and brawls on the streets in-between). Nowadays, things are a bit more sedate, and this swish bar is a great place for a pint.

You can get Dublin Pizza Company (p71) delivered here, too.

LUCKY'S

BAR

Map p278 (☎01-556 2397; www.luckys.ie; 78 Meath St; ⏰11.30am-midnight Mon-Thu, to 1am Fri, 1pm-1am Sat, 1-11.30pm Sun; 🚌13, 40, 123 from city centre) A bright spot on a street that draws the crowds after dark, Lucky's comes with sleek wood and a nice selection of local craft beer. Coke Lane Pizza (p136) has also set up shop in the beer garden to cook fresh pizzas all night.

OPEN GATE BREWERY

BREWERY

Map p278 (☎01-471 2455; www.guinnessopengate.com; St James's Gate; ⏰5.30-10.30pm Thu & Fri, 2-8pm Sat; 🚌13, 40, 123 from city centre) If the Storehouse (p123) isn't enough to satisfy the beer lover in you, try the results of the Guinness experimental brewery. You must book ahead online and each ticket comes with a sample tasting board. Quiz the brewers while you're there and relish the unique chance to taste beers that will probably never leave the building.

The Open Gate Brewery has been testing out brews for the last 100 years but only recently opened its doors to the public. From IPAs and stouts, to sour beers and pilsners, the team here has experimented with it all.

MVP

BAR

(☎01-558 2158; www.mvpdublin.com; 29 Upper Clanbrassil St; ⏰4pm-midnight Mon-Thu, to 1am Fri & Sat, to 11.30pm Sun; 🚌49, 54A, 77X from city centre) A small and friendly bar just off the beaten path that is home to potent and inventive cocktails. The menu is pure comfort food; baked and roast potatoes in all varieties are designed to warm your belly.

ARTHUR'S

PUB

Map p278 (☎01-402 0914; www.arthurspub.ie; 28 Thomas St; ⏰11am-11.30pm Mon-Thu, to 12.30am Fri & Sat, to 11pm Sun; 🚌21A, 51B, 78, 78A, 123 from Fleet St, 🚊James's) Given its location, Arthur's could easily be a cheesy tourist trap, and plenty of Guinness Storehouse (p123) visitors do pass through the doors tempted by another taste of the black stuff. Instead it's a friendly, cosy bar with a menu full of good comfort food. Best visited in winter so you get the full benefit of the roaring fireplace and soft candlelight.

BRAZEN HEAD

PUB

Map p278 (☎01-679 5186; www.brazenhead.com; 20 Lower Bridge St; ⏰10.30am-midnight Mon-Thu, to 12.30am Fri & Sat, 12.30pm-midnight Sun; 🚌51B, 78A, 123 from city centre) Reputedly Dublin's oldest pub, the Brazen Head has been serving thirsty patrons since 1198 when it set up as a Norman tavern. It's a bit away from the city centre, and the clientele consists of foreign-language students, tourists and some grizzly auld locals.

Though its history is uncertain, the sunken level of the courtyard indicates how much street levels have altered since its construction. Robert Emmet was believed to have been a regular visitor, while in *Ulysses,* James Joyce reckoned 'you get a decent enough do in the Brazen Head'.

THE DISTILLERY DISTRICT

The Liberties might be dominated by the world-famous Guinness brewery, but Dublin's most traditional neighbourhood has rediscovered whiskey. In 2015 the Teeling Distillery (p133) reopened after a hiatus of nearly 200 years (the original on nearby Marrowbone Lane operated between 1782 and 1822), followed in 2017 by the opening of the Pearse Lyons Distillery (p133), which began operations in the former St James' Church on James St. Pearse Lyons and his wife Deirdre own a brewery and distillery in Kentucky (as well as the giant animal nutrition company Alltech), but this new project is close to Lyons' heart as his own grandfather is buried in the church's graveyard. In 2019 two more distilleries opened: the Dublin Liberties Distillery (p133) and Roe & Co (p133), whose owners Diageo also own Guinness.

The boilerplate tours are all similar: you learn about the distilling process and finish with a tasting; for extra you get a master distiller experience, which includes more detail and more whiskey. The problem with all the new arrivals is that it takes a minimum of three years before anything they make can be officially called whiskey, so until the casks have reached maturation the whiskey you're tasting is a blend of something distilled elsewhere, usually the Cooley Distillery in County Louth.

POURING THE PERFECT GUINNESS

Like the Japanese Tea Ceremony, pouring a pint of Guinness is part ritual, part theatre and part logic. It's a five-step process that every decent Dublin bartender will use to serve the perfect pint.

The Glass

A dry, clean 20oz (568mL) tulip pint glass is used because the shape allows the nitrogen bubbles to flow down the side, and the contour 'bump' about halfway down pushes the bubbles into the centre of the pint on their way up.

The Angle

The glass is held beneath the tap at a 45-degree angle – and the tap faucet shouldn't touch the sides of the glass.

The Pour

A smooth pour should fill the glass to about three-quarters full, after which it is put on the counter 'to settle'.

The Head

As the beer flows into the glass it passes through a restrictor plate at high speed that creates nitrogen bubbles. In the glass, the agitated bubbles flow down the sides of the glass and – thanks to the contour bump – back up through the middle, settling at the top in a nice, creamy head. This should take a couple of minutes to complete.

The Top-off

Once the pint is 'settled', the bartender will top it off, creating a domed effect across the top of the glass with the head sitting comfortably just above the rim. Now it's the perfect pint.

Where to Find It?

Most Dublin pubs know how to serve a decent pint of Guinness. But for something really special, you'll need the expertise of an experienced bartender and the appropriate atmosphere in which to savour their creations. Everyone has their favourites: we recommend Kehoe's (p78), the Stag's Head (p80) and John Mulligan's (p168) on the south side; and Walshs (p160) on the north side.

ENTERTAINMENT

In the heart of the Liberties is the excellent Vicar Street, one of the best venues in town and where you'll catch a broad range of talent, from comedy to jazz. The Irish Museum of Modern Art (p131) also hosts the occasional gig.

VAULTS LIVE THEATRE

Map p278 (☎01-411 485; www.vaults.live; W John's Lane; adult/child from €25/17; ⊙11am-5pm Wed-Sun; 🚌13, 40, 123 from city centre) An immersive theatre performance in an old schoolhouse that takes you through six scenes from the darker side of Dublin history with incredibly detailed sets and impressive performances from the actors. The thrills and fun (go in a group if you can) will allow you to overlook the historical inaccuracies of the hour-long show.

VICAR STREET LIVE MUSIC

Map p278 (☎01-454 5533; www.vicarstreet.com; 58-59 Thomas St; tickets €25-60; ⊙7pm-midnight; 🚌13, 49, 54A, 56A from city centre) Vicar Street is a midsized venue with a capacity of around 1000, spread between the table-serviced group-seating downstairs and a theatre-style balcony. It offers a varied program, from comedy to soul, jazz, folk and world music.

SHOPPING

Some of the most interesting – and wackiest – shopping is done along Francis St in the Liberties, the home of antiquarians and, in recent years, art dealers of every hue. Although you mightn't fancy transporting the hand

luggage, you can have that original Edwardian fireplace you've always wanted, shipped to you by the shop.

SPACE OUT SISTER VINTAGE

Map p278 (www.spaceoutsister.com; 74 Francis St; ⏲11am-5pm Tue-Fri, to 4pm Sat; 🚌51B, 123, 206 from city centre) This utterly charming lingerie shop focuses on vintage and handmade pieces—think chiffon '60s nightgowns and men's silk pyjamas. The tiny shop feels more like a cosy boudoir, and it's set up right above Two Pups Coffee (p137).

MARROWBONE BOOKS BOOKS

Map p278 (www.marrowbone.ie; 78 The Coombe; ⏲11am-7pm Mon, Wed-Sun; 🚌51B, 123, 206 from city centre) This charming neighbourhood shop is everything independent bookstores should be; cosy, inviting, run by passionate bibliophiles and a treasure trove of second-hand novels. It also hosts regular (tiny) music and comedy gigs monthly.

DUBLIN FOOD CO-OP MARKET

Map p278 (☎01-454 4258; www.dublinfood.coop; The Old Chocolate Factory, Kilmainham Sq; ⏲8am-7pm Mon-Fri, 9am-6pm Sat & Sun; 🚌49, 54A, 77X from city centre) From dog food to detergent, everything in this member-owned co-op is organic and/or ecofriendly. Thursday has a limited selection of local and imported fairtrade products, but Saturday is when it's all on display - Dubliners from all over drop in for their responsible weekly shop. There's an on-the-premises baker and even baby-changing facilities.

MARTIN FENNELLY ANTIQUES ANTIQUES

Map p278 (☎01-473 1126; www.fennelly.net; 60 Francis St; ⏲9.30am-6pm Mon-Sat; 🚌51B, 123, 206 from city centre) One of the best-known antiques dealers on Francis St is Martin Fennelly, who specialises in household items ranging from candlesticks and tea caddies to jewellery boxes and French and English porcelain. He also has an excellent collection of exquisite Irish furniture.

O'SULLIVAN ANTIQUES ANTIQUES

Map p278 (☎01-454 1143; www.osullivanantiques.com; 43-44 Francis St; ⏲10am-6pm Mon-Sat; 🚌51B, 123, 206 from city centre) Fine furniture and furnishings from the Georgian, Victorian and Edwardian eras are the speciality of this respected antiques shop (which also has a branch in New York). A rummage might also reveal some distinctive bits of ceramic and crystal, not to mention medals and uniforms from a bygone era that will win you first prize at the costume ball.

OXFAM HOME HOMEWARES

Map p278 (☎01-402 0555; www.oxfamireland.org; 86 Francis St; ⏲9.30am-5.30pm Mon-Sat; 🚌51B, 123, 206 from city centre) They say charity begins at home, so get rummaging among the veneer cast-offs in this furniture branch of the charity chain where you might stumble across the odd 1960s Subbuteo table or art deco dresser. Esoteric vinyl from the '80s is another speciality of the house.

IRISH MUSEUM OF MODERN ART GIFT SHOP BOOKS

Map p278 (☎01-612 9965; www.theimmashop.com; Military Rd; ⏲11.30am-5.30pm Tue-Fri, from 10am Sat, from noon Sun; 🚌51, 51D, 51X, 69, 78, 79 from Aston Quay, 🚊Heuston) Offers a comprehensive selection of coffee-table books on Irish contemporary art.

SPORTS & ACTIVITIES

★SECRET STREET TOURS WALKING

Map p278 (www.secretstreettours.org; standard/supporter/premium supporter €10/20/30) Former rough sleeper Derek McGuire leads this eye-opening and revealing two-hour tour of the Liberties beginning at St Patrick's Tower. The 1.3km route includes areas where McGuire slept rough for two years. Along the way, Derek shares homeless tips on staying safe and blending into crowds. Some of the proceeds go towards homeless charity the Simon Community.

North of the Liffey

Neighbourhood Top Five

❶ **Hugh Lane Gallery, Dublin** (p144) Nodding sagely at the exquisite collection of modern and contemporary art.

❷ **Jameson Distillery Bow Street** (p149) Sampling a snifter of the hard stuff – that's whiskey to you and me – after discovering how it's made in this converted distillery museum.

❸ **14 Henrietta Street** (p149) Renovated Georgian mansion that tells the story of Dublin, from grandeur through difficult times.

❹ **National Museum of Ireland – Decorative Arts & History** (p149) Wandering about the glorious yard of Collins Barracks, without forgetting the collection itself – which includes fascinating exhibits on Ireland's struggle for independence and the history of design.

❺ **Tantalising Your Taste Buds** (p159) Eating in the Northside's new breed of restaurants, like Mr Fox or Grano.

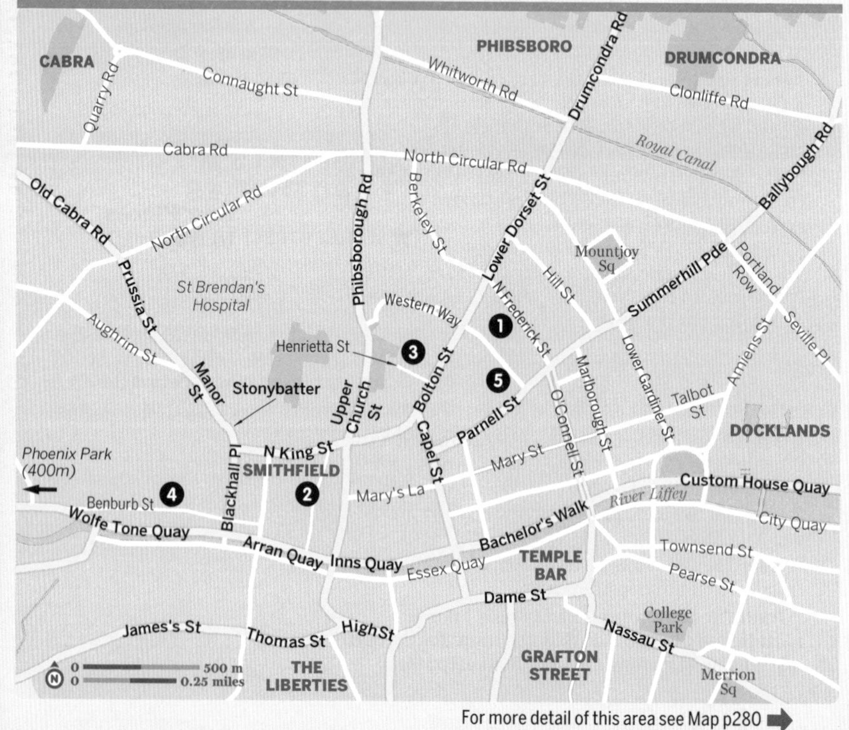

For more detail of this area see Map p280 ➡

Explore North of the Liffey

With the biggest geographical spread of any of Dublin's neighbourhoods, the area north of the Liffey requires a little planning and a bit of transport in order to be fully explored. O'Connell St and its attractions are pretty straightforward and can be explored with ease on foot, with the biggest demand on your time being the fabulous collection at the Hugh Lane Gallery, Dublin (p144) and the collection of the National Museum of Ireland – Decorative Arts & History (p149) at Collins Barracks. The Northside's other attractions are to the west, and the best way to get to them is by the Luas tram, which will reduce your journey to mere minutes. The Jameson Distillery Bow Street (p149) and Collins Barracks are within walking distance of each other, on either side of Smithfield, but you'll be under your own steam to explore Europe's largest enclosed city park, Phoenix Park (p146), home to the president, the US ambassador, the zoo and a herd of red deer, not to mention visiting Dubliners when the weather is good.

Beyond the Royal Canal, which encloses the northern edge of the city centre, are a bunch of attractions that are well worth the effort: you could devote the guts of half a day each to visiting the Croke Park museum (p150), Glasnevin Cemetery (p150) and the National Botanic Gardens (p153).

Local Life

➡ **Hangout** Go to Brother Hubbard (p157) on Capel St for great coffee and an easygoing atmosphere; equally good is Third Space (p157) in Smithfield.

➡ **Food** The Northside's culinary credentials are elevated by the likes of Oxmantown (p157), Mr Fox (p159), Grano (p158) and Fish Shop (p159) – but don't ignore stalwarts such as 101 Talbot (p159) either!

➡ **Park Life** Do as Dubliners do on a fine day and take in the massive expanse of Phoenix Park (p146), where you can run, cycle, play, walk or just lie down, depending on your fancy.

Getting There & Away

➡ **Bus** All city-centre buses stop on O'Connell St or the nearby quays. City buses serve Glasnevin and Croke Park, while national bus services, operated by Bus Éireann, arrive and depart from the Busáras (p243) depot on Store St.

➡ **Tram** The Luas runs east–west parallel to the Liffey from the Point to Heuston Station.

➡ **Train** The DART runs from Connolly Station northeast to Clontarf Rd. Mainline trains for the north and northwest go from Connolly Station (p244).

Lonely Planet's Top Tip

The area between Smithfield and Manor St is one of the Dublin's most exciting districts, home to a clutch of new restaurants and shops that have also served to reinvigorate more traditional spots, including a handful of pubs that are among the best in the city.

Best Places to Eat

➡ Legal Eagle (p158)
➡ Chapter One (p159)
➡ Fegan's 1924 (p156)
➡ Fish Shop (p159)
➡ Mr Fox (p159)

For reviews, see p156 ➡

Best Places to Drink

➡ Dice Bar (p161)
➡ Pantibar (p161)
➡ Cobblestone (p159)
➡ Confession Box (p160)

For reviews, see p159 ➡

Best Places to Buy Irish

➡ Eason's (p162)
➡ Winding Stair (p162)
➡ Moore Street Market (p162)
➡ Louis Copeland (p162)

For reviews, see p162 ➡

TOP SIGHT
HUGH LANE GALLERY, DUBLIN

Whatever reputation Dublin may have as a repository of top-class art is in large part due to the collection at this magnificent gallery, home to impressionist masterpieces, the best of modern Irish work from 1950 onward, and the actual studio of Francis Bacon.

The Gallery

Founded in 1908, the gallery has been housed since 1933 in the stunning **Charlemont House**, designed by Georgian superstar architect William Chambers in 1763. A modernist extension, which opened in 2006, has seen the addition of 13 bright galleries spread across three floors.

Hugh Lane

The gallery owes its origins to one Sir Hugh Lane (1875–1915). Born in County Cork, Lane worked in London art galleries before setting up his own gallery in Dublin. He had a connoisseur's eye and a good nose for the directions of the market, which enabled him to build up a superb collection, particularly strong in impressionists.

Unfortunately for Ireland, neither his talents nor his collection were much appreciated. Irish rejection led him to rewrite his will and bequeath some of the finest works in his collection to the National Gallery in London. Later he relented and added a rider to his will leaving the collection to Dublin but failed to have it witnessed, thus causing a long legal squabble over which gallery had rightful ownership.

DON'T MISS

- The Hugh Lane Bequest 1917 paintings
- Francis Bacon Studio
- Sean Scully collection

PRACTICALITIES

- Map p280, E3
- ☎01-222 5550
- www.hughlane.ie
- 22 N Parnell Sq
- admission free
- 9.45am-6pm Tue-Thu, to 5pm Fri, 10am-5pm Sat, 11am-5pm Sun
- 🚌7, 11, 13, 16, 38, 40, 46A, 123 from city centre

The Hugh Lane Bequest

The collection (known as the Hugh Lane Bequest 1917) was split in a complicated 1959 settlement that sees the eight masterpieces divided into two groups and alternated between Dublin and London every six years. The paintings currently on show (until 2021) are *Les Parapluies* (The Umbrellas) by Auguste Renoir, *Portrait of Eva Gonzales* by Edouard Manet, *Jour d'Été* (Summer's Day) by Berthe Morisot and *View of Louveciennes* by Camille Pissarro.

Francis Bacon Studio

Impressionist masterpieces notwithstanding, the gallery's most popular exhibit is the Francis Bacon Studio, which was painstakingly moved, in all its shambolic mess, from 7 Reece Mews, South Kensington, London, where the Dublin-born artist (1909–92) lived for 31 years. The display features some 80,000 items madly strewn about the place, including slashed canvases, the last painting he was working on, tables piled with materials, walls daubed with colour samples, portraits with heads cut out, favourite bits of furniture and many assorted piles of crap. It's a teasing and tantalising, riveting and ridiculous masterpiece that provides the viewer with no real sense of the artist himself. Far more revealing is the 10-minute profile of him with Melvyn Bragg and the immensely sad photographs of Bacon's immaculately tidy bachelor pad, which suggest a deep, personal loneliness.

Elsewhere in the Gallery

Just by the main reception desk is the **Stained Glass gallery**, whose highlight is Harry Clarke's wonderful *The Eve of St Agnes* (1924). His masterpiece is made up of 22 separate panels, each a depiction of a stanza of John Keats' eponymous poem about the doomed love between Madeline and Porphyro, who cannot meet because their families are sworn enemies.

The gallery's newest wing (opened 2006) is a two-storey extension with – on the ground floor – a gallery dedicated to seven abstract paintings by Irish-born **Sean Scully**, probably Ireland's most famous living painter. Elsewhere in the new wing is work by other contemporary Irish artists including Dorothy Cross, Brian Maguire and Norah McGuinness.

ART FIGHT

The Lane Bequest has long been the subject of legal wranglings between the Dublin gallery and the National Gallery in London, with the former laying permanent claim to the paintings which remain under the control of the latter. But in 2015 National Gallery director Nicholas Penny acknowledged that the Hugh Lane had 'moral claim' to the collection, which may result in a resolution of the claim once the current agreement is up in 2021.

The gallery has developed a decent app and a growing online catalogue of its collection, which allows you to search by artist and view their work before (or after) your visit.

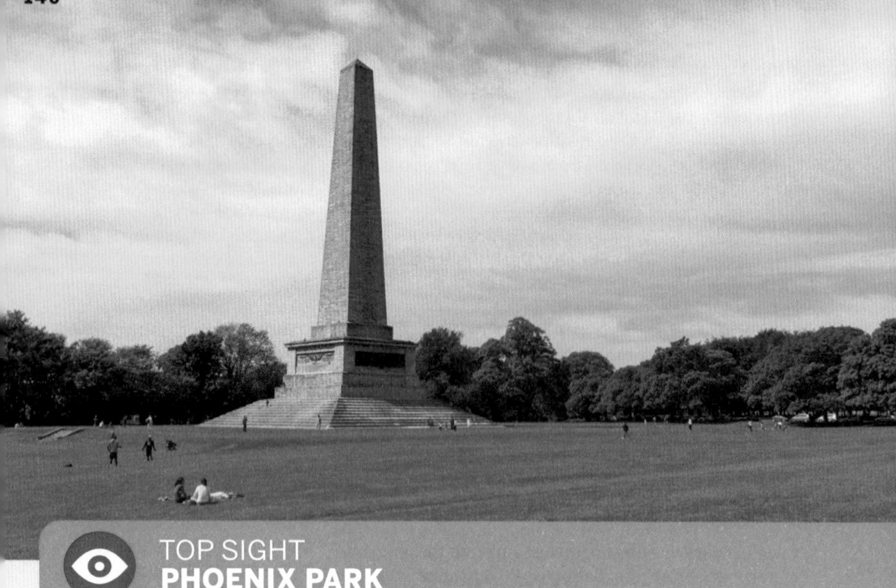

TOP SIGHT
PHOENIX PARK

The hugely impressive 709 hectares that comprise Phoenix Park are not just a magnificent playground for all kinds of sport from running to polo, but are also home to the president of Ireland, the American ambassador and a shy herd of fallow deer. It is also where you'll find Europe's oldest zoo. How's that for a place to stretch your legs?

Dublin Zoo

Established in 1831, the 28-hectare **Dublin Zoo** (www.dublinzoo.ie; adult/child/family €19.50/14/53; ⏲9.30am-6pm Mar-Sep, to dusk Oct-Feb; 👪), just north of the Hollow, is one of the oldest in the world. It is well known for its lion-breeding program, which dates back to 1857 and includes among its offspring the lion that roars at the start of MGM films. You'll see these tough cats, from a distance, on the 'African Savanna', just one of several habitats created since 2005.

The zoo is home to roughly 400 animals from 100 different species, and you can visit all of them across the eight different habitats that range from an Asian jungle to a family farm, where kids get to meet the inhabitants up close and even milk a (model) cow. Sadly, a strain of avian flu in 2017 meant that all of the zoo's birds were moved indoors so as to avoid interaction with native, wild species. There are restaurants, cafes and even a train to get you round.

Áras an Uachtaráin

The residence of the Irish president is a Palladian **lodge** (www.president.ie; ⏲guided tours hourly 10.30am-3.30pm Sat) FREE that was built in 1751 and has been enlarged a couple of times since, most recently in 1816. It was home to the British viceroys from 1782 to 1922,

DON'T MISS

- Wellington Monument
- Tour of Áras an Uachtaráin
- Dublin Zoo

PRACTICALITIES

- www.phoenixpark.ie
- admission free
- ⏲24hr
- 🚌10 from O'Connell St, 25, 26 from Middle Abbey St

and then to the governors general until Ireland cut ties with the British Crown and created the office of president in 1937. Queen Victoria stayed here during her visit in 1849, when she appeared not to even notice the Famine. The candle burning in the window is an old Irish tradition, to guide 'the Irish diaspora' home.

Tickets for the free one-hour Saturday **tours** can be collected from the **Phoenix Park Visitor Centre** (☎01-677 0095; www.phoenixpark.ie; ⏰10am-6pm Apr-Dec, 9.30am-5.30pm Wed-Sun Jan-Mar), the converted former stables of the papal nunciate, where you'll see a 10-minute introductory video before being shuttled to the Áras itself to inspect five state rooms and the president's study. If you can't make it on a Saturday, just become elected president of your own country or become a Nobel laureate or something, and then wrangle a personal invite.

The Park

Chesterfield Ave runs northwest through the length of the park from the Parkgate St entrance to the Castleknock Gate. Near the Parkgate St entrance is the 63m-high **Wellington Monument** obelisk (pictured), which was completed in 1861. Nearby is the **People's Garden**, dating from 1864, and the **bandstand** in the Hollow. Across Chesterfield Ave from the Áras an Uachtaráin – and easily visible from the road – is the massive **Papal Cross**, which marks the site where Pope John Paul II preached to 1.25 million people in 1979. In the centre of the park the **Phoenix Monument**, erected by Lord Chesterfield in 1747, looks so unlike a phoenix that it's often referred to as the Eagle Monument.

Ashtown Castle

Next door to Áras an Uachtaráin is the restored four-storey **Ashtown Castle**, a 17th-century tower house 'discovered' inside the 18th-century nuncio's mansion when the latter was demolished in 1986 due to dry rot. You can visit the castle only on a guided tour from the visitor centre.

Elsewhere in the Park

The southern part of the park has many **football** and **hurling pitches**; although they actually occupy about 80 hectares (200 acres), the area is known as the **Fifteen Acres**. To the west, the rural-looking **Glen Pond** corner of the park is extremely attractive. At weekends the football pitches at the Fifteen Acres are used by local league teams that can be fun to watch.

FARMLEIGH HOUSE

Situated in the northwest corner of Phoenix Park, opulent **Farmleigh House** (☎01-815 5900; www.farmleigh.ie; Phoenix Park, Castleknock; adult/child €8/4; ⏰10am-5.30pm, last entry 4.30pm, entry by guided tour only; 🚌37 from city centre) can only be visited by joining one of the 30-minute house tours. However, the real highlight of the 32-hectare estate is the garden, where regular shows are held. There is also an extensive program of cultural events in summer, ranging from food fairs to classical concerts. The 37m clock tower once housed an 8000L water tank that serviced the estate; views from the top are sensational.

Although the park is open 24 hours a day, it is not advised to hang around after dark.

DID YOU KNOW?

At 709 hectares, Phoenix Park is big – but when it was first developed it was even larger, as it stretched across the Liffey to the south. Part of the original park was on the site of a Viking burial ground (in the Islandbridge/Kilmainham area) that was the biggest Viking cemetery outside of Scandinavia.

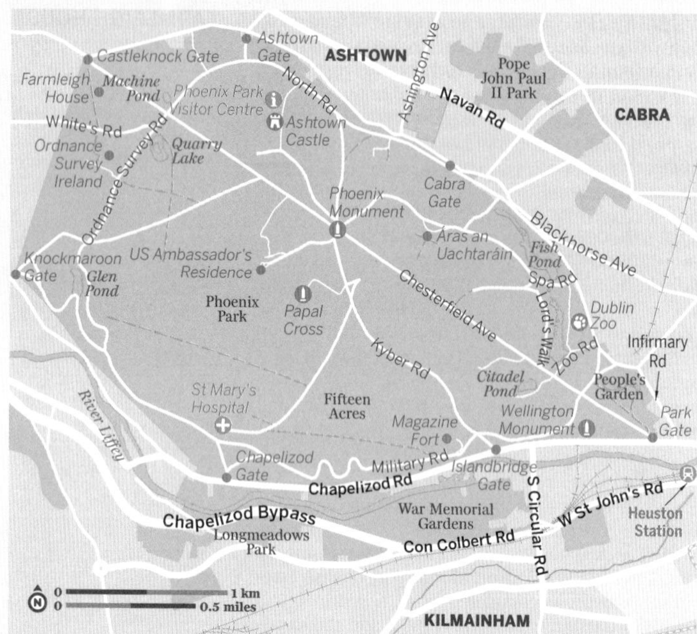

At the northwestern end of the park, near the White's Gate entrance, are the offices of **Ordnance Survey Ireland**, the government mapping department. This building was originally built in 1728 by Luke Gardiner, who was responsible for the architecture in O'Connell St and Mountjoy Sq in north Dublin.

Back towards the Parkgate St entrance is the **Magazine Fort** (see www.phoenixpark.ie for tours) on Thomas's Hill. The fort was no quick construction, the process taking from 1734 to 1801. It provided useful target practice during the 1916 Easter Rising, and was raided by the Irish Republican Army (IRA) in 1940 when the entire ammunition reserve of the Irish army was nabbed, but recovered a few weeks later.

SIGHTS

The Northside's most important attractions are evenly divided across the neighbourhood, from O'Connell St to the east right along the Liffey as far as the entrance to Phoenix Park, where you'll find Arbour Hill and Collins Barracks. To get around, use the convenient Luas tram.

HUGH LANE GALLERY, DUBLIN — GALLERY

See p144.

PHOENIX PARK — PARK

See p146.

★14 HENRIETTA STREET — MUSEUM

Map p280 (☎01-524 0383; www.14henriettastreet.ie; 14 Henrietta St; adult/child €9/6; ⌚tours hourly 10am-4pm Wed-Sat, from noon Sun; 🚌9, 13, 16, 40 from city centre) Explore one of Dublin's Georgian townhouses, carefully restored to gently peel back layers of complex social history over 250 years. Part museum, part community archive, it covers the magnificent elegance of upper-class life in the 1740s to the destitution of the early 20th century, when the house was occupied by 100 tenants living in near squalor. Access is by 75-minute guided tour only, which means visitors get the benefit of lots of interesting detail.

★NATIONAL MUSEUM OF IRELAND – DECORATIVE ARTS & HISTORY — MUSEUM

Map p280 (www.museum.ie; Benburb St; ⌚10am-5pm Tue-Sat, from 2pm Sun; 🚌25, 66, 67, 90 from city centre, 🚊Museum) FREE Once the world's largest military barracks, this splendid early neoclassical grey-stone building on the Liffey's northern banks was completed in 1704 according to the design of Thomas Burgh (he of Trinity College's Old Library). It is now home to the Decorative Arts & History collection of the National Museum of Ireland, with a range of superb permanent exhibits ranging from a history of the **1916 Easter Rising** to the work of iconic Irish designer **Eileen Gray** (1878–1976).

The building's central square held six entire regiments and is a truly awesome space, surrounded by arcaded colonnades and blocks linked by walking bridges. Following the handover to the new Irish government in 1922, the barracks were renamed to honour Michael Collins, a hero of the struggle for independence, who was killed that year in the Civil War; to this day most Dubliners refer to the museum as the **Collins Barracks**. Indeed, the army coat Collins wore on the day of his death (there's still mud on the sleeve) is part of the **Soldiers and Chiefs** exhibit, which covers the history of Irish soldiery at home and abroad from 1550 to the 21st century.

The museum's exhibits include a treasure trove of artefacts ranging from silver, ceramics and glassware to weaponry, furniture and folk-life displays. The fascinating **Way We Wore** exhibit displays Irish clothing and jewellery from the past 250 years. An intriguing sociocultural study, it highlights the symbolism jewellery and clothing had in bestowing messages of mourning, love and identity.

The old Riding School is home to **Proclaiming a Republic: The 1916 Rising**, which opened in 2016 as an enhanced and updated version of the long-standing exhibit dedicated to the rebellion. The display explores the complicated socio-historical background to the Rising and also includes visceral memorabilia such as firsthand accounts of the violence of the Black and Tans and post-Rising hunger strikes, and the handwritten death certificates of the Republican prisoners and their postcards from Holloway prison. Some of the best pieces are gathered in the **Curator's Choice** exhibition, which is a collection of 25 objects hand-picked by different curators and displayed alongside an account of why they were chosen.

★JAMESON DISTILLERY BOW STREET — MUSEUM

Map p280 (www.jamesonwhiskey.com; Bow St; adult/student/child €19/18/11, masterclasses €60; ⌚10am-5pm Mon-Sat, from 10.30am Sun; 🚌25, 66, 67, 90 from city centre, 🚊Smithfield) Smithfield's biggest draw is devoted to *uisce beatha* (ish-kuh ba-ha, 'the water of life'); that's Irish for whiskey. To its more serious devotees, that is precisely what whiskey is, although they may be put off by the slickness of this museum (occupying part of the old distillery that stopped production in 1971), which shepherds visitors through a compulsory tour of the recreated factory (the tasting at the end is a lot of fun) and into the ubiquitous gift shop.

If you're really serious about whiskey, you can deepen your knowledge with the

Whiskey Makers or the Whiskey Shakers, two 90-minute masterclasses that deconstruct the creation of Jameson whiskies and teach you how to make a range of whiskey-based cocktails. If you're just buying whiskey, go for the stuff you can't buy at home, such as the excellent Red Breast or the super-exclusive Midleton, a very limited reserve that is appropriately expensive.

GENERAL POST OFFICE HISTORIC BUILDING

Map p280 (01-705 7000; www.anpost.ie; Lower O'Connell St; 8am-8pm Mon-Sat; all city centre, Abbey) It's not just the country's main post office, or an eye-catching neoclassical building: the General Post Office is at the heart of Ireland's struggle for independence. The GPO served as command HQ for the rebels during the 1916 Easter Rising and as a result has become the focal point for all kinds of protests, parades and remembrances, as well as home to an interactive visitor centre.

The building – a neoclassical masterpiece designed by Francis Johnston in 1818 – was burnt out in the siege that resulted from the Rising, but that wasn't the end of it. There was bitter fighting in and around the GPO during the Civil War of 1922; you can still see the pockmarks of the struggle in the Doric columns. Since its reopening in 1929 it has lived through quieter times, although its role in Irish history is commemorated inside the visitor centre.

GPO WITNESS HISTORY MUSEUM

Map p280 (www.gpowitnesshistory.ie; General Post Office, Lower O'Connell St; adult/child €14/7; 10am-4.30pm Mon-Sat, from noon Sun; all city centre, Abbey) Inside the General Post Office is this wonderful museum that also serves as a fitting tribute to the 1916 Easter Rising and its key role in the creation of the Irish state. Interactive and full of touchscreens, the exhibit explores all facets of the Rising, from its origins to the events of Easter Week and on to its aftermath. Most visits are self-guided, but there are also guided tours (€18; also includes entry) at 3.30pm Monday to Friday and 11am on Saturday.

GLASNEVIN CEMETERY CEMETERY

Map p280 (Prospect Cemetery; www.glasnevintrust.ie; Finglas Rd; tours €13.50; 10am-5pm, tours hourly 10.30am-4.30pm; 40, 40A, 40B from Parnell St) FREE The tombstones at Ireland's largest and most historically important burial site read like a 'who's who' of Irish history, as most of the leading names of the last 150 years are buried here, including Daniel O'Connell and Charles Stewart Parnell. It was established in 1832 by O'Connell as a burial ground for people of all faiths – a high-minded response to Protestant cemeteries' refusal to bury Catholics. The selection of themed tours are all highly recommended.

A modern replica of a round tower acts as a handy landmark for locating the tomb of O'Connell, who died in 1847 and was re-interred here in 1869 when the tower was completed. It opened to visitors in 2018 for the first time in nearly half a century; the reward for a climb to the top is a sweet view of the city. Charles Stewart Parnell's tomb is topped with a large granite rock, on which only his name is inscribed – a remarkably simple tribute to a figure of such historical importance. Other notable people buried here include Sir Roger Casement, executed for treason by the British in 1916; the Republican leader Michael Collins, who died in the Civil War; the docker and trade unionist Jim Larkin, a prime force in the 1913 general strike; and the poet Gerard Manley Hopkins.

The history of the cemetery is told in wonderful detail in the **Glasnevin Cemetery Museum** (www.glasnevinmuseum.ie; museum €6.75, museum & tour €13.50; 10am-5pm Oct-May, until 6pm Jun-Sep).

The best way to visit the cemetery is to take one of the daily **tours** that will (ahem) bring to life the rich and important stories of those buried in what is jokingly referred to by Dubs as 'Croak Park'.

CROKE PARK STADIUM & MUSEUM MUSEUM

Map p280 (www.crokepark.ie; Clonliffe Rd, New Stand, Croke Park; adult/child museum €7/6, museum & tour €14/9; 9.30am-6pm Mon-Sat, 10.30am-5pm Sun Jun-Aug, 9.30am-5pm Mon-Sat, 10.30am-5pm Sun Sep-May; 3, 11, 11A, 16, 16A, 123 from O'Connell St) This museum is all about the history and importance of Gaelic sports in Ireland and the role of the Gaelic Athletic Association (GAA) as the stout defender of a proud cultural identity. It helps if you're a sporting enthusiast.

The twice-daily tours (except match days) of the impressive Croke Park stadium are excellent, and well worth the extra cost. Admission to the tour includes a museum visit.

The stadium's other attraction is the **Skyline** (adult/child €20/12; half-hourly 10.30am-3.30pm Mon-Sat, from 11.30am Sun Jul

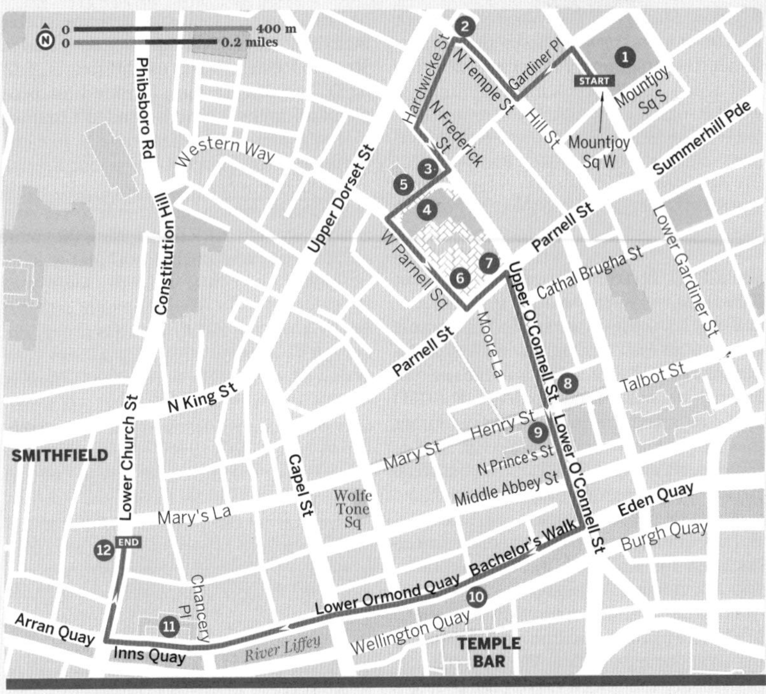

Neighbourhood Walk
A Walk on the Northside

START MOUNTJOY SQ
END ST MICHAN'S CHURCH
LENGTH 2.5KM; TWO HOURS

From ❶ **Mountjoy Square**, take a left at the northwestern corner and walk down Gardiner Pl, turning right onto N Temple St. Up ahead is the fine but now deconsecrated Georgian ❷ **St George's Church** (p155), designed by architect Francis Johnston.

Take a left onto Hardwicke St and left again onto N Frederick St. On your right you'll spot the distinctive ❸ **Abbey Presbyterian Church**, built in 1864.

The northern slice of Parnell Sq houses the ❹ **Garden of Remembrance** (p156), opened in 1966 to commemorate the 50th anniversary of the 1916 Easter Rising. North of the square, facing the park, is the excellent ❺ **Hugh Lane Gallery, Dublin** (p144), home to some of the best modern art in Europe.

In the southern part of Parnell Sq is the ❻ **Rotunda Hospital** (p154), a wonderful example of public architecture in the Georgian style and now one of the city's three main maternity hospitals. The southeastern corner of the square has the ❼ **Gate Theatre** (p161), one of the city's most important theatres.

Head south down O'Connell St, passing by the 120m-high ❽ **Spire** (p155). Erected in 2001, it has become an iconic symbol of the city. On the western side of O'Connell St, the stunning neoclassical ❾ **General Post Office** (p150) towers over the street.

When you hit the river, turn right and walk along the boardwalk until you reach the city's most distinctive crossing point, the ❿ **Ha'Penny Bridge** (p110), named for the charge levied on those who used it.

Continue west along Ormond Quay to one of James Gandon's Georgian masterpieces, the ⓫ **Four Courts** (p152), home to the most important law courts in Ireland. Finally take a right onto Church St to admire ⓬ **St Michan's Church** (p152), with grisly vaults of the long departed.

& Aug, 11.30am & 2.30pm Mon-Fri, half-hourly 10.30am-2.30pm Sat, from 11.30am Sun Sep-Jun), a guided tour around Croke Park's roof.

JAMES JOYCE CULTURAL CENTRE CULTURAL CENTRE

Map p280 (www.jamesjoyce.ie; 35 N Great George's St; adult/child €5/free; ⊙10am-5pm Tue-Sat, from noon Sun Apr-Sep, closed Mon Oct-Mar; 🚌3, 10, 11, 11A, 13, 16, 16A, 19, 19A, 22 from city centre) James Joyce is brought to virtual life in this beautifully restored Georgian house. As well as some wonderful interactive details, the exhibits include some of the furniture from Joyce's Paris apartment; a life-size recreation of a typical Edwardian bedroom (not Joyce's, but one similar to what he would have used); and the original door of 7 Eccles St, the home of Leopold and Molly Bloom in *Ulysses*, which was demolished in real life to make way for a private hospital.

Professor Denis Maginni, the exuberant, flamboyant dance instructor and 'confirmed bachelor' immortalised by James Joyce in *Ulysses*, taught the finer points of dance out of here, and if the house survived at all it's down to the efforts of Joycean scholar and gay rights activist Senator David Norris.

If the house lacks a lot of period detail, it's more than compensated for by the superb interactive displays, which include three short documentary films on various aspects of Joyce's life and work, and – the highlight of the whole place – computers that allow you to explore the content of *Ulysses* episode by episode and trace Joyce's life year by year. It's enough to demolish the myth that Joyce's works are an impenetrable mystery and render him as he should be to the contemporary reader: a writer of enormous talent who sought to challenge and entertain his audience with his breathtaking wit and use of language.

While here, you can also admire the fine plastered ceilings, some of which are restored originals while others are meticulous reproductions of Dublin stuccodore Michael Stapleton's designs. The street has also been given a facelift and now boasts some of the finest Georgian doorways and fanlights in the city.

Walking tours (p163) based on Joyce and his literary works run from the house.

ST MICHAN'S CHURCH CHURCH

Map p280 (☎01-872 4154; Lower Church St; adult/child €6/4; ⊙10am-12.45pm & 2-4.45pm Mon-Fri, 10am-12.45pm Sat; 🚊Smithfield) Macabre remains are the main attraction at this church, which was founded by the Danes in 1095 and named after one of their saints. Among the 'attractions' is an 800-year-old Norman crusader who was so tall that his feet were lopped off so he could fit in a coffin. Visits are by guided tour only.

St Michan's was the Northside's only church until 1686, a year after it was almost completely rebuilt (it was remodelled in 1825 and again after the Civil War), leaving only the 15th-century battlement tower as its oldest bit. The courtroom-like interior hasn't changed much since the 19th century: still in place is the organ from 1724, which Handel may have played for the first-ever performance of his *Messiah*. The organ case is distinguished by the fine oak carving of 17 entwined musical instruments on its front. A skull on the floor on one side of the altar is said to represent Oliver Cromwell. On the opposite side is the Stool of Repentance, where 'open and notoriously naughty livers' did public penance.

The tours of the underground vaults are the real draw, however. The bodies within are aged between 400 and 800 years, and have been preserved by a combination of methane gas coming from rotting vegetation beneath the church, the magnesium limestone of the masonry (which absorbs moisture from the air) and the perfectly constant temperature. Although there are caskets strewn about the place, the main attractions are 'the big four' – mummified bodies labelled The Unknown (a female about whom nothing is known), The Thief (his hands and feet are missing; some say as punishment for his crimes), The Nun and The Crusader: if he is indeed 800 years old then he may have participated in the piratical free-for-all crusades of the 13th century that resulted in the sack of Constantinople but which weren't sanctioned by the church. Also in the crypt are the bodies of John and Henry Sheares, two brothers executed following the Rising of 1798 and – it is claimed – the remains of Robert Emmett, the fallen leader of the 1803 rebellion. Bram Stoker is said to have visited the crypt, which may have inspired him to write a story about a certain vampire who slept in a coffin...

FOUR COURTS HISTORIC BUILDING

Map p280 (☎01-886 8000; Inns Quay; ⊙9am-5pm Mon-Fri; 🚌25, 66, 67, 90 from city centre, 🚊Four Courts) FREE This masterpiece by James Gandon (1743–1823) is a mammoth complex stretching 130m along Inns Quay, as fine an example of Georgian public architecture as there is in Dublin. Despite the construction of a brand-new criminal courts building further west along the Liffey, the Four Courts is still the enduring symbol of Irish law going about its daily business. Visitors are allowed to wander through the building, but not to enter courts or other restricted areas.

The Corinthian-columned central block, connected to flanking wings with enclosed quadrangles, was begun in 1786 and not completed until 1802. The original four courts (Exchequer, Common Pleas, King's Bench and Chancery) all branch off the central rotunda. In the lobby of the central rotunda you'll see bewigged barristers conferring and police officers handcuffed to their charges.

ARBOUR HILL CEMETERY CEMETERY

Map p280 (☎01-821 3021; www.heritageireland.ie; Arbour Hill; ⏲8am-4pm Mon-Fri, from 11am Sat, from 9.30am Sun; 🚌25, 25A, 37, 38, 39, 66, 67, 90, 134 from city centre, 🚋Museum) FREE This small cemetery is the final resting place of all 14 of the executed leaders of the 1916 Easter Rising. The burial ground is plain, with the 14 names inscribed in stone. Beside the graves is a cenotaph bearing the Easter Proclamation, a focal point for official and national commemorations. There are excellent guided tours (p163) during summer.

The front of the cemetery incongruously, but poignantly, contains the graves of British personnel killed in the War of Independence. Here, in the oldest part of the cemetery, as the gravestones toppled, they were lined up against the boundary walls where they still stand solemnly today.

NATIONAL BOTANIC GARDENS GARDENS

(www.botanicgardens.ie; Botanic Rd; ⏲9am-5pm Mon-Fri, 10am-6pm Sat & Sun Mar-Oct, 9am-4.30pm Mon-Sat, 10am-4.30pm Sun Nov-Feb; 🚌13, 13A, 19 from O'Connell St, 34, 34A from Middle Abbey St) FREE Founded in 1795, these 19.5-hectare botanic gardens are home to a series of curvilinear glasshouses, dating from 1843 to 1869 and created by Richard Turner, who was also responsible for the glasshouse at Belfast Botanic Gardens and the Palm House in London's Kew Gardens. Within these Victorian masterpieces you will find the latest in botanical technology, including a series of computer-controlled climates reproducing environments from different parts of the world.

O'CONNELL STREET STATUARY

O'Connell St is lined with statues of Irish history's good and great. The big daddy of them all is the 'Liberator' himself, **Daniel O'Connell** (1775–1847), whose massive bronze statue (Lower O'Connell St; 🚌all city centre, 🚋Abbey) soars above the street at the bridge end. The four winged figures at his feet represent O'Connell's supposed virtues: patriotism, courage, fidelity and eloquence. Dubs began to refer to the street as O'Connell St soon after the monument was erected; its name was officially changed after independence.

Heading away from the river, past a monument to **William Smith O'Brien** (1803–64), leader of the Young Irelanders, is a statue that easily rivals O'Connell's for drama: just outside the GPO is the spread-armed figure of trade-union leader **Jim Larkin** (1876–1947). His big moment came when he helped organise the general strike in 1913 – the pose catches him in full flow, urging workers to rise up for their rights. We're with you, comrade.

Next up and difficult to miss is the Spire (p155), but just below it, on pedestrianised North Earl St, is the detached figure of **James Joyce**, looking on the fast and shiny version of 21st-century O'Connell St with a bemused air. Dubs have lovingly dubbed him the 'prick with the stick' and we're sure Joyce would have loved the vulgar rhyme.

Further on is **Father Theobald Mathew** (1790–1856) the 'apostle of temperance'. There can't have been a tougher gig in Ireland, but he led a spirited campaign against 'the demon drink' in the 1840s and converted hundreds of thousands to teetotalism.

The top of the street is completed by the imposing statue of **Charles Stewart Parnell** (1846–91), the 'uncrowned king of Ireland', who was an advocate of Home Rule and became a political victim of Irish intolerance.

NATIONAL LEPRECHAUN MUSEUM — MUSEUM

Map p280 (www.leprechaunmuseum.ie; Twilfit House, Jervis St; adult/child €16/10, Darkland Tour €18; ⌚10am-6.30pm, also 7-8.30pm Fri & Sat; 🚌all city centre, 🚊Jervis) Ostensibly designed as a child-friendly museum of Irish folklore, this is really a romper room for kids sprinkled with bits of fairy tale. Which is no bad thing, even if the picture of the leprechaun painted here is more Lucky Charms and Walt Disney than sinister creature of pre-Christian mythology.

There's the optical illusion tunnel (which makes you appear smaller to those at the other end), the room full of oversized furniture, the wishing wells and, inevitably, the pot of gold; all of which is strictly for the kids. But if Walt Disney himself went on a leprechaun hunt when visiting Ireland during the filming of *Darby O'Gill and the Little People* in 1948, what the hell do we know?

The summertime Darkland Tour, a night-time storytelling session of dark and haunting tales of folklore, is a little more in keeping with the original purpose of most folklore tales – imparting moral lessons through a little bit of fear!

ROTUNDA HOSPITAL — ARCHITECTURE

Map p280 (☎01-873 0700; Parnell Sq; ⌚visiting hours 6-8pm; 🚌3, 10, 11, 13, 16, 19, 22 from city centre) Irish public hospitals aren't usually attractions, but this one – founded in 1748 as the first maternity hospital in the British Isles – makes for an interesting walk-by or an unofficial wander inside if you're interested in Victorian plasterwork. It shares its basic design with Leinster House (p97) because the architect of both, Richard Cassels, used the same floor plan to economise.

DUBLIN WRITERS MUSEUM — MUSEUM

Map p280 (www.writersmuseum.com; 18 N Parnell Sq; adult/child €7/6; ⌚9.45am-4.45pm Mon-Sat, 11am-4.30pm Sun; 🚌3, 7, 10, 11, 13, 16, 19, 46A, 123 from city centre) Memorabilia aplenty and lots of literary ephemera line the walls and display cabinets of this elegant museum devoted to preserving the city's rich literary tradition up to 1970. The building, comprising two 18th-century houses, is worth exploring on its own; Dublin stuccodore Michael Stapleton decorated the upstairs gallery.

However, the curious decision to omit living writers limits its appeal – no account at all is given to contemporary writers, who would arguably be more popular with today's readers.

Although the busts and portraits of the greats in the gallery upstairs warrant more than a cursory peek, the real draws are the ground-floor displays, which include Samuel Beckett's phone (with a button for excluding incoming calls, of course), a letter from the 'tenement aristocrat' Brendan Behan to his brother, and a 1st edition of Bram Stoker's *Dracula*.

The **Gorham Library** next door is worth a visit, and there's also a calming Zen garden. The basement restaurant, Chapter One (p159), is one of the city's best.

While the museum focuses on the dearly departed, the **Irish Writers Centre** (☎01-872 1302; www.irishwriterscentre.ie; 19 N Parnell Sq; ⌚10am-9pm Mon-Thu, to 5pm Fri) next door provides a meeting and working place for their living successors.

ST MARY'S ABBEY — MUSEUM

Map p280 (☎01-833 1618; www.heritageireland.ie; Meeting House Lane; ⌚closed; 🚊Jervis, Four Courts) Where now the glories of Babylon? All that remains of what was once Ireland's wealthiest and most powerful monastery is the chapter house, so forgotten that most Dubliners are unaware of its existence. It has been closed since late 2015 pending the upgrade of an exhibition put together by Heritage Ireland, the Dublin Archaeological Society and the History of Art Department at Trinity College, and it won't reopen until at least 2020.

Founded in 1139, this Cistercian abbey ran the show when it came to Irish church politics for much of the Middle Ages, although its reputation with the authorities was somewhat sullied when it became a favourite meeting place for rebels against the crown. On 11 June 1534 'Silken' Thomas Fitzgerald, the most important of Leinster's Anglo-Norman lords, entered the chapter house flanked by 140 horsemen with silk fringes on their helmets (hence his name) and flung his Sword of State on the ground in front of the awaiting King's Council – a ceremonial two-fingered salute to King Henry VIII and his authority. Fitzgerald's abbey antics feature in the 'Wandering Rocks' chapter of Joyce's *Ulysses*.

ST MARY'S PRO-CATHEDRAL — CHURCH

Map p280 (www.procathedral.ie; Marlborough St; ⌚8am-6.30pm; 🚌all city centre, 🚊Abbey) FREE Dublin's most important Catholic church is

14 Henrietta Street (p149)

not quite the showcase you'd expect. It's in the wrong place for starters. The large neoclassical building, built between 1816 and 1825, was intended to stand where the GPO is, but Protestant objections resulted in its location on a cramped street that was then at the heart of Monto, the red-light district.

In fact, it's so cramped for space around here that you'd hardly notice the church's six Doric columns, which were modelled on the Temple of Theseus in Athens, much less be able to admire them. The interior is fairly functional, and its few highlights include a carved altar by Peter Turnerelli and the high relief representation of the Ascension by John Smyth. The best time to visit is 11am on Sunday when the Latin Mass is sung by the Palestrina Choir, with whom Ireland's most celebrated tenor, John McCormack, began his career in 1904. If you log on to the website during Mass times you'll hear a live stream of the service.

ST GEORGE'S CHURCH CHURCH

Map p280 (Hardwicke Pl; closed to public; 11, 16, 41 from city centre) One of Dublin's most beautiful buildings is this deconsecrated church, built by Francis Johnston between 1802 and 1813 in Greek Ionic style. It is topped by an eye-catching, 60m-high steeple modelled on that of St Martin-in-the-Fields in London. Alas, it has fallen into serious disrepair and has been shrouded in scaffolding for more than a decade.

Although this was one of Johnston's finest works, and the Duke of Wellington was married here, the building's neglect is largely due to the fact that it's Church of Ireland and not Roman Catholic – the Protestant (and largely moneyed) community for whom it was built has shrunk to the point of disappearance. The bells that Leopold Bloom heard in *Ulysses* were removed, the ornate pulpit was carved up and used to decorate a pub, and the spire is in danger of crumbling, which has resulted in the scaffolding.

SPIRE MONUMENT

Map p280 (O'Connell St; all city centre, Abbey) The city's most visible landmark soars over O'Connell St and is an impressive bit of architectural engineering that was erected in 2001: from a base only 3m in diameter, it soars more than 120m into the sky and tapers into a 15cm-wide beam of light…it's tall and shiny and it does the trick rather nicely.

The brainchild of London-based architect Ian Ritchie, it is apparently the highest sculpture in the world, but much like the Parisian reaction to the construction of the Eiffel Tower, Dubliners are divided as to its aesthetic value and have regularly made fun of it. Among other names, we like 'the erection in the intersection', the 'stiletto in the ghetto' and the altogether brilliant 'eye-ful tower'.

ST MARY'S CHURCH CHURCH

Map p280 (Mary St; closed; Jervis) Designed by William Robinson in 1697, this is the most important church to survive from that period (although it's no longer in use and is closed to the public). John Wesley, founder of Methodism, delivered his first Irish sermon here in 1747 and it was the preferred church of Dublin's 18th-century social elite. Many famous Dubliners were baptised in its font, and Arthur Guinness was married here in 1793.

BELVEDERE HOUSE HISTORIC BUILDING

Map p280 (6 Great Denmark St; closed to public; 3, 10, 11, 13, 16, 19, 22 from city centre) This handsome building has been the home of Jesuit Belvedere College (a secondary school) since 1841. James Joyce studied here between 1893 and 1898 (and described his experiences in *A Portrait of the Artist as a Young Man*), and we can only wonder whether he ever took a moment to admire the magnificent plasterwork by master stuccodore Michael Stapleton in between catechism classes and arithmetic homework.

GARDEN OF REMEMBRANCE PARK

Map p280 (www.heritageireland.ie; E Parnell Sq; 8.30am-6pm Apr-Sep, 9.30am-4pm Oct-Mar; 3, 10, 11, 13, 16, 19, 22 from city centre) This rather austere little park was opened by President Eamon de Valera in 1966 for the 50th anniversary of the 1916 Easter Rising. The most interesting feature in the garden is a bronze statue of the **Children of Lir** by Oisín Kelly; according to Irish legend the children were turned into swans by their wicked stepmother.

KING'S INNS HISTORIC BUILDING

Map p280 (www.kingsinns.ie; Henrietta St; closed to public; 25, 25A, 66, 67, 90, 134 from city centre, Four Courts) Home to Dublin's legal profession (and where barristers are still trained), King's Inns occupies a classical building constructed by James Gandon between 1795 and 1817 on Constitution Hill, with Francis Johnston chipping in with the cupola. A fine example of Georgian public architecture, the building itself is, alas, only open to members and their guests.

EATING

The Northside may play second fiddle to the Southside when it comes to fine dining, but the culinary revolution that has transformed Dublin in the last decade is more dramatically obvious north of the Liffey, where cheaper rents and more available retail space has given budding restaurateurs the opportunity to express themselves. O'Connell St is lined with fast-food factories, although there are a couple of cracking restaurants close by. Some of the most interesting options are roughly between Smithfield and Stoneybatter, while the area around Capel St is worth checking out for its choice of cool cafes and ethnic spots.

CAMERINO BAKERY €

Map p280 (01-537 7755; www.camerino.ie; 158 Capel St; sandwiches €5.50; 7.30am-5pm Mon-Fri, 11am-4.30pm Sat; all city centre) You can pick up some tasty sandwiches at this cute bakery (marinated kale and feta on focaccia, free-range chicken with homemade slaw and sriracha mayo) but the baked treats steal the show. We love the chocolate raspberry cheesecake brownies and rocky-road squares. There's no seating.

★FEGAN'S 1924 CAFE €

Map p280 (01-872 2788; www.fegans1924.com; 13 Chancery St; mains €6-9; 7.30am-4pm Mon-Fri, from 11am Sat & Sun; ; 25, 66, 67, 90 from city centre, Four Courts) A slice of rural Ireland in the city centre: this wonderful cafe is all distressed furniture and rustic charm, but there's nothing old-fashioned about the food and coffee. Fluffy scrambled eggs, perfectly made French toast and excellent brews...this is a place designed for lingering. Weekends also feature 40-minute creative workshops for kids (€6 each). No cash; cards only.

★DA MIMMO'S ITALIAN €

Off Map p280 (01-856 1714; www.damimmo.ie; 148 North Strand Rd; mains €12-24; noon-10pm; 53 from Talbot St) The son of the original owners converted what was once a traditional fish-and-chip shop into this sit-down restaurant, now serving some of the best Italian food in the city. Everything here – from the Caprese salad to the lasagne – is as authentic as if you were dining in Tino's hometown of Casalattico (between Naples and Rome).

BOCO
PIZZA €

Map p280 (☎01-547 5696; www.boco.ie; 57 Bolton St; pizzas €12-16; ⏲4pm-midnight Mon-Wed, from noon Thu, to 1am Fri, 2pm-1am Sat, 2-11.30pm Sun; Dominick) Buzzing pizza joint that's handy if you're heading to the Cineworld (p161) cinema on Parnell St. If you have any room for dessert, the Bean & Goose sharing board features smashed artisanal chocolate bars from Wexford.

OXMANTOWN
CAFE €

Map p280 (www.oxmantown.com; 16 Mary's Abbey, City Markets; sandwiches €6.50; ⏲8am-4pm Mon-Fri; Four Courts, Jervis) Delicious breakfasts and excellent sandwiches make this cafe one of the standout places for daytime eating on the north side of the Liffey. Locally baked bread, coffee supplied by Cloud Picker (Dublin's only microroastery) and meats sourced from Irish farms are the ingredients, but it's the way it's all put together that makes it so worthwhile.

M&L
CHINESE €

Map p280 (☎01-874 8038; www.mlchineserestaurant.com; 13/14 Cathedral St; mains €11-20; ⏲11.30am-10pm Mon-Sat, from noon Sun; all city centre) Beyond the plain frontage and the cheap-looking decor is Dublin's best Chinese restaurant…by some distance. It's usually full of Chinese customers, who come for the authentic Szechuan-style cuisine – spicier than Cantonese and with none of the concessions usually made to Western palates (no prawn crackers or curry chips).

TEA GARDEN
TEAHOUSE €

Map p280 (☎086-219 1010; www.facebook.com/TeagardenDublin; 7 Lower Ormond Quay; ⏲11am-11pm Sun-Thu, to midnight Fri & Sat; all city centre) A tranquil escape on the quays, this teahouse boasts an exhaustive menu of brews and shishas. They are all served with a sense of ritual and expertise, and you can linger as long as you want at the traditional tatami tables. Limited snack menu.

TRAM CAFE
CAFE €

Map p280 (www.thetramcafe.ie; Wolfe Tone Sq; mains €5-6.50; ⏲8am-6pm Mon-Wed, to 9pm Thu & Fri, 10am-6pm Sat & Sun; Jervis) The coffee and sandwiches are tasty, but it's the location that's special: a 1902 tram built by Brill in Philadelphia that lay in a field in County Cavan before being restored and transported to Dublin by its two owners. The 1920s musical soundtrack adds a touch of class.

MUSASHI NOODLES & SUSHI BAR
JAPANESE €

Map p280 (☎01-532 8057; www.musashidublin.com; 15 Capel St; mains €12-17; ⏲noon-10pm; all city centre, Jervis) One of the better Japanese restaurants in town is this low-lit spot that serves freshly crafted sushi and other Japanese specialities for those who don't fancy raw fish. The lunch bento deals are a steal. It's BYOB (corkage charged), and evening bookings are recommended. There is a branch in the IFSC (p168) and another near Merrion Sq (p101).

BROTHER HUBBARD
CAFE €

Map p280 (☎01-441 6595; www.brotherhubbard.ie; 153 Capel St; dishes €7-14; ⏲7.30am-4.30pm Mon, to 10pm Tue-Fri, 9am-10pm Sat, 9am-4.30pm Sun; all city centre, Jervis) Anchored by its excellent baristas (beans by coffee experts 3FE), this cafe also does a fantastic menu of sandwiches, flatbreads and salads. The recent expansion means there's no longer a long line for tables, and the dinner menu has a strong Middle Eastern influence. It's a great brunch spot, too. There's another **branch** (Map p274; 46 Harrington St; mains €7-13; ⏲7.45am-4pm Mon-Fri, 9am-4.30pm Sat & Sun) south of the river.

THIRD SPACE
CAFE €

Map p280 (www.thirdspace.ie; Unit 14, Block C, Smithfield Market; sandwiches €6.50; ⏲7am-6pm Mon-Fri, 9am-3pm Sat & Sun; Smithfield) One of the most welcoming cafes in town is this wonderful spot in Smithfield, which serves excellent breakfasts and fine sandwiches, as well as a lovely salad for that healthier option. Sit in the window, take out a book and just relax. The staff is fabulous.

SOUP DRAGON
FAST FOOD €

Map p280 (☎01-872 3277; www.soupdragon.com; 168 Capel St; mains €5-8; ⏲8am-5pm Mon-Fri; ; all city centre, Jervis) Queues are a regular feature outside this fabulous spot which specialises in soups on the go – but it also does superb stews, sandwiches, bagels and salads. The all-day breakfast options are excellent – we especially like the mini breakfast quiche of sausage, egg and bacon. Bowls come in two sizes and prices include fresh bread and a piece of fruit.

PANEM
CAFE €

Map p280 (www.panem.ie; 21 Lower Ormond Quay; sandwiches from €4.80; ⏲8am-5.30pm Mon-Fri, from 9am Sat, from 9.30am Sun; all city centre)

Not the capital from the *Hunger Games* but a long-standing quayside cafe that serves delicious sandwiches and wickedly sweet and savoury pastries, which are all made on-site. The croissants and brioche – filled with Belgian chocolate, almond cream or hazelnut *amaretti* – are the perfect snack for a holiday stroll. Lunchtimes are chaotic.

HAN SUNG KOREAN €

Map p280 (22 Great Strand St; mains €7-9; ⊙10am-9pm Mon-Sat, 11.30am-8.30pm Sun; Jervis) At the back of this Korean supermarket is one of Dublin's best-kept secrets. Order up bowls of *bibimbap* (rice bowl with meat, vegetables and egg) or *jjigae* (spicy stew) and you'll be well fed for under a tenner.

HATCH & SONS INTERNATIONAL €

Map p280 (01-874 1903; www.hughlane.ie; 22 N Parnell Sq; mains €6-14; ⊙9.45am-5.45pm Tue-Thu, to 4.45pm Fri, 10am-4.45pm Sat, 11am-4.45pm Sun; 3, 10, 11, 13, 16, 19, 22 from city centre) There's hardly a better way to ruminate over the art in the gallery (p144) than over lunch in the basement cafe. The menu features *blaas* (filled soft bread rolls) and hot stews as well as a selection of salad platters. There's another branch below the Little Museum of Dublin (p66).

★LEGAL EAGLE IRISH €€

Map p280 (01-555 2971; www.thelegaleagle.ie; 1/2 Chancery Pl; mains €22-30; ⊙9.30am-4pm Mon & Tue, to 10pm Wed-Fri, noon-10pm Sat, noon-9pm Sun; Four Courts) With the aesthetic of an old Dublin pub, combined with a kitchen churning out top-notch comfort food, this is one of Dublin's best new restaurants. There's a wood oven for potato flatbreads topped with Toonsbridge mozzarella and oxtail, and the retro-influenced Sunday menu is a contender for the best roast in town.

L MULLIGAN GROCER IRISH €€

Map p280 (01-670 9889; www.lmulligangrocer.com; 18 Stoneybatter; mains €17-23; ⊙4-10pm Mon-Fri, from 12.30pm Sat, 12.30-9pm Sun; 25, 25A, 66, 67 from city centre, Museum) It's a great traditional pub, but the main reason to come here is for the food, all sourced locally and made by expert hands. The menu includes an excellent free-range chicken Kiev, and a hefty artisanal Scotch egg (along with a vegetarian counterpart). There is an extensive selection of beers and whiskeys on offer, too.

GRANO ITALIAN €€

Map p280 (01-538 2003; www.grano.ie; 5 Norseman Ct; ⊙mains €14-24; 37, 39, 39A, 70 from city centre) An exceptional Italian restaurant in Stoneybatter, with a rotating menu of homemade pastas and a killer tiramisu. Its lunch menu offers incredible value at €12 for two courses, and the early bird (5pm to 7pm Tuesday to Thursday and noon to 7pm Sunday) is a bargain €19/24 for two/three courses.

TERRA MADRE ITALIAN €€

Map p280 (01-873 5300; www.terramadre.ie; 13A Bachelor's Walk; mains €15-21; ⊙12.30-3pm & 5-10pm; all city centre) It would be easy to walk past the entrance to this basement restaurant. But if you did, you'd be missing out on some of the most authentic Italian food in Dublin. The menu is small and constantly changing, but will always feature a few pastas (like pappardelle with duck ragu) and *secondi* (like Tuscan tripe). Exceptional.

YARN PIZZA €€

Map p280 (01-828 0839; www.theyarnpizza.com; 37 Lower Liffey St; pizzas €9-15; ⊙5-9pm Sun-Tue, to 10pm Wed-Sat; all city centre) With a 1st-floor terrace view of the Ha'Penny Bridge, this might be the city's coolest pizza joint. Add that it serves excellent drinks (pizza and Aperol, anyone?) and its credentials are rock solid. Oh, and the pizza – thin base, pomodoro San Marzano and delicious mozzarella – is delicious. It's the sister restaurant to the **Woollen Mills** (Map p280; 01-828 0835; www.thewoollenmills.com; 42 Lower Ormond Quay) – hence the name.

FISH SHOP FISH & CHIPS €€

Map p280 (01-557 1473; www.fish-shop.ie; 76 Benburb St; fish & chips €15; ⊙noon-1pm Tue-Fri, 4-10pm Sat & Sun; 25, 25A, 66, 67 from city centre, Museum) A classic fish-and-chip shop with a gourmet, sit-down twist – not only is the fish the best you'll taste in battered form, but you'll wash it down with a fine wine from its carefully selected list. It's the original Fish Shop that moved from Queen St, where its fancier sister restaurant is now installed.

THUNDERCUT ALLEY INTERNATIONAL €€

Map p280 (www.facebook.com/ThunderCutAlleyD7; Thundercut Alley; mains €11-15; ⊙5-10pm Wed-Thu, to 11pm Fri, 11.30am-11pm Sat, 11.30am-10pm Sun; Smithfield) This tiny, hipper-than-thou joint is a great little spot full of electric-bright '80s decor with a menu of delicious cocktails and mouthwatering nibbles. It's great for a boozy (bottomless) brunch, too.

FISH SHOP SEAFOOD €€

Map p280 (☎01-430 8594; www.fish-shop.ie; 6 Queen St; 4-course set menu €45; ⊙6-10pm Wed-Sat; 🚌25, 25A, 66, 67 from city centre, 🚊Smithfield) The menu changes daily at this tiny restaurant (it has only 16 seats) to reflect what's good and fresh, but you'll have to trust them: your only choice is a four-course or tasting menu. One day you might fancy line-caught mackerel with a green sauce, another day slip sole with caper butter. Maybe the best seafood restaurant in town.

WINDING STAIR IRISH €€

Map p280 (☎01-873 7320; www.winding-stair.com; 40 Lower Ormond Quay; 2-course lunch €24, mains €25-32; ⊙noon-3.30pm & 5.30-10.30pm; 🚌all city centre) In a beautiful Georgian building that once housed the city's most beloved bookshop – the ground floor still is one (p162) – the Winding Stair's conversion to elegant restaurant has been faultless. The wonderful Irish menu (potted crab, haddock poached in milk, steamed mussels and gorgeous fat chips) coupled with an excellent wine list makes for a memorable meal.

YAMAMORI SUSHI JAPANESE €€

Map p280 (☎01-872 0003; www.yamamori.ie; 38-39 Lower Ormond Quay; sushi €4-5, mains €20-25; ⊙5.30-9.30pm Mon & Tue, to 10pm Wed & Thu, to 10.30pm Fri, noon-10.30pm Sat, noon-10pm Sun; 🚌all city centre) A sibling of the long-established Yamamori (p76) on S Great George's St, this large restaurant – spread across two converted Georgian houses and including a bamboo garden – does Japanese with great aplomb, serving all kinds of favourites from steaming bowls of ramen to delicious sushi platters.

101 TALBOT IRISH €€

Map p280 (www.101talbot.ie; 100-102 Talbot St; mains €17-24; ⊙noon-3pm & 5-10pm Tue-Thu, to 11pm Fri & Sat; 🚌all city centre) This Dublin classic has expertly resisted every trendy wave and has been a stalwart of good Irish cooking since opening more than two decades ago. Its speciality is traditional meat-and-two-veg dinners, but with Mediterranean influences: pan-fried cod with white bean cassoulet; vegan chickpea cakes with avocado salad; and confit duck with garlic crushed potato. Superb.

★CHAPTER ONE IRISH €€€

Map p280 (☎01-873 2266; www.chapterone restaurant.com; 18 N Parnell Sq; 2-course lunch €36.50, 4-course dinner €80; ⊙12.30-2pm Fri, 5-10.30pm Tue-Sat; 🚌3, 10, 11, 13, 16, 19, 22 from city centre) Flawless haute cuisine and a relaxed, welcoming atmosphere make this Michelin-starred restaurant in the basement of the Dublin Writers Museum our choice for the best dinner experience in town. The food is French-inspired contemporary Irish; the menus change regularly; and the service is top-notch. The three-course pre-theatre menu (€44) is great if you're going to the Gate (p161) around the corner.

★MR FOX IRISH €€€

Map p280 (☎01-874 7778; www.mrfox.ie; 38 W Parnell Sq; mains €20-30; ⊙noon-2pm & 5-9.30pm Tue-Sat; 🚊Parnell) In a gorgeous Georgian townhouse on Parnell Sq, the fantastic Mr Fox is cooking some of the finest food in the city. The plates celebrate Irish ingredients with a cheeky twist – think venison with black pudding, chestnut and blackberries, or pheasant with lentils and Toulouse sausage. A Michelin star can't be too far away.

DRINKING & NIGHTLIFE

The Northside's pubs just don't get the same numbers of visitors as their Southside brethren, which means that if you're looking for a truly authentic pub experience, you're more likely to get it here. Around O'Connell St you'll also get the rough with the smooth, and we suggest you keep your wits about you late at night so as to avoid the potential for trouble that can sadly beset the city's main thoroughfare after dark.

★COBBLESTONE PUB

Map p280 (www.cobblestonepub.ie; N King St; ⊙4.30-11.30pm Mon-Thu, 2pm-12.30am Fri & Sat, 1.30-11pm Sun; 🚊Smithfield) It advertises itself as a 'drinking pub with a music problem', which is an apt description for this Smithfield stalwart – although the traditional music sessions that run throughout the week can hardly be described as problematic. Wednesday's Balaclava session (from 7.30pm) is for any musician who is learning

WORTH A DETOUR

ONE FOOT IN THE GRAVE

A contender for best pub in Dublin is **John Kavanagh's** (Gravediggers; 01-830 7978; www.facebook.com/JohnKavanaghTheGravediggers; 1 Prospect Sq; 10.30am-11.30pm Mon-Thu, to midnight Fri & Sat, to 11pm Sun; 13, 19, 19A from O'Connell St) of Glasnevin, more commonly known as the Gravediggers because the employees from the adjacent cemetery had a secret serving hatch so that they could drink on the job. Founded in 1833, it is reputedly Dublin's oldest family-owned pub: the current owners are the sixth generation of Kavanaghs to be in charge. Inside, it's as traditional a boozer as you could hope: stone floors, lacquered wooden wall panels and all. In summer the green of the square is full of drinkers basking in the sun, while inside the hardened locals ensure that ne'er a hint of sunshine disturbs some of the best Guinness in town. An absolute classic.

an instrument, with musician Síomha Mulligan on hand to teach.

TOKEN BAR

Map p280 (01-532 2699; www.tokendublin.ie; 72-74 Queen St, Smithfield; 4-11pm; 25, 26, 37, 39, 66, 67, 69, 70, 79A from city centre, Smithfield, Red Line) This arcade-style bar is fitted out with retro video games and pinball machines. As well as a full bar, the restaurant serves generous portions of innovative, gourmet fast food. Book ahead for groups of more than four if you want to eat. Over 18s only.

WALSHS PUB

Map p280 (www.walshsstoneybatter.ie; 6 Stoneybatter; 3-11pm Mon-Thu, to 12.30am Fri & Sat, 3-11pm Sun; 25, 25A, 66, 67 from city centre, Museum) If the snug is free, a drink in Walshs is about as pure a traditional experience as you'll have in any pub in the city; if it isn't, you'll have to make do with the old-fashioned bar, where the friendly staff and brilliant clientele (a mix of locals and trendsetting imports) are a treat. A proper Dublin pub.

CAFFE CAGLIOSTRO COFFEE

Map p280 (www.facebook.com/cagliostrodublin; Bloom's Lane; 7am-6.30pm Mon-Thu, to 10pm Fri, from 8.30am Sat, 10am-6pm Sun; Jervis) In the middle of the 'Italian Quarter' this tiny cafe serves brilliant Italian-style coffee at a reasonable price, alongside miniature doughnuts, cannoli and paninis. On Friday evenings, the little patio turns into a *Spritzeria*, with drinkers tucking into Aperol spritzers and Italian nibbles.

YAMAMORI TENGU CLUB

Map p280 (01-558 8405; www.yamamori.ie; 37 Great Strand St; 6-11.30pm Wed & Thu, to 3am Fri & Sat; all city centre) These two floors are the sweaty home to a mix of house, techno, soul and disco. There's lots of space to dance, a great sound system and a bar serving cocktails and Japanese beers. When your feet are sore, chill out in the bamboo smoking area. Find it through the back of Yamamori Sushi (p159) when open or from Great Strand St.

LAINE, MY LOVE COFFEE

Map p280 (www.lainemylove.com; 38 Talbot St; 7.30am-3pm Mon-Fri; Connolly) There's a small menu of breakfast nibbles (porridge and pastries) and sandwiches at lunch (made with delicious Le Levain bread). But really, the focus here is on the coffee, which is so good it'll distract you from the cafe's eye-roll inducing name. Almost.

BARBERS PUB

Map p280 (01-539 4048; www.thebarbers.ie; 19 Lower Grangegorman Rd; 4.30-11.30pm Mon-Thu, 3pm-midnight Fri, 2pm-midnight Sat, 2-11.30pm Sun; ; 37, 39, 70 from city centre, Smithfield) This barbershop-pub combo could be a bad gimmick but instead it's simply an excellent local bar that happens to give haircuts. Have a pint while getting a trim, or at night the barber shop floor transforms into a stage.

CONFESSION BOX PUB

Map p280 (01-8747339; www.c11407968.wixsite.com/ryan; 88 Marlborough St; 11am-11pm Mon-Fri, 10am-midnight Sat & Sun; Abbey) This historic pub is popular with tourists and locals alike. Run by some of the friendliest bar staff you're likely to meet, it's also a good spot to brush up on your local history: the pub was a favourite spot of Michael Collins, one of the leaders in the fight for Irish independence.

PANTIBAR GAY & LESBIAN

Map p280 (www.pantibar.com; 7-8 Capel St; ⌚4-11.30pm Mon-Thu, to 12.30am Fri & Sat, to 11pm Sun; 🚌all city centre) A raucous, fun gay bar owned by Rory O'Neill, aka Panti Bliss, star of 2015's acclaimed documentary *The Queen of Ireland,* about the struggle for equality that climaxes in the historic marriage referendum of May 2015. The bar has since become a place of LGBTQ pilgrimage – and no-holds-barred enjoyment. Its own brew, Panti's Pale Ale, is a gorgeous beer.

DICE BAR BAR

Map p280 (☎01-633 3936; www.dicebar.com; 79 Queen St; ⌚4pm-midnight Mon-Thu, 3pm-1am Fri, 1.30pm-1am Sat, 3-11.30pm Sun; 🚌25, 25A, 66, 67 from city centre, 🚊Museum) More of a New York dive bar than a traditional Dublin pub, Dice Bar was originally owned by Huey from the Fun Lovin' Criminals. He's since sold his interest, but the look has stayed the same: black-and-red painted interior, dripping candles and stressed seating. Add the rocking DJs and you've got one of the Northside's most popular bars.

GRAND SOCIAL BAR

Map p280 (☎01-874 0076; www.thegrandsocial.ie; 35 Lower Liffey St; ⌚4pm-12.30am Mon-Wed, to midnight Thu, noon-2.30am Fri & Sat, 3-11pm Sun; 🚌all city centre, 🚊Jervis) This multipurpose venue hosts club nights, comedy and live-music gigs, and is a decent bar for a drink. It's spread across three floors, each of which has a different theme: the Parlour downstairs is a cosy, old-fashioned bar; the midlevel Ballroom is where the dancing is; and the upstairs Loft hosts a variety of events.

HUGHES' BAR PUB

Map p280 (19 Chancery St; ⌚8.30am-11.30pm Mon-Thu, to 12.30am Fri & Sat, noon-11pm Sun; 🚌25, 66, 67, 90 from city centre, 🚊Four Courts) Traditional purists love the music sessions at this pub, which kick off at around 9.30pm nightly Saturday through Tuesday. By day, the pub caters to the sobering conversations of barristers, solicitors and their clients from the nearby Four Courts (p152).

WIGWAM BAR

Map p280 (www.wigwamdublin.com; 54 Middle Abbey St; ⌚11am-11.30pm Mon-Thu, to 2.30am Fri & Sat; 🚌all city centre, 🚊Abbey) The latest venture by the Bodytonic crew, this excellent new bar serves 50 types of craft beer and 100 different rums on the ground floor and excellent music in the basement bar, where top-notch DJs play regularly. It also does Brazilian-influenced bar grub.

ENTERTAINMENT

★LIGHT HOUSE CINEMA CINEMA

Map p280 (☎01-872 8006; www.lighthousecinema.ie; Smithfield Plaza; 🚌all city centre, 🚊Smithfield) The most impressive cinema in town is this snazzy four-screener in a stylish building just off Smithfield Plaza. The menu offers a mix of art-house and mainstream releases, documentaries and Irish films.

ABBEY THEATRE THEATRE

Map p280 (☎01-878 7222; www.abbeytheatre.ie; Lower Abbey St; 🚌all city centre, 🚊Abbey) Ireland's national theatre was founded by WB Yeats in 1904 and was a central player in the development of a consciously native cultural identity. Expect to see a mix of homegrown theatre from Irish playwrights, as well as touring performances from around the world.

ACADEMY LIVE MUSIC

Map p280 (☎01-877 9999; www.theacademydublin.com; 57 Middle Abbey St; 🚌all city centre, 🚊Abbey) A terrific midsize venue, the Academy's stage has been graced by an impressive list of performers on the way up – and down – the ladder of success, from Ron Sexsmith to the Wedding Present.

GATE THEATRE THEATRE

Map p280 (☎01-874 4045; www.gatetheatre.ie; 1 Cavendish Row; ⌚performances 7.30pm Tue-Fri, 2.30pm & 7.30pm Sat; 🚌all city centre) The city's most elegant theatre, housed in a late 18th-century building, features a generally unflappable repertory of classic Irish, American and European plays. Orson Welles and James Mason played here early in their careers. Even today it is the only theatre in town where you might see established international movie stars work on their credibility with a theatre run.

CINEWORLD MULTIPLEX CINEMA

Map p280 (☎0818 304 204; www.cineworld.ie; Parnell Centre, Parnell St; 🚌all city centre) This 17-screen cinema shows only commercial releases. The seats are comfy, the concession stand is huge and the selection of pick

STREET SMART

By day, O'Connell St is a bustle of activity, with shoppers, hawkers, walkers and others going about their business. At night, however, it can be a different story, as alcohol and drugs can give the street an air of menace and, sadly, the odd spot of trouble. Dubliners are sick of complaining that the police presence is virtually nonexistent (the police counter by declaring they're sick of their valuable resources constantly being cut), so you'll have to keep your wits about you.

'n' mix could induce a sugar seizure. It lacks the charm of the older-style cinemas, but we like it anyway.

LAUGHTER LOUNGE COMEDY

Map p280 (01-878 3003; www.laughterlounge.com; 4-8 Eden Quay; from €26; doors open 7pm; all city centre) Dublin's only specially designated comedy theatre is where you'll find those comics too famous for the smaller pub stages but not famous enough to sell out the city's bigger venues. Think comedians on the way up (or on the way down).

SAVOY CINEMA

Map p280 (01-874 8822; www.imccinemas.ie; Upper O'Connell St; from 2pm; all city centre) The Savoy is a five-screen, first-run cinema, and has late-night shows at weekends. Savoy Cinema 1 is the largest in the city and its enormous screen is the perfect way to view really spectacular blockbuster movies.

SHOPPING

With only a handful of exceptions, Northside shopping is all about the high-street chain store and the easy-access shopping centre, especially along Henry St, which is the Northside's answer to Grafton St. Here you'll find crowds of Dubliners looking for the best bargains and the latest street fashions.

WINDING STAIR BOOKS

Map p280 (01-872 6576; www.winding-stair.com; 40 Lower Ormond Quay; 10am-6pm Mon & Fri, to 7pm Tue-Thu & Sat, noon-6pm Sun; all city centre) This handsome old bookshop is in a ground-floor room when once upon a time it occupied the whole building, which is now given over to an excellent restaurant (p159) of the same name. Smaller selection, but still some excellent quality new- and old-book perusals.

ARNOTT'S DEPARTMENT STORE

Map p280 (01-805 0400; www.arnotts.ie; 12 Henry St; 9.30am-7pm Mon-Wed, to 9pm Thu, to 8pm Fri, 9am-7pm Sat, 11am-7pm Sun; all city centre) Occupying a huge block with entrances on Henry, Liffey and Abbey Sts, this is our favourite of Dublin's department stores. It stocks virtually everything, from garden furniture to high fashion, and it's all relatively affordable.

LOUIS COPELAND CLOTHING

Map p280 (01-872 1600; www.louiscopeland.com; 39-41 Capel St; 9am-6pm Mon-Wed, Fri & Sat, to 8pm Thu, noon-5pm Sun; all city centre, Jervis) A branch of the fashionable men's designer store. Dublin's answer to Savile Row.

EASON'S BOOKS

Map p280 (01-858 3800; www.easons.com; 40 Lower O'Connell St; 8am-7pm Mon-Wed & Sat, to 9pm Thu, to 8pm Fri, noon-6pm Sun; all city centre, Abbey) The biggest selection of magazines and foreign newspapers in the whole country can be found on the ground floor of this huge bookshop near the GPO, along with literally dozens of browsers leafing through mags with ne'er a thought of purchasing one.

MOORE STREET MARKET MARKET

Map p280 (Moore St; 8am-4pm Mon-Sat; all city centre) A shadow of its vibrant former self, this is the most traditional of Dublin street markets. You can get fruit, fish and flowers, while other vendors hawk cheap cigarettes and other products. Don't try to buy just one banana though – if it says 10 for €1, that's what it is.

JERVIS CENTRE SHOPPING CENTRE

Map p280 (01-878 1323; www.jervis.ie; Jervis St; 9am-6.30pm Mon-Wed, to 9pm Thu, to 7pm Fri & Sat, 11am-6.30pm Sun; all city centre) This modern, domed mall is a veritable shrine to the British chain store. Boots, Topshop, New Look, Argos, M&S and Superdrug are all here.

SPORTS & ACTIVITIES

ADVENTUREROOMS — LIVE CHALLENGE

Map p280 (☎01-872 7243; www.adventurerooms.ie; 6-7 Little Britain St, Campbell's Ct; per person €19-33; ⊙10am-8pm; Jervis) This is a good way to test your friendships: you'll be locked into a room and to win your freedom you'll need to work together to solve a series of puzzles. An excellent rainy-afternoon activity, it's very popular with stag and hen parties as well as for corporate team building. All bookings must be made in advance.

DUBLIN DISCOVERED BOAT TOURS — BOATING

Map p280 (☎01-473 4082; www.dublindiscovered.ie; Bachelor's Walk; adult/student/child €15/13/9; ⊙10.30am-4.15pm Mar-Oct; all city centre, Abbey) 'See the sights without the traffic' is the pitch; you get to hear the history of Dublin from a watery point of view aboard an (all-important) all-weather cruiser.

DUBLIN BUS TOURS — BUS

Map p280 (☎01-872 0000; www.dublinsightseeing.ie; 59 Upper O'Connell St; adult €15-28; all city centre, Abbey) A selection of bus tours including a hop-on, hop-off city tour (€22), a ghost-bus tour (€28) and two half-day tours: the four-hour South Coast & Gardens Tour (€27; including Powerscourt) and the North Coast & Castle Tour (€25; including Malahide Castle). In 2016 it added a 1916 anniversary tour (€15) that covers the sights associated with the 1916 Easter Rising.

JAMES JOYCE WALKING TOURS — WALKING

Map p280 (☎01-878 8547; www.jamesjoyce.ie; 35 N Great George's St; adult/student €10/8; ⊙2pm Tue, Thu & Sat May-Sep, Sat only Oct-Apr; 3, 10, 11, 11A, 13, 16, 16A, 19, 19A, 22 from city centre) A series of 90-minute tours run by the James Joyce Cultural Centre (p152) cover the life and work of the artist who lived, was schooled and lost his virginity on the northside. You have a choice between Joyce's Dublin, the Footsteps of Leopold Bloom (based on *Ulysses*) and a *Dubliners* tour.

ARBOUR HILL GUIDED TOURS — WALKING

Map p280 (☎01-677 0095; www.phoenixpark.ie; Arbour Hill; ⊙11am Fri Apr–mid-Oct; 37, 38, 39 from city centre) FREE Informative 45-minute guided tours of the history and names of those interred at Arbour Hill Cemetery (p153). Tours meet just inside the cemetery gates. Phone or email for bookings.

1916 EASTER RISING COACH TOUR — BUS

Map p280 (www.1916easterrisingcoachtour.ie; N Parnell Sq; adult/child €17.50/12.50; 3, 7, 10, 11, 13, 16, 19, 46A, 123 from city centre) A 90-minute tour of the sites that played a part in the 1916 Easter Rising. Buy your tickets online or at the Visit Dublin Centre (p251) in Suffolk St.

GLENDALOUGH & POWERSCOURT TOUR — BUS

Map p280 (www.dublinsightseeing.ie; 59 O'Connell St; adult/child €24.30/10.80; ⊙10.30am) This 5½-hour tour runs along the stretch of coastline between Dun Laoghaire and Killiney before turning inland into Wicklow and on to the monastic site of Glendalough and the Powerscourt Estate (admission included). All departures are from outside the Dublin Bus (p242) office on O'Connell St.

CITY SIGHTSEEING — BUS

Map p280 (www.citysightseeingdublin.ie; 14 Upper O'Connell St; adult/student €19/17; all city centre, Abbey) A typical hop-on, hop-off tour should last around 1½ hours and lead you up and down O'Connell St, past Trinity College and St Stephen's Green, before heading up to the Guinness Storehouse and back around the north quays, via the main entrance to Phoenix Park. Tours run every eight to 15 minutes, from 9am to 6pm.

Docklands

Neighbourhood Top Five

❶ **Jeanie Johnston** (p166) Visiting this working replica of a 19th-century 'coffin ship', as the barques transporting emigrants during the Famine were known.

❷ **Famine Memorial** (p166) Contemplating the Famine while walking gently among Rowan Gillespie's thought-provoking bronze statues.

❸ **Bord Gáis Energy Theatre** (p169) Attending a gig at this spectacular theatre designed by Daniel Libeskind.

❹ Poolbeg Lighthouse (p168) Enjoying stunning views of the bay and the city with a late-afternoon stroll down the south wall to this elegant lighthouse.

❺ **3 Arena** (p169) Attending a performance at Dublin's largest indoor arena.

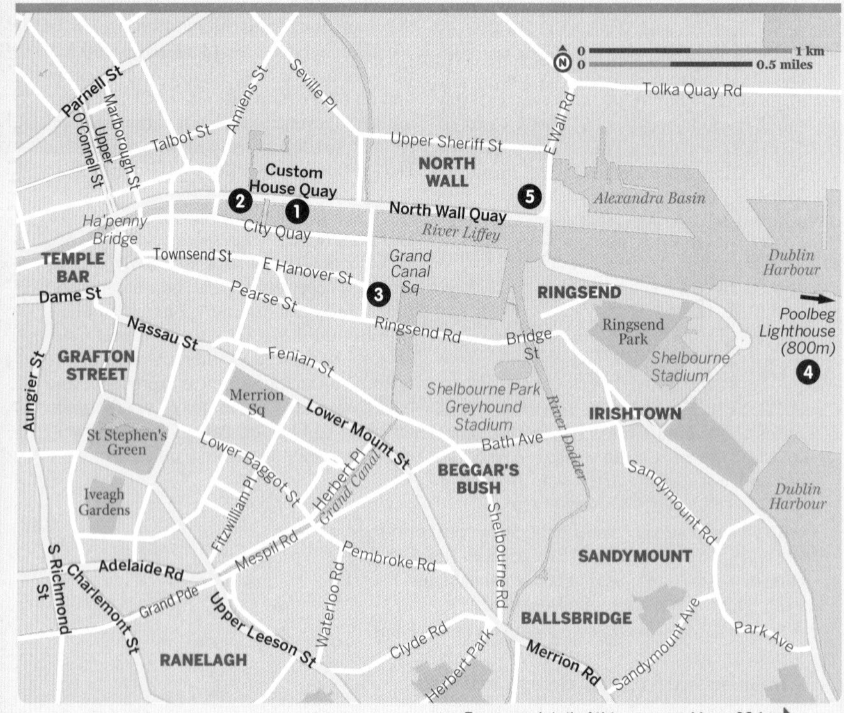

For more detail of this area see Map p284 ➡

Explore Docklands

Although much of the Docklands development that transformed the eastern end of the Liffey towards Dublin Port is given over to office and apartment blocks, there are parts of 'Canary Dwarf' (as it's jokingly named, after London's Canary Wharf) that are worth exploring, including a reconverted famine-era ship (p166) and a whole museum (p166) devoted to emigration.

The aesthetic of the area is the 10,000-sq-metre Grand Canal Sq (p167), designed by American landscape architect Martha Schwartz. Flanking its northwestern side is the magnificent 2010 Bord Gáis Energy Theatre (p169), designed by Daniel Libeskind. Stretching across the square from its entrance is a red 'carpet' – a series of red, resin-glass angled sticks that glow – and a green one – made up of polygon-shaped planters filled with marshlike vegetation.

On the north bank of the Liffey, the standout buildings are the snazzy Convention Centre (p167), designed by Kevin Roche; the Custom House (p166), a colossal Georgian building topped by a copper dome; and the city's premier indoor venue, the 3 Arena (p169), which is the main attraction in the Point Village. Dwarfing them all is the 74m-high 'Exo' on Point Sq, Dublin's tallest office block.

Local Life

- **Sustenance** For proper Neapolitan-style pizza, Paulie's Pizza (p167) is a great local choice; just around the corner is the equally popular Juniors (p167), which attracts the trendy crowd with its Brooklyn vibe.
- **Imbibe** There's a fine choice of public houses in the area, including two traditional gems: Slattery's (p168) and John Mulligan's (p168), one of the best pubs in the country.
- **Explore** Irish emigration is a major theme in the Docklands – aboard the Jeanie Johnston (p166); wandering among Rowan Gillespie's haunting statues (p166); exploring the hands-on, interactive exhibits of EPIC The Irish Emigration Museum (p166), devoted to the Irish diaspora; and exploring your own family history at the Irish Family History Centre (p166).
- **Art** Vera Klute's bust (p166) of folk singer Luke Kelly is one of the city's newest and most talked about pieces of public art.

Getting There & Away

- **Bus** The most convenient public transport option is the bus – Nos 1, 47, 56A and 77A go from Dame St to the edge of Grand Canal Sq. For the Northside, bus 151 goes from Bachelor's Walk to the Docklands.
- **Tram** The Luas Red Line terminus is at the Point Village.
- **Train** The DART stops at Grand Canal Quay.

Lonely Planet's Top Tip

Grand Canal Dock has a couple of decent spots for food, but even better ones are to be found southwest at the junction of Haddington Rd, Upper Grand Canal St and Bath Ave, where you'll find a handful of terrific restaurants and popular pubs.

Best Places to Eat

- Juniors Deli & Cafe (p167)
- Paulie's Pizza (p167)
- Workshop Gastropub (p168)

For reviews, see p167

Best Places to Drink

- Slattery's (p168)
- John Mulligan's (p168)

For reviews, see p168 

Best Place to Shop

- Design Tower (p169)

For reviews, see p169 

SIGHTS

The most memorable experiences here are tied to the exploration of Irish emigration and its global legacy.

EPIC THE IRISH EMIGRATION MUSEUM MUSEUM

Map p284 (01-906 0861; www.epicchq.com; CHQ Bldg, Custom House Quay; adult/child €15/7.50; 10am-6.45pm, last entrance 5pm; George's Dock) This is a high-tech, interactive exploration of emigration and its effect on Ireland and the 70 million or so people spread throughout the world who claim Irish ancestry. Start your visit with a 'passport' and proceed through 20 interactive galleries examining why they left, where they went and how they maintained their relationship with their ancestral home.

IRISH FAMILY HISTORY CENTRE CULTURAL CENTRE

Map p284 (01-671 0338; www.irishfamilyhistorycentre.com; CHQ Bldg, Custom House Quay; €12.50, incl EPIC The Irish Emigration Museum €24; 30/60min genealogist consultation €45/85; 10am-5pm Mon-Fri, from noon Sat; George's Dock) Discover your family history with interactive screens where you can track your surname and centuries of Irish emigration. The ticket price includes a 15-minute consultation with a genealogist, but additional 30-minute and hour-long sessions are also available. You can visit as part of the EPIC exhibition or buy a separate ticket.

FAMINE MEMORIAL MEMORIAL

Map p284 (Custom House Quay; all city centre) Just east of the Custom House is one of Dublin's most thought-provoking (and photographed) examples of public art: the set of life-size bronze figures (1997) by Rowan Gillespie known simply as *Famine*. Designed to commemorate the ravages of the Great Hunger (1845–51), their haunted, harrowed look testifies to a journey that was both hazardous and unwelcome.

The location of the sculptures is also telling, for it was from this very point in 1846 that one of the first 'coffin ships' (as they came to be known) set sail for the USA. Steerage fare on the *Perseverance* was £3 and 210 passengers made that first journey, landing in New York on 18 May 1846, with all passengers and crew intact.

In June 2007 a second series of *Famine* sculptures by Rowan Gillespie was unveiled on the quayside in Toronto's Ireland Park by then Irish president Mary McAleese to commemorate the arrival of Famine refugees in the New World.

JEANIE JOHNSTON MUSEUM

Map p284 (www.jeaniejohnston.ie; Custom House Quay; adult/student/child/family €10/9/6/28; tours hourly 10am-4pm Apr-Oct, 11am-3pm Nov-Mar; all city centre, George's Dock) One of the city's most original tourist attractions is an exact working replica of a 19th-century 'coffin ship', as the sailing boats that transported starving emigrants away from Ireland during the Famine were gruesomely known – even if the original *Jeanie Johnston* suffered no deaths in 16 journeys between 1848 and 1855, carrying a total of 2500 passengers. A small on-board museum details the harrowing plight of a typical journey, which usually took around 47 days. The ship also operates as a Sail Training vessel, with journeys taking place from May to September. If you are visiting during these times, check the website for details of when it will be in dock.

CUSTOM HOUSE LANDMARK

Map p284 (Custom House Quay; 9am-5pm Mon-Fri; all city centre) Georgian genius James Gandon (1743–1823) announced his arrival on the Dublin scene with this magnificent building constructed over 10 years between 1781 and 1791, just past Eden Quay at a wide stretch in the River Liffey. It's a colossal, neoclassical pile that stretches for 114m and is topped by a copper dome.

Best appreciated from the south side of the Liffey, its fine detail deserves closer inspection. Below the frieze are heads representing the gods of Ireland's 13 principal rivers; the sole female head, above the main door, represents the River Liffey. The cattle heads honour Dublin's beef trade, and the statues behind the building represent Africa, America, Asia and Europe. Set into the dome are four clocks and, above that, a 5m-high statue of Hope.

LUKE KELLY BUST STATUE

Map p284 (Mayor Square – NCI or Spencer Dock) An eye-catching 2m marble bust of folk singer Luke Kelly by award-winning German artist Vera Klute stands on the street where Kelly was born in 1940. Three thousand individual strands of patinated copper wire make up Kelly's famous head of curly hair and wiry beard, but it's the pose that has generated most of the commentary:

Jeanie Johnston

Klute captured Kelly with eyes firmly closed and mouth open in song – which some point out looks like he's in the throes of orgasm.

JAMES CONNOLLY MEMORIAL STATUE

Map p284 (Beresford Pl; all city centre, Abbey St, Red Line) Ireland's most famous socialist, James Connolly (1868–1916), is depicted proudly in front of the plough and stars of his Irish Citizen Army. An influential organiser for workers' rights, his role in the 1916 Easter Rising cemented his legacy, with his particularly cruel execution helping to fan the flames of Irish independence.

GRAND CANAL SQUARE SQUARE

Map p284 (Grand Canal Dock) This modern square was designed by American landscape artist Martha Schwartz and opened in 2008. Its most distinctive feature is the red 'carpet' made of bright red resin-glass paving covered with red glowing angled light sticks.

SAMUEL BECKETT BRIDGE BRIDGE

Map p284 (Spencer Dock) Spanish architect Santiago Calatrava's second Dublin bridge (his first is the James Joyce Bridge; 2003) is this wishbone-design structure (2007) in the Docklands at Spencer Dock.

CONVENTION CENTRE LANDMARK

Map p284 (Spencer Dock, North Wall Quay; closed to the public; Mayor Square – NCI) The angled, tube-like Convention Centre was designed by Kevin Roche in 2011. It looks its best at night, when it is lit up.

EATING

You may be out of the city centre, but there's a cluster of restaurants here that are well worth the effort.

ROCKET'S DINER €

Map p284 (01-524 0152; www.rockets.ie; North Wall Quay; burgers €7-8; 8am-11pm; Mayor Square – NCI) Burgers served '50s diner style. It's a 'faster' branch of Eddie Rocket's, which has locations all over the city centre.

★**JUNIORS DELI & CAFE** ITALIAN €€

Map p284 (01-664 3648; www.juniors.ie; 2 Bath Ave; mains €17-26; 8.30am-10.30am, noon-2.30pm & 5.30-10pm Mon-Fri, 11am-3pm & 5.30-10pm Sat, 11am-3.30pm Sun; 3 from city centre, Grand Canal Dock) Cramped and easily mistaken for any old cafe, Juniors is hardly ordinary. Designed to imitate a New York deli, the food (Italian-influenced, all locally sourced produce) is delicious, the atmosphere always buzzing (it's often hard to get a table) and the ethos top-notch, which is down to the two brothers who run the place.

PAULIE'S PIZZA ITALIAN €€

Map p284 (www.paulies.ie; 58 Upper Grand Canal St; pizzas €13-17; 6-10pm Mon-Thu, noon-3pm & 6-10pm Fri, 2-10pm Sat & Sun; ; 3 from city centre, Grand Canal Dock) At the heart of this lovely, occasionally boisterous restaurant is a Neapolitan pizza oven, used to create some of the best pizzas in town. Margheritas, *biancas* (no tomato sauce), calzone and other Neapolitan specialities are the real treat, but there's also room for a classic New York slice and a few local creations.

ELY BAR & GRILL FUSION €€

Map p284 (01-672 0010; www.elywinebar.ie; CHQ Bldg, ISFC, Georges Dock; mains €18-40; noon-10pm Mon-Fri, to 6pm Sun; George's Dock) Scrummy homemade burgers, bangers and mash, and perfectly charred steaks are some of the meals served in this converted tobacco warehouse in the International Financial Services Centre (IFSC). Dishes are prepared with organic produce from the owner's family farm in County Clare, so you can be assured of the quality.

WORKSHOP GASTROPUB IRISH €€

Map p284 (Kennedy's; ☎01-677 0626; www.theworkshopgastropub.com; 10 George's Quay; mains lunch €7-9, dinner €10-24; ⊙noon-3pm & 5-10pm Sun-Fri, noon-12.30am Sat; ; all city centre, Tara St) Take a traditional pub and introduce a chef with a vision: hey presto, you've got a gastropub (surprisingly one of the few in the city) serving burgers, *moules frites* (mussels served with French fries) and sandwiches, as well as a good range of salads.

MUSASHI IFSC JAPANESE €€

Map p284 (☎01-555 7373; www.musashidublin.com; Unit 2, Burton Hall, Custom House Sq; mains €13-18, sushi €5-8; ⊙noon-10pm Sun-Thu, to 11pm Fri & Sat; Mayor Square – NCI) Freshly made sushi, sashimi and other Japanese specialities, including a particularly tasty *tatsuta* chicken, served to an appreciative lunchtime and after-work crowd. It is the sister restaurant to Musashi Noodles & Sushi Bar (p157) on Capel St, and there are also locations on Parnell St and Hogan Pl.

HERBSTREET FUSION €€

Map p284 (☎01-675 3875; www.herbstreet.ie; Hanover Quay; mains €13-19; ⊙8am-2pm Mon, 8am-3pm & 5-7pm Tue-Fri, 10am-4pm & 5-7pm Sat, 10am-4pm Sun; Grand Canal Dock) Low-power hand driers, one-watt LED bulbs, secondhand furniture and strictly European wines: this restaurant is taking its green responsibilities seriously. Most of the food is sourced locally, but what really makes this place a hit is the terrific brunch menu – pancakes, Irish breakfasts, Mexican-style eggs...it's all good.

QUAY 16 FUSION €€

Map p284 (☎01-817 8760; www.mvcillairne.com; MV Cill Airne, North Wall Quay; mains €15-29; ⊙noon-3pm Mon-Fri, 6-10pm Mon-Sat; Spencer Dock) The MV *Cill Airne,* commissioned in 1961 as a passenger liner tender, is now permanently docked along the north quays, where it serves the public as a bar, bistro and fine restaurant. Dishes such as pan-roasted sea trout and Himalayan-salt-aged fillet steak are expertly prepared and served alongside an excellent variety of wines.

POOLBEG LIGHTHOUSE

One of the city's most rewarding walks is a stroll along the Great South Wall to the **Poolbeg Lighthouse** (South Wall; ⊙24hr; 1, 47, 56A, 77A, 84N from city centre), that red tower visible in the middle of Dublin Bay. The lighthouse dates from 1768, but it was redesigned and rebuilt in 1820. To get there, take the bus to Ringsend from the city centre, and then make your way past the power station to the start of the wall (it's about 1km). It's not an especially long walk out to the lighthouse – about 800m or so – but it will give you a stunning view of the bay and the city behind you, a view best enjoyed just before sunset on a summer's evening.

DRINKING & NIGHTLIFE

While you wouldn't traipse all the way out here just to get a drink, if you're in the neighbourhood there are plenty of good spots to enjoy a pint or two.

★JOHN MULLIGAN'S PUB

Map p284 (www.mulligans.ie; 8 Poolbeg St; ⊙noon-11.30pm Mon-Thu, 11am-12.30am Fri, 11.30am-12.30am Sat, 12.30-11pm Sun; all city centre) This brilliant old boozer is a cultural institution, established in 1782 and in this location since 1854. A drink (or more) here is like attending liquid services at a most sacred, secular shrine. John F Kennedy paid his respects in 1945, when he joined the cast of regulars that seems barely to have changed since.

RUIN BAR

Map p284 (☎01-499 0509; www.ruinbar.ie; 33 Tara St; ⊙noon-midnight Sun-Wed, to 1.30am Thu-Sat; all city centre, Tara St) This spacious bar is filled with colourful murals to admire and snap while working your way through the extensive drink selection. Taking inspiration from Budapest's ruin bars, it lacks the soul of the originals but is still a nice place to grab a casual meal and a pint.

SLATTERY'S PUB

Map p284 (☎01-668 5481; www.slatterysd4.ie; 62 Upper Grand Canal St; ⊙12.30-11.30pm Mon-Thu, to 12.30am Fri & Sat, 12.30-11pm Sun; 4, 7, 8, 120 from city centre) A decent boozer that is a favourite with rugby fans who didn't get tickets to the match – they congregate around the TVs and ebb and flow with each passage of the game. It's also popular on Friday and Saturday nights.

ENTERTAINMENT

BORD GÁIS ENERGY THEATRE THEATRE

Map p284 (☎01-677 7999; www.bordgaisenergy theatre.ie; Grand Canal Sq; 🚊Grand Canal Dock) Forget the uninviting sponsored name: Daniel Libeskind's masterful design is a three-tiered, 2100-capacity auditorium where you're as likely to be entertained by the Bolshoi or a touring state opera as you are to see *Dirty Dancing* or Barbra Streisand. It's a magnificent venue – designed for classical, paid for by the classics.

ODEON CINEMA CINEMA

Map p284 (www.odeoncinemas.ie; Point Village; 🚊The Point) A six-screen multiplex showing all the latest releases.

3 ARENA LIVE MUSIC

Map p284 (☎01-819 8888; www.3arena.ie; East Link Bridge, North Wall Quay; tickets €30-100; ⊙6.30-11pm; 🚊The Point) The premier indoor venue in the city has a capacity of 23,000 and plays host to the brightest touring stars in the firmament. Drake, Boyzone and Steely Dan performed here in 2019.

SHELBOURNE PARK GREYHOUND STADIUM SPECTATOR SPORT

Map p284 (☎01-525 3666; www.igb.ie; South Lotts Rd; packages €13.50-46.50; ⊙6.30-10.30pm Tue & Thu-Sat; 🚌3, 7, 7A, 8, 45, 84 from city centre) Greyhound racing's reputation has been seriously sullied due to revelations about the mistreatment of dogs, but the sport's aficionados can eat, bet and watch in luxury from the glassed-in restaurant at this dog track. There's a free **shuttle service** (⊙7pm Sat) on Saturday nights from Burgh Quay.

SHOPPING

Isn't there enough shopping for you around Grafton St? For a long time the Docklands development crowd didn't think so and imagined a new shopping oasis by the banks of the Liffey. Things didn't *quite* go as planned and the Docklands remains largely bereft of the kind of retail distractions envisaged, with the notable exception of the Design Tower.

DESIGN TOWER ARTS & CRAFTS

Map p284 (☎01-677 5655; www.thedesigntower.com; Pearse St; ⊙9am-5pm Mon-Fri; 🚊Grand Canal Dock) Housed in a 19th-century sugar refinery that was Dublin's first iron-structured building, this seven-storey design centre houses studios for around 20 local craftspeople, producing everything from Celtic-inspired jewellery to wall hangings and leather bags. Some studios are open by appointment only; check the website for details.

SPORTS & ACTIVITIES

CITY KAYAKING DUBLIN KAYAKING

Map p284 (☎085-866 7787; www.citykayaking.com; Dublin City Moorings, Custom House Quay; adult/child €33/25; ⊙tours 9am-8pm May-Oct; 🚌all city centre, 🚊George's Dock) A great way to see the city is aboard a kayak on this 90-minute guided trip that takes you up the Liffey through the city centre. There's a 30-minute instruction and prep session beforehand; a change of clothes and a towel is advisable, as you will inevitably get a little wet. Book online.

WAKEDOCK ADVENTURE SPORTS

Map p284 (☎01-664 3883; www.wakedock.ie; Grand Canal Dock; 30min tuition adult/student €60/45; ⊙noon-8pm Tue-Fri, from 10am Sat & Sun; 🚌1, 15A, 15B, 56A, 77A from city centre, 🚊Grand Canal Dock) Try the relatively new sport of cable wakeboarding – waterskiing by holding on to a fixed overhead cable instead of a motorboat. You can then graduate to flips and jumps over obstacles in the water. The sport is shortlisted for the 2020 Olympics. You can also rent wetsuits (€2).

SPORTS & FITNESS MARKIEVICZ HEALTH & FITNESS

Map p284 (☎01-672 9121; www.dublincity.ie; Townsend St; adult/child €7.50/3.75; ⊙7am-9.45pm Mon-Thu, to 8.45pm Fri, 9am-5.45pm Sat, 10am-3.45pm Sun; 🚌all city centre, 🚊Tara St) This excellent fitness centre has a swimming pool, a workout room (with plenty of gym machines) and a sauna. You can swim for as long as you please, but children are only allowed at off-peak times (10am to 5.30pm Monday to Saturday).

The Southside

Neighbourhood Top Five

❶ **Aviva Stadium** (p175) Cheering on Leinster or Ireland (in either rugby or football) is a memorable way to spend a few hours.

❷ **Herbert Park** (p172) Strolling, sitting or jogging around this glorious stretch of greenery - an ideal way to spend a sunny day in Dublin.

❸ **Stella Theatre** (p175) Visiting the city's fanciest cinema, a restored art deco classic.

❹ **Southside Dining** (p172) Dining in handsome Ranelagh or bustling Rathmines - always a treat, especially in spots like the Manifesto.

❺ **National Print Museum** (p172) Exploring the surprisingly interesting history of printing in Ireland at this terrific little museum.

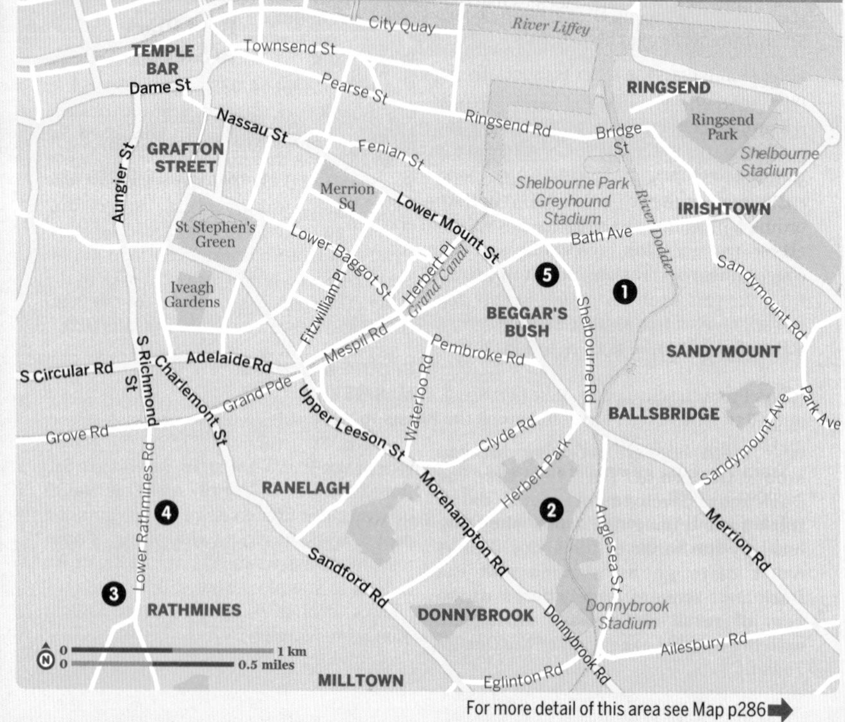

For more detail of this area see Map p286

Explore Southside

Ballsbridge is 2km southeast of St Stephen's Green and so within walking distance; another 2km to the south is Donnybrook, home to the Royal Dublin Society Showground (p175) and Donnybrook Stadium (p175) – the glorious expanse of Herbert Park (p172) is nearby.

Ranelagh is the loveliest of the villages immediately south of the Grand Canal; it's a pleasant, 2km walk south along Camden St and across the bridge; it's also easily accessible on the Luas green line. Rathmines, immediately west of Ranelagh, is accessible by bus 14 or 15 from the city centre, but it's not as pleasant a spot to amble about in. Rathgar, southwest of Rathmines, is the other village in Dublin 6, but it's strictly residential.

Local Life

- **Sustenance** Gourmands from all over the city trek to the likes of Butcher Grill (p173) in Ranelagh, Manifesto (p172) in Rathmines and Farmer Brown's (p173) on Bath Ave for the relaxed weekend brunch.
- **Sleeping** Even Dubliners take a night away from home...in their own city. Luxury B&Bs like Ariel House (p208) are great choices, while for a little glam there's always the Dylan (p208).
- **Drinking** Neighbourhood locales like the Taphouse (p174) in Ranelagh and Beggar's Bush (p174) on Haddington Rd are hugely popular with locals and other Dubliners – the latter is especially popular with fans going to and from a match in the Aviva.
- **Exercise** Herbert Park (p172) is one of the most popular parks in the city for all kinds of exercise, from running to tennis.
- **Cinema** The Stella Theatre (p175) in Rathmines is no ordinary cinema, but a sumptuously restored art deco classic where you can sip cocktails and recline on a couch while watching the latest release.

Getting There & Away

- **Bus** From the city centre, take bus Nos 5, 7, 7A, 8, 45 and 46 to Ballsbridge; for Donnybrook the 10A or 46; and for Rathmines No 14 or 15.
- **Tram** The Luas green line serves Ranelagh from St Stephen's Green.
- **Train** The DART serves Sandymount (for Bath Ave) and Lansdowne Rd.

Lonely Planet's Top Tip

Herbert Park (p172) is an excellent spot for a run and can be easily reached on foot from most city-centre hotels.

Best Places to Eat

- Farmer Brown's (p173)
- Dillinger's (p174)
- Manifesto (p172)
- Chophouse (p174)
- Kinara (p173)

For reviews, see p172

Best Places to Drink

- Beggar's Bush (p174)
- Taphouse (p174)

For reviews, see p174

Best Places to Sleep

- Dylan (p208)
- Devlin (p208)
- Ariel House (p208)

For reviews, see p208

SIGHTS

The southside neighbourhoods of Ballsbridge, Donnybrook, Ranelagh and Rathmines are short on visitor attractions – the sole exception being the National Print Museum near Sandymount.

NATIONAL PRINT MUSEUM MUSEUM

Map p286 (☎01-660 3770; www.nationalprint-museum.ie; Haddington Rd, Garrison Chapel, Beggar's Bush; ⏰9am-5pm Mon-Fri, from 2pm Sat & Sun; 🚌4, 7 from city centre, 🚆Grand Canal Dock, Lansdowne Rd) FREE You don't have to be into printing to enjoy this quirky little museum, where personalised guided tours (11.30am daily and 2.30pm Monday to Friday) are offered in a delightfully casual and compelling way. A video looks at the history of printing in Ireland and then you wander through the various (still working) antique presses amid the smell of ink and metal.

The guides are excellent and can tailor the tours to suit your special interests – for example, anyone interested in history can get a detailed account of the difficulties encountered by the rebels of 1916 when they tried to have the proclamation printed. Upstairs there are lots of old newspaper pages recording important episodes in Irish history over the last century.

HERBERT PARK PARK

Map p286 (Ballsbridge; ⏰dawn-dusk; 🚌5, 7, 7A, 8, 45, 46 from city centre, 🚆Sandymount, Lansdowne Rd) A gorgeous swathe of green lawns, ponds and flower beds near the Royal Dublin Society Showground (p175). Sandwiched between prosperous Ballsbridge and Donnybrook, the park runs along the River Dodder. There are tennis courts and a kids' playground here too.

EATING

Affluent neighbourhoods tend to attract a better quality of restaurant, and so it is with the southside: even the ordinary pub will tend to produce some excellent cuisine, while the established restaurants are all uniformly good. The restaurants in Ranelagh and Rathmines are incredibly popular most evenings and especially at weekends for brunch, so be sure to book your table in advance to avoid disappointment.

NICK'S COFFEE COMPANY CAFE €

Map p286 (☎086 383 8203; www.facebook.com/NicksCoffeeCompanyLtd; 22 Ranelagh Rd; 7am-8pm Mon-Thu, to 9pm Fri-Sun; 🚊Ranelagh) This little coffee hut is a Ranelagh institution and there are frequently lines in the morning for its strong espresso-based coffee, beans and range of speciality teas. Service is quick and, if the weather is warm, there's limited open-air seating and sometimes a wall of rotating street art to admire.

★**MANIFESTO** ITALIAN €€

Map p286 (☎01-496 8096; www.manifestorestaurant.ie; 208 Lower Rathmines Rd; pizzas €12-17, mains €19-25; ⏰5-10pm; 🚌14, 15, 140 from city centre) A table at this tiny Italian joint, which has a loyal legion of fans, is worth the wait. Pizzas are expertly charred with

DA NORT'SOYID & THE SOUTHSYDE

It was traditionally assumed that the southside is totally posh and the northside is a derelict slum – at least before gentrification began transforming virtually the whole of the city centre. But while most of the city has been given the developer's lick of paint, attitudes about the city's various neighbourhoods remain entrenched.

The 'southside' generally refers to Dublin 4 and the fancy suburbs immediately west and south – conveniently ignoring the traditionally working-class neighbourhoods in southwestern Dublin such as Bluebell and Tallaght. North Dublin is huge, but the northside tag is usually applied to the inner suburbs, where incomes are typically lower, accents are more pronouncedly Dublin and – most recently – the influx of foreign nationals is more in evidence.

All Dubliners are familiar with the 'posh twit' stereotype born and raised on the southside, but there's another kind of Dubliner, usually from the middle-class districts of northern Dublin, who affects a salt-of-the-earth accent while talking about the 'gee-gees' and says things like 'tis far from sushi we was rared' while tucking into a maki roll.

Rathmines Town Hall

carefully curated toppings like tender-stem broccoli and Sicilian capers, and the wine list is inventive and vast, with a generous selection available by the glass.

★FARMER BROWN'S INTERNATIONAL **€€**

Map p286 (☎01-660 2326; www.farmerbrowns.ie; 25A Bath Ave; brunch €7-12, dinner €15-28; ⏰10am-4pm & 5-8.30pm; 📶; 🚌7, 8 from city centre, 🚆Grand Canal Dock) The hicky-chic decor and mismatched furniture won't be to everyone's liking, but there's no disagreement about the food, which makes this spot our choice for best brunch in Dublin. From healthy smashed avocado to a stunning Cuban pork sandwich, it has all your lazy breakfast needs covered. Very much worth the effort. There's another branch (p174) in Rathmines.

STELLA DINER DINER **€€**

Map p286 (☎01-496 7063; www.stelladiner.ie; 211 Lower Rathmines Rd; mains €8-20; ⏰8am-10pm; 🚌14, 15, 140 from city centre) Unsurprisingly, American comfort food is at the heart of this stylish spot, where diners tuck into hot dogs and burgers from red-leather booths. If you have a craving for American pancakes, these are some of the best in town – fluffy, light and accompanied by a generous jug of maple syrup. Unlimited filter coffee is a nice touch, too.

BUTCHER GRILL INTERNATIONAL **€€**

Map p286 (☎01-498 1805; www.thebutchergrill.ie; 92 Ranelagh Rd; mains €20-36; ⏰5.30-9.30pm Sun-Wed, to 10.30pm Thu-Sat, plus noon-3.30pm Sat & Sun; 🚊Ranelagh) No surprise that this terrific spot specialises in meat, which is locally sourced and cooked to perfection in its wood-smoked grill. From venison to a superb *côte de boeuf* (rib steak) to share – there are few spots in town where the meat sweats are so welcome. The weekend roasts are top notch too, with duck fat roasties and Yorkshire pudding.

KINARA PAKISTANI **€€**

Map p286 (☎01-406 0066; www.kinarakitchen.ie; 17 Ranelagh Rd; mains €19-30; ⏰5-11pm daily, plus noon-3pm Thu & Fri, 1-5pm Sun; 🚊Ranelagh) Connoisseurs of the various cuisines of South Asia can distinguish between Indian and Pakistani fare; this exceptional restaurant specialising in the latter will soon educate even the most inexperienced palate. Curries such as the *nehari gosht* (made with beef) are superb, as are fish dishes, including the *machali achari* (fillet of red snapper simmered with pickles).

WORTH A DETOUR

SOUTHSIDE SEAFOOD

Michael's (☎01-278 0377; www.michaels.ie; 57 Deerpark Rd; mains €18-33; ⊙noon-10pm Tue-Sat; 🚌47 from city centre) Sure, it's a little bit of a trek from the city centre. But a trip to Michael's is well worth the effort – this is probably the best seafood in the city. Huge platters of Dublin Bay prawns, sole, mussels and lobster emerge from the kitchen bathed in garlic butter, with copper pots of handcut chips and pots of aioli for dunking. Heavenly.

Little Mike's (www.littlemikes.ie; 63 Deerpark Rd; mains €15-32; ⊙noon-10pm Thu-Sun; 🚌47 from city centre) At Little Mike's, opened in 2019, you can sit at the counter for a few glasses of wine and some smaller plates of the seafood that Michael's, its sister restaurant, is known (and loved) for. This spot, a few doors down from Michael's, is a more casual iteration.

FARMER BROWN'S INTERNATIONAL €€

Map p286 (☎086-046 8837; www.farmerbrowns.ie; 170 Lower Rathmines Rd; mains €16-28; ⊙10am-4pm & 5-10pm; 🚌14, 15 from city centre) A second branch of the much-loved restaurant on Bath Ave (p173), offering virtually the same delicious menu. Its juicy burgers are a contender for the best in the city.

DILLINGER'S AMERICAN €€

Map p286 (☎01-497 8010; www.dillingers.ie; 47 Ranelagh Rd; mains €16-28; ⊙5.30-9.30pm Mon & Tue, to 10.30pm Wed & Thu, to 11pm Fri, 10.30am-4pm & 5.30-11pm Sat, 10.30am-4pm & 5.30-9.30pm Sun; 🚊Ranelagh) This trendy American-style diner is small, so expect a wait if you want to go for the (excellent) weekend brunch. It's worth it just to taste the amazing things they can do with pulled pork, and if you're craving American-style pancakes, this is the place for you.

CHOPHOUSE GASTROPUB €€

Map p286 (☎01-660 2390; www.thechophouse.ie; 2 Shelbourne Rd; lunch €15-25, dinner €16-35; ⊙restaurant noon-2.30pm & 6-10pm Mon-Fri, 5-10pm Sat, 1-8pm Sun; 🚌4, 7, 8, 120 from city centre) This fine sprawling bar is a terrific gastropub where the focus is on juicy cuts of steak, but reluctant carnivores also have a choice of fish, chicken or lamb dishes. It does an excellent Sunday lunch – the slow-braised pork belly is delicious. It's a popular watering hole when there's a match on at the Aviva Stadium.

SABA ASIAN €€

Map p286 (www.sabadublin.com; 22 Upper Baggot St; mains lunch €14-22, dinner €18-26; ⊙noon-9.30pm Mon-Wed, to 10pm Thu, to 10.30pm Fri, 11.30am-10.30pm Sat, 11.30am-9.30pm Sun; 🚌5, 7, 7A, 8, 18, 45 from city centre) Asian fusion – mostly Thai and Vietnamese – is a popular hit at this thoroughly contemporary restaurant. It's a branch of the original restaurant on Clarendon St (p74).

DRINKING & NIGHTLIFE

The neighbourhood pubs and bars attract a mixed clientele of local residents, sports fans and Sunday drivers looking to inhale the fine air of southside's leafy suburbs.

BLACKBIRD PUB

Map p286 (☎01-559 1940; www.facebook.com/BlackbirdRathmines; 82-84 Lower Rathmines Rd; ⊙4pm-midnight Mon-Thu & Sun, to 1am Fri & Sat; 📶; 🚌14, 15, 140 from city centre) Candelit and cosy, this boozer epitomises the new-style of Irish pub, full of mismatching furniture, interesting curios and private snugs, with some retro video games thrown in. A good mix of traditional and craft drinks.

TAPHOUSE BAR

Map p286 (☎01-491 3436; www.taphouse.ie; 60 Ranelagh Rd; ⊙12.30pm-11.30am Mon-Thu, to 12.30am Fri & Sat, to 11pm Sun; 🚊Ranelagh) Locals refer to it by its original name of Russell's, but that doesn't mean that the regulars aren't delighted with the new owners' sprucing up of a village favourite. What they didn't change was the beloved balcony – the best spot to have a drink on a warm day.

BEGGAR'S BUSH PUB

Map p286 (Jack Ryan's; www.beggarsbush.com; 115 Haddington Rd; ⊙10.30am-11pm Mon-Thu, to 12.30am Fri & Sat, 12.30-11pm Sun; 🚌4, 7, 8,

120 from city centre, 🚉Grand Canal Dock) A staunch defender of the traditional pub aesthetic, Ryan's (as it's referred to by its older clientele) has adjusted to the modern age by adding an outside patio for good weather. Everything else, though, has remained the same, which is precisely why it's so popular with flat-capped pensioners and employees from nearby Google.

ENTERTAINMENT

★STELLA THEATRE CINEMA

Map p286 (☎01-496 7014; www.stellatheatre.ie; 207-209 Lower Rathmines Rd; tickets from €19; ⏰5pm-late Mon-Fri, from 9am Sat & Sun; 🚌14, 15, 140 from city centre) A cinema night may not always be a glamorous event, but at the Stella Theatre it is. A narrow entrance opens up to sumptuous art deco glory with comfortable leather seats paired with tables and footstools. Leave extra time to order food that will be delivered during the film or book ahead to go to the cocktail club upstairs.

BOWERY LIVE MUSIC

Map p286 (www.facebook.com/thebowerydublin; 196 Lower Rathmines Rd; ⏰4-11.30pm Mon-Thu, to 12.30am Fri & Sat, to 11pm Sun; 🚌14, 65, 140 from city centre) With its burnished wood, intricate chandeliers and ship-shaped stage, this music venue is one of the best-looking bars in the city. It features live performances every night of the week, from ska to disco to reggae, and upstairs is an excellent people-watching spot.

DONNYBROOK STADIUM STADIUM

Map p286 (www.leinsterrugby.ie; Donnybrook Rd; 🚌10, 46A from city centre) This purpose-built 6000-capacity arena is shared by a bunch of rugby teams, including the Ireland Wolfhounds (the junior national side), the Ireland Women's Team, Leinster 'A' and local club sides Old Wesley and Bective Rangers. Tickets are easily available for virtually all games.

AVIVA STADIUM STADIUM

Map p286 (☎01-238 2300; www.avivastadium.ie; 11-12 Lansdowne Rd; 🚉Lansdowne Rd) Gleaming 50,000-capacity ground with an eye-catching curvilinear stand in the swanky neighbourhood of Donnybrook. Home to Irish rugby and football internationals.

ROYAL DUBLIN SOCIETY SHOWGROUND SPECTATOR SPORT

Map p286 (RDS Showground; ☎01-668 9878; www.rds.ie; Merrion Rd, Ballsbridge; 🚌7 from Trinity College) This impressive, Victorian-era showground is used for various exhibitions throughout the year. The most important annual event here is the late-July **Dublin Horse Show**, which includes an international showjumping contest. Leinster rugby also plays its home matches in the 35,000-capacity arena. Ask at the tourist office for other events.

The Royal Dublin Society Showground was founded in 1731 and has had its headquarters in a number of well-known Dublin buildings, including Leinster House from 1814 to 1925. The society was involved in the foundation of the National Museum, the National Library, the National Gallery and the National Botanic Gardens.

SHOPPING

There are some shopping opportunities in Ranelagh and Ballsbridge, but the best shopping is south of both (and easily reached on the Luas) at the Dundrum Town Centre (p45) – the largest shopping centre in the country.

APRIL AND THE BEAR HOMEWARES

Map p286 (☎01-558 3527; www.aprilandthebear.com; 2 Wynnefield Rd; ⏰10.30am-6pm Wed-Sat; 🚌14, 15, 140 from city centre) This quirky homewares store moved from Temple Bar to Rathmines in April 2019, and is the place to go if you fancy a mounted dinosaur head or a monkey lamp for your wall. And really, who doesn't?

1

3

DAVID SOANES PHOTOGRAPHY/GETTY IMAGES ©; ARCHITECTS: POPULOUS AND SCOTT TALLON WALKER

1. Aviva Stadium (p175)
Home to Irish rugby and football internationals, Aviva has 50,000 seating capacity.

2. Bowery (p175)
One of the most attractive bars in the city, the Bowery has live performances every night of the week.

3. Herbert Park (p172)
The glorious expanse of popular Herbert Park runs along the River Dodder.

2

SAM MELLISH/IN PICTURES VIA GETTY IMAGES ©

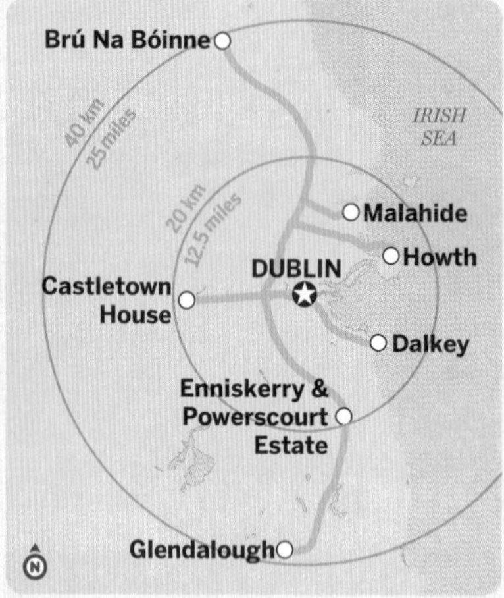

Day Trips from Dublin

Howth 189

A seaside village with terrific restaurants at the foot of a bulbous head with fine walks.

Enniskerry & Powerscourt Estate 192

A Palladian mansion with a stunning garden and even better views of the surrounding countryside.

Castletown House & Around 193

Ireland's largest Palladian home, built for the 18th century's richest man.

Dalkey 173

A picturesque, compact village by the sea with a nice harbour and coastal walks.

Malahide 174

A delightful north Dublin village with a 12th-century castle and 101 hectares of tended gardens.

TOP SIGHT
BRÚ NA BÓINNE

STEPHAN HOEROLD/GETTY IMAGES ©

The vast Neolithic necropolis known as Brú na Bóinne (the Boyne Palace) is one of the most extraordinary sites in Europe. A thousand years older than Stonehenge, it's a powerful testament to the mind-boggling achievements of prehistoric humankind.

History

The complex was built to house the remains of those in the top social tier and its tombs were the largest artificial structures in Ireland until the construction of the Anglo-Norman castles 4000 years later. The area consists of many different sites; the three principal ones are Newgrange, Knowth and Dowth.

Over the centuries the tombs decayed, were covered by grass and trees, and were plundered by everybody from Vikings to Victorian treasure hunters, whose carved initials can be seen on the great stones of Newgrange. The countryside around the tombs is home to countless other ancient tumuli (burial mounds) and standing stones.

Brú na Bóinne Visitor Centre

Built in a spiral design echoing Newgrange, this superb interpretive centre houses interactive exhibits on prehistoric Ireland and its passage tombs. It has regional tourism info and an excellent cafe, plus a book and souvenir shop. Upstairs, a glassed-in observation mezzanine looks out over Newgrange.

All visits to Newgrange and/or Knowth depart from here.

DON'T MISS

- Brú na Bóinne Visitor Centre
- Newgrange
- Winter Solstice experience
- Knowth

PRACTICALITIES

- ☎041-988 0300
- www.worldheritageireland.ie
- Donore
- adult/child visitor centre €4/3, visitor centre & Newgrange €7/4, visitor centre & Knowth €6/4, all 3 sites €13/8
- 9am-7pm Jun–mid-Sep, 9am-6.30pm May & mid-Sep–early Oct, 9.30am-5.30pm Feb-Apr & early Oct-early Nov, 9am-5pm early Nov-Jan

Brú na Bóinne

All visits start at the ❶ **visitor centre**, which has a terrific exhibit that includes a short context-setting film. From here, you board a shuttle bus that takes you to ❷ **Newgrange**, where you'll go past the ❸ **kerbstone** into the ❹ **main passage** and the ❺ **burial chamber**. If you're not a lucky lottery winner for the solstice, fear not – there's an artificial illumination ceremony that replicates it. If you're continuing on to tour ❻ **Knowth**, you'll need to go back to the visitor centre and get on another bus; otherwise, you can drive directly to ❼ **Dowth** and visit, but only from outside (the information panels will tell you what you're looking at).

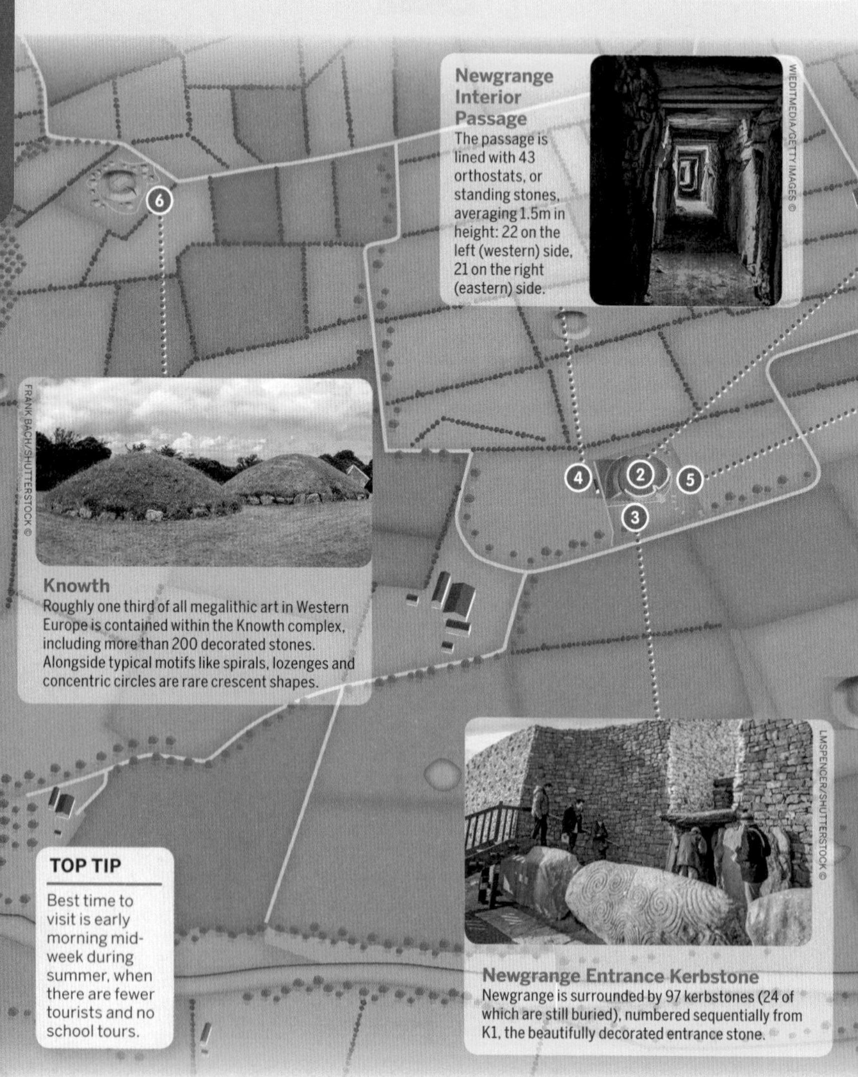

Newgrange Interior Passage
The passage is lined with 43 orthostats, or standing stones, averaging 1.5m in height: 22 on the left (western) side, 21 on the right (eastern) side.

WIEDITMEDIA/GETTY IMAGES ©

Knowth
Roughly one third of all megalithic art in Western Europe is contained within the Knowth complex, including more than 200 decorated stones. Alongside typical motifs like spirals, lozenges and concentric circles are rare crescent shapes.

FRANK BACH/SHUTTERSTOCK ©

Newgrange Entrance Kerbstone
Newgrange is surrounded by 97 kerbstones (24 of which are still buried), numbered sequentially from K1, the beautifully decorated entrance stone.

LMSPENCER/SHUTTERSTOCK ©

TOP TIP

Best time to visit is early morning mid-week during summer, when there are fewer tourists and no school tours.

MICHELLE MCMAHON/GETTY IMAGES ©

Newgrange
Newgrange's passage grave is designed to allow for a solar alignment during the winter solstice

FACT FILE

The winter solstice event is witnessed by a maximum of 50 people selected by lottery and their guests (one each). In 2017, 32,522 people applied.

Dowth
There is no public access to the two passage chambers at Dowth. The crater at the top was due to a clumsy attempt at excavation in 1847.

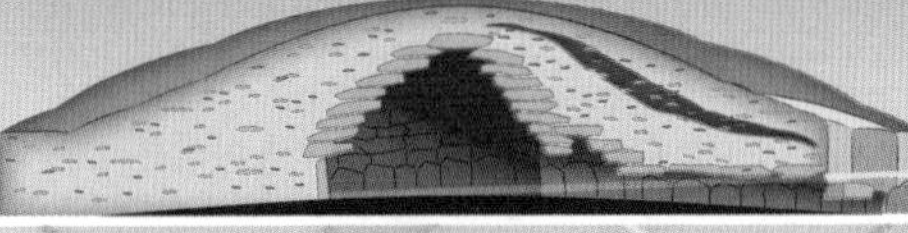

Newgrange Burial Chamber
The corbelled roof of the chamber has remained intact since its construction, and is considered one of the finest of its kind in Europe.

©NATIONAL MONUMENTS SERVICE DEPT OF ARTS, HERITAGE AND THE GAELTACHT

Brú na Bóinne Visitor Centre
Opened in 1997, the modern visitor centre was heavily criticised at first as being unsuitable, but then gained plaudits for the way it was integrated into the landscape.

GUIDED TOURS

Brú na Bóinne is one of the most popular tourist attractions in Ireland, and there are plenty of organised tours. Most depart from Dublin. Options include the highly recommended **Mary Gibbons Tours** (☎086 355 1355; www.newgrangetours.com; tour incl entrance fees adult/child €40/35).

The Brú na Bóinne Visitor Centre has a cafe and a picnic area outside (no food or drink is permitted at the monuments themselves). Otherwise, Slane and Drogheda have plenty of options. Drogheda has large supermarkets.

HERITAGE CARD

If you're planning to visit several archaeological and historic sites, consider investing in a **Heritage Card** (www.heritageireland.ie; adult/child €40/10), valid for one year and available for purchase at the **Battle of the Boyne Site** (☎041-980 9950; www.battleoftheboyne.ie; Drybridge; adult/child €5/3; ⌚9am-5pm May-Sep, to 4pm Oct-Apr) ticket office, as well as other participating sites throughout the country.

Newgrange

A startling 80m in diameter and 13m high, Newgrange's white round stone walls, topped by a grass dome, look eerily futuristic. Underneath lies the finest Stone Age passage tomb in Ireland – one of the most remarkable prehistoric sites in Europe. Dating from around 3200 BC, it predates Egypt's pyramids by some six centuries.

The tomb's precise alignment with the sun at the time of the winter solstice suggests it was also designed to act as a calendar.

No one is quite sure of its original purpose, however – the most common theories are that it was a burial place for kings or a centre for ritual.

Newgrange's name derives from 'New Granary' (the tomb did in fact serve as a repository for wheat and grain at one stage), although a more popular belief is that it comes from the Irish for 'Cave of Gráinne', a reference to a popular Celtic myth. The Pursuit of Diarmuid and Gráinne tells of the illicit love between the woman betrothed to Fionn MacCumhaill (Finn McCool), leader of the Fianna, and Diarmuid, one of his most trusted lieutenants. When Diarmuid was fatally wounded, his body was brought to Newgrange by the god Aengus in a vain attempt to save him, and the despairing Gráinne followed him into the cave, where she remained long after he died. This suspiciously Arthurian tale (substitute Lancelot and Guinevere for Diarmuid and Gráinne) is undoubtedly a myth, but it's still a pretty good story. Newgrange also plays another role in Celtic mythology as the site where the hero Cúchulainn was conceived.

Over time, Newgrange, like Dowth and Knowth, deteriorated and at one stage was even used as a quarry. The site was extensively restored in 1962 and again in 1975.

A superbly carved **kerbstone** with double and triple spirals guards the tomb's main entrance, but the area has been reconstructed so that visitors don't have to clamber in over it. Above the entrance is a slit, or roof-box, which lets light in. Another beautifully decorated kerbstone stands at the exact opposite side of the mound. Some experts say that a **ring of standing stones** encircled the mound, forming a great circle about 100m in diameter, but only 12 of these stones remain, with traces of others below ground level.

Holding the whole structure together are the 97 boulders of the **kerb ring**, designed to stop the mound from collapsing outwards. Eleven of these are decorated with motifs similar to those on the main entrance stone, although only three have extensive carvings.

The white quartzite that encases the tomb was originally obtained from Wicklow, 70km south – in an age before horse and wheel, it was transported by sea and then up the River Boyne. More than 200,000 tonnes of earth and stone also went into the mound.

You can walk down the narrow 19m passage, lined with 43 stone uprights (some of them engraved), which leads into the tomb chamber about one-third of the way into the colossal mound. The chamber has three recesses, and in these are large basin stones that held cremated human bones. As well as the remains, the basins would have held funeral offerings of beads and pendants, but these were stolen long before the archaeologists arrived.

Above, the massive stones support a 6m-high corbel-vaulted roof. A complex drainage system means that not a drop of water has penetrated the interior in 40 centuries.

Newgrange Winter Solstice

At 8.20am on the winter solstice (between 18 and 23 December), the rising sun's rays shine through the roof-box above the entrance, creep slowly down the long passage and illuminate the tomb chamber for 17 minutes. There is little doubt that this is one of the country's most memorable, even mystical, experiences.

There's a simulated winter sunrise for every group taken into the mound. To be in with a chance of witnessing the real thing on one of six mornings around the solstice, enter the free lottery that's drawn in late September; 50 names are drawn and each winner is allowed to take one guest (be aware, however, that over 30,000 people apply each year). Fill out the form at the Brú na Bóinne Visitor Centre or email brunaboinne@opw.ie.

Knowth

Northwest of Newgrange, the burial mound of Knowth was built around the same time. It has the greatest collection of passage-grave art ever uncovered in Western Europe. Early excavations cleared a passage leading to the central chamber which, at 34m, is much longer than the one at Newgrange. In 1968, a 40m passage was unearthed on the opposite side of the mound.

Excavations continue, and were due to close the site from November 2017 to Easter 2018.

Also in the mound are the remains of six early-Christian souterrains (underground chambers) built into the side. Some 300 carved slabs and 17 satellite graves surround the main mound.

Human activity at Knowth continued for thousands of years after its construction, which accounts for the site's complexity. The Beaker folk, so called because they buried their dead with drinking vessels, occupied the site in the Early Bronze Age (c 1800 BC), as did the Celts in the Iron Age (c 500 BC). Remnants of bronze and iron workings from these periods have been discovered. Around AD 800 to 900, it was turned into a *ráth* (earthen ring fort), a stronghold of the very powerful O'Neill clan. In 965 it was the seat of Cormac MacMaelmithic, later Ireland's high king for nine years, and in the 12th century the Normans built a motte and bailey (a raised mound with a walled keep) here. The site was finally abandoned around 1400.

Visits start only from the visitor centre.

Dowth

The circular mound at Dowth is similar in size to Newgrange – about 63m in diameter – but is slightly taller at 14m high. Due to safety issues, Dowth's tombs are closed to visitors, though you can visit the mound (and its resident grazing sheep) from the L1607 road between Newgrange and Drogheda.

North of the tumulus are the ruins of **Dowth Castle** and **Dowth House**.

PETER ZELEI IMAGES/GETTY IMAGES ©

TOP SIGHT
GLENDALOUGH

If you've come to Wicklow, chances are that a visit to Glendalough (Gleann dá Loch, meaning 'Valley of the Two Lakes') is one of your main reasons. And rightly so, for this is one of the most beautiful corners of the whole country and the epitome of Ireland's rugged, romantic landscape.

The substantial remains of this important monastic settlement are certainly impressive, but an added draw is the splendid setting: two dark and mysterious lakes tucked into a long, glacial valley fringed by forest. It is, despite its immense popularity, a deeply tranquil and spiritual place, and you will have little difficulty in understanding why those solitude-seeking monks came here in the first place.

DON'T MISS

- Monastic Site
- Reefert Church
- St Kevin's Cell
- Walking options
- Visitor Centre

PRACTICALITIES

- www.glendalough.ie
- admission free
- 24hr

History

In AD 498 a young monk named Kevin arrived in the Glendalough Valley looking for somewhere to kick back, meditate and be at one with nature. He pitched up in what had been a Bronze Age tomb on the southern side of the Upper Lake and for the next seven years slept on stones, wore animal skins, maintained a near-starvation diet and – according to the legend – became bosom buddies with the birds and animals. Kevin's ecofriendly lifestyle soon attracted a bunch of disciples, all seemingly unaware of the irony that they were flocking to hang out with a hermit who wanted to live as far away from other people as possible. Over the next couple of centuries his one-man undertaking mushroomed into an established settlement and by the 9th century Glendalough rivalled Clonmacnoise as the island's premier monastic city. Thousands of students studied and lived in a thriving community that was spread over a considerable area.

Inevitably Glendalough's success made it a key target for Viking raiders, who sacked the monastery at least four times between 775 and 1071. The final blow came in 1398, when English forces from Dublin almost destroyed it. Efforts were made to rebuild and some life lingered on here as late as the 17th century when, under renewed repression, the monastery finally died.

Lower Lake

Monastic Site

One of the most significant monastic sites in Ireland, Glendalough is centred on a 1000-year-old **round tower** (pictured), a ruined **cathedral** and the tiny church known as **St Kevin's Kitchen**. It was founded in the 6th century by St Kevin, a bishop who established a monastery on the Upper Lake's southern shore and about whom there is much folklore.

During the Middle Ages, when Ireland was known as 'the island of saints and scholars', Glendalough became a monastic city catering to thousands of students and teachers. The site is entered through the only surviving **monastic gateway** in Ireland.

At the centre of Glendalough's graveyard, to the southwest of the cathedral, is the **Priest's House**. This odd building dates from 1170 but has been heavily reconstructed. It may have been the location of shrines of St Kevin. Later, during penal times, it became a burial site for local priests – hence the name.

St Mary's Church

The 10th-century St Mary's Church, to the southwest of the round tower, stands outside the walls of the monastic site and belonged to local nuns. It has a lovely western doorway.

Deer Stone

At the junction with Green Rd as you cross the river just south of the monastic site is the Deer Stone, set in the middle of a group of rocks. Legend claims that when St Kevin needed milk for two orphaned babies, a doe stood here waiting to be milked. The stone is actually a *bullaun* (a stone used as a mortar for grinding medicines or food).

Many such stones are thought to be prehistoric, and they were widely regarded as having supernatural properties: women who bathed their faces with water from the hollow were supposed to keep their looks forever. The early churchmen brought the stones into their monasteries, perhaps hoping to inherit some of their powers.

Upper Lake

Teampall na Skellig

The original site of St Kevin's settlement, Teampall na Skellig is at the base of the cliffs towering over the southern side of the Upper Lake and accessible only by boat; unfortunately, there's no boat service to the site so you'll have to settle for looking at it from across the lake. The terraced shelf has the reconstructed ruins of a church and early graveyard. Rough wattle huts once stood on the raised ground nearby. Scattered around are some early grave slabs and simple stone crosses.

TIME YOUR VISIT

Visitors swarm to Glendalough in summer, so it's best to arrive early and/or stay late, preferably on a weekday, as the site is free and open 24 hours. The lower car park gates are locked when the visitor centre closes.

The National Park Information Office (☎0404-45425; www.wicklowmountainsnationalpark.ie; Bolger's Cottage, Upper Lake car park; ⏲10am-5.30pm May-Sep, to dusk Sat & Sun Oct-Apr) provides info about Wicklow Mountains National Park, and is the place to pick up maps and leaflets about local hiking trails. It's located by the Upper Lake car park, 1.5km west of the **Glendalough Visitor Centre** (☎0404-45352; www.heritageireland.ie; adult/child €5/3; ⏲9.30am-6pm mid-Mar–mid-Oct, to 5pm mid-Oct–mid-Mar).

LOCAL EATS

Laragh is the place for dining, as only the **Glendalough Hotel** (☎0404-45135; www.glendaloughhotel.com; Main St; s/d/f from €129/149/179; P 📶 👪) serves food near the monastic site.

Glendalough

A WALKING TOUR

A visit to Glendalough is a trip through ancient history and a refreshing hike in the hills. The ancient monastic settlement founded by St Kevin in the 5th century grew to be quite powerful by the 9th century, but it started falling into ruin from 1398 onwards. Still, you won't find more evocative clumps of stones anywhere.

Start at the ❶ **Main Gateway** to the monastic city, where you will find a cluster of important ruins, including the (nearly perfect) 10th-century ❷ **Round Tower**, the ❸ **cathedral** dedicated to Sts Peter and Paul, and ❹ **St Kevin's Kitchen**, which is really a church. Cross the stream past the famous ❺ **Deer Stone**, where Kevin was supposed to have milked a doe, and turn west along the path. It's a 1.5km walk to the ❻ **Upper Lake**. On the lake's southern shore is another cluster of sites, including the ❼ **Reefert Church**, a plain 11th-century Romanesque church where the powerful O'Toole family buried their kin, and ❽ **St Kevin's Cell**, the remains of a beehive hut where Kevin is said to have lived.

ST KEVIN

St Kevin came to the valley as a young monk in AD 498, in search of a peaceful retreat. He was reportedly led by an angel to a Bronze Age tomb now known as St Kevin's Bed. For seven years he slept on stones, wore animal skins, survived on nettles and herbs and – according to legend – developed an affinity with the birds and animals. One legend has it that, when Kevin needed milk for two orphaned babies, a doe stood waiting at the Deer Stone to be milked.

Kevin soon attracted a group of disciples and the monastic settlement grew, until by the 9th century Glendalough rivalled Clonmacnoise as Ireland's premier monastic city. According to legend, Kevin lived to the age of 120. He was canonised in 1903.

OLOS/SHUTTERSTOCK ©

Round Tower
Glendalough's most famous landmark is the 33m-high Round Tower, which is exactly as it was when it was built a thousand years ago except for the roof; this was replaced in 1876 after a lightning strike.

Deer Stone
The spot where St Kevin is said to have truly become one with the animals is really just a large mortar called a *bullaun*, used for grinding food and medicine.

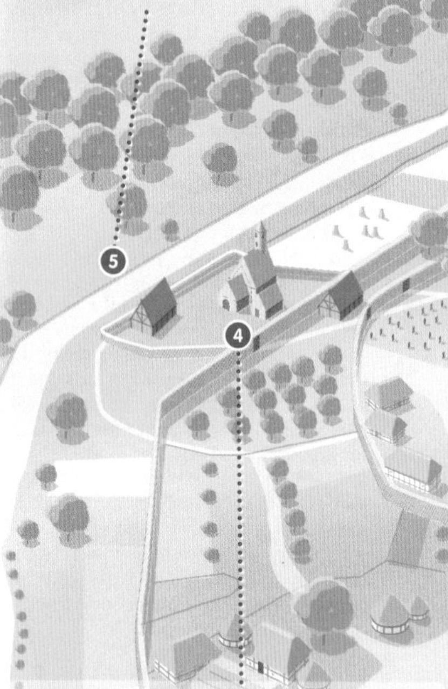

St Kevin's Kitchen
This small church is unusual in that it has a round tower sticking out of the roof – it looks like a chimney, hence the church's nickname.

SIR FRANCIS CANKER PHOTOGRAPHY/GETTY IMAGES ©

St Kevin's Cell

This beehive hut is reputedly where St Kevin would go for prayer and meditation; not to be confused with St Kevin's Bed, a cave where he used to sleep.

Reefert Church

Its name derives from the Irish *righ fearta*, which means 'burial place of the kings'. Seven princes of the powerful O'Toole family are buried in this simple structure.

Upper Lake

The site of St Kevin's original settlement is on the banks of the Upper Lake, one of the two lakes that give Glendalough its name – the 'Valley of the Two Lakes'.

RAFAL STACHURA/GETTY IMAGES ©

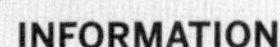

NORTH

INFORMATION

At the eastern end of the Upper Lake is the National Park Information Office, which has leaflets and maps on the site, local walks etc. The grassy spot in front of the office is a popular picnic spot in summer.

MICHAEL J THOMPSON/SHUTTERSTOCK ©

Cathedral of St Peter & St Paul

The largest of Glendalough's seven churches, the cathedral was built gradually between the 10th and 13th centuries. The earliest part is the nave, where you can still see the *antae* (slightly projecting column at the end of the wall) used for supporting a wooden roof.

Main Gateway

The only surviving entrance to the ecclesiastical settlement is a double arch; notice that the inner arch rises higher than the outer one in order to compensate for the upward slope of the causeway.

GERARDO BORBOLLA/SHUTTERSTOCK ©

St Kevin's Bed

Just east of Teampall na Skellig, and 10m above the Upper Lake's waters, is the 2m-deep artificial cave called St Kevin's Bed, said to be where Kevin lived. The earliest human habitation of the cave was long before St Kevin's era – there's evidence that people lived in the valley for thousands of years before the monks arrived.

Reefert Church

The considerable remains of Reefert Church sit above the tiny River Poulanass, south of the Upper Lake car park. It's a small, plain, 11th-century Romanesque nave-and-chancel church with some reassembled arches and walls. Traditionally, Reefert (literally 'Royal Burial Place') was the burial site of the chiefs of the local O'Toole family. The surrounding graveyard contains a number of rough stone crosses and slabs, most made of shiny mica schist.

St Kevin's Cell

Climb the steps at the back of the Reefert Churchyard and follow the path to the west and you'll find, at the top of a rise overlooking the Upper Lake, the scant remains of St Kevin's Cell, a small beehive hut.

Stone Fort

In the green area just south of the Upper Lake car park is a large circular wall thought to be the remains of an early Christian stone fort (caher).

WALKING IN GLENDALOUGH

The Glendalough Valley is all about walking. There are nine waymarked trails in the valley, the longest of which is about 10km, or about four hours' walking. Before you set off, drop by the National Park Information Office (p185) and pick up the relevant leaflet and trail map. It also has a number of excellent guides for sale – you won't go far wrong with Joss Lynam's *Easy Walks Near Dublin* or Helen Fairbairn's *Dublin & Wicklow: A Walking Guide*.

A word of warning: don't be fooled by the relative gentleness of the surrounding countryside or the fact that the Wicklow Mountains are really no taller than big hills. The weather can be merciless here, so be sure to take the usual precautions, have the right equipment and tell someone where you're going and when you should be back. For Mountain Rescue call 112 or 999.

The easiest and most popular walk is the gentle hike along the northern shore of the Upper Lake to the old lead and zinc **mine workings**, which date from 1800. The better route is along the lake shore rather than on the road (which runs 30m in from the shore), a distance of about 2.5km one way from the Glendalough Visitor Centre. Continue up to the head of the valley if you wish.

Alternatively you can walk up the **Spink** (from the Irish for 'pointed hill'; 380m), the steep ridge with vertical cliffs running along the southern flanks of the Upper Lake. You can go part of the way and turn back, or complete a circuit of the Upper Lake by following the top of the cliff, eventually coming down by the mine workings and going back along the northern shore. This circuit is about 6km long and takes around three hours.

The third option is a hike up **Camaderry Mountain** (700m), hidden behind the hills that flank the northern side of the valley. The path (not waymarked) begins opposite the entrance to the Upper Lake car park (near a 'Wicklow Mountains National Park' sign). Head straight up the steep hill to the north and you come out on open mountains with sweeping views in all directions. You can then continue west up the ridge to Camaderry summit. To the top of Camaderry and back is about 7.5km and takes around four hours.

Howth

Explore

Tidily positioned at the foot of a bulbous peninsula, the pretty port village of Howth (the name rhymes with 'both') is a major fishing centre, a yachting harbour and one of the most sought-after addresses in town.

Howth is divided between the upper headland – where the best properties are, discreetly spread atop the gorse-rich hill where there are some fine walks and spectacular views of Dublin Bay – and the busy port town, where all the restaurants are (as is an excellent weekend farmers market).

The Best...

- **Sight** Howth Summit
- **Place to Eat** House (p191)
- **Place to Drink** Abbey Tavern (p191)

Top Tip

Howth's 'hidden' beach is **Claremont Beach** (31, 31A from Beresford Pl, Howth), on the other side of the railway facing Ireland's Eye. To get here, go past the semi-industrial area by the West Pier.

Getting There & Away

DART The 20-minute train ride from Dublin city centre to Howth Village costs €3.25.

Bus Services 31 and 31A from Beresford Pl near Busáras run up to Howth Summit for €2.70.

Need to Know

- **Area Code** 01
- **Population** 8706
- **Location** 15km northeast of Dublin

SIGHTS

HOWTH SUMMIT — VIEWPOINT

Howth Summit (171m) has excellent views across Dublin Bay right down to County Wicklow. From the top of Howth hill you can walk to the top of the Ben of Howth, a headland near the village, which has a cairn said to mark a 2000-year-old Celtic **royal grave**. The 1814 **Baily Lighthouse**, at the southeastern corner, is on the site of an old stone fort and can be reached by a dramatic clifftop walk.

HOWTH CASTLE — CASTLE

Most of Howth backs onto the extensive grounds of Howth Castle, built in 1564 but much changed over the years, most recently in 1910 when Sir Edwin Lutyens gave it a modernist makeover. Today the castle is divided into four very posh and private residences (the grounds are open to the public). The **castle gardens** (24hr; 31, 31A from Beresford Pl, Howth) FREE are worth visiting, as they're noted for their rhododendrons (which bloom in May and June), azaleas and a long, 10m-high beech hedge planted in 1710.

The original estate was acquired in 1177 by the Norman noble Sir Almeric Tristram, who changed his surname to St Lawrence after winning a battle at the behest (or so he believed) of his favourite saint. The family has owned the land ever since, though the unbroken chain of male succession came to an end in 1909.

On the grounds are the ruins of the 16th-century Corr Castle and an ancient dolmen (a tomb chamber or portal tomb made of vertical stones topped by a huge capstone) known as Aideen's Grave. Legend has it that Aideen died of a broken heart after her husband was killed at the Battle of Gavra near Tara in AD 184, but the the dolmen is at least 300 years older than that.

Also within the grounds are the ruins of **St Mary's Abbey** (Abbey St; 31, 31A from Beresford Pl, Howth) FREE, originally founded in 1042 by the Viking King Sitric, who also founded the original church on the site of Christ Church Cathedral. The abbey was amalgamated with the monastery on Ireland's Eye in 1235. Some parts of the ruins date from that time, but most are from the 15th and 16th centuries. The tomb of Christopher St Lawrence (Lord Howth), in the southeastern corner, dates from around 1470. See the caretaker or read the instructions on the gate for opening times.

YE OLDE HURDY GURDY MUSEUM OF VINTAGE RADIO — MUSEUM

(www.hurdygurdyradiomuseum.wordpress.com; €5; 11am-4pm daily May-Oct, Sat & Sun only Nov-Apr) Housed in the old Martello tower overlooking the harbour is this museum of

Howth

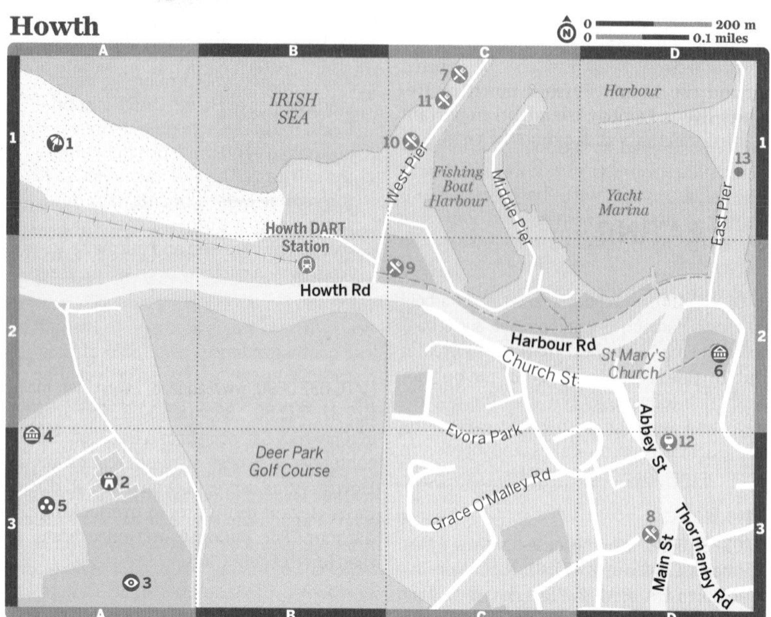

Howth

Sights

1 Claremont Beach ... A1
2 Howth Castle ... A3
3 Howth Castle Gardens ... A3
4 National Transport Museum ... A3
5 St Mary's Abbey ... A3
6 Ye Olde Hurdy Gurdy Museum of Vintage Radio ... D2

Eating

7 Aqua ... C1
8 House ... D3
9 Howth Market ... C2
10 Oar House ... C1
11 Octopussy's Seafood Tapas ... C1

Drinking & Nightlife

12 Abbey Tavern ... D3

Sports & Activities

13 Doyle & Sons ... D1

wonderful curiosities collected by Pat Herbert. Inside you'll find artefacts related to all forms of communication, from radios to gramophones and early TVs. The name derives from a comment made by former Taoiseach (prime minister) Seán Lemass, who asked a radio controller in the 1950s, 'How's the hurdy-gurdy?' (A hurdy-gurdy is a type of string instrument.)

NATIONAL TRANSPORT MUSEUM MUSEUM

(☎01-832 0427; www.nationaltransportmuseum.org; Howth Castle; adult €3, child & student €1.25; ⏱2-5pm Sat & Sun) The rather ramshackle National Transport Museum has a range of exhibits including double-decker buses, a bakery van, fire engines and trams – most notably a Hill of Howth electric one that operated from 1901 to 1959. To reach the museum, go through the castle gates and turn right just before the castle.

IRELAND'S EYE BIRD SANCTUARY

(☎01-831 4200) A short distance offshore from Howth is Ireland's Eye, a rocky seabird sanctuary with the ruins of a 6th-century monastery. There's a Martello tower at the northwestern end of the island, where boats from Howth land, while a spectacularly sheer rock face plummets into the sea at the eastern end. It's really only worth exploring if you're interested in birds, although the boat trip out here, with Doyle & Sons, affords some lovely views of Dublin Bay.

As well as the seabirds overhead, you can see young birds on the ground during the nesting season. Seals can also be spotted around the island. Further north of Ireland's Eye is Lambay Island, an important seabird sanctuary that cannot be visited.

EATING

HOWTH MARKET MARKET €

(☎01-839 4141; www.howthmarket.ie; 3 Harbour Rd, Howth Harbour; ⏲9am-6pm Sat, Sun & bank holidays) One of the best markets in greater Dublin, this is the place to come not only for fresh fish (obviously) but also for organic meat and veg, and homemade everything else, including jams, cakes and breads. A great option for Sunday lunch.

★HOUSE IRISH €€

(☎01-839 6388; www.thehouse-howth.ie; 4 Main St; mains €18-25; ⏲8.45am-9.30pm Mon-Thu, to 10.30pm Fri, 10am-10.30pm Sat, to 9.30pm Sun) A wonderful spot on the main street leading away from the harbour where you can feast on dishes such as squash and potato gnocchi or wild Wicklow venison with smoked black-pudding croquette, as well as a fine selection of fish. The brunch is one of the best you'll find on the north side of the city.

OAR HOUSE SEAFOOD €€

(☎01-839 4568; www.oarhouse.ie; 8 West Pier; mains €18-32; ⏲12.30-9pm Mon-Thu, to 9.30pm Fri & Sat, to 8.30pm Sun) A feast-o-fish – of the locally caught variety – is what the menu is all about at this restaurant. While this might be par for the course in a fishing village, this place stands out both for the way the fish is prepared and because you can get many dishes as smaller, tapas-style portions as well as mains.

OCTOPUSSY'S SEAFOOD TAPAS SEAFOOD €€

(☎01-839 0822; www.octopussys.ie; 7-8 West Pier; tapas €8-17; ⏲noon-9pm) Best known for its tasty seafood tapas, Octopussy's is a firm local favourite. All of the seafood comes from the fish shop next door, which in turn buys it from the fishing boats that dock right in front. You can't get any fresher than that.

LOCAL KNOWLEDGE

HOWTH SUMMIT WALK

A 6km looped walk around the headlands begins at Howth DART station – follow the green arrow along the promenade and then turn right onto the cliff path. The walk takes you up to the summit before looping back down again. There are other, longer, walks marked by blue, red and purple arrows (which partially overlap the green route).

AQUA SEAFOOD €€€

(☎01-832 0690; www.aqua.ie; 1 West Pier; mains €29-37; ⏲12.30-3.30pm & 5.30-9.30pm Tue-Thu, to 10pm Fri & Sat, noon-5pm & 6-8.30pm Sun) A contender for best seafood restaurant in Howth, Aqua serves top-quality fish dishes in its elegant dining room overlooking the harbour. The building was once home to the Howth Yacht Club.

DRINKING & NIGHTLIFE

ABBEY TAVERN PUB

(www.abbeytavern.ie; 28 Abbey St; ⏲12.30-11.30pm Mon-Thu, to 12.30am Fri & Sat, to 11pm Sun) At the front is an old-style tavern frequented by a mix of locals and visitors; at the back is the venue for a nightly traditional Irish music and dance show (from 7.30pm), which also includes a four-course meal. A bit of fun, but strictly for tourists!

SPORTS & ACTIVITIES

DOYLE & SONS BOATING

(☎01-831 4200; www.howth-boats.com; from €200) Doyle & Sons takes boats out to the bird-sanctuary island of Ireland's Eye from the East Pier of Howth Harbour. It also conducts half- (€300) and full-day (€500) angling trips as well as general sightseeing and birdwatching excursions.

Rates are for the whole boat, which takes up to 10 passengers.

Enniskerry & Powerscourt Estate

Explore

At the top of the '21 Bends', as the steep and winding R117 road from Bray is known, the handsome village of Enniskerry is home to upmarket shops and organic cafes. It's a far cry from the village's origins, when Richard Wingfield, earl of nearby Powerscourt, commissioned a row of terraced cottages for his labourers in 1760. These days you'd need to have laboured pretty successfully to get your hands on one of them.

The Best...

- **Sight** Powerscourt Estate
- **Place to Eat** Johnnie Fox's
- **Place to Stay** Powerscourt Hotel & Spa

Getting There & Away

Car Enniskerry is 18km south of Dublin, just 3km west of the M11 along the R117.

Bus Dublin Bus (www.dublinbus.ie) services link Dublin (Dublin City University) with Enniskerry (€3.30, 1½ hours, hourly).

Tour The estate is hard to visit via public transport, so a good option is a guided tour. DoDublin Bus Tour (p163) includes both Powerscourt and Glendalough, and departs from Dublin city centre.

Need to Know

- **Area Code** ☎01
- **Population** 1889
- **Location** 18km south of Dublin

SIGHTS

★**POWERSCOURT ESTATE** GARDENS

(☎01-204 6000; www.powerscourt.com; Bray Rd; house free, gardens adult/child Mar-Oct €10/5, Nov-Feb €7.50/3.50; ⊙9.30am-5.30pm Mar-Oct, to dusk Nov-Feb) Wicklow's most visited attraction is this magnificent 64-sq-km estate, whose main entrance is 500m south of Enniskerry. At the heart of it is an elegant Palladian mansion, but the real draws are the formal gardens and the stunning views that accompany them. Most of the house is not open to the public, but there's a fine cafe and several gift and homewares shops, while the grounds are home to two golf courses and the best hotel in Wicklow.

The estate has existed more or less since 1300, when the LePoer (later anglicised to Power) family built themselves a castle here. The property changed Anglo-Norman hands a few times before coming into the possession of Richard Wingfield, newly appointed Marshall of Ireland, in 1603. His descendants were to live here for the next 350 years. In 1730 the Georgian wunderkind Richard Cassels (or Castle) was given the job of building a 68-room Palladian-style mansion around the core of the old castle. He finished the job in 1741, but an extra storey was added in 1787 and other alterations were made in the 19th century.

The Wingfields left in the 1950s, after which the house had a massive restoration. Then, on the eve of its opening to the public in 1974, a fire gutted the whole building. The estate was eventually bought by the Slazenger sporting-goods family, who have overseen a second restoration as well as the addition of all the amenities the estate now has to offer, including the two golf courses and the fabulous hotel, part of Marriott's Autograph collection.

The 20-hectare **landscaped gardens** are the star attraction, originally laid out in the 1740s but redesigned in the 19th century by gardener Daniel Robinson. Robinson was one of the foremost horticulturalists of his day, and his passion for growing things was matched only by his love of booze: the story goes that by a certain point in the day he was too drunk to stand and so insisted on being wheeled around the estate in a barrow.

Perhaps this influenced his largely informal style, which resulted in a magnificent blend of landscaped gardens, sweeping terraces, statuary, ornamental lakes, secret hollows, rambling walks and walled enclosures replete with more than 200 types of trees and shrubs, all designed to frame the stunning natural backdrop of the Great Sugarloaf mountain. Tickets come with a map laying out 40-minute and hour-long walks around the gardens. Don't miss the exquisite **Japanese Gardens** or the **Pepperpot Tower**, modelled on a 3in actual pepper pot owned by Lady Wingfield. The **animal cemetery** is the final resting place of the Wingfield pets and even one of the family's favourite milking cows. Some of the epitaphs are surprisingly personal.

The house itself is every bit as grand as the gardens, but with most areas closed to the public, there's not much to see beyond the bustle of the ground-floor cafe and gift shop.

A 6km drive to a separate part of the estate takes you to the 121m-high **Powerscourt Waterfall** (adult/child €6/3.50; 9.30am-7pm May-Aug, 10.30am-5.30pm Mar, Apr, Sep & Oct, 10.30am-4pm Nov-Feb) – walking from house to falls is not recommended as the route lies on narrow roads with no footpath. It's the highest waterfall in Ireland, and at its most impressive after heavy rain. A nature trail has been laid out around the base of the waterfall, taking you past giant redwoods, ancient oaks, beech, birch and rowan trees. There are plenty of birds in the vicinity, including the chaffinch, cuckoo, chiffchaff, raven and willow warbler.

EATING

JOHNNIE FOX'S SEAFOOD €€

(01-295 5647; www.johnniefoxs.com; Glencullen; mains €15-26, seafood platters €28-130, 3-course Hooley menu €59.50; kitchen 12.30-9.30pm, bar 11am-11.30pm Mon-Thu, to 12.30am Fri & Sat, noon-11pm Sun;) Just over the County Dublin border, 5.5km northwest of Enniskerry, traditional 19th-century pub Johnnie Fox's fills with busloads of tourists for its knees-up Hooley Show of Irish music and dancing. But it's even more worthwhile entering its warren of rooms, nooks and crannies for standout seafood spanning Roaring Bay oysters, Dublin Bay prawns, Annagassan crab, Kilmore Quay lobster and more. Vegetarian, kids and babies menus are available.

POPPIES COUNTRY COOKING CAFE €

(01-282 8869; www.facebook.com/poppiesireland; The Square; mains €6.50-12; 8am-5pm Mon-Fri, to 6pm Sat & Sun) Hearty Irish breakfasts are served until noon at this poppy-red-painted cafe with a butter-yellow interior, while wholesome salads, filling sandwiches and daily specials such as shepherd's pie and veggie quiches make it a great option for lunch. You can also drop by for cakes, pastries and scones served with Kilmurry-made jam.

EMILIA'S RISTORANTE ITALIAN €€

(01-276 1834; www.emilias.ie; The Square; mains €11-24; 5-9pm Tue-Sat) A lovely 1st-floor dining room is the backdrop for Italian dishes such as Tuscan-wine-simmered cod, house-made Puglian pasta with clams and chicken breast in lemon sauce, as well as crispy thin-crust pizzas – try the Nettuno, with prawns, artichokes and black olives.

SLEEPING

★POWERSCOURT HOTEL & SPA LUXURY HOTEL €€€

(01-274 8888; www.powerscourthotel.com; Powerscourt Estate; d/ste from €244/333; P) Wicklow's most luxurious hotel is this 200-room stunner on the grounds of the Powerscourt Estate. Inside this Marriott-managed property, the decor is a thoroughly contemporary version of the estate's Georgian style. Rooms are massive; some have balconies. There's a gourmet restaurant (three-course evening menu €65), a lounge serving afternoon tea, a traditional bar and a holistic ESPA spa.

Castletown House & Around

Explore

Of all of Ireland's Palladian mansions, Castletown House is undoubtedly the grandest. It is a testament to the wealth and ambition of its original owner, William Conolly, who also happened to be the richest man in Ireland during the 18th century. Although parts of the house have been damaged, there's enough on display to give you an intimate look at the extravagant luxuries enjoyed by the Anglo-Irish gentry of the period.

The Best...

➡ **Sight** Castletown House (p194)

➡ **Place to Stay Carton House** (01-505 2000; www.cartonhouse.com; d/ste from €250/340; P)

Top Tip

The guided tour of the house is informative and full of detail about its construction and larger-than-life occupiers, not least Lady Louisa.

Getting There & Away

Bus No 67 runs from Dublin to Celbridge (€3.50, one hour, hourly).

Car Take the N4 to Celbridge.

Need to Know

- **Area Code** ☎01
- **Location** 21km west of Dublin

SIGHTS

★CASTLETOWN HOUSE HISTORIC BUILDING

(☎01-628 8252; www.castletown.ie; Celbridge; house adult/child €8/3.50, with guided tour €10/5, grounds free; ⊙house 10am-6pm daily Mar-Oct, to 5.30pm Wed-Sun Nov–mid-Dec, grounds dawn-dusk year-round) Magnificent Castletown House is Ireland's single-most imposing Georgian estate, and a testament to the vast wealth enjoyed by the Anglo-Irish gentry during the 18th century. Hour-long guided tours beginning at noon and 3pm provide an insight into how the 1% lived in the 18th century; otherwise you can wander at will. Don't miss a stroll down to the river for grand views back to the house. Castletown is signposted from junction 6 on the M4.

The house was built between the years 1722 and 1732 for William Conolly (1662–1729), speaker of the Irish House of Commons and, at the time, Ireland's richest man. Born into relatively humble circumstances in Ballyshannon, County Donegal, Conolly made his fortune through land transactions in the uncertain aftermath of the Battle of the Boyne (1690).

The job of building a palace fit for a prince was entrusted to Sir Edward Lovett Pearce (1699–1733) – hence the colonnades and terminating pavilions. His design was an extension of a preexisting 16th-century Italian palazzo-style building, created by Italian architect Alessandro Galilei (1691–1737) in 1718, but Conolly wanted something even grander, hence Pearce's appearance on the job in 1724. A highlight of the opulent interior is the Long Gallery, replete with family portraits and exquisite stucco work by the Francini brothers.

Conolly didn't live to see the completion of his wonder-palace. His widow, Katherine, continued to live at the unfinished house after his death in 1729, and instigated many improvements. Her main architectural contribution was the curious 42.6m obelisk, known locally as the Conolly Folly. Her other offering was the Heath Robinson–esque (or Rube Goldberg–esque, if you prefer) **Wonderful Barn**, six teetering storeys wrapped by an exterior spiral staircase, on private property just outside Leixlip, which is closed to the public.

Castletown House remained in the family's hands until 1965, when it was purchased by Desmond Guinness, who restored the house to its original splendour. His investment was continued from 1979 by the Castletown Foundation. In 1994 Castletown House was transferred to state care and today it is managed by the Heritage Service.

Dalkey

Explore

Dublin's most important medieval port has long since settled into its role as an elegant dormitory village, but there are some revealing vestiges of its illustrious past, most notably the remains of three of the eight castles that once lorded over the area.

Dalkey is small enough that you can get around on foot. Most visitors will be arriving by DART, so start your exploration in the middle of town: the main sights are on Castle St, as are most of the cafes (or on the streets just off it). Coliemore Harbour is where you can get boat trips; overlooking the adjoining Bullock Harbour are the remains of Bullock Castle.

The waters around the island are popular with scuba divers; qualified divers can rent gear in Dun Laoghaire, further north, from Ocean Divers (p196).

The Best...

- **Festival** Dalkey Book Festival (p224)
- **Place to Eat** Select Stores (p195)
- **Place to Drink** Finnegan's (p196)

Dalkey

Top Tip

To the south there are good views from the small park at Sorrento Point and from Killiney Hill. A number of rocky swimming pools are also found along the Dalkey coast.

Getting There & Away

DART The best way to get to Dalkey is by train from Pearse or Connolly stations – a one-way ticket costs €3.30 (€3 with a Leap Card).

Bus Service 7 takes a slow route from Mountjoy Sq through the Dublin city centre to Dalkey – the fare is €3.30.

Boat Dalkey native **Ken the Ferryman** (www.kentheferryman.com; Coliemore Harbour; adult/child €8/5; 10am-6pm) takes passengers to and from Dalkey Island aboard the *Lilly Rose*.

Need to Know

- **Area Code** 01
- **Population** 8083
- **Location** 8km south of Dublin

SIGHTS

DALKEY CASTLE & HERITAGE CENTRE MUSEUM

(01-285 8366; www.dalkeycastle.com; Castle St, Dalkey; adult/child €10/8; 10am-6pm Mon-Fri, from 11am Sat & Sun, closed Tue Sep-May) Spread across Goat Castle and St Begnet's Church, this heritage centre has models, displays and exhibitions on Dalkey's history. There's a Living History tour in the format of a theatre performance, and a Writers' Gallery covering the town's rich literary heritage – from Samuel Beckett (who was born here) and Maeve Binchy (who was born near here) to Joseph O'Connor (who lives here). The centre also organises **guided tours** (€10; 11am & noon Wed & Fri Jun-Aug).

DALKEY ISLAND ISLAND

Dalkey Island's main sight is **St Begnet's Holy Well**, but it's also a popular spot for fishing, with shoals of pollock, mackerel and coalfish feeding in its waters. It's also a lovely spot to spend a couple of hours with a picnic – but be sure to take everything off the island with you when you leave. Ken the Ferryman provides transport to and from the island.

BULLOCK CASTLE RUINS

(Bullock Harbour) These are the ruins of a castle built by the monks of Dublin's St Mary's Abbey in around 1150.

EATING

★**SELECT STORES** HEALTH FOOD €

(01-285 9611; www.facebook.com/selectstoresdalkey; 1 Railway Rd; mains €6-12; 8am-6pm Mon-Sat) This long-established food emporium has been transformed into a one-stop shop for all things good for you: the award-winning kitchen rolls out veggie burgers, fresh juices, salads and, in the mornings, a range of healthy breakfasts. Bono is a fan, apparently.

MAGPIE INN PUB FOOD €€

(01-202 3909; www.magpieinn.com; 115-116 Coliemore Rd; mains €15-24; 12.30-11.30pm Mon-Thu, to 12.30am Fri & Sat, to 11pm Sun) The main strength of the excellent menu here

WORTH A DETOUR

SANDYCOVE

Sandycove, situated just 1km north of Dalkey, has a pretty little beach and a Martello tower – built by British forces as a lookout for signs of a Napoleonic invasion – which is now home to the **James Joyce Museum** (01-280 9265; www.joycetower.ie; 10am-6pm May-Sep, to 4pm Oct-Apr; Sandycove & Glasthule) FREE.

There are really only two things to do here: visit the Martello Tower and, if you're brave enough, get into the water at the adjacent **Forty Foot Pool**.

is, obviously, seafood, including a range of mouth-watering lunch options such as fresh Galway mussels *marinière* with toasted sourdough, and more substantial dinner mains like ale-battered fish with pea puree, tartar sauce and chips. Wash it all down with a choice of craft beer.

DRINKING & NIGHTLIFE

FINNEGAN'S PUB

(www.finnegans.ie; 1 Sorrento Rd; noon-midnight) There's a fabulous local atmosphere in this lovely traditional pub, which has been a staple here for over 40 years.

SPORTS & ACTIVITIES

OCEAN DIVERS DIVING

(www.oceandivers.ie; The Boat Yard, Dun Laoghaire Harbour, Dun Laoghaire; boat dives €45-69; 9.30am-5pm Tue-Sat) A PADI diving school operating out of Dun Laoghaire Harbour, Ocean Divers offers boat diving around Dalkey Island, the site of two wrecks: the MV *Leinster* (which sank in 1918) and the *Bolivar* (a 1947 sinking).

Malahide

Explore

Malahide (Mullach Íde) was once a small village with its own harbour, a long way from the urban jungle of Dublin. The only thing protecting it from the northwards expansion of Dublin's suburbs is Malahide Demesne, 101 well-tended hectares of parkland dominated by a castle once owned by the powerful Talbot family.

The handsome village remains relatively intact, but the once-quiet marina has been massively developed and is now a bustling centre with a pleasant promenade and plenty of restaurants and shops.

The Best...

- **Sight** Malahide Castle
- **Activity** Portmarnock Golf Club
- **Place to Eat** Greedy Goose

Top Tip

If travelling by DART, be sure to get on the right train from Dublin city centre as the line splits at Howth Junction.

Getting There & Away

Bus Services 42 and 142 (€3.50) from Talbot St take around 45 minutes.

DART Stops in Malahide (€3.50).

Need to Know

- **Area Code** 01
- **PopulationLocation** 16,550
- **Location** 18km northeast of Dublin

SIGHTS

MALAHIDE CASTLE CASTLE

(01-816 9538; www.malahidecastleandgardens.ie; adult/child €14/6.50; 9.30am-5.30pm) The oldest part of this hotchpotch castle, which was in the hands of the Talbot family from 1185 to 1976, is the three-storey 12th-century tower house. The facade is flanked by circular towers that were

Malahide Castle

tacked on in 1765. The castle, now owned by Fingal County Council, is accessible via guided tour only (last tour 4.30pm; 3.30pm November to March). The impressive gardens are self-guided.

The castle is packed with furniture and paintings; highlights are a 16th-century oak room with decorative carvings, and the medieval Great Hall, which has family portraits, a minstrel's gallery and a painting of the Battle of the Boyne. Puck, the Talbot family ghost, is said to have last appeared in 1975.

EATING

CHEZ SARA FRENCH €€

(01-845 1882; www.chezsara.ie; 3 Old St; mains €19-24; 5pm-midnight Tue-Sun) Irish lamb, seafood linguine and beautifully cooked steak are just three of the highlights at this cosy French restaurant in the middle of the village.

GREEDY GOOSE INTERNATIONAL €€

(01-845 1299; www.greedygoose.ie; 15 Townyard Lane; menus €25-31; 5-11pm Mon-Fri, 1-11pm Sat & Sun; 42, 142 from city centre, Malahide) The menu at this pleasant restaurant overlooking the marina has dishes from all over the globe: take your pick from Thai crab cakes, chana masala, wild mushroom arancini and more. The food is best enjoyed as part of three separate menus: pick three dishes from one and eat portions roughly equivalent to Spanish *raciones* – bigger than starters, smaller than mains.

SALE E PEPE INTERNATIONAL €€

(01-845 4600; www.saleepepe.ie; The Diamond, Main St; mains €17-29; 5-10.30pm Mon-Sat, 4-10.30pm Sun) Despite the name, there's only a handful of Italian dishes here on a menu that emphasises well-prepared steaks, homemade organic burgers and fish and chips.

DRINKING & NIGHTLIFE

GIBNEY'S PUB

(www.gibneys.com; 6 New St; 10.30am-11.30pm Mon-Thu, to 12.30am Fri & Sat, 11.30am-11pm Sun) Malahide's best-known and best-loved pub is a huge place, spread over a number of rooms and outdoor areas. At weekends it's always packed with locals.

SPORTS & ACTIVITIES

★PORTMARNOCK GOLF CLUB GOLF

(01-846 2968; www.portmarnockgolfclub.ie; Golf Links Rd, Portmarnock; green fees weekday/weekend €225/250) Founded in 1894, this is one of the world's outstanding links courses and a former long-time host of the Irish Open. Visitor tee times are spread throughout the day, with 11.30am to 2.30pm reserved exclusively for members.

Sleeping

A surge in tourist numbers and a relative lack of beds means hotel prices can skyrocket, particularly at weekends and during the high season (May to September). There are good midrange options north of the Liffey, but the biggest spread of accommodation is south of the river, from midrange Georgian townhouses to the city's top hotels. Budget travellers rely on the decent hostels, many of which have private rooms as well as dorms.

Accommodation Styles

Top-end and deluxe hotels fall into two categories – period Georgian elegance and cool, minimalist chic. No matter what the decor, you can expect luxurious surrounds, king-sized beds, satellite TV, full room service, wi-fi and discreet, professional pampering. While the luxury of the best places is undeniable, their inevitable affiliation to the world's most celebrated hotel chains has introduced the whiff of corporate homogeneity into the carefully ventilated air.

Dublin's midrange accommodation is more of a mixed bag, ranging from no-nonsense but soulless chains to small B&Bs in old Georgian townhouses. These days, hotel connoisseurs the world over have discovered the intimate but luxurious boutique hotel, where the personal touch is maintained through fewer rooms, each of which is given lavish attention. Dublin's townhouses and guesthouses – usually beautiful Georgian homes converted into lodgings – are this city's version of the boutique hotel, and there are some truly outstanding ones to choose from. These are beautifully decked out and extremely comfortable, while at the lower end, rooms are simple, a little worn and often rather overbearingly decorated. Here you can look forward to kitsch knick-knacks, chintzy curtains, lace doilies and clashing floral fabrics so loud they'll burn your retinas. Breakfast can range from home-baked breads, fruit and farmhouse cheeses to a traditional, fat-laden fry-up.

Budget options are few and far between in a city that has undergone a dramatic tourist revolution, so if you want to stay anywhere close to the city centre, you'll have to settle for a hostel. Thankfully, most of them maintain a pretty high standard of hygiene and comfort. Many offer various sleeping arrangements, from a bed in a large dorm to a four-bed room or a double. There are plenty to pick from, but they tend to fill up very quickly and stay full.

There are also central self-catering apartments for groups, families or those on extended stays who may prefer to do their own thing. And there are hundreds of rental options in the city, ranging from basic rooms in apartments to fully furnished Georgian homes. New rules on short-term lettings were introduced in July 2019 for landlords in rent pressure zones (all of the city centre), restricting them to 90 days or less of renting per year.

Useful Websites

All Dublin Hotels (www.irelandhotels.com/hotels) Decent spread of accommodation in the city centre and suburbs.

Daft.ie (www.daft.ie) If you're looking to rent in Dublin, this is the site to search.

Dublin Hotels (www.dublinhotels.com) Hotels in the city centre and beyond.

Dublin Tourism (www.visitdublin.com) Good selection of rated accommodation.

Hostel Dublin (www.hosteldublin.com) Good resource for hostel accommodation.

Lonely Planet (lonelyplanet.com/ireland/dublin/hotels) Recommendations and bookings.

Lonely Planet's Top Choices

Merrion (p204) The city's best hotel.

Grafton Guesthouse (p201) Lofty rooms at an excellent price.

Cliff Townhouse (p203) Boutique luxury in a beautiful townhouse.

Conrad Dublin (p203) Exquisite business hotel.

Aloft Dublin City (p205) Brilliant new midrange hotel.

Shelbourne (p204) Historic and very elegant.

Best By Budget

€

Grafton Guesthouse (p201) Cool, lofty style in a gorgeous red-brick building.

Generator Hostel (p206) Funky hostel on the north side.

Kelly's Hotel (p201) Minimalist boutique chic smack in the middle of the action.

€€

Cliff Townhouse (p203) Terrific boutique bolthole.

Brooks Hotel (p202) Welcoming and cosy, with an in-house cinema.

Aloft Dublin City (p205) Amazing views from the rooftop terrace.

€€€

Merrion (p204) Sophisticated, elegant and central.

Shelbourne (p204) A Dublin institution.

Conrad Dublin (p203) Superb, modern rooms.

Best Comfy Pillows

Brooks Hotel (p202) Everyone needs a pillow menu.

Merrion (p204) Nestle your head in luxury.

Westbury Hotel (p203) The beds are heavenly.

Best Boutique Beds

Cliff Townhouse (p203) Ten magnificent rooms.

Devlin (p208) Artsy retreat in Ranelagh.

Number 31 (p203) Architect-designed marvel.

Best Cool Hostels

Avalon House (p201) Lively, with a generous breakfast.

Kinlay House (p204) Unbeatable prices in a gorgeous building.

Isaacs Hostel (p206) Best bunks in the city.

Best Landmark Lodges

Wilder Townhouse (p203) A beautiful, Victorian red-brick building.

Shelbourne (p204) The building in which the Irish Constitution was signed.

Schoolhouse Hotel (p208) A historic school dating back to 1861.

Best Super Spas

Merrion (p204) Impeccable treatments in a serene setting.

Intercontinental Dublin (p208) Super plush and inviting.

Marker (p207) Killer infinity pool.

NEED TO KNOW

Price Ranges

The following price ranges refer to the cost per night of a standard double room in high season.

€	less than €150
€€	€150–€250
€€€	over €250

Discounted Rates

- Keep an eye out for online offers.
- Flexibility is a must.
- Hotels that cater to business customers offer cheaper weekend rates.

Check-In & Checkout Times

Checkout at most establishments is noon, but some of the smaller guesthouses and B&Bs require that you check out a little earlier, usually around 11am. Check-in is usually between 2pm and 3pm.

Tipping

It's customary to tip bellhops €1 per bag, and concierges up to €5 for any additional service they provide, such as booking restaurants, taxis or advice on what to do or where to go.

Where to Stay

NEIGHBOURHOOD	FOR	AGAINST
Grafton Street & St Stephen's Green	Close to sights, nightlife and pretty much everything; a good choice of midrange and top-end hotels.	Generally more expensive than elsewhere; not always good value for money and rooms tend to be smaller.
Merrion Square & Georgian Dublin	Lovely neighbourhood, elegant hotels and townhouse accommodation.	Not a lot of choice; virtually no budget accommodation. Also relatively quiet after dark.
Temple Bar	In the heart of the action; close to everything, especially the party.	Noisy and touristy; not especially good value for money; rooms are very small and often less than pristine.
Kilmainham & the Liberties	Close to the old city and the sights of west Dublin. An up-and-coming spot for great restaurants, too.	If you want to hit the main city sights, you're facing a bit more of a walk in and out of town.
North of the Liffey	Good range of choices; within walking distance of sights and nightlife.	Budget accommodation not always good quality; some locations not especially comfortable after dark.
Docklands	Excellent contemporary hotels with good service, including some top-end choices.	Isolated in neighbourhood that doesn't have a lot of life after dark; reliant on taxis or public transport to get to city centre.
Southside	More bang for your buck; generally bigger rooms and properties with gardens.	If not on the Luas line, bus transfers into town can take up valuable time.

BOOKING IN ADVANCE

Getting the hotel of your choice without a reservation can be tricky in high season (May to September), so always book your room in advance. You can book through Dublin Tourism's online booking service (www.visitdublin.com). Advance internet bookings are your best bet for deals.

Grafton St & St Stephen's Green

Grafton St itself has only one hotel – one of the city's best – but you'll find a host of choices in the area surrounding it. Not surprisingly, being so close to the choicest street in town comes at a premium, but the competition for business is fierce, which ensures quality is top rate.

★GRAFTON GUESTHOUSE BOUTIQUE HOTEL €
Map p270 (☎01-648 0025; www.graftonguesthouse.com; 27 S Great George's St; s/d from €100/125; @📶; 🚌all city centre, 🚊St Stephen's Green) Following a hefty refurbishment in 2018, Grafton Guesthouse is one of the standout budget hotels in the city. Exposed brick walls, subway-tiled bathrooms and period features give the rooms a distinct Brooklyn vibe, and it's bang in the middle of the action on George's St. Street-facing rooms are noisy, especially at weekends.

KELLY'S HOTEL BOUTIQUE HOTEL €
Map p270 (☎01-648 0010; www.kellysdublin.com; 36 S Great George's St; r from €130; ❄@📶; 🚌all city centre) A trendy boutique hotel in an original Victorian red-brick. The interiors are thoroughly modern: rooms are small and tastefully decorated with polished wooden floors and elegant minimalist furnishings. It's part of a complex that includes Grafton Guesthouse, two bars – Hogan's (p80) and the No Name Bar (p78) – and French restaurant L'Gueuleton (p76) next door. Front-facing rooms can be quite noisy.

AVALON HOUSE HOSTEL €
Map p270 (☎01-475 0001; www.avalon-house.ie; 55 Aungier St; dm/s/d from €19/36/72; @📶; 🚌15, 16, 16A, 16C, 19, 19A, 19C, 65, 65B, 83, 122) Pared-back dorms with high ceilings and old-fashioned sinks, metal-framed bunks and shared bathrooms give this an old-school look at odds with newer hostels, but it's popular – because of its location and nice common room. Book well in advance.

TRINITY COLLEGE APARTMENT €
Map p270 (☎01-896 1177; www.tcd.ie/summeraccommodation; Accommodations Office, Trinity College; s/d from €85/140; ⊙May–mid-Sep; P@📶; 🚌all cross-city) The closest thing to living like a student at this stunningly beautiful university is crashing in their rooms when they're on holidays. The best choice is on campus, in the older blocks with shared facilities or in newer blocks, which have two-bed apartments with private bathroom. There's also a new block immediately off campus on Westland Row.

RADISSON BLU ROYAL HOTEL HOTEL €€
Map p274 (☎01-898 2900; www.radissonblu.ie/royalhotel-dublin; Golden Lane; r from €250; P❄@📶; 🚌all city centre, 🚊St Stephen's Green) A business hotel that is an excellent example of how sleek lines and muted colours combine beautifully with luxury, ensuring a memorable night's stay. From hugely impressive public areas to sophisticated bedrooms – each with a flat-screen digital TV embedded in the wall to go along with all the other little touches – this hotel will not disappoint.

CENTRAL HOTEL HOTEL €€
Map p270 (☎01-679 7302; www.centralhoteldublin.com; 1-5 Exchequer St; r from €150; @📶; 🚌all city centre, 🚊St Stephen's Green) The rooms are a modern – if miniaturised – version of Edwardian luxury. Heavy velvet curtains and custom-made Irish furnishings (including beds with draped backboards) fit a bit too snugly into the space afforded them, but they do lend a touch of class. Note that street-facing rooms can get a little noisy. Location-wise, the name says it all.

DEAN HOTEL €€
Map p274 (☎01-607 8110; www.deanhoteldublin.ie; 33 Harcourt St; r/ste from €155/315; P@📶; 🚌10, 11, 13, 14, 15A, 🚊St Stephen's Green) Every room at this newish designer hotel comes with earplugs, vodka, wine and Berocca – so you know what to expect (light sleepers, beware). Take your pick from elegant and well-appointed Mod Pods (single bed on a couch), Punk Bunks (yup, bunk beds) or deluxe doubles (SupeRooms or Hi-Fis) and suites. The more expensive rooms come with Netflix and a turntable.

The hotel deliberately advertises as an upmarket party hotel that borrows its ethos (if not its look) from the Ace Hotel in New York and the Hoxton in London: sandwiched between two of the most popular nightclubs in town the rooms can get very noisy indeed, especially those on the 1st floor. The top floor is home to Sophie's (p75), a brasserie that turns into a popular bar after 11pm.

CAMPUS ACCOMMODATION

During the summer months (and sometimes during term time), visitors can opt to stay in campus accommodation, which is both convenient and comfortable.

Trinity College (p201) The extensive range of student accommodation includes modern apartments with all mod cons and older (more atmospheric) rooms with shared bathrooms. They're on campus and just off it, on Pearse St.

Dublin City University (DCU; ☎01-700 5736; www.dcurooms.com; Larkfield Apts, Campus Residences, Dublin City University; s/d from €80/110; P; 🚌11, 11A, 11B, 13, 13A, 19, 19A from city centre) This accommodation is proof that students slum it in relative luxury. The modern rooms have plenty of amenities at hand, including a kitchen, a common room and a fully equipped health centre. The Glasnevin campus is only 15 minutes by bus or car from the city centre.

It has discounted parking arrangements with a car park five-minutes' walk away.

DAWSON — BOUTIQUE HOTEL €€

Map p270 (☎01-612 7900; www.thedawson.ie; 35 Dawson St; r from €160; @📶; 🚌all city centre, 🚊St Stephen's Green) A boutique hotel with a range of elegant rooms designed in a variety of styles, from classical French to more exotic Moroccan. Crisp white sheets throughout and luxe amenities in the bathrooms. There's also a fancy spa and the trendy Sam's Bar (p81) below.

BROOKS HOTEL — HOTEL €€

Map p270 (☎01-670 4000; www.brookshotel.ie; 59-62 Drury St; r from €210; P❄@📶; 🚌all cross-city, 🚊St Stephen's Green) A small, plush hotel just west of Grafton St that emphasises friendly, top-notch service. The bedrooms have a subtle elegance, but the clinchers are the king- and superking-sized beds, the pillow menu, and the portable smartphone that includes unlimited internet usage and local calls.

BUSWELL'S HOTEL — HOTEL €€

Map p270 (☎01-614 6500; www.buswells.ie; 23-27 Molesworth St; s/d from €165/180; P❄@; 🚌all cross-city, 🚊St Stephen's Green) This Dublin institution, open since 1882, has a long association with politicians, who wander across the road from Dáil Éireann (Irish Assembly) to wet their beaks at the hotel bar. The 69 bedrooms have all been given the once-over, but have kept their Georgian charm intact.

IVEAGH GARDEN HOTEL — HOTEL €€

Map p274 (☎01-568 5500; www.iveaghgardenhotel.ie; r from €180; 🚊Harcourt) Instagrammers flock to this ever-so-stylish hotel on Harcourt St, with its art deco couches and geometric light fittings. Rooms vary from snug City Pods to lofty suites, some of which overlook the beautiful Iveagh Gardens.

TRINITY LODGE — GUESTHOUSE €€

Map p270 (☎01-617 0900; www.trinitylodge.com; 12 S Frederick St; r from €180; 📶; 🚌all city centre, 🚊St Stephen's Green) Martin Sheen's grin greets you upon entering this award-winning guesthouse, which he declared his favourite spot for an Irish stay. Marty's not the only one: this place is so popular it's added a second townhouse across the road, which has also been kitted out to the highest standards. Room 2 of the original house has a lovely bay window.

Discounted parking (€17.50) is available in an adjacent covered car park.

HARRINGTON HALL — GUESTHOUSE €€

Map p274 (☎01-475 3497; www.harringtonhall.com; 69-70 Harcourt St; r from €180; @📶; 🚊Harcourt) Want to fluff up the pillows in the home of a former Lord Mayor of Dublin? The traditional Georgian style of Timothy Charles Harrington's home – he wore the gold chain from 1901 to 1903 – has thankfully been retained and this smart guesthouse stands out for its understated elegance. The 1st- and 2nd-floor rooms have their original fireplaces and ornamental ceilings.

GREEN — HOTEL €€

Map p274 (☎01-607 3600; www.thegreenhotel.ie; 1-5 Harcourt St; r from €180; P@📶; 🚌all cross-city, 🚊St Stephen's Green) Fresh out of a big refurb (and rebrand), the former O'Callaghan hotel is now a much cooler spot simply known as the Green. With an ultra-slick new bar area, stylish rooms and a great location right on St Stephen's Green, it makes for a great base in the city.

★WESTBURY HOTEL HOTEL €€€

Map p270 (☎01-679 1122; www.doylecollection.com; Grafton St; r/ste from €430/580; P@; all city centre, St Stephen's Green) Tucked away just off Grafton St is one of the most elegant hotels in town. The upstairs lobby is a great spot for afternoon tea or a drink, and the two restaurants on-site – Balfes and Wilde – are both exceptional.

★CLIFF TOWNHOUSE BOUTIQUE HOTEL €€€

Map p270 (☎01-638 3939; www.theclifftownhouse.com; 22 St Stephen's Green N; r from €220; @; all city centre, St Stephen's Green) As pieds-à-terre go, this is a doozy: there are 10 exquisitely appointed bedrooms spread across a wonderful Georgian property whose best views overlook St Stephen's Green. Downstairs is Sean Smith's superb restaurant Cliff Townhouse (p77).

FITZWILLIAM HOTEL HOTEL €€€

Map p270 (☎01-478 7000; www.fitzwilliamhoteldublin.com; St Stephen's Green W; r from €350; P❄@; all cross-city, Stephen's Green) You couldn't pick a more prestigious spot on the Dublin Monopoly board than this minimalist Terence Conrad–designed number overlooking the Green. Ask for a corner room on the 5th floor (502 or 508), with balmy balcony and a view. The mezzanine-level Citron restaurant serves modern Irish cuisine. It's contemporary elegance at its very best.

WESTIN DUBLIN HOTEL €€€

Map p270 (☎01-645 1000; www.thewestindublin.com; Westmoreland St; r from €350; P@; all city centre) Once a fancy bank branch, now a fancier hotel: rooms are decorated in elegant mahogany and soft colours that are reminiscent of the USA's finest. You will sleep on 10 layers of the Westin's own trademark Heavenly Bed, which is damn comfortable indeed. The old bank vault is now the basement bar.

Merrion Square & Around

It's the most sought-after real estate in town, so it's hardly surprising that it's home to the lion's share of the city's top hotels. But although you'll pay for the privilege of bedding down in luxury, there are some excellent deals available at many of these well-located properties, which are within a gentle stroll of the best restaurants, bars and attractions the city has to offer.

★NUMBER 31 GUESTHOUSE €€

Map p276 (☎01-676 5011; www.number31.ie; 31 Leeson Close; r from €220; P; all city centre) The city's most distinctive property is the former home of modernist architect Sam Stephenson, who successfully fused 1960s style with 18th-century grace. Its 21 bedrooms are split between the retro coach house, with its modern rooms, and the more elegant Georgian house, where rooms are individually furnished with tasteful French antiques and big, comfortable beds.

Gourmet breakfasts with kippers, homemade breads and granola are served in the conservatory.

ALEX HOTEL €€

Map p276 (☎01-607 3700; www.thealexhotel.ie; 41-47 Fenian St; r from €229; @; Pearse) The first of the O'Callaghan Collection to get a rebrand in 2018, the Alex is a beautifully sleek hotel where gorgeous design meets decadent comfort. Think herringbone blankets on the bed, plump velvet cushions and retro rotary telephones. There's a cool coworking area in the lobby, along with excellent Cloud Picker coffee in the cafe.

WILDER TOWNHOUSE HOTEL €€

Map p276 (☎01-969 6598; www.thewilder.ie; 22 Adelaide Rd; r from €180; P@; Harcourt) Set in a striking red-brick building, the Wilder has a delightfully quirky vibe, with cute little ornaments and tailor's mannequins in the rooms, which vary wildly in size. The bar is deliciously atmospheric, and you couldn't ask for a more peaceful location.

DAVENPORT HOTEL €€

Map p276 (☎01-607 3500; www.davenporthotel.ie; Merrion Sq N; r from €240; P@; all city centre) Recently renovated, The Davenport is housed within the old Merrion Hall, a striking building built in 1863 for the Plymouth Brethren. The new rooms are a modern version of Art Deco, with padded headboards and woollen throws on the beds. The best museums in the city are just a few minutes away on foot, as is Merrion Square.

★CONRAD DUBLIN HOTEL €€€

Map p276 (☎01-602 8900; www.conradhotels.com; Earlsfort Tce; r from €350; P@; all city centre) A €13 million refit has transformed this standard business hotel into an exceptional five-star property. The style is contemporary chic – marble bathrooms, wonderfully comfortable beds and a clutter-free aesthetic that doesn't skimp on mod cons (bedside docking stations for iPhones, USB sockets and HD flat-screen TVs) – and it works. The Coburg Brasserie (p101) is exceptional.

★MERRION HOTEL €€€

Map p276 (☎01-603 0600; www.merrionhotel.com; Upper Merrion St; r/ste from €410/900; P@ᯤ≋; 🚌all city centre) This resplendent five-star hotel, in a terrace of beautifully restored Georgian townhouses, opened in 1988 but looks like it's been around a lot longer. Try to get a room in the old house (with the largest private art collection in the city), rather than the newer wing, to sample its truly elegant comforts.

Located opposite Government Buildings, its marble corridors are patronised by politicos, visiting dignitaries and the odd celeb. Even if you don't stay, book a table for the superb Art Afternoon Tea (€55 per person), with endless cups of tea served out of silver pots by a raging fire.

★SHELBOURNE HOTEL €€€

Map p276 (☎01-676 6471; www.theshelbourne.ie; 27 St Stephen's Green N; r from €385; P@ᯤ≋; 🚌all city centre, 🚊St Stephen's Green) Dublin's most famous hotel was founded in 1824 and has been the preferred halting post of the powerful and wealthy ever since. Several owners and refurbs later it is now part of Marriott's Renaissance portfolio, and while it has a couple of rivals in the luxury stakes, it cannot be beaten for heritage.

Guests are staying in a slice of history: it was here that the Irish Constitution was drafted in 1921, and this is the hotel in Elizabeth Bowen's eponymous novel. Afternoon tea in the refurbished Lord Mayor's Lounge remains one of the best experiences in town.

MERRION MEWS GUESTHOUSE €€€

Map p276 (Irish Landmark Trust; www.irishlandmark.com; Fitzwilliam Lane; 2 nights from €860; Pᯤ; 🚌7, 46A from city centre) This carefully restored Georgian mews dating from 1792 is managed by the Irish Landmark Trust. There are three beautifully appointed double bedrooms that sleep six, a living area and a fully equipped kitchen above a stables – which is still used by the mounted unit of the police. Outside is a garden, one of the few left in the area.

Bookings are for a minimum of two nights and as it's a period home – with thick walls – the wi-fi can be a bit sketchy.

Temple Bar

If you're here for a weekend of wild abandon and can't fathom anything more than a quick stumble into bed, then Temple Bar's choice of hotels and hostels will suit you perfectly. Generally speaking the rooms are small, the prices are large and you must be able to handle the late-night symphonies of diehard revellers.

ASHFIELD HOUSE HOSTEL €

Map p268, H3 (☎01-679 7734; www.ashfieldhostel.com; 19-20 D'Olier St; dm/d from €19/90; @ᯤ; 🚌all city centre) A stone's throw from Temple Bar and O'Connell Bridge, this modern hostel in a converted church has a selection of tidy four- and six-bed rooms, one large dorm and 25 rooms, all with a private bathroom. A generous continental-style breakfast is included.

BARNACLES HOSTEL €

Map p268, E4 (☎01-671 6277; www.barnacles.ie; 19 Temple Lane S; dm/d from €15/120; Pᯤ; 🚌all city centre) If you're here for a good time, not a long time, then this bustling Temple Bar hostel is the ideal spot to meet fellow revellers and tap up the helpful and knowledgable staff for the best places to cause mischief. Rooms are quieter at the back.

GOGARTY'S TEMPLE BAR HOSTEL HOSTEL €

Map p268, F3 (☎01-671 1822; www.gogartys.ie; 58-59 Fleet St; dm/d €18/120; Pᯤ; 🚌all city centre) Sleeping isn't really the activity of choice for anyone staying in this compact, decent hostel in the middle of Temple Bar, next to the pub of the same name (p115). It tends to get booked up with stag and hen parties so, depending on your mood, bring either your earplugs or your bunny ears. Six self-catering apartments are also available.

KINLAY HOUSE HOSTEL €

Map p268, B5 (☎01-679 6644; www.kinlaydublin.ie; 2-12 Lord Edward St; dm/tw from €25/60; ᯤ; 🚌all city centre) This former boarding house for boys has massive, mixed dormitories (for up to 24), and smaller rooms, including doubles. It's on the edge of Temple Bar, so it's occasionally raucous. Staff are friendly, and there are cooking facilities and a cafe. Breakfast is included.

CLARENCE HOTEL HOTEL €€
Map p268, C4 (01-407 0800; www.theclarence.ie; 6-8 Wellington Quay; r/ste from €200/350; P @ ; all city centre) Once owned by Bono and the Edge, this handsome hotel was the hottest bed in town, but now it's just another elegant Dublin four-star designed to reflect the aesthetic of a 1930s gentlemen's club, complete with Shaker oak beds draped in Irish linen, an excellent bar and a fine restaurant.

DUBLIN CITI HOTEL HOTEL €€
Map p268, E4 (01-6794455; www.dublincitihotel.com; 46-49 Dame St; r from €195; @ ; all city centre) An unusual turreted 19th-century building right next to the Central Bank is home to this midrange hotel. Rooms aren't huge, are simply furnished and have fresh white quilts. It's only a stagger (literally) from the heart of Temple Bar, hic.

★**MORGAN HOTEL** BOUTIQUE HOTEL €€€
Map p268, F3 (01-643 7000; www.themorgan.com; 10 Fleet St; r from €280; @ ; all city centre) Fresh out of a €15 million redesign in 2018, the Morgan is one of the sleekest hotels in town. The rooms are contemporary and calming, with a pale grey decor and slick marble bathrooms. The restaurant, 10 Fleet Street, is exceptional, as are the cocktails whizzed up with smoke and pizazz.

Kilmainham & the Liberties

Accommodation was traditionally thin on the ground in this part of the city, but with two new hotels launched in 2018 and 2019 and another couple on the way, that's all set to change. And a good thing too, as this is one of Dublin's hottest neighbourhoods.

★**ALOFT DUBLIN CITY** HOTEL €€
Map p278 (01-963 1800; www.alofthotels.com; 1 Mill St; r from €180; P ; 49, 54A from city centre) 'This must be the place' is emblazoned in bright neon across the wall of the 7th-floor breakfast room, and you'd be hard pushed to disagree. Modern rooms adorned with cool local artwork; huge, floor-to-ceiling windows; and – back up on the 7th floor, where you'll also find the reception – a swish rooftop bar with fab views over the city.

MALDRON KEVIN STREET HOTEL €€
Map p278(01-906 8900; www.maldronhotelkevinstreet.com; Upper Kevin St; r from €200; ; 49, 54A from city centre) Handy for all the sights you'll find within the Liberties – St Patrick's Cathedral, the Teeling Distillery

HOME AWAY FROM HOME

Self-catering apartments are a good option for visitors staying a few days, for groups of friends, or for families with kids. There are literally hundreds of short-term letting options in Dublin, the overwhelming majority of them listed on Airbnb. From beds squeezed into what was once a broom closet to deluxe, duplex apartments with views, there's plenty of choice to be had.

Alternatively, there are smaller companies in town with a stock of self-catering apartments, ranging from one-room studios to two-bedroom flats with lounge areas, bathrooms and kitchenettes. A decent two-bedroom apartment will cost from €150 a night, with most topping €200 in anything but the low season. Good, central places include the following:

Premier Suites (Map p276; 01-638 1111; www.premiersuitesdublinleesonstreet.com; 14-17 Lower Leeson St; ste from €190; P @; all city centre) Contemporary deluxe studios and suites.

Latchfords (Map p276; 01-676 0784; www.latchfords.ie; 99-100 Lower Baggot St; studio/2-bedroom apt from €180/210; all city centre) An elegant Georgian townhouse with studio and two-bedroom apartments.

Oliver St John Gogarty's Penthouse Apartments (Map p268; 01-671 1822; www.gogartys.ie; 18-21 Anglesea St; 2-bed apt from €99; all city centre) Self-catering accommodation above the pub of the same name.

and, of course, the Guinness Storehouse – the latest outpost from the Maldron group is modern and clean, if a little soulless. Still, it makes for a handy base, and you can often score great rates at the last minute.

North of the Liffey

There is a scattering of decent midrange options between O'Connell St and Smithfield, with a fair number of hostels in the mix. Gardiner St, to the east of O'Connell St, was the traditional B&B district of town, but with only a few exceptions it has been rendered largely obsolete by chain hotels throughout the city.

★ISAACS HOSTEL HOSTEL €

Map p280 (☎01-855 6215; www.isaacs.ie; 2-5 Frenchman's Lane; dm/tw from €22/99; @ wi-fi; bus all city centre, tram Connolly) The Northside's best hostel – actually for atmosphere alone it's the best in town – is in a 200-year-old wine vault just around the corner from the main bus station. With summer barbecues, live music in the lounge, internet access, colourful dorms and even a sauna, this terrific place generates consistently good reviews from backpackers and other travellers.

★GENERATOR HOSTEL HOSTEL €

Map p280 (☎01-901 0222; www.staygenerator.com; Smithfield Sq; dm/tw from €18/150; @ wi-fi; tram Smithfield) This European chain brings its own brand of funky, fun design to Dublin's hostel scene, with bright colours, comfortable dorms (including women-only) and a lively social scene. It even has a screening room for movies. Good location right on Smithfield Sq, next to the Jameson Distillery Bow Street (p149).

JACOB'S INN HOSTEL €

Map p280 (☎01-855 5660; www.jacobsinn.com; 21-28 Talbot Pl; dm/d from €26/139; wi-fi; bus all city centre, train Connolly) Sister hostel to Isaacs around the corner, this clean and modern hostel offers spacious accommodation with private bathrooms and outstanding facilities, including its brand-new Pod Beds, which come with a privacy curtain, and USB and plug sockets.

MEC HOSTEL HOSTEL €

Map p280 (☎01-873 0826; www.mechostel.com; 42 N Great George's St; dm/ste from €17/125; wi-fi; bus 36, 36A from city centre) A Georgian classic on one of Dublin's most beautiful streets, this popular hostel has a host of dorms and apartment-style suites, all with private bathroom. Facilities include a full kitchen, two lounges and a bureau de change. Breakfast is free and there's decent wi-fi throughout.

CLIFDEN GUESTHOUSE GUESTHOUSE €

Map p280 (☎01-874 6364; www.clifdenhouse.com; 32 Gardiner Pl; r from €100; P wi-fi; bus 36, 36A from city centre) The Clifden is a very nicely refurbished Georgian house with 14 tastefully decorated rooms. They all come with bathroom, and are immaculately clean and extremely comfortable. It offers exceptional online deals.

ABBEY COURT HOSTEL HOSTEL €

Map p280 (☎01-878 0700; www.abbey-court.com; 29 Bachelor's Walk; dm/d from €13/90; wi-fi; bus all city centre) Spread over two buildings, this large, well-run hostel has 33 clean dorm beds and good storage. Its excellent facilities include a dining hall, a conservatory and a barbecue area. Doubles with bathrooms are in the newer building where a light breakfast is provided in the adjacent cafe. Not surprisingly, this is a popular spot; reservations are advised.

ADDRESS AT DUBLIN 1 HOTEL €€

Off Map p280 (☎01-704 0770; www.theaddressatdublin1.ie; Amiens St; r from €200; @ wi-fi; tram Connolly, train Connolly) Ostensibly part of the old North Star Hotel, the Address has surprisingly stylish and plush bedrooms, some of which overlook the passing trains gliding into Connolly Station — so give the commuters a little wave as they pass. The tiny rooftop lounge is an added bonus.

RIU PLAZA GRESHAM HOTEL HOTEL €€

Map p280 (☎01-874 6881; www.gresham-hotels.com; 23 Upper O'Connell St; r from €200; P air-con @ wi-fi; bus all city centre) The landmark Gresham has been hosting guests since 1817, and the fabulous open-plan foyer is one of the city's most impressive hotel lobbies. Its 323 rooms and 10 suites are spacious and well serviced.

MALDRON HOTEL SMITHFIELD HOTEL €€

Map p280 (☎01-485 0900; www.maldronhotels.com; Smithfield Village; r €189; wi-fi; bus 25, 25A, 25B, 66, 66A, 66B, 67, 90, 151 to Upper Ormond Quay, tram Smithfield) With big bedrooms and plenty of earth tones to soften the contemporary edges, this functionally modern hotel is your best bet in this part of town. We love the floor-to-ceiling windows: great for checking out what's going on below in the square.

JURY'S INN PARNELL ST HOTEL €€

Map p280 (01-878 4900; www.jurysinns.com; Moore St Plaza, Parnell St; r from €180; 36, 36A from city centre) Jury's hotels are nothing if not reliable, and this edition of Ireland's most popular hotel chain is no exception. What do you care that the furnishings were mass-produced and flat-packed and that the decor was created to be utterly inoffensive to everything save good taste? The location – just off Upper O'Connell St – is terrific.

ACADEMY PLAZA HOTEL HOTEL €€

Map p280 (01-878 0666; www.academyplazahotel.ie; Findlater Pl; r from €160; all city centre) Only a few steps from O'Connell St, this solidly three-star hotel offers a comfortable, if unmemorable, night's sleep. The deluxe suites come with free wi-fi and flat-screen digital TV.

CASTLE HOTEL HOTEL €€

Map p280 (01-874 6949; www.castle-hotel.ie; 3-4 Great Denmark St; r from €180; all city centre, Connolly) In business since 1809, the Castle Hotel may be slightly rough around the edges but it's one of the most pleasant hotels this side of the Liffey. The fabulous palazzo-style grand staircase leads to 50-odd bedrooms, whose furnishings are traditional and a tad antiquated, but perfectly good throughout – check out the original Georgian cornicing around the high ceilings.

MORRISON HOTEL HOTEL €€€

Map p280 (01-887 2400; www.morrisonhotel.ie; Lower Ormond Quay; r €350; all city centre, Jervis) Space-age funky design is the template at this hip hotel, part of the Hilton Doubletree group. King-sized beds (with fancy mattresses), 40in LCD TVs, free wi-fi and deluxe toiletries are just some of the hotel's offerings. Probably the Northside's most luxurious address.

Docklands

Staying in the Docklands area means you'll be relying on public transport or taxis to get you in and out of the city centre.

GIBSON HOTEL HOTEL €€

Map p284 (01-618 5000; www.thegibsonhotel.ie; Point Village; r from €225; 151 from city centre, The Point) Built for business travellers and out-of-towners taking in a gig at the 3 Arena (p169) next door, the Gibson is impressive: 250-odd ultramodern rooms decked out in deluxe beds, flat-screen TVs and internet work stations. You might catch last night's star act having breakfast the next morning in the snazzy restaurant area.

SPENCER HOTEL HOTEL €€

Map p284 (01-433 8800; www.thespencerhotel.com; Custom House Quay; r/ste from €240/330; George's Dock) This swanky business hotel in the heart of the Irish Financial Services Centre (IFSC) has beautiful rooms decorated with contemporary light oak furnishings, designer beds and rainforest power showers. Guests have free use of the health club. Weekend rates are substantially cheaper.

TRINITY CITY HOTEL HOTEL €€

Map p284 (01-648 1000; www.trinitycityhotel.com; Pearse St; r from €220; Trinity) While the bedrooms have a slight corporate feel, the public spaces in Trinity City really shine, particularly the Brunswick Terrace and courtyard garden, where you can enjoy a drink alfresco (which is something of a rarity in Dublin).

CLAYTON HOTEL CARDIFF LANE HOTEL €€

Map p284 (01-643 9500; www.claytonhotelcardifflane.com; Cardiff Lane; r from €230; Grand Canal Dock) A good midrange hotel with excellent amenities (two restaurants, a bar and a fitness centre), this hotel suffers only because of its location, on an isolated street far from the city-centre action. Its saving graces are the nearby Grand Canal Dock, its selection of bars and restaurants, and its swimming pool.

★MARKER HOTEL €€€

Map p284 (01-687 5100; www.themarkerhoteldublin.com; Grand Canal Sq; r/ste from €350/520; Grand Canal Dock) Behind the eye-catching chequerboard facade created by Manuel Aires Mateus are 187 swanky rooms and suites decked out in a wintry palette (washed-out citruses and cobalts) and starkly elegant furnishings, which give them an atmosphere of cool sophistication. The public areas are a little wilder and the rooftop bar is a summer favourite with the 'in' crowd.

Southside

Some of the city's most elegant B&Bs are scattered about these leafy suburbs, including a handful that can rival even the best hotels in town for comfort and service.

★ARIEL HOUSE INN €

Map p286 (01-668 5512; www.ariel-house.net; 52 Lansdowne Rd; r from €130; P; 4, 7, 8, 84 from city centre) Our favourite lodging in Ballsbridge is this wonderful Victorian-era property that is somewhere between a boutique hotel and a luxury B&B. Its 28 rooms are all individually decorated with period furniture, which lends the place an air of genuine luxury. A far better choice than most hotels.

★DEVLIN BOUTIQUE HOTEL €€

Map p286 (01-406 6550; www.thedevlin.ie; 117-119 Ranelagh Rd; r from €150; P@; 4, 15, 15A, 15B, 65, 83, 140 from city centre, Beechwood) Following the lead of its hip sister hotel the Dean (p201), this Ranelagh outpost is an artsy spot in one of Dublin's fanciest boroughs. Though definitely on the small side, the rooms (or ModPods) are well designed, with navy-coloured walls, local artwork and a stash of Irish treats – there are Dyson hairdryers in the rooms and a cinema in the basement.

SCHOOLHOUSE HOTEL BOUTIQUE HOTEL €€

Map p286 (01-667 5014; www.schoolhousehotel.com; 2-8 Northumberland Rd; r from €180; P; 5, 7, 7A, 8, 18, 27X, 44 from city centre) A Victorian schoolhouse dating from 1861, this beautiful building has been successfully converted into an exquisite boutique hotel that is (ahem) ahead of its class. Its 31 cosy bedrooms, named after famous Irish people, all have king-sized beds, big white quilts and loudly patterned headboards. The Canteen bar and patio bustles with local businessfolk in summer.

PEMBROKE TOWNHOUSE INN €€

Map p286 (01-660 0277; www.pembroketownhouse.ie; 90 Pembroke Rd; r from €150; P; 5, 7, 7A, 8, 18, 45 from city centre) This elegant boutique hotel in a handsome Georgian townhouse underwent a much-needed makeover in 2019, making it once again one of the most stylish guesthouses in the city. It's supremely comfortable and its location – on a leafy street near the bustling Baggot St – is excellent.

WATERLOO HOUSE INN €€

Map p286 (01-660 1888; www.waterloohouse.ie; 8-10 Waterloo Rd; s/d from €170/200; P; 5, 7, 7A, 8, 18, 45 from city centre) Within walking distance of St Stephen's Green, this lovely guesthouse is spread over two ivy-clad Georgian houses off Baggot St. Rooms are tastefully decorated with high-quality furnishings in authentic Farrow & Ball Georgian colours. Home-cooked breakfast is served in the conservatory, or in the garden on sunny days.

HERBERT PARK HOTEL HOTEL €€

Map p286 (01-667 2200; www.herbertparkhotel.ie; Merrion Rd; r from €160; 5, 7, 7A, 8, 18, 45 from Trinity College) This hotel features a bright, modernist foyer that opens onto two busy bars, and spacious comfortable rooms, designed with chichi New York in mind, with huge windows and balconies overlooking gorgeous 19-hectare Herbert Park. Rooms also come with Nespresso machines. The Royal Dublin Society Showground (p175) is 100m away.

DYLAN HOTEL €€€

Map p286 (01-660 3000; www.dylan.ie; Eastmoreland Pl; r from €270; @; 5, 7, 7A, 8, 18, 27X, 44 from city centre) The Dylan's baroque-meets-Scandinavian-sleek designer look makes for a wonderfully quirky hotel, and a €10 million renovation in 2017 saw the addition of 28 new bedrooms. Downstairs, you'll find a buzzy bar and terrace where the beautiful people gather in force.

INTERCONTINENTAL DUBLIN HOTEL €€€

Map p286 (01-665-4000; www.intercontinentaldublin.ie; Simmonscourt Rd; r from €280; P@; Sandymount) Formerly the Four Seasons, this seriously plush hotel makes for a decadent getaway. But it's got a fair amount of character, too — as well as a killer spa and a cocktail bar that lures plenty of visiting celebrities. It's just a short tram ride from town.

Understand Dublin

DUBLIN TODAY 210

Dublin is growing, thriving and preparing to catch the Brexit wave.

HISTORY 212

Over 1000 years of ups and downs make for a most eventful story.

LITERARY DUBLIN 224

A Unesco World City of Literature, Dublin's literary credentials are being renewed by a new generation of talent.

MUSICAL DUBLIN 230

All manner of music – from folk to electronica – drawing at the bottomless well of musical genius.

ARCHITECTURE 233

A hodgepodge of styles, but the longest shadow is cast by the city's extraordinary wealth of Georgian architecture.

THE IRISH WAY OF LIFE 238

They might be easy-going, but the Irish are not that easy to figure out!

Dublin Today

Dublin is very much a city on the rise. The skyline is dotted with cranes, just one of the more visible signs of the renewal that's continued apace over the last several years. New hotels are opening along with so many new cafes and restaurants that it's almost impossible to keep count, while the city's infrastructure is once again being improved after nearly a decade of stagnation. But with greater prosperity comes deep challenges, including a rising cost of living and a major homelessness crisis.

Best on Film

Sing Street (2016) John Carney's delightful coming-of-age musical set in 1980s Dublin is about a boy's efforts to start a band to impress a girl.

What Richard Did (2012) The story of what happens when a privileged youth assaults a romantic rival who dies of his injuries; loosely based on real events that occurred in 2000.

The Dead (1987) Stunning rendition of James Joyce's story from *Dubliners*, starring Donal McCann and Anjelica Huston.

Best in Print

Dubliners (James Joyce; 1914) Fifteen poignant and powerful tales of Dubliners and the moments that define their lives. Even if you never visit, read this book.

Conversations with Friends (Sally Rooney; 2017) A wonderfully forensic examination of relationships in post-crash Dublin.

The Barrytown Trilogy (Roddy Doyle) *The Commitments* (1987), *The Snapper* (1990) and *The Van* (1991) – yes, they've all been made into films, but the books are still better.

Rooms Available

The year 2018 was a bumper one for tourism, with a record number of visitors to the city. To meet growing demand, dozens of new hotels are being added to the existing stock: 15 hotel developments have already been approved by the city council, with another 20 awaiting the thumbs up and a further 11 going through the tender process. Tourism chiefs say that the new hotels will mean 5000 extra jobs and €250 million more in tourist revenue.

More hotels won't necessarily mean lower prices, however, as the government has raised value-added tax (VAT) on the hospitality industry back to 13.5% – up from the 9% lifeline thrown in 2011 to help the sector weather the effects of the global financial crisis. Many hoteliers and restaurateurs have responded negatively, arguing that the rise puts pressure on operators' margins already stretched by rising wage and rent costs.

What is almost certain is that the VAT hike will be passed on to the consumer. Many cafes and restaurants have already raised their prices, while hotel owners will be forced to mitigate what is effectively a 50% increase in their VAT bill by bumping up their room rates even more than the standard rise from year-on-year inflation.

Short-Term Letting Restrictions

The construction of new hotels coincides with a raft of new regulations governing short-term lets, including a prohibition on homeowners letting a second property in the city centre on a short-term basis, as well as an annual cap of 90 days for all short-term lets. The proliferation of short-term lets has been a major issue in Dublin, and is seen as a contributor to the serious housing shortage crisis arising from landlords being tempted by the substantial profits of short-term letting over the more regulated income they would earn from longer-term leasing to those living in the city.

Short-term letting specialists like Airbnb argue that the new rules are unenforceable and impossible to police, with some suggesting that in practice the rules will merely appear to be a solution but will do little to alleviate the problem.

Visible Homelessness

As Dublin booms, the problem of homelessness is getting more acute. In the winter of 2018 there were 156 rough sleepers in the city centre, the most visible element of a crisis where the overall number of homeless has risen by 268% since 2015 – 82 families lost their homes in March 2019 alone.

Most homeless charities agree that the problem is caused by structural factors such as a lack of affordable housing, unemployment, poverty and inadequate mental health services, as well as personal factors including addiction, family breakdown and mental health.

The issue has galvanised public opinion and has become something of a cause célèbre, with several well-known names involved, not least Oscar-winning musician Glen Hansard. He has lent his name and time to several activist-led protests against homelessness, and every Christmas Eve leads a charity busk at the top of Grafton St. This impromptu street concert has become a big deal, attracting large crowds and with a few famous names joining in, including Hozier, Damien Rice and Bono.

The Shadow of Brexit

Whatever government plans to shore up the tourism sector, sort out the economy and fix social ills may yet be undone by Brexit, the spectre of which continues to loom over Ireland. As Britain stumbles over exactly what to do, Ireland waits. And worries.

Dublin is desperate to make the best out of a bad situation (Brexit will inevitably be bad for Ireland, as Britain is one of its key trading partners), and as London's financial star is dimmed in the face of Brexit, the Irish capital is keen to offer itself as a viable alternative to London for firms looking to keep a foothold in the EU. Dublin has plenty of competition, however, with Luxembourg and a handful of cities in Germany attempting to slice off some of London's financial-sector pie.

Dublin's case is a strong one, not least because of an attractive corporate tax rate that has seen some of the world's biggest tech names set up here, including Facebook, Google, Twitter and LinkedIn. The city's English-speaking, highly educated workforce is another plus. A number of British firms have already made the move, including Somerset Capital, a London-based hedge fund who set up a Dublin office in 2018 and whose major shareholder is leading Brexiteer Jacob Rees-Mogg.

if Dublin were 100 people

85 would be Irish
5 would be from the EU
3 would be Asian
3 would be African
1 would be British
3 would be other

age of Dubliners

(% of population)

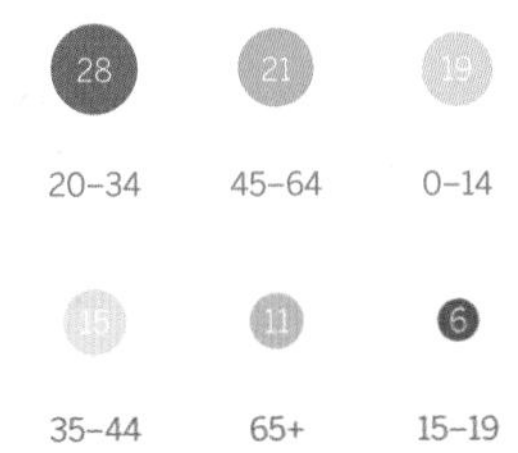

population per sq km

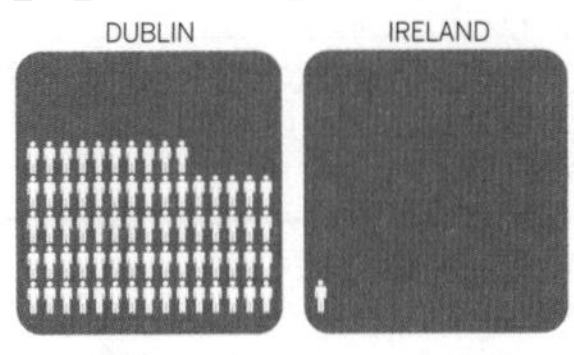

History

Until a couple of decades ago, if you'd asked your average Dubliner the key to the city's complex history, they'd most likely give you a version of the past punctuated with '800 years'. This refers to the duration of the English (then British) occupation, the sine qua non of everything that happened to this city. Yet within that narrative is a rich and storied tale of invasion, rebellion and transformation, as Dublin works its way through the various epochs, from Viking to Georgian and beyond.

Early Footprints & Celtic Highways

Stone Age farmers who arrived in Ireland between 10,000 and 8000 BC provided the country's genetic stock and lay the foundations of its agricultural economy. During the following Bronze Age, in addition to discovering and crafting metals to stock the future National Museum, they also found time to refine their farming techniques and raise livestock.

Iron Age warriors from Eastern Europe, who were known as the Celts, arrived in the country around 500 BC and divided Ireland into provinces and numerous districts ruled by chieftains. Roads connecting these provinces converged at a ford over the River Liffey called Átha Cliath (Ford of the Hurdles) – which Ptolemy wrote about in AD 140 as Eblana Civitas – and the town that grew up at this junction during the 9th century was to give Dublin its Irish name, Baile Átha Cliath (Town of the Hurdle Ford).

The Coming of Christianity

Celtic society was ruled by Brehon Law, the tenets of which still form the basis of Ireland's ethical code today.

St Patrick founded the See of Dublin sometime in the mid-5th century and went about the business of conversion in present-day Wicklow and Malahide, before laying hands on Leoghaire, the King of Ireland, using water from a well next to St Patrick's Cathedral. Or so the story goes. Irrespective of the details, Patrick and his monk buddies were successful because they managed to fuse the strong tradition of druidism and pagan ritual with the new Christian teaching, which created an exciting hybrid known as Celtic, or Insular, Christianity.

TIMELINE

10,000 BC

Human beings arrive in Ireland during the mesolithic era, originally crossing a land bridge between Scotland and Ireland and later the sea in hide-covered boats.

500 BC

Iron Age warriors from Eastern Europe, known as the Celts, divide Ireland into provinces and myriad districts ruled by chieftains.

AD 431–432

Pope Celestine I sends Bishop Palladius to Ireland to minister to those who were already believers; St Patrick arrives the following year to continue the mission.

Compared to new hotspots like Clonmacnoise in County Offaly and Glendalough in County Wicklow, Dublin was a rural backwater and didn't really figure in the Golden Age, when Irish Christian scholars excelled in the study of Latin and Greek learning and Christian theology. They studied in the monasteries that were, in essence, Europe's most important universities, producing brilliant students, magnificent illuminated books such as the *Book of Kells* (now housed in Trinity College), ornate jewellery and the many carved stone crosses that dot the island 'of saints and scholars'.

The nature of Christianity in Ireland was one of marked independence from Rome, especially in the areas of monastic rule and penitential practice, which emphasised private confession to a priest followed by penances levied by the priest in reparation – which is the spirit and letter of the practice of confession that exists to this day.

St Patrick showed a remarkable understanding of Celtic power structures by working to convert chieftains rather than ordinary Celts, who inevitably followed their leaders into adopting the new religion.

The Vikings

Raids by marauding Vikings had been a fact of Irish life for quite some time, before a group of them decided to take a break from their hell-raising to build a harbour (*longphort,* in Irish) on the banks of the Liffey in 837. Although a Celtic army forced them out some 65 years later, they returned in 917 with a massive fleet, established a stronghold by the black pool at Wood Quay, just behind Christ Church Cathedral, and dug their heels in. They went back to plundering the countryside but also laid down guidelines on plot sizes and town boundaries for their town of Dyfflin (derived from the Irish for 'black pool', *dubh linn),* which became the most prominent trading centre in the Viking world.

But their good times came to an end in 1014 when an alliance of Irish clans led by Brian Ború decisively whipped them (and the Irish clans that *didn't* side with Brian Ború) at the Battle of Clontarf, forever breaking the Scandinavian grip on the eastern seaboard. However, rather than abandoning the place in defeat, the Vikings enjoyed Dublin so much that they decided to stay and integrate.

During the 12th century Dublin became a pilgrimage city, in part because it housed the Bacall Íosa (staff of Jesus), St Patrick's legendary crozier.

Strongbow & the Normans

The next wave of invaders came in 1169, when an army of Cambro-Norman knights led by Richard de Clare (better known as Strongbow) landed in Wexford at the urging of Dermot MacMurrough, ousted King of Leinster, who needed help to regain his throne. As a gesture of thanks, MacMurrough made Strongbow his heir and gave him Aoife, his daughter, as a wife. Strongbow and his knights then took Dublin in 1170 and decided to make it their new capital.

917

Plundering Vikings establish a new settlement at the mouth of the harbour and call it 'Dyfflin', which soon becomes a centre of economic power.

988

High King Mael Seachlainn II leads the permanent Irish conquest of Dyfflin, giving the settlement its modern name in Irish – Baile Átha Cliath, meaning 'Town of the Hurdle Ford'.

1170

Strongbow captures Dublin and then takes Aoife, daughter of the High King Dermot MacMurroughs, as his wife before being crowned King of Leinster.

1172

King Henry II of England invades Ireland, forcing the Cambro-Norman warlords and some of the Gaelic Irish kings to accept him as their overlord.

Meanwhile, King Henry II of England, concerned that the Normans might set up a rival power base in Ireland, organised his own invading force, and landed his army in 1171 – with the blessing of Pope Adrian IV, who wanted Henry to make Ireland's renegade monks toe the Roman line.

For all their might, the Anglo-Normans' dominance was limited to a walled area surrounding what today is loosely Greater Dublin, and was then called 'the Pale'. Beyond the Pale – a phrase that entered the English language to mean 'beyond convention' – Ireland remained unbowed and unconquered.

The Normans declared their fealty to the English throne and set about reconstructing and fortifying their new capital. In 1172 construction began on Christ Church Cathedral, and 20 years later work began on St Patrick's Cathedral, a few hundred metres to the south.

Henry II's son, King John, commissioned the construction of Dublin Castle in 1204 'for the custody of our treasure...and...the defence of the city'. As capital of the English 'colony' in Ireland, Dublin expanded. Trade was organised and craft guilds developed, although membership was limited to those of English name and blood.

As Dublin grew bigger so did its problems, and over the next few centuries misery seemed to pile upon mishap. In 1317 Ireland's worst famine of the Middle Ages killed off thousands and reduced some to cannibalism. In 1348 the country was decimated by the Black Death; the devastating recurrence over the following century was an indication of the terrible squalor of medieval Dublin.

In the 15th century the English extended their influence beyond the Pale by throwing their weight behind the dominant Irish lords. The atmosphere was becoming markedly cosier as the Anglo-Norman occupiers began to follow previous invaders by integrating into Irish culture.

The Tudors & the Protestant Ascendancy

Ireland presented a particular challenge to Henry VIII (r 1509–47), in part due to the Anglo-Norman lords' more or less unfettered power over the country, which didn't sit well with Henry's belief in strong monarchical rule. He decreed absolute royal power over Ireland, but the Irish lords weren't going to take it lying down.

In 1534 the most powerful of Leinster's Anglo-Normans, 'Silken' Thomas Fitzgerald, renounced his allegiance to the king, and Henry came at him ferociously: Fitzgerald was executed and all his lands confiscated. Henry ordered the surrender of all lands to the English Crown and, three years later, after his spat with Rome, he dissolved the monasteries and all Church lands passed to the newly constituted Anglican Church. Dublin was declared an Anglican city and relics such as the Bacall Íosa (staff of Jesus) were destroyed.

Elizabeth I (r 1558–1603) came to the throne with the same uncompromising attitude to Ireland as her father. Ulster was the most hostile

1297

Dublin becomes the main seat of the Parliament of Ireland, comprised of merchants and landowners.

1315

A Scottish army led by Edward de Bruce attacks the city; waning English interest in defending Dublin forces the Earls of Kildare to become the city's main protectors.

1317

Ireland's worst famine of the Middle Ages kills off thousands and reduces some to cannibalism.

1348

Roughly half of the city's population of 30,000 succumbs to the Black Death; victims are buried in mass graves in an area of the Liberties still known as the 'Blackpitts'.

to her, with the Irish fighting doggedly under the command of Hugh O'Neill, the Earl of Tyrone, but they too were finally defeated in 1603.

O'Neill's defeat signalled the end of Gaelic Ireland and the renewed colonisation of the country through plantation. Loyal Protestants from England and Scotland were awarded the confiscated rich agricultural lands of Ulster, sowing the bitter seeds of division that blight the province to this day. Unlike previous arrivals, these new colonists kept very much apart from the native Irish, who were left disenfranchised, landless and reduced to a state of near misery.

All the while, Dublin prospered as the bulwark of English domination and became a bastion of Protestantism. A chasm developed between the 'English' city and the 'Irish' countryside, where there was continuing unrest and growing resentment. After winning the English Civil War (1641–51), Oliver Cromwell came to Ireland to personally reassert English control and, while Protestant Dublin was left untouched (save the use of St Patrick's Cathedral as a stable for English horses), his troops were uncompromising in their dealing with rebellion up and down the eastern coast.

Hugh O'Neill achieved something of a pyrrhic victory in 1603 when he refused to surrender until after he heard of Elizabeth I's death. He and his fellow earls then fled the country in what become known as the Flight of the Earls.

Georgian Dublin & the Golden Age

Following the Restoration of 1660 and the coronation of Charles II (r 1660–85), Dublin embarked upon a century of unparalleled development and essentially waved two fingers at the rest of the country, which was being brought to its knees. In 1690 most of Ireland backed the losing side when it took up arms for the Catholic King of England, James II (r 1685–88), who was ultimately defeated by the Protestant William of Orange at the Battle of the Boyne, not far from Dublin.

William's victory ushered in the punitive Penal Code, which stripped Catholics of most basic rights in a single, sweeping legislative blow. Again, however, the country's misfortune proved the capital's gain as the city was flooded with landless refugees willing to work for a pittance.

With plenty of cash to go around and an eagerness to live in a city that reflected their new-found wealth, the Protestant nobility overhauled Dublin during the reigns of the four Georges (1714–1830). Speculators bought up swathes of land and commissioned substantial projects of urban renewal, including the creation of new streets, the laying out of city parks and the construction of magnificent new buildings and residences.

It was impossible to build in the heart of the medieval city, so the nouveau riche moved north across the river, creating a new Dublin of stately squares surrounded by fine Georgian mansions. The elegantly made-over Dublin became the second city in the British Empire and the fifth largest in Europe.

The end of the 17th century saw an influx of Huguenot weavers, who settled in Dublin after fleeing anti-Protestant legislation in France and established a successful cloth industry, largely in the Liberties, that helped fuel the city's growth.

1350–1530

The Anglo-Norman barons establish power bases independent of the English Crown. English control gradually extends to an area around Dublin known as 'the Pale'.

1487

Gerard Mór Fitzgerald, Earl of Kildare, occupies Dublin with the help of troops from Burgundy, in direct defiance of King Henry VII.

1487

Fitzgerald supports claims of Yorkist pretender Lambert Simnel, a 10-year-old who is crowned King Edward VI in Christ Church Cathedral.

1537

'Silken' Thomas Fitzgerald, son of the Earl of Kildare, storms Dublin and its English garrisons. The rebellion is squashed; Thomas and his followers are executed.

Dublin's teeming, mostly Catholic, slums soon spread north in pursuit of the rich, who turned back south to grand new homes around Merrion Sq, St Stephen's Green and Fitzwilliam Sq.

In 1745 when James Fitzgerald, the Earl of Kildare, started construction of Leinster House he was mocked for his move into the wilds. 'Where I go society will follow', he confidently predicted. He was right; today Leinster House is the seat of Irish parliament and is in modern Dublin's centre.

Dublin Declines, Catholicism Rises

Constant migration from the countryside into Dublin meant that, by the end of the 18th century, the capital had a Catholic majority, most of whom lived in terrible conditions in ever-worsening slums. Inspired by the Enlightenment and the principles of the French Revolution of 1789, many leading Irish figures (nearly all of whom were Protestant) began to question the quality and legitimacy of British rule.

Rebellion was in the air by the turn of the century, starting with the abortive French invasion at the urging of Dubliner Wolfe Tone (1763–98) and his United Irishmen in 1798. The 'Year of the French' resulted in defeat for the invaders and the death of Tone, but in 1803 the United Irishmen tried again, this time under the leadership of Robert Emmet (1778–1803), which also resulted in failure and Emmet's execution on Thomas St, near the Guinness brewery.

It was only a matter of time before Dublin's bubble burst, and the pin came in the form of the 1801 Act of Union, which dissolved the Irish Parliament (originally established in 1297) and reintroduced direct rule from Westminster. Many of the upper classes fled to London, the dramatic growth that had characterised Dublin in the previous century came to an almost immediate halt, and the city fell into a steady decline.

While Dublin was licking its wounds, a Kerry lawyer called Daniel O'Connell (1775–1847) launched his campaign to recover basic rights for Catholics, achieving much with the Catholic Emancipation Act of 1829. The 'Liberator', as he came to be known, became the first Catholic lord mayor of Dublin, in 1841.

A Nation's Soup Kitchen

Rural Ireland had become overwhelmingly dependent on the easily grown potato. Blight – a disease that rots tubers – had always been an occasional hazard, but when three successive crops failed between 1845 and 1847, it spelled disaster. The human cost was cataclysmic: up to one million people died from disease and starvation, while more again fled the country for Britain and the United States. The damage was compounded by the British government's adoption of a laissez-faire economic policy, which opposed food aid for famine occurring within the Empire. In Ireland, landowners refused to countenance any forbearance on rents, all the while exporting crops to foreign markets. Defaulters – starving or not – were penalised with incarceration in workhouses or prison.

1584

Mayoress Margaret Ball dies following imprisonment for her Catholic sympathies. Archbishop Dermot O'Hurley is hanged for his support of a rebellion against the English Crown.

1592

Trinity College is founded on the grounds of a former monastery, on the basis of a charter granted by Elizabeth I to stop Ireland being 'infected with popery'.

1594–1603

The Nine Years' War between English and Irish chieftains led by Hugh O'Neill brings English troops to Dublin, who force the citizenry to house them.

1603

Hugh O'Neill and the Irish fighting under his command in Ulster are defeated by Elizabeth I's forces. He and his fellow earls flee the country in what is known as the Flight of the Earls.

The British government's uncompromising stance hardened the steel of opposition. The deaths and mass exodus caused by the Great Famine had a profound social and cultural effect on Ireland and left a scar on the Irish psyche that cannot be overestimated. Urban Dublin escaped the worst ravages, but desperate migrants flooded into the city looking for relief – soup kitchens were set up all over the city, including in the bucolic Merrion Sq, where presumably its affluent residents bore direct witness to the tragedy.

The horrors of the Famine and its impact on Dublin's centre saw the wealthy abandon the city for a new set of salubrious suburbs south of Dublin along the coast, now accessible via Ireland's first railway line, built in 1834 to connect the city to Kingstown (present-day Dun Laoghaire). The flight from the city continued for the next 70 years and many of the fine Georgian residences became slum dwellings. With such squalor came a host of social ills, including alcohol, which had always been a source of solace but now became a chronic problem.

British Prime Minister William Gladstone introduced Home Rule bills three times into the House of Commons between 1886 and 1895, but the House of Lords voted them down on each occasion.

The Blossoming of National Pride

In the second half of the 19th century, Dublin was staunchly divided along sectarian lines and, although Catholics were still partly second-class citizens, a burgeoning Catholic middle class provided the impetus for Ireland's march towards independence.

It was the dashing figure of Protestant landlord Charles Stewart Parnell (1846–91), from County Wicklow, who first harnessed the broad public support for Home Rule. Elected to Westminster in 1875, the 'Uncrowned King of Ireland' campaigned tirelessly for land reform and a Dublin parliament.

He appeared to have an ally in the British prime minister, William Gladstone, who lightened the burden on tenants by passing Land Acts enabling them to buy property. Gladstone was also converted to the cause of Home Rule, for both principled reasons and practical ones: the granting of some form of self-government would at least have the effect of reconciling Irish nationalism to the British state.

In the twilight of the 19th century there was a move to preserve all things Irish. The Gaelic Athletic Association (GAA) was set up in 1884 to promote Irish sports, while Douglas Hyde and Eoin McNeill formed the Gaelic League in 1893 to encourage Irish arts and language. The success of the Gaelic League paved the way for the Celtic Revival Movement, spearheaded by WB Yeats and Lady Gregory, who founded the Abbey Theatre in 1904.

Charles Stewart Parnell suffered a swift fall from grace after it was made public that he had been having an affair with a married woman, Kitty O'Shea. He was ditched as leader of his own Irish Parliamentary Party in 1890 and died a broken man the following year.

1680

The architectural style known as Anglo-Dutch results in the construction of notable buildings such as the Royal Hospital Kilmainham, now the Irish Museum of Modern Art.

1695

Penal Laws prohibit Catholics from owning a horse, marrying outside their religion, and buying or inheriting property; within 100 years Catholics will own only 5% of Irish land.

1757

The Wide Street Commission is set up to design the framework of a modern city: new parks are laid out, streets widened and new public buildings commissioned.

1801

The Act of Union unites Ireland politically with Britain. The Irish Parliament votes itself out of existence following an intensive campaign of bribery.

The Struggle for Independence

Although Irish culture was thriving at the start of the 20th century, the country's peaceful efforts to free itself from British rule were thwarted at every juncture. Dublin's slums were the worst in Europe, and the emergence of militant trade unionism introduced a socialist agenda to the struggle for self-determination.

By 1910 it was reckoned that 20,000 Dublin families each occupied a single room; a good example is the house at 14 Henrietta St.

In 1905 Arthur Griffith (1871–1922) founded a new political movement called Sinn Féin ('Ourselves Alone'), which sought to achieve Home Rule through passive resistance rather than political lobbying. It urged the Irish to withhold taxes and its MPs to form an Irish government in Dublin.

Meanwhile, trade union leaders Jim Larkin and James Connolly agitated against low wages and corporate greed, culminating in the Dublin Lockout of 1913, where 300 employers 'locked out' 20,000 workers for five months. During this time Connolly established the Irish Citizen Army (ICA) to defend striking workers from the police. Things were heating up.

Home Rule was finally passed by Westminster in 1914, but its provisions were suspended for the duration of WWI. Bowing to pressure from Protestant-dominated Ulster, where 140,000 members of the newly formed Ulster Volunteer Force (UVF) swore to resist any attempts to weaken British rule in Ireland, the bill also made provisions for the 'temporary' exclusion of the North from the workings of the future Act. How temporary was 'temporary' was anybody's guess – and it was in such political fudging that the seeds of trouble were sown. To counter the potential threat from the UVF, Irish nationalists formed the Irish Volunteer Force (IVF), but a stand-off was avoided when the vast majority of them enlisted in the British Army: if Britain was going to war in defence of small nations, then loyalty to the Allied cause would help Ireland's long-term aspirations.

The Easter Rising

The more radical factions within Sinn Féin, the IVF and the ICA saw Britain's difficulty as Ireland's opportunity, and planned to rise up against the Crown on Easter Sunday, 1916. In typical fashion, the rhetoric of the rebellion outweighed the quality of the planning. When the head of the IVF, Eoin McNeill, got wind of the plans, he published an advertisement in the newspaper cancelling the planned 'manoeuvres'. The leaders rescheduled the revolution for the following day but word never spread beyond the capital, where a motley band of about a thousand rebels assembled and seized strategic buildings. The main gar-

1829

Following a powerful campaign by Daniel O'Connell, the 'Liberator', the Catholic Emancipation Act is passed, repealing the remaining Penal Laws.

1840

The Corporation Act allows Catholics to vote in local elections for the first time since the 1690s, giving them a two-to-one majority.

1841

Daniel O'Connell is elected the first Catholic mayor of Dublin in 150 years; one of his first acts is to found a multi-denominational cemetery in Glasnevin.

1845–51

A mould called phytophthora ravages the potato harvest. The Great Famine is the single greatest catastrophe in Irish history, with the deaths of up to one million people.

rison was the General Post Office, outside which the poet and school teacher Pádraig Pearse read out the 'Proclamation of the Republic'.

The British Army didn't take the insurgence seriously at first, but after a few soldiers were killed they sent a gunboat down the Liffey to rain shells on the rebels. After six days of fighting the city centre was ravaged and the death toll stood at 300 civilians, 130 British troops (many of whom were Irish) and 60 rebels.

The rebels, prompted by Pearse's fear of further civilian casualties, surrendered and were arrested. Crowds gathered to mock and jeer at them as they were led away. Initially, Dubliners resented them for the damage they had caused with their futile rising, but their attitudes began to change following the executions of the leaders in Kilmainham Gaol. The hostility shown to the rebels turned to outright sympathy and support.

Many Dubliners were appalled at the sentences received by the leaders of the Rising, especially the fate suffered by 18-year-old Willie Pearse, whose main offence was that he was Pádraig's brother. James Connolly was severely injured during the Rising, so was strapped to a chair and shot.

The War of Independence

In the 1918 general election, the more radical Sinn Féin party won three-quarters of the Irish seats. In May 1919 they declared independence and established the first Dáil Éireann (Irish Assembly) in Dublin's Mansion House, led by Éamon de Valera. This was effectively a declaration of war.

Mindful that they could never match the British on the battlefield, Sinn Féin's military wing – made up of Irish Volunteers now renamed the Irish Republican Army (IRA) – began attacking arms dumps and barracks in guerrilla strikes. The British countered by strengthening the Royal Irish Constabulary (RIC) and introducing a tough auxiliary force made up of returning WWI servicemen known as the Black and Tans (after the colour of their uniforms).

They met their match in Michael Collins, the IRA's commander and a master of guerrilla warfare. Although the British knew his name, Collins masterfully concealed his identity and throughout the war was able to freewheel around the city on his bicycle like he didn't have a care in the world.

On 10 November 1920, Collins learned that 14 undercover British intelligence operatives known as the 'Cairo Gang' had just arrived in Dublin. The following morning he had his own crack squad ('the Apostles') assassinate each one of them as they lay in their beds. That afternoon, British troops retaliated by opening fire on the crowd at a hurling match in Croke Park, resulting in the deaths of 10 spectators and one player, Michael Hogan, whose death was later commemorated when the main stand at the stadium was named after him. The events of 'Bloody

By 1918, when WWI ended, 50,000 Irish citizens had lost their lives.

1867

Several thousand supporters of the Irish Republican Brotherhood (IRB) fight the police in Tallaght; they disperse and some 200 agitators are arrested.

1905

Journalist Arthur Griffiths founds a new movement whose aim is independence under a dual monarchy; he names the movement Sinn Féin, meaning 'Ourselves Alone'.

1913

The largest labour dispute in Irish history sees 20,000 Dublin workers 'locked out' for five months by defiant employers.

1916

Republicans take the GPO in Dublin and announce the formation of an Irish Republic. After less than a week of fighting, the rebels surrender and are summarily executed.

Sunday' galvanised both sides in the conflict and served to quash any moral doubts over what was becoming an increasingly brutal struggle.

Brutalities notwithstanding, the war resulted in relatively few casualties – 2014 in total – and by mid-1921 had ground to a kind of stalemate. Both sides were under pressure to end it: the international community was urging Britain to resolve the issue one way or another, while, unbeknown to the British, the IRA was on the verge of collapse. A truce was signed on 11 July 1921.

Éamon de Valera, the leader of the first Dáil Éireann (Irish Assembly), was spared the firing squad in 1916 because of his US birth; killing him would have been a public-relations disaster.

Treaty & Civil War

The terms of – and the circumstances surrounding – the Treaty that ended the War of Independence make up the single most divisive episode in Irish politics, one that still breeds prejudice, inflames passions and shapes the political landscape in parts of the country.

After months of argument and facing the threat of, in the words of British Prime Minister Lloyd George, an 'immediate and terrible war', the Irish negotiating team, led by Michael Collins, signed the Anglo-Irish Treaty on 6 December 1921. Instead of establishing the Irish Republic for which the IRA had fought, it created an Irish Free State, effectively a British dominion, in which members of the newly constituted parliament would have to swear allegiance to the British Crown before they could participate in government. The six counties comprising Northern Ireland were given the choice of becoming part of the Free State or remaining in the United Kingdom; they chose the latter, sowing the seeds of discontent that would lead to further rounds of the Troubles in the North. Although Collins was dissatisfied with the deal, he hoped it would be the 'first step' in the journey towards an Irish republic. Nevertheless, he also foresaw trouble and remarked prophetically, 'I've just signed my own death warrant'.

Éamon de Valera vehemently opposed the Treaty and the two erstwhile comrades were pitted against one another into pro-Treaty and

BEST BOOKS ON DUBLIN HISTORY

- *Dublin: The Making of a Capital City* (2014) David Dickson
- *Come Here to Me: Dublin's Other History* (2013) Donal Fallon, Sam McGrath and Ciaran Murray
- *Dublin: A Cultural & Literary History* (2005) Siobhán Kilfeather
- *Stones of Dublin: A History of Dublin in Ten Buildings* (2014) Lisa Marie Griffith
- *A Short History of Dublin* (2010) Richard Killeen

1919–21

The Irish War of Independence begins in January 1919. Two years (and 2014 casualties) later, the war ends in a truce on 11 July 1921, leading to peace talks.

1921–22

The Anglo-Irish Treaty is signed on 6 December 1921. It gives 26 counties of Ireland independence and six Ulster counties the choice of opting out. The Irish Free State is founded in 1922.

1948

Fine Gael, in coalition with the new Republican Clann na Poblachta, wins the 1948 general election and declares the Free State a republic.

1960s

A construction boom sees the growth of new suburbs north and south of the city in an effort to rehouse Dubliners removed from dangerous city-centre tenements.

anti-Treaty camps. Although the Dáil narrowly ratified the Treaty and the electorate accepted it by a large majority, Ireland slid into civil conflict in June 1922.

Ironically, the Civil War was more brutal than the struggle that preceded it. In 11 months roughly 3000 Irish died – including 77 executed by the state – but the vindictive nature of the fighting left indelible scars that have yet to be fully healed. The assassination of Michael Collins in his home county of Cork on 22 August 1922 rocked the country; 500,000 people (almost one-fifth of the population) attended his funeral. The last few months of fighting were especially ugly, with both sides engaging in tit-for-tat atrocities. On 24 May 1923, de Valera ordered the anti-Treaty forces to drop their arms.

The 1922 Civil War began when anti-Treaty IRA forces occupied Dublin's Four Courts and were shelled by pro-Treaty forces, led by Michael Collins. Dublin, which escaped any real damage during the War of Independence, became a primary theatre of the Civil War, which cost the lives of 250 Dubliners.

The Irish Republic

Ireland finally entered a phase of peace. Without an armed struggle to pursue – at least not one pursued by the majority – the IRA became a marginalised force in independent Ireland and Sinn Féin fell apart. In 1926 de Valera created a new party, Fianna Fáil (Soldiers of Destiny), which has been the dominant force in Irish politics ever since. Over the following decades Fianna Fáil gradually eliminated most of the clauses of the Treaty with which it had disagreed (including the oath of allegiance).

In 1932 a freshly painted Dublin hosted the 31st Eucharistic Congress, which drew visitors from around the world. The Catholic Church began to wield disproportionate control over the affairs of the state; contraception was made illegal in the 1930s and the age of consent was raised from 16 to 17.

In 1936, when the IRA refused to disarm, de Valera had it banned. The following year the Civil War–tainted moniker 'Free State' was dropped in favour of Eire as the country's official name in a rewrite of the constitution.

Despite having done much of the groundwork, Fianna Fáil lost out to its rivals Fine Gael, descendants of the original pro-Treaty Free State government, on declaring the 26 counties a republic in 1949.

Author and Treaty negotiator Robert Erskine Childers was executed by the government on 24 November 1922. Childers ended up on the anti-Treaty side during the Civil War, but was arrested for possessing a gun given to him by (the now pro-Treaty) Michael Collins and sentenced to death.

The Stroll to Modernisation

Sean Lemass succeeded de Valera as Taoiseach (Prime Minister) in 1959 and set about fixing the Irish economy, which he did so effectively that the rate of emigration soon halved. While neighbouring London was swinging in the '60s, Dublin was definitely swaying. Youngsters from rural communities poured into the expanding city and it seemed like the good times were never going to end. But, almost inevitably, the economy slid back into recession.

1969

Marches in Derry are disrupted by Loyalist attacks and heavy-handed police action, culminating in the 'Battle of the Bogside' (12–14 August). It marks the beginning of the 'Troubles'.

1972

Angry demonstrators burn the British Embassy in Dublin in response to the killing of 13 civilians in Derry by British paratroopers.

1974

Simultaneous bombings in Monaghan and Dublin on 17 May leave 33 dead and 300 injured, the biggest loss of life in any single day during the Troubles.

1990s

Low corporate tax, decades of investment in higher education, transfer payments from the EU and a low-cost labour market lead to the 'Celtic Tiger' boom.

On the 50th anniversary of the 1916 Easter Rising, Nelson's Pillar on O'Connell St was partially blown up by the IRA and crowds cheered as the remainder was removed the following week. Republicanism was still prevalent and a new round of the Troubles were about to flair up in the North.

Although Ireland remained neutral during WWII – as a way of pushing its independence – Dublin's North Strand was hit by a 227kg German bomb on 31 May 1941, killing more than 30 and injuring 90.

In 1973 Ireland joined the European Economic Community (EEC), a forerunner to the European Union (EU), and got a significant leg-up from the organisation's coffers over the following decades. But the tides of change were coming once again. Political instability and an international recession did little to help hopes of economic recovery, and by the early '80s emigration was once again a major issue. But Ireland – and Dublin in particular – was growing increasingly liberal, and was straining at the shackles imposed on its social and moral mores by a largely conservative Catholic Church. Politicians too were seen in a new light as stories of corruption and cronyism became increasingly commonplace.

Dublin was hardly touched by the sectarian tensions that would pull Northern Ireland asunder, although 25 people died after three Loyalist car bombs exploded in the city in 1974.

From Celtic Tiger...

In the early 1990s European funds helped kick-start economic growth. Huge sums of money were invested in education and physical infrastructure, while the policy of low corporate tax rates coupled with attractive incentives made Ireland very appealing to high-tech businesses looking for a door into EU markets. In less than a decade Ireland went from being one of the poorest countries in Europe to one of the wealthiest: unemployment fell from 18% to 3.5%, the average industrial wage leapt to the top of the European league, and the dramatic rise in GDP meant that the country laid claim to an economic model of success that was the envy of the entire world. Ireland became synonymous with the term 'Celtic Tiger'.

The visit of Pope John Paul II in 1979 saw more than one million people flock to Phoenix Park to hear him say Mass; around 130,000 were there in 2018 for Pope Francis' visit.

In Dublin, an impressive programme of construction began with the Irish Financial Services and then expanded down both sides of the Liffey towards Dublin port; the city's population grew dramatically and suburbs were expanded to accommodate the new arrivals from other parts of Ireland and beyond.

...To Rescue Cat

From 2002 the Irish economy was kept buoyant by a gigantic construction boom that was completely out of step with any measure of responsible growth forecasting. The out-of-control international derivatives market flooded Irish banks with cheap money, and they lent it freely.

1993

About 20,000 demonstrators call for an end to IRA violence as a result of the bomb that killed two children in Warrington, England.

2005

The IRA ends its campaign of violence on 28 July, ordering its units 'to assist the development of purely political and democratic programmes through exclusively peaceful means'.

2008

The global financial crisis triggers the collapse of the Irish banking system and the property boom; Ireland's economy goes into financial free fall.

2009

The publication of the Murphy Report reveals a vast network of secrecy and cover-up of widespread crimes of sexual abuse by serving priests within the Dublin diocese.

Luas tram

Then Lehman Bros and the credit crunch happened. The Irish banks nearly went to the wall, but were bailed out at the last minute and, before Ireland could draw breath, the International Monetary Fund (IMF) and the EU held the chits of the country's mid-term economic future. Ireland found itself yet again confronting the familiar demons of high unemployment and emigration, but a deep-cutting programme of austerity saw the corner turned by the end of 2014.

In Dublin the signs of recovery were evidenced by a renewed spate of construction, including the addition of a city-centre spur line linking two Luas lines and the ongoing construction of the city's tallest building, rising up from Point Sq near the 3 Arena.

Taoiseach Leo Varadkar is the eighth Dubliner to become prime minister. He is also the youngest and first openly gay man to hold the office.

2011

Queen Elizabeth II visits Dublin as part of her Irish trip, the first by a British monarch since the visit of George V in 1911.

2015

The Marriage Equality referendum is passed by a large majority; the results are announced in Dublin Castle and the city centre explodes in celebration.

2017

Dubliner Leo Varadkar, the gay son of an Indian immigrant, becomes Taoiseach (prime minister). At 38 he is the youngest person to hold the office.

2018

Ireland votes to remove the constitutional ban on abortion; in Dublin, the 'yes' vote exceeds 73%, with Dublin Bay South having the widest margin in Ireland at 78.49%.

Literary Dublin

Dubliners know a thing or two about the written word. No other city of comparable size can claim four winners of the Nobel Prize in Literature, but the city's impact on the English-reading world extends far beyond the fab four of George Bernard Shaw, William Butler Yeats, Samuel Beckett and Seamus Heaney...one name, folks: James Joyce.

Creative Capital

Before Dublin was even a glint in a Viking's eye, Ireland was the land of saints and scholars, thanks to the monastic universities that sprang up around the country to foster the spread of Christianity and the education of Europe's privileged elite. But for our purposes, we need to fast-forward 1000 years to the 18th century and the glory days of Georgian Dublin, when the Irish and English languages began to cross-fertilise. Experimenting with English, using turns of phrase and expressions translated directly from Gaeilge, and combining these with a uniquely Irish perspective on life, Irish writers have dazzled and delighted readers for centuries. British theatre critic Kenneth Tynan summed it up in the *Observer* thus: 'The English hoard words like misers: the Irish spend them like sailors'.

Dublin has as many would-be sailors as Hollywood has frustrated waitresses, and it often seems like a bottomless well of creativity. The section given over to Irish writers is often the largest and busiest in any local bookstore, reflecting not only a rich literary tradition and thriving contemporary scene, but also an appreciative, knowledgeable and hungry local audience that attends readings and poetry recitals like rock-music fans at a gig.

Indeed, Dublin has produced so many writers, and has been written about so much, that you could easily plan a Dublin literary holiday. *A Literary Guide to Dublin,* by Vivien Igoe, includes detailed route maps, a guide to cemeteries and an eight-page section on literary and historical

LITERARY FESTIVALS

Dublin's literary festivals are a great opportunity to meet Irish and international authors. Dublin has a handful of festivals of note:

International Literature Festival Dublin (☎01-969 5259; www.ilfdublin.com; ⏱May) The city's biggest literary event is a great showcase of local and international talent.

Dublin Book Festival (www.dublinbookfestival.com; ⏱mid-Nov) A three-day festival of literature with readings and talks.

Dalkey Book Festival (www.dalkeybookfestival.org; ⏱mid-Jun) A small festival with an impressive line-up.

Mountains to the Sea Dlr Book Festival (www.mountainstosea.ie; ⏱Mar) The southside suburb of Dun Laoghaire gets literary.

FIVE BOOKS ABOUT DUBLIN

The Barrytown Trilogy (Roddy Doyle; 1992) Doyle's much-loved trilogy tells the story of the Northside working-class Rabbitte family. The three novels – *The Commitments* (1987), *The Snapper* (1990) and *The Van* (1991) – were published together in 1992.

Montpelier Parade (Karl Geary; 2017) The tale of the troubled relationship between the teenage Sonny and the much older Vera, set in the south Dublin neighbourhood of Monkstown, brings 1980s Dublin to life.

Dublin 4 (Maeve Binchy; 1982) Although written more than three decades ago, Binchy's examination of the tumult that afflicts a group of residents in Dublin's most affluent neighbourhood is just as poignant and relevant today.

Dubliners (James Joyce; 1914) Dublin serves as the unifying bedrock for this classic collection of 15 short stories that chronicle the travails of the capital and its middle-class residents at the turn of the 20th century.

Conversations with Friends (Sally Rooney; 2017) A brilliantly observed story of four characters – aspiring writer Frances, her ex Bobbi and older married couple Nick and Melissa – set against the backdrop of a post-economic-crash Dublin.

pubs. A. Norman Jeffares' *O'Brien Pocket History of Irish Writers: From Swift to Heaney* also has detailed and accessible summaries of writers and their work.

A Rich Writing History

Modern Irish literature begins with Jonathan Swift (1667–1745), the master satirist, social commentator, dean of St Patrick's Cathedral and author of *Gulliver's Travels*. Fast-forward a couple of centuries and you're in the company of acclaimed dramatist Oscar Wilde (1854–1900); *Dracula* creator Bram Stoker (1847–1912) – some have claimed that the name of the count may have come from the Irish *droch fhola* (bad blood); and playwright and essayist George Bernard Shaw (1856–1950), author of *Pygmalion* (which was later turned into *My Fair Lady*), who hailed from Synge St near the Grand Canal.

Towering above all of them – in reputation if not popularity – is James Joyce (1882–1941), whose name and books elicit enormous pride in Ireland. The majority of Joyce's literary output came when he had left Ireland for the artistic hotbed that was Paris, which was also true for another great experimenter in language and style, Samuel Beckett (1906–89). Beckett's work centres on fundamental existential questions about the human condition and the nature of self. He is probably best known for his play *Waiting for Godot*, but his unassailable reputation is based on a series of stark novels and plays.

Of the dozens of 20th-century Irish authors to have achieved published renown, some names to look out for include playwright and novelist Brendan Behan (1923–64), who wove tragedy, wit and a turbulent life into his best works, including *Borstal Boy*, *The Quare Fellow* and *The Hostage*, before dying young of alcoholism. A collection of his newspaper columns was published under the title *Hold Your Hour and Have Another*.

Dublin's Nobel Laureates

- *William Butler Yeats (1923)*
- *George Bernard Shaw (1925)*
- *Samuel Beckett (1969)*
- *Seamus Heaney (1995)*

The Contemporary Scene

The literary scene is flourishing, thanks in part to the proliferation of smaller presses and printing houses giving authors a chance to publish, which in turn has helped engender a generation of new writers more confident in seeing the fruits of their labours reach an audience.

JAMES JOYCE

Uppermost among Dublin writers is James Joyce, author of *Ulysses*, considered by some to be the greatest book of the 20th century – although we've yet to meet five people who've actually finished it. Still, Dubliners are immensely proud of the writer once castigated as a literary pornographer by locals and luminaries alike – even George Bernard Shaw dismissed him as vulgar. Joyce was so unappreciated that he left the city, never to reside in it again, though he continued to live here through his imagination and literature.

His Life

Born in Rathgar in 1882, the young Joyce had three short stories published in an Irish farmers' magazine under the pen name Stephen Dedalus in 1904. The same year he fled town with the love of his life, Nora Barnacle (when Joyce's father heard her name he commented that she would surely stick to him). He spent most of the next 10 years in Trieste, now part of Italy, where he wrote prolifically but struggled to get published. His career was further hampered by recurrent eye problems: he had 25 operations for glaucoma, cataracts and other conditions.

The first major prose he finally had published was *Dubliners* (1914), a collection of short stories set in the city, including the three he had written in Ireland. Publishers began to take notice and his autobiographical *A Portrait of the Artist as a Young Man* (1916) followed. In 1918 the US magazine *Little Review* started to publish extracts from *Ulysses* but notoriety was already pursuing his epic work and the censors prevented publication of further episodes after 1920.

Passing through Paris on a rare visit to Dublin, he was persuaded by Ezra Pound to stay a while in the French capital. What he intended to be a brief visit turned into a 20-year stay. It was a good move for the struggling writer for, in 1922, he met Sylvia Beach of the Paris bookshop Shakespeare & Co, who finally managed to put *Ulysses* (1922) into print. The publicity from its earlier censorship ensured instant success.

Buoyed by the success of the inventive *Ulysses*, Joyce went for broke with *Finnegans Wake* (1939), 'set' in the dreamscape of a Dublin publican. Perhaps not one to read at the airport, the book is a daunting and often obscure tome about eternal recurrence. It is even more complex than *Ulysses* and took the author 17 years to write.

In 1940, WWII drove the Joyce family back to Zürich, Switzerland, where the author died the following year.

Ulysses

Ulysses is the ultimate chronicle of the city in which, Joyce once said, he intended 'to give a picture of Dublin so complete that if the city one day suddenly disappeared from the earth it could be reconstructed out of my book'. It is set here on 16 June 1904 – the day of Joyce's first date with Nora Barnacle – and follows its characters as their journeys around town parallel the voyage of Homer's *Odyssey*.

The experimental literary style makes it difficult to read, but there's much for even the slightly bemused reader to relish. It ends with Molly Bloom's famous stream of consciousness discourse, a chapter of eight huge, unpunctuated paragraphs. Because of its sexual explicitness, the book was banned in the USA and the UK until 1933 and 1937 respectively.

As a testament to the book's enduring relevance and extraordinary innovation, it has inspired writers of every generation since. Joyce admirers from around the world descend on Dublin every year on 16 June to celebrate Bloomsday and retrace the steps of *Ulysses'* central character, Leopold Bloom. It is a slightly gimmicky and touristy phenomenon that is aimed at Joyce fanatics and tourists, but it's plenty of fun and a great way to lay the groundwork for actually reading the book.

The #MeToo movement has also played its indirect part, with publishers keen to promote female voices that in previous eras may not have been given the opportunity to be heard. The best of these include Sally Rooney, who has emerged as the brightest star in the new, more female-focused firmament. Her first novel, *Conversations with Friends* (2017) established her as a writer of huge talent, but it was her follow-up, *Normal People* (2018), that really made her a star. The story of a difficult relationship between two friends during the economic downturn, *Normal People* won Best Novel at the Costa Book Awards, Book of the Year at the British Book Awards and was a *New York Times* bestseller. Another new name to look out for is Emilie Pine, who burst onto the scene in 2018 with a superb collection of nonfiction essays, *Notes to Self,* an unflinching look at addiction, sexual assault and mental health.

Karl Whitney's debut book, *Hidden City: Adventures & Explorations in Dublin* (2015), is a stunning exploration of the city's hidden nooks and crevices. It received the blessing of Colm Tóibín, who reckons it's a more useful guide to the city than *Ulysses* or an official guidebook.

Melatu Uche Okorie was born in Nigeria, but moved to Ireland in 2006, where she spent 8½ years in direct provision (the processing system for asylum seekers), an experience she recounts in the three stories of *This Hostel Life* (2018), which cast a light on the migrant experience in Ireland.

Sinéad Gleeson is another important voice on the literary scene: her 2019 memoir, *Constellations: Reflections from Life,* is a stunning collection of linked essays exploring the fraught relationship between the physical body and identity. Dubliner Karl Geary left home for New York in the late 1980s, but tells the story of a love affair between a teenager and an older woman in his debut novel set in south Dublin, *Montpelier Parade* (2017).

Small Towns & Recession

The theme of small-town life is a popular one these days, as many authors explore the changes wrought by the economic crash of 2008. Gone is the nostalgic, repression-infused prose of yesteryear, replaced by a more brazen, often darkly comic style reflective of a new generation of writers raised on the optimistic confidence of the Celtic Tiger yet forced to grapple with the frequently harsh realities of post-crash austerity.

Both of Sally Rooney's novels are set against the backdrop of post-crash Dublin, but it's also a familiar landscape for the likes of Cork-born Lisa McInerney, author of *The Glorious Heresies* (2015), and Colin Barrett, who won the Guardian First Book Award for *Young Skins* (2013). Alan McMonagle's *Ithaca* (2017) treads similar ground, telling the story of a lonely boy's search for his elusive 'Da', and how in hunting for something we've lost, we risk losing sight of what we have. *Multitudes* (2016), by Lucy Caldwell, is a heart-warming debut collection of short stories set almost entirely in Belfast, with series of young female protagonists going through life's growing pains. Another recession-era novel of note is Donal Ryan's *The Spinning Heart* (2012), in which the effects of the crash on rural Ireland are explored through 21 different voices.

The Big Hitters

Rooney, Pine and others have joined the existing canon of established names. This includes Dubliner Colum McCann (1965–), who left Ireland in 1986, eventually settling in New York, where his sixth novel, the post–September 11 *Let the Great World Spin* (2009), catapulted him to the top of the literary tree and won him the National Book Award for fiction as well as the International IMPAC Dublin Literary Award.

BOOKS FOR YOUNG ADULTS

Irish authors have had a fair amount of success with the lucrative young adult market. John Boyne's *The Boy in the Striped Pyjamas* can rightfully be considered a YA masterpiece, while 2019's *My Brother's Name is Jessica* tackles the trans experience in a novel aimed at teenagers.

One of the most successful Irish authors is Eoin Colfer, creator of the Artemis Fowl series, eight fantasy novels following the adventures of Artemis Fowl II as he grows from criminal antihero to saviour of the fairies.

Dublin-born Sarah Crossan has established herself as one of the most successful authors for young adults, with books like *The Weight of Water* (2011), *Apple and Rain* (2014) and *One* (2015), a touching story about conjoined twins. Young readers have been delighted by Shane Hegarty's Darkmouth series, set in a fictional Irish town (Darkmouth), where young Finn is learning about girls and fighting monsters; 2018 saw the fourth book in the series, *Hero Rising*.

Established heavyweights continue to add to the country's literary works. There's Roddy Doyle (1958–), of course, whose mega-successful Barrytown novels – *The Commitments, The Snapper, The Van* and *Paddy Clarke Ha Ha Ha* – have all been made into films. His latest book, *Charlie Savage* (2019), compiles a year's worth of very funny pieces he wrote for the *Irish Independent* about a middle-aged Dubliner.

Sebastian Barry (1955–) has been shortlisted twice for the Man Booker Prize, for his WWI drama *A Long Long Way* (2005) and the absolutely compelling *The Secret Scripture* (2008), about a 100-year-old inmate of a mental hospital who decides to write an autobiography. In 2016 he published the fourth McNulty family novel, *Days Without End,* an award-winning epic set partly during the American Civil War.

Anne Enright (1962–) did nab the Booker for *The Gathering* (2007), a zeitgeist tale of alcoholism and abuse – she described it as 'the intellectual equivalent of a Hollywood weepie'. Her most recent novel, *The Green Road* (2015), also mines the murky waters of the Irish family.

Another Booker Prize winner is heavyweight John Banville (1945–), who won it for *The Sea* (2005); we also recommend either *The Book of Evidence* (1989) or the masterful roman à clef *The Untouchable* (1997), based loosely on the secret-agent life of art historian Anthony Blunt. Banville's literary alter ego is Benjamin Black, author of a series of eight hard-boiled detective thrillers set in the 1950s and starring a troubled pathologist called Quirke – the latest book is *Wolf on a String* (2017). Another big hitter is Wexford-born Colm Tóibín (1955–), author of nine novels including *Brooklyn* (2009; made into an Oscar-nominated film in 2015 starring Saoirse Ronan) and *Nora Webster* (2014), a powerful study of widowhood.

If you want to see Beckett's phone, Behan's union card and a first edition of *Dracula* all under the one roof, the Dublin Writers Museum has extensive collections from the city's most famous (dead) writers.

Emma Donoghue (1969–) followed the award-winning *Room* (2010) with *Frog Music* (2014), about the real-life shooting of cross-dressing gamine Jenny Bonnet in late-19th-century San Francisco, and *The Wonder* (2016), about a fasting child in 1850s Ireland. And finally there's John Boyne (1971–), whose Holocaust novel *The Boy in the Striped Pyjamas* (2006; the film version came out in 2008) made him Ireland's most successful author. He's added a few works since then, most recently *My Brother's Name is Jessica* (2019), which has generated some controversy among trans-rights activists, who accuse Boyne of misgendering and deadnaming (referring to someone by their birthname after they've transitioned).

Seamus Heaney

Modern-day Poets

Ireland's greatest modern bard was Derry-born but Dublin-resident Nobel Laureate Seamus Heaney (1939–2013), whose enormous personal warmth and wry humour flow through each of his evocative works. He was, unquestionably, the successor to Yeats and one of the most important contemporary poets of the English language. After winning the Nobel Prize in 1995 he compared the ensuing attention to someone mentioning sex in front of their mammy. *Opened Ground: Poems 1966–1996* (1998) is our favourite of his books.

Dubliner Paul Durcan (1944–) is one of the most reliable chroniclers of changing Dublin. He won the prestigious Whitbread Prize for Poetry in 1990 for *Daddy, Daddy* and is a funny, engaging, tender and savage writer. Eavan Boland (1944–) is a prolific and much-admired writer, best known for her poetry, who combines Irish politics with outspoken feminism; *In a Time of Violence* (1994) and *The Lost Land* (1998) are two of her most celebrated collections. More recently, Derek Mahon's (1941–) *Against the Clock* (2018) is as much a melancholic meditation on the passage of time as it is a light-hearted acceptance of the fact. Galway-born Elaine Feeney (1979–) is one of the country's best-known contemporary poets: 2017's *Rise* is her fourth collection of poems.

If you're interested in finding out more about poetry in Ireland, visit the website of the excellent Poetry Ireland (www.poetryireland.ie), which showcases the work of new and established poets.

Musical Dublin

Dublin's literary tradition may have the intellectuals nodding sagely, but it's the city's musical credentials that have everyone else bopping, for it's no cliché to say that music is as intrinsic to the local lifestyle as a good night out. Even the streets – well, Grafton St and Temple Bar – are abuzz with the sounds of music, and you can hardly get around without stubbing your toe on the next international superstar busking their way to a record contract.

Traditional & Folk

Irish music – commonly referred to as 'traditional' or simply 'trad' – has retained a vibrancy not found in other traditional European forms. This is probably because, although Irish music has kept many of its traditional aspects, it has itself influenced many forms of music, most notably US country and western – a fusion of Mississippi Delta blues and Irish traditional tunes that, combined with other influences like gospel, is at the root of rock and roll. Other reasons for its current success include the willingness of its exponents to update the way it's played (in ensembles rather than the customary *céilidh* – communal dance – bands) and the popularity of pub sessions.

Dublin Albums

- *Boy (1980)* U2
- *I Do Not Want What I Haven't Got (1990)* Sinéad O'Connor
- *Music in Mouth (2003)* Bell X1
- *Loveless (1991)* My Bloody Valentine
- *Becoming a Jackal (2010)* Villagers

The pub session is still the best way to hear the music at its rich, lively best – and, thanks largely to the tourist demand, there are some terrific sessions in pubs throughout the city. Thankfully, though, the best musicians have also gone into the recording studio. If you want to hear musical skill that will both tear out your heart and restore your faith in humanity, go no further than the fiddle-playing of Tommy Peoples on *The Quiet Glen* (1998), the beauty of Paddy Keenan's uillean pipes on his self-titled 1975 album, or the stunning guitar playing of Andy Irvine on albums such as *Compendium: The Best of Patrick Street* (2000).

The most famous traditional band is The Chieftains, who spend most of their time these days playing in the US, and marked their 50th anniversary in 2012 with the ambitious *Voice of Ages,* a collaboration with the likes of Bon Iver and Paolo Nutini. More folksy than traditional were The Dubliners, founded in O'Donoghue's on Merrion Row the same year as The Chieftains. Most of the original members, including the utterly brilliant Luke Kelly and fellow frontman Ronnie Drew, have died, but the group still plays the odd nostalgia gig. In 2006 it released *Live at Vicar St,* which captures some of its brilliance.

Another band whose career has been stitched into the fabric of Dublin life is The Fureys, comprising four brothers originally from the travelling community (no, not like the Wilburys) along with guitarist Davey Arthur. And if it's rousing renditions of Irish rebel songs you're after, you can't go past The Wolfe Tones. Ireland is packed with traditional talent and we strongly recommend that you spend some time in a specialised traditional shop such as Claddagh Records, which has branches on Cecilia St in Temple Bar and Westmoreland St.

Since the 1970s various bands have tried to blend traditional with more progressive genres with mixed success. The first band to pull it

LUKE KELLY: THE ORIGINAL DUBLINER

With a halo of wiry ginger hair and a voice like hardened honey, Luke Kelly (1940–84) was perhaps the greatest Irish folk singer of the 20th century, a performer who used his voice in the manner of the American blues singers he admired so much to express the anguish of being lonely and afraid in a world they never made (to paraphrase AE Housman).

He was a founding member of The Dubliners, along with Ronnie Drew (1934–2008), Barney McKenna (1939–2012) and Ciarán Bourke (1935–88), but he treated Dublin's most famous folk group as more of a temporary cooperative enterprise. He shared the singing duties with Drew, lending his distinctive voice to classic drinking ditties like 'Dirty Old Town' and rousing rebel songs like 'A Nation Once Again', but it was his mastery of the more reflective ballad that made him peerless. His rendition of 'On Raglan Road', from a poem by Patrick Kavanagh that the poet himself insisted he sing, is the most beautiful song about Dublin we've ever heard, but it is his version of Phil Coulter's 'Scorn Not His Simplicity' that grants him his place among the immortals. Coulter wrote the song following the birth of a son with Down's syndrome, and even though it became one of Kelly's best-loved songs, he had such respect for it that he only sang it a handful of times, and only in the most respectful of settings.

In January 2019, on the 35th anniversary of his death, two sculptures of Kelly were unveiled in Dublin, one on South King St (p70) and another on Sheriff St (p166), the street where he was born.

Luke Kelly: The Collection is recommended listening.

off was Moving Hearts, led by Christy Moore, who went on to become an important folk musician in his own right.

Popular Music

From the 1960s onwards, Dublin became a hotbed of rock and pop; most of the artists have now faded into obscurity. Notable exceptions are Thin Lizzy, led by Phil Lynott (1949–86), and Bob Geldof's new wave Boomtown Rats, who didn't like Mondays or much else either.

But they all paled in comparison to the supernova that is U2, formed in 1976 in North Dublin and by the late 1980s one of the world's most successful rock bands. What else can we say about them that hasn't already been said? After 14 studio albums, 22 Grammy awards and 150 million album sales, they have nothing to prove to anyone – and not even their minor faux pas in 2014, when Apple 'gave' copies of *Songs of Innocence* to iTunes subscribers whether they wanted it or not, has dampened their popularity. The 2017 Joshua Tree Tour, staged to commemorate the 30th anniversary of their groundbreaking album, was a huge commercial and critical success.

Of all the Irish acts that followed in U2's wake during the 1980s and early 1990s, a few managed to comfortably avoid being tarred with 'the next U2' burden. The Pogues' mix of punk and Irish folk kept everyone going for a while, but the real story there was the empathetic songwriting of Shane MacGowan, whose genius has been overshadowed by his heavy drinking – but he still managed to pen Ireland's favourite song, 'Fairytale of New York', sung with emotional fervour by everyone around Christmas. Sinéad O'Connor thrived by acting like a U2 antidote – whatever they were into she was not – and by having a damn fine voice; the raw emotion on *The Lion and the Cobra* (1987) makes it a great offering. And then there was My Bloody Valentine, the pioneers of late-1980s guitar-distorted shoegazer rock: *Loveless* (1991) is one of the best Dublin albums of all time.

Traditional Playlist

Compendium: The Best of Patrick Street (2001) Patrick Street

Old Hag You Have Killed Me (1976) The Bothy Band

Paddy Keenan (1975) Paddy Keenan

The 1990s were largely dominated by DJs, dance music and a whole new spin on an old notion, the boy band. Behind Ireland's most successful groups (Boyzone and Westlife) is impresario Louis Walsh, whose musical sensibilities seem mired in '60s showband schmaltz. Walsh, who became a judge on *The X Factor* in the UK, also unleashed Jedward on the world – identical twins who endeared themselves to everyone with their wacky antics.

Dublin Songs

'Lay Me Down' (2001) The Frames

'One' (1991) U2

'On Raglan Road' (1972) Luke Kelly and The Dubliners

'Molly Malone' (2002) Sinéad O'Connor

'Old Town' (1982) Phil Lynott

The Contemporary Scene

Alternative music has never been in ruder health in Ireland – and Dublin, as the largest city in the country, is where everyone comes to make noise. Local artists to look out for include Saint Sister, whose 'atmos-folk' sound is a blend of harp, synth and harmony; their 2018 debut album *Shape of Silence* was one of the year's best releases.

Wyvern Lingo's eponymous debut album was also very well received, their harmonious R&B sound a harbinger of even better things to come, while Kojaque, aka Kevin Smith, is one of the most interesting new voices of recent years; his unique brand of hip-hop is flawlessly expressed on his debut album, *Deli Daydreams.*

More established artists still making waves include Kodaline, whose fusion of American rock and British pop has made them one of Ireland's most popular bands; their third album, *Politics of Living,* was released in 2018. Bray-born, blues-influenced Hozier (full name Andrew Hozier-Byrne), whose 2013 smash *Take Me to Church* made him a global name, released his second album, *Wasteland, Baby!* in 2019, debuting at the top of the US Billboard 200 chart. Although he spends a lot of his time in New York these days, Glen Hansard (of *Once* fame) is still a major presence in Ireland; in 2019 he released his fourth solo album, *The Wild Willing.*

Hugely successful Dublin trio The Script have parlayed their melodic brand of pop-rock onto all kinds of TV shows, from *90210* to *Made in Chelsea.* In 2017 they released their fifth album, the chart-topping *Freedom Child.* They mightn't sell as many records, but Villagers (which is really just Conor O'Brien and a selection of collaborators) has earned universal acclaim for its brand of indie-folk rock – and in 2018 their album *The Art of Pretending to Swim* moved them away from the more folksy sound of earlier stuff into a more electronic feel, without foregoing the brilliant songwriting that cemented O'Brien's position as one of the country's best talents.

But it's not just about musicians with grave intent: if Boyzone and Westlife were big, their success pales in comparison to that of One Direction, another product of 'the X Factory'. We mention them because one of their members, Niall Horan, is from Mullingar, County Westmeath – about an hour west of Dublin – which inevitably meant that when One Direction played Croke Park in 2015 it was a kind of homecoming. The band has since split, but Niall has launched a successful solo career – 2017 saw the release of his first solo album, *Flicker.* Inevitably, it debuted at the top of the US album charts.

Architecture

Dublin's skyline is a clue to its age, with visible peaks of its architectural history dating back to the Middle Ages. Of course, Dublin is older still, but there are no traces left of its Viking origins and you'll have to begin your architectural exploration in the 12th century, with the construction of the city's castle and two cathedrals. Its finest buildings, however, date from much later – built during the golden century that came to be known as the Georgian period.

Medieval Dublin

Viking Dublin was largely built of not-so-durable wood, of which there's virtually no trace left. The Norman footprint is a little deeper, but even its most impressive structures have been heavily reconstructed. The imposing Dublin Castle – or the complex of buildings that are known as Dublin Castle – bears little resemblance to the fortress that was erected by

Above National Museum of Ireland - Decorative Arts & History (p149)

the Anglo-Normans at the beginning of the 13th century and more to the neoclassical style of the 17th century. However, there are some fascinating glimpses of the lower reaches of the original, which you can visit on a tour.

Although the 12th-century cathedrals of Christ Church and St Patrick's were heavily rebuilt in Victorian times, there are some original features, including the crypt in Christ Church, which has a 12th-century Romanesque door. The older of the two St Audoen's Churches dates from 1190 and it too has a few Norman odds and ends, including a late-12th-century doorway.

Archéire (www.archiseek.com) is a comprehensive website covering all things to do with Irish architecture and design. If you want something in book form, look no further than Christine Casey's superb *The Buildings of Ireland: Dublin* (2005; Yale University Press), which goes through the city literally street by street.

Anglo-Dutch Period

After the Restoration of Charles II in 1660, Dublin embarked upon almost a century and a half of unparalleled growth as the city raced to become the second most important in the British Empire. The most impressive examples of the style are the Royal Hospital Kilmainham (1680), designed by William Robinson and now home to the Irish Museum of Modern Art; and the Royal Barracks (now Collins Barracks; 1701) built by Thomas Burgh and now home to a branch of the National Museum of Ireland.

Georgian Dublin

Dublin's architectural apogee can roughly be placed in the period spanning the rule of the four English Georges, between the accession of George I in 1714 and the death of George IV in 1830. The greatest influence on the shape of modern Dublin throughout this period came from the Wide Street Commissioners, appointed in 1757 and responsible for designing civic spaces and the framework of the modern city. Their efforts were complemented by Dublin's Anglo-Irish Protestant gentry who, flush with unprecedented wealth, dedicated themselves wholeheartedly towards improving their city.

Their inspiration was the work of the Italian architect Andrea Palladio (1508–80), who revived the symmetry and harmony of classical architecture. When the Palladian style reached these shores in the 1720s, the architects of the time tweaked it and introduced a number of, let's call them, 'refinements'. Most obvious were the elegant brick exteriors and decorative touches, such as coloured doors, fanlights and ironwork, which broke the sometimes austere uniformity of the fashion. Consequently, Dublin came to be known for its 'Georgian style'.

Sir Edward Lovett Pearce

The architect credited with the introduction of the Georgian style to Dublin's cityscape was Sir Edward Lovett Pearce (1699–1733), who first arrived in Dublin in 1725 and turned heads with the building of Par

GEORGIAN PLASTERERS

The handsome exteriors of Dublin's finest Georgian houses are often matched by superbly crafted plasterwork within. The fine work of Michael Stapleton (1747–1801) can be seen in Trinity College, Ely House near St Stephen's Green, and Belvedere House in north Dublin. The LaFranchini brothers, Paolo (1695–1776) and Filippo (1702–79), are responsible for the outstanding decoration in Newman House on St Stephen's Green. But perhaps Dublin's most famous plastered surfaces are in the chapel at the heart of the Rotunda Hospital. Although hospitals are never the most pleasant places to visit, this one's worth it for the German stuccadore Bartholomew Cramillion's fantastic rococo plasterwork.

Leinster House

liament House (now Bank of Ireland; 1728–39). It was the first two-chamber debating house in the world and the main chamber, the House of Commons, is topped by a massive pantheon-style dome.

Pearce also created the blueprint for the city's Georgian townhouses, the most distinguishing architectural feature of Dublin. The local version typically consists of four storeys, including the basement, with symmetrically arranged windows and an imposing, often brightly painted front door. Granite steps lead up to the door, which is often further embellished with a delicate leaded fanlight. The most celebrated examples are on the Southside, particularly around Merrion and Fitzwilliam Sqs, but the Northside also has some magnificent streets, including North Great George's and Henrietta Sts. The latter features two of Pearce's originals (at Nos 9 and 10) and is still Dublin's most unified Georgian street. Mountjoy Sq, the most elegant address in 18th-century Dublin, is currently being renewed after a century of neglect.

Sir William Chambers designed the Examination Hall (1791) and the Chapel (1798) that flank the elegant 18th-century quadrangle of Trinity College, known as Parliament Sq. However, Trinity College's most magnificent feature, the Old Library Building, with its breathtaking Long Room (1712), was designed by Thomas Burgh.

Richard Cassels

German architect Richard Cassels (aka Richard Castle; 1690–1751) hit town in 1728. While his most impressive country houses are outside Dublin, he did design Nos 85 and 86 St Stephen's Green (1738), which were combined in the 19th century and renamed Newman House, and No 80 (1736), which was later joined with No 81 to create Iveagh House, now the Department of Foreign Affairs; you can visit the peaceful gardens there still. The Rotunda Hospital (1748), at the top of O'Connell St, is also one of Cassels' works. As splendid as these buildings are, it seems he was only warming up for Leinster House (1745–48), the magnificent country residence built on what was then the countryside, but is now the centre of government.

Busáras

Sir William Chambers

Dublin's boom attracted such notable architects as Swedish-born Sir William Chambers (1723–96), who designed some of Dublin's most impressive buildings, though he never actually bothered to visit the city. It was the north side of the Liffey that benefited most from Chambers' genius: the chaste and elegant Charlemont House (now Hugh Lane Gallery; 1763) lords over Parnell Sq, while the Casino at Marino (1755–79) is his most stunning and bewitching work.

James Gandon & Thomas Cooley

It was towards the end of the 18th century that Dublin's developers really kicked into gear, when the power and confidence of the Anglo-Irish Ascendancy seemed boundless. Of several great architects of the time, James Gandon (1743–1823) stood out, and he built two of Dublin's most enduring and elegant neoclassical landmarks: the Custom House (1781–91) and the Four Courts (1786–1802). They were both built on the quays to afford plenty of space in which to admire them.

Regency & Victorian

The Act of Union (1801) turned Dublin from glorious capital to Empire backwater, which resulted in precious little construction for much of the 19th century. Exceptions include the General Post Office (GPO), designed in 1818 by Francis Johnston (1760–1829), and the stunning series of curvilinear glasshouses in the National Botanic Gardens, which were created in the mid-19th century by the Dublin ironmaster Richard Turner (1798–1881).

After Catholic Emancipation in 1829, there was a wave of church building, and later the two great Protestant cathedrals of Christ Church and St Patrick's were reconstructed. One especially beautiful example is the splendidly ornate and incongruous Newman University Church (1856), built in a Byzantine style by John Hungerford Pollen (1820–1902) because Cardinal Newman was none too keen on the Gothic style that was all the rage at the time.

James Gandon's greatest rival was Thomas Cooley (1740–84), who died too young to reach his full potential. His greatest building, the Royal Exchange (now City Hall; 1779), was butchered to provide office space in the mid-19th century, but returned to its breathtaking splendour in a stunning 2000 restoration.

Modern Architecture

Without any blank slate like a mass demolition or an architecturally convenient fire (like Chicago suffered in 1871), the architecture of modern Dublin has largely been squeezed in between other periods and has been low on avant-garde examples of international movements.

Exceptions include modernist buildings such as Busáras (1953) and Liberty Hall (1965), which have divided critics. The 1960s and 1970s saw the erection of several buildings in the Brutalist style, including the Irish Life Centre (1977) on Lower Abbey St, the Central Bank building (1970; currently being revamped) on Dame St and Paul Koralek's bold and brazen Berkeley Library (1967) on the grounds of Trinity College. The style is divisive among critics, who either embrace its block-like forms and raw concrete construction or reject it as indelicate and ugly. The style's name doesn't help its case: from the French 'brut', meaning 'raw', in Dublin it's considered 'brutal', slang for 'awful'.

It wasn't until the explosive growth of the 1990s that the city's modern landscape really began to improve, even if some of the early constructions – such as the Irish Financial Services Centre (IFSC; 1987) and the Waterways Visitor Centre (1994) – don't seem as impressive now as they did when they first opened.

The most stunning makeover has occurred in the Docklands, which has been transformed from quasi-wasteland to a fine example of contemporary urban design. You'll find the best examples on Grand Canal Sq, dominated by Daniel Libeskind's elegant Bord Gáis Energy Theatre (2010) and Manuel Aires Mateus' Marker Hotel (2011), and the plaza itself, designed by American landscape artist Martha Schwartz in 2008, is equally eye-catching.

The financial crash of 2008 put the kibosh on new building, but in 2017 construction began in the Docklands on the 17-storey 'Exo' office block, named in reference to the 'exoskeleton' external supporting structure. It will be 74m high, 7m taller than the Montevetro building, Google's HQ on Barrow St. The Exo is expected to be completed by March 2020.

MODERN BRIDGES

Over the last few years the Liffey has been spanned by a handful of new bridges that are all pretty good examples of modern design. Santiago Calatrava's James Joyce Bridge (2003) at Usher's Island gave the city its first piece of design with the imprimatur of a 'starchitect', and he outdid himself again in 2009 with the harp-like Samuel Beckett Bridge at Spencer Dock. In between them is the award-winning pedestrian Sean O'Casey Bridge (2005), designed by Cyril O'Neill, while the latest addition is the Rosie Hackett Bridge, joining Hawkins St and Marlborough St. It opened in 2014 and is the only bridge in Dublin named after a woman; Hackett was a prominent trade unionist and participated in the Easter Rising of 1916.

The Irish Way of Life

The Irish reputation for being affable is largely well deserved, but it only hints at a more profound character, one that is more complex and contradictory than the image of the silver-tongued master of blarney might suggest. This dichotomy is best summarised by a quote usually ascribed to the poet William Butler Yeats: 'Being Irish, he had an abiding sense of tragedy, which sustained him through temporary periods of joy.'

The Dublin Pulse

1,904,806 people live in the Greater Dublin area, which accounts for 40% of the population of the State.

Dubliners are famous for being warm and friendly, which is just another way of saying they love a chat, whether with friends or strangers. They will entertain you with their humour, alarm you with their willingness to get stuck into a good debate, and cut you down with their razor-sharp wit. Slagging – the Irish version of teasing – is an art form, which may seem caustic to unfamiliar ears, but is quickly revealed as an intrinsic element of how Dubliners – and the Irish generally – relate to one another. It is commonly assumed that the mettle of friendship is proven by how well you can take a joke rather than by the payment of a cheap compliment.

Yet beneath all of the garrulous sociability and self-deprecating talk lurks a dark secret, which is that, at heart, the Irish have traditionally been low on self-esteem. This is partly why they're so suspicious of easy compliments, but the last three decades have seen a paradigm shift in the Irish character. Prosperity and its related growth in expectations have gone a long way towards transforming Dubliners from a people who underestimated themselves, to a city eager to celebrate its achievements and successes.

Prosperity and its related growth in expectations have gone a long way towards transforming Dubliners from a people who wallowed in false modesty like a sport, to a city eager to celebrate its achievements and successes. Inevitably this personality shift has been largely driven by the appetites and demands of Generation Y, but there's no doubt that many older Dubs, for too long muted by a fear of appearing unseemly or boastful, have wholeheartedly embraced the change.

This cultural shift survived the trauma of the financial crash and the austerity that followed, even if many blamed a tawdry and materialistic culture of exaggerated excess for the country's woes, an attitude memorably summarised by a government minister who sheepishly declared on TV that 'we all partied!' But with the economy (largely) back on track, Dublin is once again hammering down on the pedal of its ambitions and watching the worst ravages of austerity quickly disappear in its rear-view mirror.

Nurse & Curse of the People

Despite a 25% drop-off in alcohol consumption over the last decade (according to a 2017 report by the World Health Organization), Ireland has a fractious relationship with alcohol - and Dublin is no different.

Supporters of marriage equality celebrating on May 23, 2015

The country regularly tops the list of the world's biggest binge drinkers, and while there is an increasing awareness of, and alarm at, the devastation caused by alcohol to Irish society (especially to young people), drinking remains the country's most popular social pastime, with no sign of letting up. Spend a weekend night walking around any town in the country and you'll get a firsthand feel of the influence and effect of the booze.

Some experts put Ireland's binge-drinking antics down to the dramatic rise in the country's economic fortunes, but statistics have long suggested that Ireland has had an unhealthy fondness for 'taking the cure', though the acceptability of public drunkenness is a far more recent phenomenon – the older generations regularly remind the youngsters that they would *never* have been seen staggering in public.

Lifestyle

Dubliners may like to grumble – about work, the weather, the government and those *feckin' eejits* on reality TV shows – but, if pressed, will tell you that they live in the best city on earth. There's loads *wrong* with the place, but isn't it the same way everywhere else?

Traditional Ireland – of the large family, closely linked to church and community – has largely disappeared as the increased urbanisation of the country continues to break up the social fabric of community interdependence that was a necessary element of relative poverty. Contemporary Ireland is therefore not altogether different from any other European country, and you have to travel further to the margins of the country – the islands and the isolated rural communities – to find an older version of society.

RELIGION

According to the census of 2016, about 3.7 million residents in the Republic (or 78% of the population) call themselves Roman Catholic, followed by 2.6% Church of Ireland (Protestant), 1.3% Muslim, 1.3% Orthodox, and 3.9% other religions; 9.8% declared themselves to have no religion – a 74% rise on 2011.

Catholicism remains a powerful cultural identifier, but more in a secular rather than religious way, as many Irish now reject the Church's stance on a host of social issues, from contraception to divorce and homosexuality. In part this is the natural reaction of an increasingly cosmopolitan country with an ever-broadening international outlook, but the Church's failure to satisfactorily take responsibility and atone for its role in the clerical abuse of decades past has breached the bond of trust between many parishioners and their parish.

LGBT-Friendly Ireland

A gay Taoiseach (Republic of Ireland Prime Minister). The first country in the world to introduce marriage equality for same-sex couples by popular vote. It's been an extraordinary road for a country that only decriminalised same-sex activity in 1993.

The rise to power of Dublin-born-and-raised Taoiseach Leo Varadkar, who only came out five months before the country voted for marriage equality in May 2015, is a powerful example of the paradigm shift that has occurred in attitudes toward the LGBT community in Ireland. The vote in favour of same-sex marriage was 62.4% – all but one constituency voted in favour.

Varadkar is very much a product of a new Ireland, where sexual orientation is considered not quite irrelevant, but not worthy of any kind of discrimination. In this new Ireland, pride celebrations – in Dublin, Cork, Galway and elsewhere – are now firmly fixed on the festival calendar, with rural Ireland lagging not too far behind its urban brethren.

Multiculturalism

Ireland has long been a pretty homogenous country, but the arrival of thousands of immigrants from all over the world – 17% of the population is foreign-born – has challenged the mores of racial tolerance and integration. To a large extent it has been successful – though, if you scratch beneath the surface, racial tensions can be exposed.

Just over 21% of all Dublin residents are born outside of Ireland, making the capital home to more non-Irish than any other part of the country. For example, almost two-thirds of Ireland's Chinese population live in Dublin.

The tanking of the economy exacerbated these tensions and the 'Irish jobs for Irish people' opinion has been expressed with greater vehemence and authority: the rise of right-wing movements across Europe and the US has emboldened Irish ultranationalists to take a more vocal and visible stance, but their numbers remain relatively insignificant for now, even if in 2019 one of these groups was involved in a series of protests against plans to house groups of immigrants in several Irish towns.

Antiracism groups have reported a rise in racist incidents, particularly Islamophobia, but the bulk of these are generally verbal and non-physical, which perhaps also explains another statistic that says that 75% of these incidents go unreported. In spite of this, most Muslims and people of colour living in Ireland feel that the country is safe and welcoming and that racism is not the norm for the vast majority of the white Irish population.

Survival Guide

TRANSPORT 242

ARRIVING IN DUBLIN 242

Air 242

Boat 243

Bus 243

Car & Motorcycle........243

Train 244

GETTING AROUND..... 244

Bus 244

Tram 244

Car & Motorcycle........244

Bicycle 245

Train 246

TOURS 246

DIRECTORY A–Z.... 247

Accessible Travel 247

Customs Regulations 247

Discount Cards..........247

Electricity 248

Embassies & Consulates 248

Emergency & Important Numbers......248

Health.................248

Internet Access..........248

Legal Matters 248

LGBT+ Travellers 248

Medical Services 249

Money.................249

Opening Hours 250

Post.................. 250

Public Holidays......... 250

Safe Travel............. 250

Taxes & Refunds........ 250

Telephone 250

Time..................251

Toilets.................251

Tourist Information.............251

Visas..................251

Women Travellers........251

LANGUAGE 252

Transport

ARRIVING IN DUBLIN

Ireland's capital and biggest city is the most important point of entry and departure for the country – almost all airlines fly in and out of Dublin Airport. Ferries from the UK arrive at the Dublin Port terminal, while ferries from France arrive in the southern port of Rosslare. Dublin is also the nation's primary rail hub. Flights, cars and tours can be booked online at lonelyplanet.com/bookings.

Air

Dublin Airport (☎01-814 1111; www.dublinairport.com) is 13km north of the city centre and has two terminals: most international flights (including most US flights) use Terminal 2; Ryanair and select others use Terminal 1. Both terminals have the usual selection of pubs, restaurants, shops, ATMs and car-hire desks.

There are direct flights to Dublin from all major European centres (including many options from the UK) and from Atlanta, Boston, Charlotte, Chicago, Los Angeles, New York, Orlando, Philadelphia, San Francisco and Washington, DC in the USA. Flights from further afield (Australasia and Africa) are usually routed through another European hub such as London; one recently introduced exception is a direct service from Addis Ababa (Ethiopia).

Most airlines have walk-up counters at Dublin Airport; those that don't have their ticketing handled by other airlines.

There is no train service from the airport to the city centre.

Bus

It takes about 45 minutes to get into the city by bus.

Aircoach (☎01-844 7118; www.aircoach.ie; one way/return €7/10) Private coach service with three routes from the airport to more than 20 destinations throughout the city, including the main streets of the city centre. Coaches run every 10 to 15 minutes between 6am and midnight, then hourly from midnight until 6am.

Airlink Express Coach (☎01-873 4222; www.dublinbus.ie; one way/return €7/12) Bus 747 runs every 10 to 20 minutes from 5.45am to 12.30am between the airport, the central bus station (Busáras) and the Dublin Bus office on Upper O'Connell St. Bus 757 runs every 15 to 30 minutes from 5am to 12.25am between the airport and various stops in the city, including Grand Canal Dock, Merrion Sq and Camden St.

Dublin Bus (Map p280; ☎01-873 4222; www.dublinbus.ie;

CLIMATE CHANGE & TRAVEL

Every form of transport that relies on carbon-based fuel generates CO_2, the main cause of human-induced climate change. Modern travel is dependent on aeroplanes, which might use less fuel per kilometre per person than most cars but travel much greater distances. The altitude at which aircraft emit gases (including CO_2) and particles also contributes to their climate change impact. Many websites offer 'carbon calculators' that allow people to estimate the carbon emissions generated by their journey and, for those who wish to do so, to offset the impact of the greenhouse gases emitted with contributions to portfolios of climate-friendly initiatives throughout the world. Lonely Planet offsets the carbon footprint of all staff and author travel.

59 Upper O'Connell St; ⌚9am-5.30pm Tue-Fri, to 2pm Sat, 8.30am-5.30pm Mon; 🚌all city centre) A number of buses serve the airport from various points in Dublin, including buses 16 (Rathfarnham), 41 (Lower Abbey St) and 102 (Sutton/Howth); all cross the city centre on their way to the airport.

Taxi

There is a taxi rank directly outside the arrivals concourse of both terminals. It should take about 45 minutes to get into the city centre by taxi, and cost around €25, including an initial charge of €3.80 (€4.20 between 10pm and 8am and on Sundays and bank holidays). Make sure the meter is switched on.

Boat

Dublin Port Terminal

The **Dublin Port Terminal** (☎01-855 2222; Alexandra Rd; 🚌53 from Talbot St) is 3km northeast of the city centre. Services include the following:

Irish Ferries (☎0818 300 400; www.irishferries.com; Ferryport, Terminal Rd South) Holyhead, Wales (€200 return, three hours)

P&O Irish Sea (☎01-686 9467; www.poferries.com; Terminal 3, Dublin Port) Liverpool, England (€180 return, 8½ hours, or four hours by fast boat)

Isle of Man Steam Packet Company/Sea Cat (www.steam-packet.com; Terminal 1, Dublin Port; ⌚4.30am-10pm) Isle of Man (€110 return, 1½ hours)

BUS

An express bus transfer to and from Dublin Port is operated by **Morton's Bus** (Map p268; www.mortonscoaches.ie; adult/child €3.50/2; ⌚7.15am, 12.30pm, 2pm & 7pm), leaving from Westmoreland St and timed to coincide with ferry departures. Otherwise, regular bus 53 serves the port from Talbot St. Inbound ferries are met by timed bus services that run to the city centre.

CAR

If you've brought your own car on the ferry, the city is easily accessed in around 15 minutes via East Wall Rd, North Wall Quay or the Thomas Clarke Bridge.

TAXI

There are taxi ranks outside the main terminals. It costs around €19 and take approximately 15 minutes to get to the city centre.

GREENER ARRIVALS

Although the vast majority of visitors will enter and exit Dublin via the airport, you can do your bit for the environment and arrive by boat – and have a bit of an adventure along the way. From Britain it's a cinch: you can buy a combined train-and-ferry ticket (known as SailRail) for under €50 (see www.irishrail.ie for travel from Ireland or www.thetrainline.com for travel from the UK). Or if you're really on a budget, get a bus-and-ferry ticket – from London it won't cost you more than the price of a meal.

You can also arrive at another Irish port. Rosslare in County Wexford has ferry services from France and southwestern Britain, while Larne, a short hop outside Belfast, is served from Stranraer in Scotland. Not only will you get to Dublin easily enough, but you can do some exploring on the way.

Bus

Dublin's central bus station, **Busáras** (Map p280; ☎01-836 6111; www.buseireann.ie; Store St; 🚉Connolly) is just north of the River Liffey, behind the Custom House. It has different-sized luggage lockers costing from €6 to €10 per day.

It's possible to combine bus and ferry tickets from major UK centres to Dublin on the bus network. The journey between London and Dublin takes about 12 hours and costs from €32 return (but note it's €47 one way). For more London details, contact **Eurolines** (☎01-836 6111; https://eurolines.buseireann.ie).

From here, **Bus Éireann** (☎1850 836 6111; www.buseireann.ie) serves the whole national network, including buses to towns and cities in Northern Ireland.

Car & Motorcycle

Road access to and from Dublin is pretty straightforward. A network of motorways radiates outward from the M50 ring road that surrounds Dublin, serving the following towns and cities:

M1 North to Drogheda, Dundalk and Belfast

M3 Northwest to Navan, Cavan and Donegal

M4 West to Galway and Sligo

M7 Southwest to Limerick; also (via M8) to Cork

M9 Southeast to Kilkenny and Waterford

M11 Southeast to Wexford

Motorway Tolls

There are tolls on limited sections of most motorways, costing between €1.40 and €2.90 for a car and between

€0.70 and €1.50 for a motorcycle. The M50 ring road has a barrier-free toll between junctions 6 and 7 (crossing the Liffey): vehicles not registered with e-tags are charged €3.10; motorcycles are free.

Many rental cars come equipped with tags that automatically take account of M50 charges and add them to your final bill (a sticker on the rental car will indicate it); otherwise, go to www.eflow.ie and pay the toll before 8pm the following day to avoid penalties.

Train

All trains in the Republic are run by **Irish Rail** (Iarnród Éireann; ☎01-836 6222; www.irishrail.ie). Dublin has two main train stations: **Heuston Station** (☎01-836 6222; Heuston), on the western side of town near the Liffey; and **Connolly Station** (☎01-703 2359; Connolly, Connolly Station), a short walk northeast of Busáras, behind the Custom House.

Connolly Station is a stop on the DART line into town; the Luas Red Line serves both Connolly and Heuston stations.

GETTING AROUND

Bus

The office of **Dublin Bus** (Map p280; ☎01-873 4222; www.dublinbus.ie; 59 Upper O'Connell St; 9am-5.30pm Tue-Fri, to 2pm Sat, 8.30am-5.30pm Mon; all city centre) has free single-route timetables for all its services. Buses run from around 6am (some start at 5.30am) to about 11.30pm.

Bus Fares

Fares are calculated according to stages (stops):

STAGES	CASH FARE (€)	LEAP CARD (€)
1-3	2.15	1.55
4-13	3	2.25
over 13	3.30	2.50

A Leap Card (www.leapcard.ie), available from most newsagents, is not just cheaper but also more convenient, as you don't have to worry about tendering exact fares (required with cash, otherwise you will get a receipt for reimbursement, which is only possible at the Dublin Bus main office). Register the card online and top it up with whatever amount you need. When you board a bus, DART, Luas (light rail) or suburban train, just swipe your card and the fare is automatically deducted.

Fare-Saver Passes

Fare-saver passes include the following:

DoDublin Card (adult/child €35/10) Three-day unlimited travel on all bus services, including Airlink and Dublin Bus hop-on, hop-off tours as well as entry to the Little Museum of Dublin and a walking tour.

Luas Flexi Ticket (1/7/30 days from €7/16.50/66) Unlimited travel on all Luas services. The one-day pass covers all zones; the multiday passes start at one zone.

Rambler Pass (5/30 days €33/165) Valid for unlimited travel on all Dublin Bus and Airlink services, except Nitelink.

Visitor Leap Card (1/3/7 days €10/19.50/40) Unlimited travel on bus, Luas and DART, including Airlink, Nitelink and Xpresso buses.

Nitelink

Nitelink late-night buses run from the College, Westmoreland and D'Olier Sts triangle. On Fridays and Saturdays, departures are at 12.30am, then every 20 minutes until 4.30am on the more popular routes, and until 3.30am on the less-frequented ones; there are no services from Sunday to Thursday. Fares are €6.60 (€4.50 with Leap Card). See www.dublinbus.ie for route details.

Tram

The Luas (www.luas.ie) light-rail system has two lines: the Green Line (running every five to 15 minutes) runs from Broombridge in the north of the city down through O'Connell St and St Stephen's Green to Sandyford in south Dublin (via Ranelagh and Dundrum); the Red Line (every 20 minutes) runs from the Point Village to Tallaght via the north quays and Heuston Station.

There are ticket machines at every stop or you can use a tap-on, tap-off Leap Card, which is available from most newsagents. A typical short-hop fare (around four stops) is €2.80. Services run from 5.30am to 12.30am Monday to Friday, from 6.30am to 12.30am Saturday and from 7am to 11.30pm Sunday.

Car & Motorcycle

Traffic in Dublin is a nightmare and parking is an expensive headache. There are no free spots to park anywhere in the city centre during business hours (7am to 7pm Monday to Saturday), but there is plenty of paid parking, priced according to zone: €2.90 per hour in the yellow (central) zone down to €0.60 in the blue (suburban). Supervised and sheltered car parks cost around €4 per hour, with most offering a low-cost evening flat rate.

Clamping of illegally parked cars is thoroughly enforced, and there is an €80 charge for removal. Parking is free after 7pm Monday to Saturday, and all day Sunday, in most metered spots (unless indicated) and on single yellow lines.

Car theft and break-ins are an occasional nuisance, so never leave anything visible or of value in your car. When you're booking accommodation, check on parking facilities.

Hire

All the main agencies are represented in Dublin. Book in advance for the best rates, especially at weekends and during summer months, when demand is highest.

Motorbikes and mopeds are not available for rent. People aged under 21 are not allowed to hire a car; for the majority of rental companies you have to be at least 23 and have had a valid driving licence for a minimum of one year. Many rental agencies will not rent to people over 70 or 75.

The following rental agencies have several branches across the capital and at the airport:

Avis Rent-a-Car (☎01-605 7500; www.avis.ie; 35 Old Kilmainham Rd; ⏰8.30am-5.45pm Mon-Fri, to 2.30pm Sat & Sun; 🚌23, 25, 25A, 26, 68, 69 from city centre)

Budget Rent-a-Car (☎01-837 9611; www.budget.ie; 151 Lower Drumcondra Rd; ⏰9am-6pm; 🚌41 from O'Connell St)

Europcar (☎01-812 2800; www.europcar.ie; 1 Mark St; ⏰8am-6pm Mon-Fri, 8.30am-3pm Sat & Sun; 🚌all city centre)

Hertz Rent-a-Car (☎01-709 3060; www.hertz.com; 151 S Circular Rd; ⏰8.30am-5.30pm Mon-Fri, 9am-4.30pm Sat, 9am-3.30pm Sun; 🚌9, 16, 77, 79 from city centre)

Thrifty (☎01-844 1944; www.thrifty.ie; 26 E Lombard St; ⏰8am-6pm Mon-Fri, to 3pm Sat & Sun; 🚌all city centre)

ROAD SAFETY RULES

➡ Drive on the left, overtake to the right.

➡ Seat belts must be worn by the driver and all passengers.

➡ Children aged under 12 are not allowed to sit in front seats.

➡ Motorcyclists and their passengers must wear helmets.

➡ When entering a roundabout, give way to the right.

➡ Speed limits are 50km/h or as signposted in the city, 100km/h on all roads outside city limits and 120km/h on motorways (marked in blue).

➡ The legal alcohol limit is 50mg of alcohol per 100mL of blood, or 22mg on the breath (roughly one unit of alcohol for a man and less than that for a woman).

Bicycle

Relatively flat and compact, Dublin is ideal cycling territory. Getting from one end of the city centre to the other is a cinch, and a bike makes the nearby suburbs readily accessible. There is a (growing) network of cycle lanes, but encroachment by larger vehicles such as buses and trucks is a major problem in the city centre, so you'll have to keep your wits about you.

There are plenty of spots to lock your bike throughout the city, but be sure to do so thoroughly as bike theft can be a problem, and never leave your bike on the street overnight as even the toughest lock can be broken. Dublin City Cycling (www.cycledublin.ie) is an excellent online resource.

Bikes are only allowed on suburban trains (not the DART), either stowed in the guard's van or in a special compartment at the opposite end of the train from the engine.

Dublinbikes

One of the most popular ways to get around the city is with the blue bikes of Dublinbikes (www.dublinbikes.ie), a public bicycle-rental scheme with more than 100 stations spread across the city centre. Purchase a €5 three-day card (as well as a credit-card deposit of €150) online or at select stations where credit cards can be used. You'll be issued a ticket with an ID and PIN that you'll need to use to free a bike for use, which is then free of charge for the first 30 minutes and €0.50 for each half-hour thereafter.

Hire, Purchase & Repair

Bike rental has become tougher due to the Dublinbikes scheme. The typical rental costs for a hybrid or touring bike are around €25 a day or €140 per week.

Cycleways (www.cycleways.com; 31 Lower Ormond Quay; ⏰8.30am-6pm Mon-Fri, from 10am Sat; 🚌all city centre) An excellent bike shop that rents out hybrids and touring bikes during the summer months (May to September).

2Wheels (www.2wheels.ie; 57 S William St; ⏰10am-6pm Mon, Tue & Sat, to 8pm Wed, Thu & Fri, noon-6pm Sun; 🚌all city centre) New bikes, all the gear you could possibly need and a decent repair service; but be sure to book an appointment as it is generally quite busy.

Train

The **Dublin Area Rapid Transport** (DART; ☎01-836 6222; www.irishrail.ie) provides quick train access to the coast as far north as Howth (about 30 minutes) and as far south as Greystones in County Wicklow. Pearse Station is convenient for central Dublin south of the Liffey, and Connolly Station for north of the Liffey. There are services every 10 to 20 minutes, sometimes more frequently, from around 6.30am to midnight Monday to Saturday. Services are less frequent on Sunday. A one-way DART ticket from Dublin to Dun Laoghaire or Howth costs €3.30 (€2.40 with a Leap Card).

There are also suburban rail services north as far as Dundalk, inland to Mullingar and south past Bray to Arklow.

Train Passes

DART passes include the following:

Adult All Day Rail (one/three days €12.15/28.50) Valid for unlimited travel on DART and suburban rail travel.

Family All Day Rail (€20) Valid for travel on rail services for one day for a family of two adults and two children aged under 16.

TOURS

Dublin isn't that big, so a straightforward sightseeing tour is only really necessary if you're looking to cram in the sights or avoid blistered feet. What is worth considering, however, is a specialised guided tour, especially for those with a culinary, historical or literary bent. There are bus tours aplenty – Dublin Bus Tours, the city's bus company, runs a variety of tours, all of which can be booked at its **office** (Map p280; ☎01-872 0000; www.dublinsightseeing.ie; 59 Upper O'Connell St; adult €15-28; 🚌all city centre, 🚊Abbey), or at the Bus Éireann counter at the **Visit Dublin Centre** (Map p270; www.visitdublin.com; 25 Suffolk St; ⌚9am-5.30pm Mon-Sat, 10.30am-3pm Sun; 🚌all city centre). There are even boat tours as well, but the best way to get around is on foot, in the company of an expert.

Directory A–Z

Accessible Travel

Dublin's compact city centre is mostly flat, with a few cobblestoned areas and a relatively accessible public-transport network, making it an attractive destination for people with disabilities. While most DART stations are disability-friendly, DART and train services require 24 hours' notice before boarding with a wheelchair. All city buses are wheelchair-accessible, but Luas is the way to go for maximum accessibility.

Resources

Download Lonely Planet's free Accessible Travel guides from http://lptravel.to/AccessibleTravel.

Accessible Ireland (www.accessibleireland.com) Reviews, plus short introductions to public transport.

Ireland.com (www.ireland.com/en-us/accommodation/articles/accessibility) Informative article with links to accessibility information for transport and tourist attractions.

Irish Wheelchair Association (☎01-818 6400; www.iwa.ie) Useful national association.

Mobility Mojo (www.mobilitymojo.com) More than 500 reviews of establishments in a searchable database, mostly in the Dublin and Galway areas but expanding all the time.

Trip-Ability (www.trip-ability.com) Review site that should soon feature a booking facility.

Customs Regulations

Getting into the country is easy, so long as you have the right documentation. Immigration channels at airports are divided between holders of EU and non-EU passports. The former usually results in a cursory glance at your passport, while visitors in the latter category are scrutinised a little more.

Duty-Free

For duty-free goods from outside the EU, limits include 200 cigarettes, 1L of spirits or 2L of wine, 60mL of perfume and 250mL of *eau de toilette*.

Tax & Duty Paid

Amounts that officially constitute personal use include 3200 cigarettes (or 400 cigarillos, 200 cigars or 3kg of tobacco) and either 10L of spirits, 20L of fortified wine, 60L of sparkling wine, 90L of still wine or 110L of beer.

Discount Cards

Senior citizens are entitled to discounts on public transport and museum fees. Students and under-26s also get discounts with the appropriate student or youth card. Local discount passes include the following:

Dublin Pass (adult/child one-day €62/33, three-day €92/49) For heavy-duty sightseeing, the Dublin Pass will save you a packet. It provides free entry to over 25 attractions (including the Guinness Storehouse), discounts at 20

PRACTICALITIES

Newspapers *Irish Independent* (www.independent.ie), *Irish Times* (www.irishtimes.com), *Irish Examiner* (www.examiner.ie), *The Herald* (www.herald.ie).

Radio RTE Radio 1 (88-90MHz), RTE Radio 2 (90-92MHz), Today FM (100-103MHz), Newstalk 106-108 (106-108MHz).

Smoking It is illegal to smoke indoors everywhere except private residences and prisons.

Weights & Measures The metric system is used; the exception is for liquid measures of alcohol, where pints are used.

others and guaranteed fast-track entry to some of the busiest sights. To avail of the free Aircoach transfer to and from the airport, download the app before you arrive. Otherwise, it's available from any Discover Ireland Dublin Tourism Centre.

Heritage Card (adult/child/student €40/10/10) This card entitles you to free access to all sights in and around Dublin managed by the Office of Public Works (OPW). You can buy it at OPW sites or Dublin Tourism offices.

Electricity

Type G
230V/50Hz

Embassies & Consulates

Australian Embassy (☎01-664 5300; www.ireland.embassy.gov.au; 3rd fl, 47-49 St Stephen's Green E; ⏰8.30am-4.30pm Mon-Fri; 🚌37 from city centre)

Canadian Embassy (☎01-234 4000; www.canada.ie; 7-8 Wilton Tce; ⏰9am-1pm & 2-4.30pm; 🚌37 from city centre)

Dutch Embassy (☎01-269 3444; www.netherlandsandyou.nl/your-country-and-the-netherlands/ireland; 160 Merrion Rd, Ballsbridge; ⏰By appointment only; 🚌4, 7, 8 from city centre)

French Embassy (☎01-277 5000; www.ambafrance-ie.org; 66 Fitzwilliam Lane; ⏰9-10am & noon-4pm Mon-Fri; 🚌46A from city centre)

German Embassy (☎01-269 3011; www.dublin.diplo.de; 31 Trimleston Ave, Booterstown, Blackrock; ⏰8am-5pm Mon-Thu, to 2pm Fri, consular service 9am-noon Mon, Tue & Fri, 8.30-11.30am & 2-4pm Wed; 🚆Booterstown)

Italian Embassy (☎01-660 1744; www.ambdublino.esteri.it/Ambasciata_Dublino; 63 Northumberland Rd, Ballsbridge, Dublin 4; ⏰by appointment only; 🚌4, 7, 63, 84 from city centre)

UK Embassy (☎01-205 3700; www.gov.uk; 29 Merrion Rd, Ballsbridge; ⏰9am-5pm Mon-Fri; 🚌4, 7, 8 from city centre)

US Embassy (☎01-630 6200; http://ie.usembassy.gov/embassy; 42 Elgin Rd, Ballsbridge; ⏰by appointment only; 🚌4, 7, 8 from city centre)

Emergency & Important Numbers

Ambulance, Fire, Police (Gardaí), Boat or Coastal Rescue	☎999 or 112
Rape Crisis Centre	☎1800 778 888
Country Code	☎+353
International Access Code	☎00

Health

EU citizens equipped with a European Health Insurance Card (EHIC), available from health centres or, in the UK, post offices, will be covered for most medical care – but not non-emergencies or emergency repatriation. While other countries, such as Australia, also have reciprocal agreements with Ireland, many do not.

Tap Water

Don't bother with bottled water in restaurants; Dublin's tap water is perfectly safe, free and generally excellent.

Internet Access

Wi-fi and 3G/4G networks are making internet cafes largely redundant (except to gamers); the few that are left will charge around €6 per hour. Most accommodation has wi-fi service, either free or for a daily charge (up to €10 per day).

Legal Matters

The possession of small quantities of marijuana attracts a fine or warning, but harder drugs are treated more seriously. Public drunkenness is illegal but commonplace – the police will usually ignore it unless you're causing trouble. If you need legal assistance, contact the **Legal Aid Board** (☎066-947 1000, in Republic 1890 615 200; www.legalaidboard.ie; ⏰9am-5pm Mon-Fri).

LGBT+ Travellers

Dublin is a pretty good place to be LGBTIQ+. Being gay or lesbian in the city is completely unremarkable, while in recent years members of the trans community have also found greater acceptance. However, LGBTIQ+

people can still be harrassed or worse, so if you do encounter any sort of trouble, call the **Crime Victims Helpline** (☎116006; 24hr) or the **Sexual Assault Investigation Unit** (☎01-666 3430; www.garda.ie; ⏱24hr).

Resources include the following:

Gaire (www.gaire.com) Online message board and resource centre.

Gay Men's Health Project (☎01-660 2189; www.hse.ie/go/GMHS) Practical advice on men's health issues.

National LGBT Federation (☎01-675 5025; www.nxf.ie; 2 Upper Exchange St, Temple Bar; 🚌all city centre) Publishers of *Gay Community News*.

Outhouse (☎01-873 4932; www.outhouse.ie; 105 Capel St; ⏱10am-6pm Mon-Fri, noon-5pm Sat; 🚌all city centre) Top LGBTIQ+ resource centre, and a great stop-off point to see what's on, check noticeboards and meet people. It publishes the free *Ireland's Pink Pages*, a directory of gay-centric services, which is also accessible on the website.

Medical Services

Dentists

Dental care is a costly business in Dublin. Unless you have a medical card (only available to registered residents), you can expect to pay from €85 for a basic check, and about €100 for a cleaning and €120 for a filling appointment.

Doctors

If you don't have a medical card, you'll have to pay for all visits to a doctor. Charges begin at €50 for even a cursory examination. You can request a doctor to visit your accommodation at any time with the private service **Doctor on Duty** (☎01-420 0880; www.mediserve.ie; ⏱24hr).

The **Health Service Executive** (HSE; ☎01-679 0700, 1800 520 520; www.hse.ie; Dr Steevens' Hospital, Steevens' Lane; ⏱9.30am-5.30pm Mon-Fri; 🚌25A, 25B, 26, 66 from city centre) has a Choice of Doctor Scheme, which can advise you on a suitable general practitioner (GP) from 9am to 5pm Monday to Friday. The HSE also provides information services for those with physical and mental disabilities.

Your hotel or embassy can also suggest a doctor, but the **Grafton Medical Centre** (☎01-671 2122; www.graftonmedical.ie; 34 Grafton St; ⏱8.30am-6pm Mon-Thu, to 5pm Fri; 🚌all city centre) is also a good clinic. If you need a doctor after 6pm or at weekends, **Caredoc** (☎1850 334 999; www.caredoc.ie; ⏱6pm-8am Mon-Fri, 24hr Sat & Sun) is an excellent service that will provide a doctor, usually within an hour.

Hospitals

EU citizens are encouraged to obtain a European Health Insurance Card (EHIC) before they leave home, which will cover hospital costs should they require hospitalisation. This card provides cover for a year and is easily obtained from a local health authority or, in the UK, post offices. The main Dublin city-centre hospitals are the following:

Mater Misericordiae Hospital (☎01-830 1122; www.mater.ie; Eccles St; 🚌120, 122 from city centre)

St James's Hospital (☎01-410 3000; www.stjames.ie; James's St; 🚊James's)

Pharmacies

For minor, self-limiting illnesses, pharmacists can give valuable advice and sell over-the-counter medication. They can also advise when more specialised help is required and point you in the right direction.

All pharmacies in Dublin are clearly designated by a green cross. There are branches of the English chain pharmacy, Boots, spread throughout the city centre. Most pharmacies are open until 7pm or 8pm, but the City, Hickey's and O'Connell's pharmacies in the city centre stay open until 10pm.

Money

ATMs are widespread. Credit cards (with PIN) are widely accepted in restaurants, hotels and shops.

ATMs

Most banks have ATMs that are linked to international money systems such as Cirrus, Maestro or Plus. Each transaction incurs a currency conversion fee, and credit cards can incur immediate and exorbitant cash-advance interest-rate charges. Also it is strongly recommended that if you're staying in the city centre, you get your money out early on a Friday to avoid the long queues that can form after 8pm.

Changing Money

The best exchange rates are at banks, although bureaux de change and other exchange facilities usually open for longer hours. There's a cluster of banks located around College Green opposite Trinity College and all have exchange facilities.

Credit Cards

Visa and MasterCard credit and debit cards are widely accepted in Dublin. Smaller businesses prefer debit cards (and will charge a fee for credit cards). Nearly all credit and debit cards use the chip-and-PIN system, and an increasing number of places will not accept your card if you don't have your PIN.

Opening Hours

Standard opening hours in relatively late-rising Dublin are as follows:

Banks 10am to 4pm Monday to Wednesday and Friday, 10am–5pm Thursday

Offices 9am to 5pm Monday to Friday

Post Offices 9am to 6pm Monday to Friday, 9am to 1pm Saturday

Restaurants noon to 10pm (or midnight); food service generally ends around 9pm; top-end restaurants often close 3 to 6pm; restaurants serving brunch open around 11am

Shops 9.30am to 6pm Monday to Wednesday, Friday and Saturday, 9.30am to 8pm Thursday (to 9pm for bigger shopping centres and supermarkets), noon to 6pm Sunday

Post

The Irish postal service, An Post, is reliable, efficient and generally on time. Postboxes in Dublin are usually green and have two slots: one for 'Dublin only', the other for 'All Other Places'. There are a couple of post offices in the city centre, including **An Post** (Map p270; 01-705 8206; www.anpost.ie; St Andrew's St; 8.30am-5pm Mon-Fri; all city centre) and the **General Post Office** (Map p280; 01-705 7000; www.anpost.ie; Lower O'Connell St; 8am-8pm Mon-Sat; all city centre, Abbey).

Public Holidays

Good Friday and Christmas Day are the only two days in the year when all pubs close. Otherwise, the half-dozen or so bank holidays (most of which fall on a Monday) mean just that – the banks are closed, along with about half the shops. St Patrick's Day and St Stephen's Day holidays are taken on the following Monday should they fall on a weekend.

New Year's Day 1 January

St Patrick's Day 17 March

Easter (Good Friday to Easter Monday inclusive) March/April

May Bank Holiday First Monday in May

June Bank Holiday First Monday in June

August Bank Holiday First Monday in August

October Bank Holiday Last Monday in October

Christmas Day 25 December

St Stephen's Day 26 December

Safe Travel

Dublin is a safe city by any standards, except maybe those set by the Swiss. Basically, act as you would at home.

- Don't leave anything visible in your car when you park.
- Skimming at ATMs is an ongoing problem; be sure to cover the keypad with your hand when you input your PIN.
- Take care around the western edge of Thomas St (onto James St), where drug addicts are often present.
- The northern end of Gardiner St and the areas northeast of there have crime-related problems.

Police Stations

Police stations are in the following areas of Dublin:

Docklands (01-677 8141; Pearse St; all city centre)

Merrion Sq area (01-676 3481; Harcourt Tce; 24hr; Harcourt)

North of the Liffey (Store St; Connolly) Plus another **east of Mountjoy Sq** (Fitzgibbon St; 122 from city centre).

Taxes & Refunds

A standard value-added tax (VAT) rate of 23% is applied to all goods sold in Dublin excluding books, children's clothing and educational items. Non-EU residents can claim the VAT back so long as the store operates either the Cashback or Taxback refund programme. You'll get a voucher with your purchase that must be stamped at the last point of exit from the EU.

Telephone

When calling Dublin from abroad, dial your international access code, followed by 353 and 1 (dropping the 0 that precedes it). To make international calls from Dublin, first dial 00, then the country code, followed by the local area code and number.

Country Code	+353
City Code	01
International Access Code	00
Directory Enquiries	11811 or 11850
International Directory Enquiries	11818

Mobile Phones

All European and Australasian mobile phones work in Dublin, as do North American phones not locked to a local network. Check with your provider. Prepaid SIM cards start from €20.

Phone cards

Virtually every newsagent sells a range of different phonecards, which can be used to make cut-rate international calls. Cards come in €7, €15 or €20 values and give you plenty of minutes to call abroad with.

Time

In winter, Dublin (and the rest of Ireland) is on GMT, also known as Universal Time Coordinated (UTC); the same as Britain. In summer, the clock shifts to GMT plus one hour. When it's noon in Dublin in summer, it's 4am in Los Angeles and Vancouver, 7am in New York and Toronto, 1pm in Paris, 7pm in Singapore and 9pm in Sydney.

Toilets

There are no on-street facilities in Dublin. All shopping centres have public toilets; if you're stranded, go into any bar or hotel.

Tourist Information

Visit Dublin Centre (Map p270; www.visitdublin.com; 25 Suffolk St; 9am-5.30pm Mon-Sat, 10.30am-3pm Sun; all city centre) has general visitor information on Dublin and Ireland, as well as an accommodation and booking service.

Visas

Not required for citizens of Australia, New Zealand, the USA or Canada, or citizens of European nations that belong to the European Economic Area (EEA).

Women Travellers

Dublin should pose no problems for women travellers.

The morning-after pill is available without a prescription from pharmacies.

In the unlikely event of a sexual assault, get in touch with the *gardaí* (police) and the **Rape Crisis Centre** (24hr 1800 778 888; www.drcc.ie; 70 Lower Leeson St; 8am-7pm Mon-Fri, 9am-4pm Sat; all city centre).

Language

Irish (Gaeilge) is the country's official language. In 2003 the government introduced the Official Languages Act, whereby all official documents, street signs and official titles must be either in Irish or in both Irish and English. Despite its official status, Irish is really only spoken in pockets of rural Ireland known as the Gaeltacht, the main ones being Cork (Corcaigh), Donegal (Dún na nGall), Galway (Gaillimh), Kerry (Ciarraí) and Mayo (Maigh Eo).

Ask people outside the Gaeltacht if they can speak Irish and nine out of 10 of them will probably reply, *'ah, cupla focal'* (a couple of words), and they generally mean it. Irish is a compulsory subject in both primary and secondary schools, but Irish classes have traditionally been rather academic and unimaginative, leading many students to resent it as a waste of time. As a result, many adults regret not having a greater grasp of it. In recent times, at long last, a new Irish curriculum has been introduced cutting the hours devoted to the subject but making the lessons more fun, practical and celebratory.

PRONUNCIATION

Irish divides vowels into long (those with an accent) and short (those without) and also disinguishes between broad (**a**, **á**, **o**, **ó**, **u**) and slender (**e**, **é**, **i** and **í**), which can affect the pronunciation of preceding consonants. Other than a few odd-looking clusters, such as **mh** and **bhf** (pronounced both as w), consonants are generally pronounced as they are in English.

Irish has three main dialects: Connaught Irish (in Galway and northern Mayo), Munster Irish (in Cork, Kerry and Waterford) and Ulster Irish (in Donegal). The blue pronunciation guidelines given here are an anglicised version of modern standard Irish, which is essentially an amalgam of the three – if you read them as if they were English, you'll be able to get your point across in Gaeilge without even having to think about the specifics of Irish pronunciation or spelling.

WANT MORE?

For in-depth language information and handy phrases, check out Lonely Planet's *Irish Language & Culture*. You'll find it at **shop.lonelyplanet.com**, or you can buy Lonely Planet's iPhone phrasebooks at the Apple App Store.

BASICS

Hello.	*Dia duit.*	deea gwit
Hello. (reply)	*Dia is Muire duit.*	deeas moyra gwit
Good morning.	*Maidin mhaith.*	mawjin wah
Good night.	*Oíche mhaith.*	eekheh wah
Goodbye.		
(when leaving)	*Slán leat.*	slawn lyat
(when staying)	*Slán agat.*	slawn agut
Yes.	*Tá.*	taw
It is.	*Sea.*	sheh
No.	*Níl.*	neel
It isn't.	*Ní hea.*	nee heh

Thank you (very) much.
Go raibh (míle) maith agat. — goh rev (meela) mah agut

Excuse me.
Gabh mo leithscéal. — gamoh lesh scale

I'm sorry.
Tá brón orm. — taw brohn oruhm

I don't understand.
Ní thuigim. — nee higgim

Do you speak Irish?
An bhfuil Gaeilge agat? — on wil gaylge oguht

What is this?
Cad é seo? — kod ay shoh

What is that?
Cad é sin? — kod ay shin

I'd like to go to...
Ba mhaith liom dul go dtí... — baw wah lohm dull go dee...

I'd like to buy...
Ba mhaith liom... a cheannach. — bah wah lohm... a kyanukh

another/ one more	*ceann eile*	kyawn ella
nice	*go deas*	goh dyass

MAKING CONVERSATION

Welcome.
Ceád míle fáilte. (lit: 100,000 welcomes) — kade meela fawlcha

How are you?
Conas a tá tú? — kunas aw taw too

..., (if you) please.
...más é do thoil é. — ...maws ay do hall ay

What's your name?
Cad is ainm duit? — kod is anim dwit

My name is (Sean Frayne).
(Sean Frayne) is ainm dom. — (shawn frain) is anim dohm

DAYS OF THE WEEK

Monday	*Dé Luaín*	day loon
Tuesday	*Dé Máirt*	day maart
Wednesday	*Dé Ceádaoin*	day kaydeen
Thursday	*Déardaoin*	daredeen
Friday	*Dé hAoine*	day heeneh
Saturday	*Dé Sathairn*	day sahern
Sunday	*Dé Domhnaigh*	day downick

Signs

Fir	fear	Men
Gardaí	gardee	Police
Leithreas	lehrass	Toilet
Mna	mnaw	Women
Oifig An Phoist	iffig ohn fwisht	Post office

CUPLA FOCAL

Here are a few phrases *os Gaeilge* (in Irish) to help you impress the locals:

Tóg é gobogé.
Take it easy.
tohg ay gobogay

Ní féidir é!
Impossible!
nee faydir ay

Ráiméis!
Nonsense!
rawmaysh

Go huafásach!
That's terrible!
guh hoofawsokh

Ní ólfaidh mé go brách arís!
I'm never ever drinking again!
knee ohlhee mey gu brawkh ureeshch

Slainte!
Your health!/Cheers!
slawncha

Táim go maith.
I'm fine.
thawm go mah

Nollaig shona!
Happy Christmas!
nuhlig hona

Cáisc shona!
Happy Easter!
kawshk hona

Go n-éirí an bóthar leat!
Bon voyage!
go nairee on bohhar lat

NUMBERS

1	*haon*	hayin
2	*dó*	doe
3	*trí*	tree
4	*ceathaír*	kahirr
5	*cúig*	kooig
6	*sé*	shay
7	*seacht*	shocked
8	*hocht*	hukt
9	*naoi*	nay
10	*deich*	jeh
11	*haon déag*	hayin jague
12	*dó dhéag*	doe yague
20	*fiche*	feekhe

GLOSSARY

12 July – the day the *Orange Order* marches to celebrate Protestant King William III's victory over the Catholic King James II at the Battle of the Boyne in 1690

An Óige – literally 'the Youth'; Republic of Ireland Youth Hostel Association

Anglo-Norman – Norman, English and Welsh peoples who invaded Ireland in the 12th century

Apprentice Boys – *Loyalist* organisation founded in 1814 to commemorate the Great Siege of Derry in August every year

ard – literally 'high'; Irish place name

Ascendancy – refers to the Protestant aristocracy descended from the Anglo-Normans and those who were installed here during the *Plantation*

bailey – outer wall of a castle

bawn – area surrounded by walls outside the main castle, acting as a defence and as a place to keep cattle in times of trouble

beehive hut – see *clochán*

Black & Tans – British recruits to the Royal Irish Constabulary shortly after WWI, noted for their brutality

Blarney Stone – sacred stone perched on top of Blarney Castle; bending over backwards to kiss the stone is said to bestow the gift of gab

bodhrán – hand-held goatskin drum

Bronze Age – earliest metalusing period, around 2500 BC to 300 BC in Ireland; after the Stone Age and before the *Iron Age*

B-Specials – Northern Irish auxiliary police force, disbanded in 1971

bullaun – stone with a depression, probably used as a mortar for grinding medicine or food, often found at monastic sites

caher – circular area enclosed by stone walls

cairn – mound of stones over a prehistoric grave

cashel – stone-walled *ring fort*; see also *ráth*

céilidh – session of traditional music and dancing; also called 'ceili'

Celtic Tiger – nickname of the Irish economy during the growth years from 1990 to about 2002

Celts – *Iron Age* warrior tribes that arrived in Ireland around 300 BC and controlled the country for 1000 years

chancel – eastern end of a church, where the altar is situated, reserved for the clergy and choir

chipper – slang term for fish-and-chips fast-food restaurant

cill – literally 'church'; Irish place name; also 'kill'

Claddagh ring – ring worn in much of *Connaught* since the mid-18th century, with a crowned heart nestling between two hands; if the heart points towards the hand then the wearer is partnered or married, if towards the fingertip he or she is looking for a mate

clochán – circular stone building, shaped like an oldfashioned beehive, from the early Christian period

Connaught – one of the four ancient provinces of Ireland, made up of Counties Galway, Leitrim, Mayo, Roscommon and Sligo; sometimes spelled 'Connacht'; see also *Leinster, Munster* and *Ulster*

craic – conversation, gossip, fun, good times; also known as 'crack'

crannóg – artificial island made in a lake to provide habitation in a good defensive position

currach – rowing boat made of a framework of laths covered with tarred canvas; also known as 'cúrach'

Dáil – lower house of the parliament of the Republic of Ireland; see also *Oireachtas* and *Seanad*

DART – Dublin Area Rapid Transport train line

demesne – landed property close to a house or castle

diamond – town square

dolmen – tomb chamber or portal tomb made of vertical stones topped by a huge capstone; from around 2000 BC

drumlin – rounded hill formed by retreating glaciers

Dúchas – government department in charge of parks, monuments and gardens in the Republic; formerly known as the Office of Public Works

dún – fort, usually constructed of stone

DUP – Democratic Unionist Party; founded principally by Ian Paisley in 1971 in hardline opposition to *Unionist* policies held by the *UUP*

Éire – Irish name for the Republic of Ireland

esker – raised ridge formed by glaciers

Fáilte Ireland – 'Welcome Board'; Irish Tourist Board

Fianna – mythical band of warriors who feature in many tales of ancient Ireland

Fianna Fáil – literally 'Warriors of Ireland'; a major political party in the Republic, originating from the *Sinn Féin* faction opposed to the 1921 treaty with Britain

Fine Gael – literally 'Tribe of the Gael'; a major political party in the Republic, originating from the *Sinn Féin* faction that favoured the 1921 treaty with Britain; formed the first government of independent Ireland

fir – men (singular 'fear'); sign on men's toilets; see also *leithreas* and *mná*

fleadh – festival

GAA – Gaelic Athletic Association; promotes Gaelic football and hurling, among other Irish games

Gaeltacht – Irish-speaking

gallóglí – mercenary soldiers of the 14th to 15th century; anglicised to 'gallowglasses'

garda – Irish Republic police; plural 'gardaí'

ghillie – fishing or hunting guide; also known as 'ghilly'

gort – literally 'field'; Irish place name

hill fort – a hilltop fortified with ramparts and ditches, usually dating from the *Iron Age*

HINI – Hostelling International of Northern Ireland

Hunger, the – colloquial name for the Great Famine of 1845–51

hurling – Irish sport similar to hockey

Iarnród Éireann – Republic of Ireland Railways

INLA – Irish National Liberation Association; formed in 1975 as an *IRA* splinter group; it has maintained a ceasefire since 1998

IRA – Irish Republican Army; the largest Republican paramilitary organisation, founded 80 years ago with the aim to fight for a united Ireland; in 1969 the IRA split into the Official IRA and the Provisional IRA; the Official IRA is no longer active and the PIRA has become the IRA

Iron Age – metal-using period that lasted from the end of the *Bronze Age*, around 300 BC (the arrival of the Celts), to the arrival of Christianity, around the 5th century AD

jarvey – driver of a *jaunting car*

jaunting car – Killarney's traditional horse-drawn transport; see also *jarvey*

Leinster – one of the four ancient provinces of Ireland, made up of Counties Carlow, Dublin, Kildare, Kilkenny, Laois, Longford, Louth, Meath, Offaly, West Meath, Wexford and Wicklow; see also *Connaught, Munster* and *Ulster*

leithreas – toilets; see also *mná* and *fir*

leprechaun – mischievous elf or sprite from Irish folklore

lough – lake, or long narrow bay or arm of the sea

Loyalist – person, usually a Northern Irish Protestant, insisting on the continuation of Northern Ireland's links with Britain

Luas – light-rail transit system in Dublin; Irish for 'speed'

marching season – *Orange Order* parades, which take place from Easter and throughout summer to celebrate the victory by Protestant King William III of Orange over Catholic James II in the Battle of the Boyne on 12 July 1690, and the union with Britain

Mesolithic – also known as the Middle Stone Age; time of the first human settlers in Ireland, about 8000 BC to 4000 BC; see also *Neolithic*

mná – women; sign on women's toilets; see also *fir* and *leithreas*

motte – early Norman fortification consisting of a raised, flattened mound with a keep on top; when attached to a *bailey* it is known as a motte-and-bailey fort, many of which were built in Ireland until the early 13th century

Munster – one of the four ancient provinces of Ireland, made up of Counties Clare, Cork, Kerry, Limerick, Tipperary and Waterford; see also *Connaught, Leinster* and *Ulster*

nationalism – belief in a reunited Ireland

Nationalist – proponent of a united Ireland

Neolithic – also known as the New Stone Age; a period characterised by settled agriculture lasting from around 4000 BC to 2500 BC in Ireland; followed by the *Bronze Age;* see also *Mesolithic*

NIR – Northern Ireland Railways

NITB – Northern Ireland Tourist Board

NNR – National Nature Reserves

North, the – political entity of Northern Ireland, not the northernmost geographic part of Ireland

NUI – National University of Ireland; made up of branches in Dublin, Cork, Galway and Limerick

Ogham stone – a stone etched with Ogham characters, the earliest form of writing in Ireland, with a variety of notched strokes

Oireachtas – Parliament of the Republic of Ireland, consisting of the *Dáil,* the lower house, and the *Seanad,* the upper house

Orange Order – the largest Protestant organisation in Northern Ireland, founded in 1795, with a membership of up to 100,000; name commemorates the victory of King William of Orange in the Battle of the Boyne

óstán – hotel

Palladian – style of architecture developed by Andrea Palladio (1508–80), based on ancient Roman architecture

paramilitaries – armed illegal organisations, either *Loyalist* or *Republican,* usually associated with the use of violence and crime for political and economic gain

partition – division of Ireland in 1921

passage grave – Celtic tomb with a chamber reached by a narrow passage, typically buried in a mound

penal laws – laws passed in the 18th century forbidding Catholics from buying land and holding public office

Plantation – settlement of Protestant immigrants (known as Planters) in Ireland in the 17th century

poitín – illegally brewed whiskey, also spelled 'poteen'

provisionals – Provisional IRA, formed after a break with the official *IRA* (who are now largely inconsequential); named after the provisional government declared in 1916, they have been the main force combating the British army in *the North;* also known as 'provos'

PSNI – Police Service of Northern Ireland

ráth – *ring fort* with earthen banks around a timber wall; see also *cashel*

Real IRA – splinter movement of the *IRA*; opposed to *Sinn Féin's* support of the Good Friday Agreement; responsible for the Omagh bombing in 1998 in which 29 people died; subsequently called a ceasefire but has been responsible for bombs in Britain and other acts of violence

Republic of Ireland – the 26 counties of *the South*

Republican – supporter of a united Ireland

republicanism – belief in a united Ireland, sometimes referred to as militant nationalism

ring fort – circular habitation area surrounded by banks and ditches, used from the *Bronze Age* right through to the Middle Ages, particularly in the early Christian period

RTE – Radio Telifís Éireann; the national broadcasting service of the Republic of Ireland, with two TV and four radio stations

RUC – Royal Ulster Constabulary, the former name for the armed Police Service of Northern Ireland *(PSNI)*

Seanad – upper house of the parliament of the Republic of Ireland; see also *Oireachtas* and *Dáil*

shamrock – three-leafed plant said to have been used by St Patrick to illustrate the Holy Trinity

shebeen – from the Irish 'síbín'; illicit drinking place or speakeasy

sheila-na-gig – literally 'Sheila of the teats'; female figure with exaggerated genitalia, carved in stone on the exteriors of some churches and castles; explanations include male clerics warning against the perils of sex to the idea that they represent Celtic war goddesses

Sinn Féin – literally 'We Ourselves'; a *Republican* party with the aim of a united Ireland; seen as the political wing of the *IRA* but it maintains that both organisations are completely separate

slí – hiking trail or way

snug – partitioned-off drinking area in a pub

souterrain – underground chamber usually associated with *ring* and *hill forts;* probably provided a hiding place or escape route in times of trouble and/or storage space for goods

South, the – Republic of Ireland

standing stone – upright stone set in the ground, common across Ireland and dating from a variety of periods; some are burial markers

Taoiseach – Republic of Ireland prime minister

teampall – church

trá – beach or strand

Treaty – Anglo-Irish Treaty of 1921, which divided Ireland and gave relative independence to the South; cause of the 1922–23 Civil War

tricolour – green, white and orange Irish flag symbolising the hoped-for union of the 'green' Catholic Southern Irish with the 'orange' Protestant Northern Irish

turlough – a small lake that often disappears in dry summers; from the Irish 'turlach'

UDA – Ulster Defence Association; the largest *Loyalist* paramilitary group; it has observed a ceasefire since 1994

uillean pipes – Irish bagpipes with a bellow strapped to the arm; 'uillean' is Irish for 'elbow'

Ulster – one of the four ancient provinces of Ireland; sometimes used to describe the six counties of *the North,* despite the fact that Ulster also includes Counties Cavan, Monaghan and Donegal (all in the Republic); see also *Connaught, Leinster* and *Munster*

Unionist – person who wants to retain Northern Ireland's links with Britain

United Irishmen – organisation founded in 1791 aiming to reduce British power in Ireland; it led a series of unsuccessful risings and invasions

UUP – Ulster Unionist Party; the largest *Unionist* party in Northern Ireland and the majority party in the Assembly; founded in 1905 and led by *Unionist* hero Edward Carson from 1910 to 1921; from 1921 to 1972 the sole *Unionist* organisation but is now under threat from the *DUP*

UVF – Ulster Volunteer Force; an illegal *Loyalist* Northern Irish paramilitary organisation

Volunteers – offshoot of the IRB that came to be known as the *IRA*

Behind the Scenes

SEND US YOUR FEEDBACK

We love to hear from travellers – your comments keep us on our toes and help make our books better. Our well-travelled team reads every word on what you loved or loathed about this book. Although we cannot reply individually to your submissions, we always guarantee that your feedback goes straight to the appropriate authors, in time for the next edition. Each person who sends us information is thanked in the next edition – the most useful submissions are rewarded with a selection of digital PDF chapters.

Visit **lonelyplanet.com/contact** to submit your updates and suggestions or to ask for help. Our award-winning website also features inspirational travel stories, news and discussions.

Note: We may edit, reproduce and incorporate your comments in Lonely Planet products such as guidebooks, websites and digital products, so let us know if you don't want your comments reproduced or your name acknowledged. For a copy of our privacy policy visit lonelyplanet.com/privacy.

WRITER THANKS

Fionn Davenport

Dublin's forever changing, and to update it properly I need more than two eyes and one brain, so a huge thanks to everyone who helped me along. To the staff in the Dublin office, thanks for your tips, suggestions and recommendations; to Nicola Brady, for her invaluable assistance in knowing all of the right places to eat; and to Cliff Wilkinson, the ever-present, ever-helpful editor who answered all of my questions.

ACKNOWLEDGEMENTS

Cover photograph: Samuel Beckett Bridge, mady70 / Alamy ©

Illustrations: p180-1 by Michael Weldon, p58-9, p92-3 and p186-7 by Javier Zarracina

THIS BOOK

This 12th edition of Lonely Planet's *Dublin* guidebook was researched and written by Fionn Davenport, who also wrote the previous two editions. This guidebook was produced by the following:

Destination Editor Clifton Wilkinson
Senior Product Editor Jessica Ryan
Regional Senior Cartographer Mark Griffiths
Product Editor Kate Kiely
Book Designer Gwen Cotter
Assisting Editors Andrew Bain, Imogen Bannister, Janice Bird, Nigel Chin, Shona Gray, Carly Hall, Victoria Harrison, Kellie Langdon, Rosie Nicholson, Katie O'Connell, Kristin Odijk, Gabrielle Stefanos, Simon Williamson
Assisting Cartographer Julie Sheridan
Cover Researcher Meri Blazevski
Thanks to Fergal Condon, Sasha Drew, John McCullough, Genna Patterson

See also separate subindexes for:
- EATING P261
- DRINKING & NIGHTLIFE P262
- ENTERTAINMENT P262
- SHOPPING P263
- SPORTS & ACTIVITIES P263
- SLEEPING P263

Index

14 Henrietta Street 13, 143, **155**
1916 Easter Rising 149

A

accessible travel 247
accommodation 15, 198-208, *see also* Sleeping *subindex, individual neighbourhoods*
  Docklands 207-8
  Grafton St & St Stephen's Green 201-3
  Kilmainham & Liberties, the 205-6
  Merrion Square & Around 203-4
  North of the Liffey 206-7
  self-catering options 205-8
  Southside 208
  St Stephen's Green 201-3
  Temple Bar 204-5
activities 24-7, *see also individual activities,* Sports & Activities *subindex*
Act of Union (1801) 217, 236
air travel 242-3
airports 242-3
alcohol 238-9, *see also* drinking & nightlife
ambulance 248
ancestry, tracing 102
Áras an Uachtaráin 146
Arbour Hill Cemetery 153
architecture 22-3, 233-7, **5**
area codes 248, 250
Ark Children's Cultural Centre 28
art 21
art market 101
ATMs 249
Aviva Stadium 175, **176-7**

B

Bacon, Francis 145
Bank of Ireland 69-70
Bank of Ireland Cultural & Heritage Centre 68
bars 20-1, 38, 40, *see also* Drinking & Nightlife *subindex*
bathrooms 251
Beatty, Alfred Chester 64
Beckett, Samuel 167, 225
beer 40, 140, **40**
  Guinness Storehouse 10, 123-5, **11**
Belvedere House 156
Berkeley Library 57
bicycle travel 245, **17**
Bloody Sunday (1920) 219-20
Bloomsday 25-6, **25**
boat travel 243
Book of Kells 7, 56, 69, **59**
books 100, 210, 220, 224-9
Bord Gais Energy Theatre 3
Bowery 175, **177**
Brexit 211
Brú na Bóinne 179-83, **180**, **179**, **180**, **181**
Bullock Castle 195
bureaux de change 249
Burke, Edmund 56
bus travel 242-3, 243, 244, **236**
business hours 34, 38, 42, 45, 250
busking 44

C

cafes 38, *see also* Drinking & Nightlife *subindex*
car travel 243-4, 244-5
Caravaggio 95
Castletown House 193-4
Catholicism 216, 222, 240
cell phones 14, 250
cheese 46, 83, **46**
Chester Beatty Library 11, 64-5, 66, **11**, **64**
children, travel with 28-9
Christ Church Cathedral 107-9, 136, 234, 236, **109**, **107**
City Assembly House 68
City Hall 69
City Spectacular 26, **26**
climate 24-7
climate change 242
College Green 73
Collins, Michael 219, 220-1
comedy 43, 44
Connolly, James 167, 219
consulates 248
Contemporary Music Centre 111
Convention Centre 167
costs 14, 34, 199, 247-8, 250
credit cards 249-50
Croke Park Stadium & Museum 150-2
Cromwell, Oliver 215
Culture Night 27
currency 14
Custom House 166
customs regulations 247

D

Da Nort'soyid 172
Dalkey 194-6, **195**
Dalkey Castle & Heritage Centre 195
Dalkey Island 195
dangers, *see* safety
dental services 249
de Valera, Éamon 219, 220-1
distilleries 139
Docklands 53, 164-9, **164**, **284**
  accommodation 207-8
  activities 169
  drinking 165, 168-9
  entertainment 169
  food 165, 167-8
  highlights 164-5
  nightlife 165, 168-9
  shopping 165, 169
  sights 166-7
  sports & activities 169
  transport 165
Douglas Hyde Gallery of Modern Art 68
Dowth 183
drinking & nightlife 31, 37-40, **39**, *see also* Drinking & Nightlife *subindex, individual neighbourhoods*
drugs 248
Dublin Castle 64, 66, **63**, **61**
Dublin City Liffey Swim 26, **26**
Dublin Liberties Distillery 133
Dublin Writers Museum 154, 228
Dublin Zoo 28, 146
Dubliners, the 230, 231
Dublinia: Experience Viking & Medieval Dublin 28, 110
duty free 45

E

Easter Rising, the 218-19
economy 210-11, 222-3
electricity 248
embassies 248
emergencies 248
Enniskerry 192-3
entertainment 41-4, 82-3, *see also* Entertainment *subindex, individual neighbourhoods*
  bookings 42
  festivals 44
  listings 42
EPIC The Irish Emigration Museum 166
events 24-7

Sights 000
Map Pages **000**
Photo Pages **000**

F

Famine, the 166, 216-17
Famine Memorial 166
fashion 45, 46
festivals 24-7
  entertainment 44
  literary 244
  theatre 43
Fianna Fáil 221, 254
film 43, 210
Fine Gael 220, 221
fire 248
Fitzwilliam Square 98
food 9, 22, 33-6, **9**, **33**, **34**, *see also* Eating *subindex*, *see also individual neighbourhoods*
  costs 34
  opening hours 34
football 47-8, 49, **47**
Forbidden Fruit 25
Four Courts 152-3
free attractions 32

G

Gaeilge 252-6
galleries, *see* museums & galleries
Gallery of Photography 110
Garden of Remembrance 156
gardens 22
Gate Theatre 41, **71**
Geldof, Bob 231
General Post Office 150
Georgian architecture 234-6
Glasnevin Cemetery 150
Glendalough 184-8, **186-7**, **184**, **186**, **187**
glossary 254-6
Goldsmith, Oliver 56
golf 49
Government Buildings 100-1
GPO Witness History 150
Grafton St area 52, 54-87, **54**, **67**, **270**, **274**
  accommodation 201-3
  drinking 55, 78-82
  food 55, 71-8
  highlights 54-65
  nightlife 55, 78-82
  shopping 83-6
  sights 56-71
  transport 55
  walks 67, **67**
Grand Canal Square 167
Gray, Eileen 149
Guinness 40, 140, **30**
Guinness Storehouse 10, 123-5, **11**, **123**, **125**

H

Handel's Hotel (Site of Neal's New Musick Hall) 111
Hansard, Glen 211
Ha'penny Bridge 110, 116, **117**
health 248
Heaney, Seamus 13, 225, 229, **229**
Herbert Park 172, 177, **176**
history 4, 21, 212-23
  Act of Union (1801) 217, 236
  Anglo-Irish Treaty 220
  Battle of the Bogside 221
  Bloody Sunday (1920) 219-20
  Celtic Tiger 222
  Civil War 220-1
  Easter Rising, the 218-19
  Georgian 215-16
  global financial crisis 222-3
  Great Famine, the 216-17
  Home Rule 217-18
  Huguenots 98, 216
  Irish Republican Army 219-22
  marriage equality referendum 223, 240, **239**
  Norman 213-14
  Sinn Féin 218-21
  Troubles, the 220, 221
  Viking 213, 233-4
  War of Independence 219-20
  WWI 219
  WWII 222
holidays 250
homelessness 211
homewares 46
Horan, Niall 232
hospitals 249
Howth 189-91, **190**
Howth Castle 189
Howth Summit 189
Hozier 232
Hugh Lane Gallery, Dublin 9, 144-5, **8**, **144**
Huguenot Cemetery 98

I

Icon Factory 110
Imaginosity 28, **29**
internet access 248
Ireland's Eye 190-1
Irish Family History Centre 166
Irish language 252-6
Irish Museum of Modern Art 131-2, **131**
Irish Republican Army (IRA) 219-22
Irish Whiskey Museum 68
Irish-Jewish Museum 70
itineraries 18-19
Iveagh Gardens 68
Iveagh House 68

J

James Connolly Memorial 167
James Joyce Cultural Centre 152
Jameson Distillery Bow Street 149-50
Jeanie Johnston 166, **167**
Joyce, James 66, 152, 153, 196, 210, 225, 226

K

Kavanagh, Patrick 98
Kelly, Luke 13, 70, 166-7
Kilmainham Gaol 10, 129-30, 133, 219, **10**, **129**
Kilmainham Gate 136
Kilmainham area 53, 121-41, **121**, **135**, **278**
  accommodation 205-6
  activities 141
  drinking 122, 138-9
  eating 136-8
  entertainment 140
  food 122
  highlights 121-32
  museums 122
  nightlife 122, 138-9
  shopping 140-1
  sights 123-32, 133-6
  sports & activities 141
  transport 122
  walks 134-5
King's Inns 156
Knowth 183

L

language 14, 30-1, 252-6
Lecky, WEH 57
legal matters 248
Leinster House 97, 216, **235**
Lemass, Sean 221
LGBT+ community 240
LGBT+ travellers 248-9
Liberties, the 53, 121-41, **121**, **135**, **278**
  accommodation 205-6
  activities 141
  drinking 122, 138-9
  eating 136-8
  entertainment 140
  food 122
  highlights 121-32
  museums 122
  nightlife 122, 138-9
  shopping 140-1
  sights 123-36
  sports 141
  transport 122
  walks 134-5, **135**
lifestyle 239
literary figures 100
literature 22, 224-9
Little Museum of Dublin 20, 66-8, **20**
live music 42, 44
local life 30-1
Long Hall 38
Luke Kelly Bust 166-7
Luke Kelly Statue 70
Lynott, Phil 70, 231

M

Malahide 196-7
Malahide Castle 196-7, **197**
Mansion House 70
markets 22, 45, 46, 106, 122, *see also* Eating, Shopping *subindexes*
marriage equality referendum 223, 240, **239**
Marsh's Library 133, **23**
Mathew,Father Theobald 153
measures 247
media 247
medical services 249
Merrion Square 96
Merrion Square area 52-3, 88-104, **88**, **99**, **276**, **103**
  accommodation 203-4
  activities 104
  art 89
  drinking & nightlife 89, 103-4
  entertainment 104

Merrion Square area *continued*
food 89, 101-3
highlights 88-96
nightlife 89, 103-4
shopping 104
sights 90-100
sports 104
transport 89
walks 98-9, **99**
mobile phones 14, 250
Monet 95
money 14, 34, 199, 247-8, 249
Mosaic 110
motorcycle travel 243-4, 244-5
multiculturalism 240
Museum of Literature Ireland 13, 68-9
Museum of Natural History 97, **19**
museums & galleries 21
music 21, 21-2, 230-2

N

National Aquatic Centre 29
National Botanic Gardens 153
National Gallery 12, 95, 97, **12**, **94**
National Leprechaun Museum 29, 154
National Library of Ireland 98-100
National Museum of Ireland 9, 92-3, **92-3**, **8**, **93**
archaeology 90-3, **90**
decorative arts 49, **233**
history 149, **233**
National Photographic Archive 111
National Print Museum 172
National Transport Museum (Howth) 190
National Wax Museum Plus 110-11
Newgrange 179-83
Newman University Church 70
newspapers 247
nightlife, *see* drinking & nightlife

Sights 000
Map Pages **000**
Photo Pages **000**

North of the Liffey 53, 142-63, **142**, **151**, **280**
accommodation 206-7
activities 163
drinking 143, 159-61
entertainment 161
food 143, 156-9
highlights 142-48
nightlife 143, 159-61
shopping 162
sights 144-56
sports 163
transport 143
walks 151, **151**
Number 29 Lower Fitzwilliam Street 100

O

O'Brien, William Smith 153
O'Connell, Daniel 153, 216
O'Connell St 153, 162, *see also* North of the Liffey
O'Connor, Sinéad 231
Old Library 56, 58, 66, *see also Book of Kells*
opening hours 34, 38, 42, 45, 250
Origin Gallery 100

P

parks 22
Parnell, Charles Stewart 153, 217, 218
Patrick Kavanagh Statue 98
Pearse Lyons Distillery 133-4
Pearse, Pádraig 219
pharmacies 249
Phil Lynott Statue 70
Phoenix Park 146-8, **148**, **146**
planning
activities 48
budgeting 14-15, 32, 34
children, travel with 28-9
Dublin basics 14-15
Dublin's neighbourhoods 52-3
events 247
festivals 24-7
itineraries 18-19
local life 30-1
repeat visitors 13
sports 48
travel seasons 15
websites 14
poetry 229
Pogues, the 231
police 248, 250
Poolbeg Lighthouse 168
population 211, 238
postal services 250
Powerscourt Estate 192-3
public holidays 250
pubs 4, 7, 20, 38, 40, **6-7**, **37**, **116** *see also* Drinking & Nightlife *subindex*

R

racism 240
radio 247
Rathmines Town Hall 173, **173**
religion 240
River Liffey 51
road rules 245
Roe & Co Distillery 133
Rotunda Hospital 154
Royal Hibernian Academy (RHA) Gallagher Gallery 97-8
Royal Hospital Kilmainham 131
rugby 48, **47**

S

safety 250
Salmon, George 56
Samuel Beckett Bridge 167
Sandycove 196
Science Gallery 68
self-catering 35
Shaw, George Bernard 225
shopping 22, 45-6, *see also* Shopping *subindex, individual neighbourhoods*
Sinn Féin 218-21
slagging 30
smoking 247
Southside 53, 170-5, **170**, **286**
accommodation 171, 208
drinking 171, 174-5
entertainment 175
food 171, 172-4
highlights 170-1
nightlife 171, 174-5
shopping 175
sights 172
transport 171
Spire 155-6
sports 31, 47-9, 86-7, *see also* Sports & Activities *subindex, individual sports, individual activities*
St Audoen's Catholic Church 136
St Audoen's Church of Ireland 134-6
St George's Church 155
St James's Gate 123-4
St Kevin 184-8
St Mary's Abbey 154
St Mary's Church 156
St Mary's Pro-Cathedral 154-5
St Michan's Church 152
St Patrick 212, 213
St Patrick's Cathedral 126-8, 133, 136, 234, 237-6, **128**, **126**
St Patrick's Festival 24, **25**
St Patrick's Tower 134, 136
St Stephen's Green 12, 66, **12**
St Stephen's Green area 52, 54-87, **54**, **67**, **270**, **274**
accommodation 201-3
drinking 55, 78-82
food 55, 71-8
highlights 54-65
nightlife 55, 78-82
shopping 83-6
sights 56-71
transport 55
walks 67
St Stephen's 'Pepper Canister' Church 100
St Werburgh's Church 70-1
statuary 153
Stoker, Bram 225
Sunlight Chambers 111, 116, **116**
Swift, Jonathan 225
swimming 49

T

Taste of Dublin 26
taxes 250
taxis 243
Teeling Distillery 133, **19**
telephone services 250
Temple Bar area 53, 105-20, **105-6**, **268**
accommodation 204-5
activities 120
drinking 106, 114-15
entertainment 106, 115-18
food 106, 111-14
highlights 105-9
history 111
nightlife 106, 114-5

shopping 118-20
sights 107-11
sports 120
transport 106
Temple Bar Food Market 116, **116**
Temple Bar Gallery & Studios 110
theatres 44
time 14, 251
tipping 199
toilets 251
tourist information 14, 251
tours 246
train travel 244, 246, **236**
tram travel 244, **223**
transport 242-6, **223**, **236**
travel to Dublin 15, 242-4
travel within Dublin 15, 244-6
Trinity College 7, 56-60, 66, 78, 216, 235, **60**, **168-9**, **3**, **7**, **56**, **58-9**

U

U2 231
Ulster Volunteer Force 218
Ulysses 226

V

Varadkar, Leo 223, 240
Vaughan collection 95
Vaults Live 13
visas 14, 251

W

walking tours
1916 Rebellion 87
Glendalough Valley 188
Grafton Street 67
historical 86-7
Howth 191
James Joyce 163
St Stephen's Green 67
Trinity College 87
War Memorial Gardens 134, **23**
water sports 49
websites 14, 48, 198
weights 247
whiskey 13, 139
Whitefriars Street Carmelite Church 71
wi-fi 248
Wilde, Oscar 225, **103**
women travellers 251

Y

Ye Olde Hurdy Gurdy Museum of Vintage Radio (Howth) 189-90
Yeats, WB 94, 217

EATING

57 The Headline 138
101 Talbot 159
777 75
1837 Bar & Brasserie 137

A

Al Vesuvio 113
Aqua 191
Assassination Custard 136
Avoca 76
Azteca 73

B

Balfes 74
Bang Café 103
Banyi Japanese Dining 112
Beef and Lobster 113
Bison Bar & BBQ 112
Blazing Salads 73
Boco 157
Bonsai Bar 74-5
Bow Lane 74
Brambles 101
Brother Hubbard 157
Bunsen 72, 112
Butcher Grill 173

C

Cake Café 71
Camden Kitchen 75
Camden Rotisserie 71
Camerino 156
Chameleon 113
Chapter One 159, **53**
Chez Max 77
Chez Sara 197
Chophouse 174
Clanbrassil Coffee Shop 137
Clanbrassil House 138
Cleaver East 113
Cliff Townhouse 77
Coburg Brasserie 101
Coke Lane Pizza 136-7
Container Coffee 137
Coppinger Row 76
Cornucopia 73
Cow's Lane 112

D

Da Mimmo's 156
Dax 103
Dillinger's 174
Dollard & Co 112
Drury Buildings 76-7
Dublin Cookie Company 137
Dublin Pizza Company 71-2
Dunne & Crescenzi 76

E

Eatyard 72
Elephant & Castle 113
Ely Bar & Grill 167-8
Ely Wine Bar 101
Emilia's Ristorante 193
Etto 101

F

Fade Street Social 75
Fallon & Byrne 73
Farmer Brown's 173, 174
Featherblade 74
Fegan's 1924 156
Fish Shop 158, 159
Fumbally 137
F.X. Buckley 114

G

Gaillot et Gray 137
Glovers Alley 77
Good World 76
Govinda's 73
Grano 158
Greedy Goose 197
Greenhouse 77

H

Hang Dai 75
Han Sung 158
Hatch & Sons 158
Herbstreet 168
Honest to Goodness 73
House 101, 191
Howth Market 191

I

Itsa@IMMA 137

J

Jerusalem Restaurant 75
Johnnie Fox's 193
Juniors Deli & Cafe 167

K

Kinara 173
Klaw 112

L

L Mulligan Grocer 158
La Peniche 101-2
L'Ecrivain 102
Legal Eagle 158
Legit Coffee Co 137
Lemon 72
Leo Burdock's 138
L'Gueuleton 76
Listons 72
Little Bird 73
Little Mike's 174
Loose Canon 71
Lucky Tortoise 74

M

M&L 157
Magpie Inn 195-6
Manifesto 172-3
Marco Pierre White Steakhouse & Grill 78
Masa 71
Meet Me in the Morning 72
Michael's 174
Mr Fox 159
Murphy's Ice Cream 72
Musashi Hogan Place 101
Musashi IFSC 168
Musashi Noodles & Sushi Bar 157
Music Cafe Dublin 112

N

Neon 72
Nick's Coffee Company 172

O

Oar House 191
Octopussy's Seafood Tapas 191
Opium 77
Oxmantown 157

P

Panem 157-8
Pang 71
Paulie's Pizza 167
Pepper Pot 72
Pi Pizza 73-4
Pichet 76
Pig's Ear 76
Pitt Bros BBQ 75

Poppies Country Cooking 193
Port House 76

Q
Quay 16 168
Queen of Tarts 112

R
Restaurant Patrick Guilbaud 102
Richmond 74
Roberta's 113
Rocket's 167

S
Saba 74, 174
Sale e Pepe 197
Sano Pizza 111
Seafood Cafe 112-13
Select Stores 195
Shanahan's on the Green 78
Silk Road Café 65
Simon's Place 73
Sisu Izakaya 74
Sophie's @ the Dean 75
Soup Dragon 157
Stella Diner 173

T
Tasty 8 137
Tea Garden 157
Temple Bar Food Market 112
Terra Madre 158
The Ivy 13, 75
Third Space 157
Thundercut Alley 158-9
Tram Cafe 157
Trocadero 77
Two Pups Coffee 137

U
Unicorn 102-3
Union8 138
Uno Mas 74

V
Variety Jones 138

W
Wagamama 77
Wilde 77
Winding Stair 159
Workshop Gastropub 168
Wow Burger 72

X
Xico 101

Y
Yamamori 76
Yamamori Sushi 159
Yarn 158

Z
Zaytoon 112

DRINKING & NIGHTLIFE

9 Below 79
37 Dawson Street 81

A
Abbey Tavern 191
Against the Grain 79
Anseo 80
Arthur's 139
Auld Dubliner 114

B
Barbers 160
Beggar's Bush 174-5
Bernard Shaw 80
Bestseller 79
Blackbird 174
Brazen Head 139-40
Brogan's 115
Bruxelles 82

C
Café en Seine 82
Caffe Cagliostro 160
Camden Exchange 79
Chelsea Drug Store 79
Clement & Pekoe 82
Cobblestone 159-60
Confession Box 160
Copper Face Jacks 81

D
Darkey Kelly's Bar & Restaurant 115
Dawson Lounge 82
Dice Bar 161
Dicey's Garden 81
Doheny & Nesbitt's 104
Drop Dead Twice 138
Drury Buildings Cocktail Bar 80

F
Fallon's 138
Farrier & Draper 80
Finnegan's 196
Fitzsimons 115
Fourth Corner 138-9

G
George 81
Gibney's 197
Globe 82
Grand Social 161
Gravity Bar 125
Grogan's Castle Lounge 78

H
Hartigan's 104
Hogan's 80-1
House 104
Hughes' Bar 161

I
Idlewild 81
International Bar 81

J
J. O'Connell 79
John Kavanagh's 160
John Mulligan's 168, **6-7**

K
Kaph 82
Kehoe's 78

L
Laine, My Love 160
Liquor Rooms 114
Long Hall 78-9, **38**
Lucky Duck 79
Lucky's 139

M
Mary's Bar 80
McDaid's 80
MVP 139

N
Network 82
No Name Bar 78

O
Octagon Bar 115
O'Donoghue's 104, **37**
Old Royal Oak 138
Oliver St John Gogarty 115
Open Gate Brewery 139

P
Palace Bar 114
Pantibar 161
Peruke & Periwig 79
P.Mac's 80
Porterhouse 115
Pygmalion 81

R
Rí Rá 81
Ruin 168

S
Sam's Bar 81
Sidecar 79
Slattery's 168-9
Square Ball 104
Stag's Head 80
Street 66 114
Swan 80

T
Taphouse 174
Temple Bar 114, 116, **116**
The Oak 114
Token 160
Toner's 103-4
Turk's Head 115

V
Vintage Cocktail Club 114

W
Wall and Keogh 82
Walshs 160
Wigwam 161

Y
Yamamori Tengu 160

ENTERTAINMENT

3 Arena 169
Abbey Theatre 161
Academy 161
Ark Children's Cultural Centre 118

Aviva Stadium 175
Bord Gáis Energy Theatre 169, **3**
Bowery 175, **177**
Button Factory 118
Chaplins Comedy Club 118
Cineworld Multiplex 161-2
Devitt's 82
Donnybrook Stadium 175
Gaiety Theatre 83
Gate Theatre 161
Ha'Penny Bridge Inn 118
Irish Film Institute 118-19
Laughter Lounge 162
Light House Cinema 161
Mother 118
National Concert Hall 82
New Theatre 118
Odeon Cinema 169
O'Donoghue's 104, **37**
Olympia Theatre 118
Project Arts Centre 118
Royal Dublin Society Showground 175
Samuel Beckett Theatre 83
Savoy 162
Shelbourne Park Greyhound Stadium 169
Smock Alley Theatre 115
Stella Theatre 175
Sugar Club 104
Ticketmaster 83
Ukiyo 82-3
Vaults Live 140
Vicar Street 140-1
Whelan's 82, **44**
Workman's Club 118

SHOPPING

A

All City Records 120
April and the Bear 175
Aran Sweater Market 85
Arnott's 162
Article 84
Avoca Handweavers 83

B

Barry Doyle Design Jewellers 84-5
Brown Thomas 84

C

Chupi 83
Claddagh Records 119
Connolly Books 120
Costume 85
Cow's Lane Designer Mart 119

D

Danker Antiques 85
Design Centre 84
Design Tower 169
Designyard 86
Dublin Food Co-op 141
Dubray Books 86

E

Eason's 162

F

Find 119
Flip, Sharpsville & Helter Skelter 119
Folkster 119-20

G

George's Street Arcade 84
Gutter Bookshop 119

H

Harlequin 86
Heraldic Artists 104
Hodges Figgis 86
House of Names 85-6

I

Industry 85
Irish Design Shop 83
Irish Museum of Modern Art Gift Shop 141

J

Jam Art Factory 119, **3**
Jenny Vander 86
Jervis Centre 162-3

K

Kilkenny Shop 85
Knobs & Knockers 85

L

Library Project 120
Louis Copeland 85, 162
Loulerie 84
Lucy's Lounge 119

M

Marrowbone Books 141
Martin Fennelly Antiques 141
MoMuse 84
Moore Street Market 162

N

Nowhere 84

O

Om Diva 83
O'Sullivan Antiques 141
Oxfam Home 141

P

Parfumarija 83-4
Powerscourt Townhouse 84

R

Rhinestones 85
Rory's Fishing Tackle 120

S

Scout 119
Sheridan's Cheesemongers 83, **46**
Siopaella 84
Siopaella Design Exchange 119
Space Out Sister 141
St Stephen's Green Shopping Centre 86
Stokes Books 85

T

Tamp & Stitch 120
Temple Bar Book Market 120

U

Ulysses Rare Books 85
Urban Outfitters 120

W

Weir & Son's 84
Winding Stair 162

SPORTS & ACTIVITIES

1916 Easter Rising Coach Tour 163
1916 Rebellion Walking Tour 87
AdventureRooms 163
Arbour Hill Guided Tours 163
Carriage Tours 87
Children's Playground 87
Christ Church Guided Tours 120
City Kayaking Dublin 169
City Sightseeing 163
DoDublin Bus Tour 163
Doyle & Sons 191-2
Dublin Bus Tours 163
Dublin Discovered Boat Tours 163
Dublin Literary Pub Crawl 87
Dublin Musical Pub Crawl 120
Fab Food Trails 86
Glendalough & Powerscourt Tour 163
Green Mile 86
Guided Tour of Oireachtas 104
Historical Walking Tour 86-7
James Joyce Walking Tours 163
Little Bird 87
Melt 120
Ocean Divers 196
Pat Liddy Walking Tours 87
Portmarnock Golf Club 197
Sandeman's New Dublin Tour 87
Secret Street Tours 141
See Dublin by Bike 87
Sports & Fitness Markievicz 169
Trinity College Walking Tour 87
Viking Splash Tours 28, 87
Wakedock 169

SLEEPING

A

Abbey Court Hostel 206
Address at Dublin 1 206
Alex 203
Aloft Dublin City 205
Ariel House 208
Ashfield House 204
Avalon House 201

B

Barnacles 204
Brooks Hotel 202
Buswell's Hotel 202

C

Castle Hotel 207
Central Hotel 201

Clarence Hotel 205
Clayton Hotel Cardiff Lane 207
Clifden Guesthouse 206
Cliff Townhouse 203
Conrad Dublin 203-4

D
Davenport 203
Dawson 202
Dean 201-2
Devlin 208
Dublin Citi Hotel 205
Dylan 208

F
Fitzwilliam Hotel 203

G
Generator Hostel 206
Gibson Hotel 207
Gogarty's Temple Bar Hostel 204
Grafton Guesthouse 201
Green 202

H
Harrington Hall 202
Herbert Park Hotel 208

I
Intercontinental Dublin 208
Isaacs Hostel 206
Iveagh Garden Hotel 202

J
Jacob's Inn 206
Jury's Inn Parnell St 207

K
Kelly's Hotel 201
Kinlay House 204-5

M
Maldron Hotel Smithfield 206-7
Maldron Kevin Street 205-6
Marker 207-8
MEC Hostel 206
Merrion 204
Merrion Mews 204
Morgan Hotel 205
Morrison Hotel 207

N
Number 31 203

P
Pembroke Townhouse 208
Powerscourt Hotel & Spa 193-4

R
Radisson Blu Royal Hotel 201
Riu Plaza Gresham Hotel 206

S
Schoolhouse Hotel 208
Shelbourne 204
Spencer Hotel 207

T
Trinity City Hotel 207
Trinity College 201
Trinity Lodge 202

W
Waterloo House 208
Westbury Hotel 203
Westin Dublin 203
Wilder Townhouse 203

Sights 000
Map Pages **000**
Photo Pages **000**

Dublin Maps

Sights
- Beach
- Bird Sanctuary
- Buddhist
- Castle/Palace
- Christian
- Confucian
- Hindu
- Islamic
- Jain
- Jewish
- Monument
- Museum/Gallery/Historic Building
- Ruin
- Shinto
- Sikh
- Taoist
- Winery/Vineyard
- Zoo/Wildlife Sanctuary
- Other Sight

Activities, Courses & Tours
- Bodysurfing
- Diving
- Canoeing/Kayaking
- Course/Tour
- Sento Hot Baths/Onsen
- Skiing
- Snorkelling
- Surfing
- Swimming/Pool
- Walking
- Windsurfing
- Other Activity

Sleeping
- Sleeping
- Camping
- Hut/Shelter

Eating
- Eating

Drinking & Nightlife
- Drinking & Nightlife
- Cafe

Entertainment
- Entertainment

Shopping
- Shopping

Information
- Bank
- Embassy/Consulate
- Hospital/Medical
- Internet
- Police
- Post Office
- Telephone
- Toilet
- Tourist Information
- Other Information

Geographic
- Beach
- Gate
- Hut/Shelter
- Lighthouse
- Lookout
- Mountain/Volcano
- Oasis
- Park
- Pass
- Picnic Area
- Waterfall

Population
- Capital (National)
- Capital (State/Province)
- City/Large Town
- Town/Village

Transport
- Airport
- Border crossing
- Bus
- Cable car/Funicular
- Cycling
- Ferry
- Metro station
- Monorail
- Parking
- Petrol station
- S-Bahn/Subway station
- Taxi
- T-bane/Tunnelbana station
- Train station/Railway
- Tram
- U-Bahn/Underground station
- Other Transport

Routes
- Tollway
- Freeway
- Primary
- Secondary
- Tertiary
- Lane
- Unsealed road
- Road under construction
- Plaza/Mall
- Steps
- Tunnel
- Pedestrian overpass
- Walking Tour
- Walking Tour detour
- Path/Walking Trail

Boundaries
- International
- State/Province
- Disputed
- Regional/Suburb
- Marine Park
- Cliff
- Wall

Hydrography
- River, Creek
- Intermittent River
- Canal
- Water
- Dry/Salt/Intermittent Lake
- Reef

Areas
- Airport/Runway
- Beach/Desert
- Cemetery (Christian)
- Cemetery (Other)
- Glacier
- Mudflat
- Park/Forest
- Sight (Building)
- Sportsground
- Swamp/Mangrove

Note: Not all symbols displayed above appear on the maps in this book

MAP INDEX

Temple Bar (p268)

Grafton Street (p270)

Grafton St & St Stephen's Green (p274)

Merrion Square & Around (p276)

Kilmainham & the Liberties (p278)

North of the Liffey (p280)

Docklands (p284)

The Southside (p286)

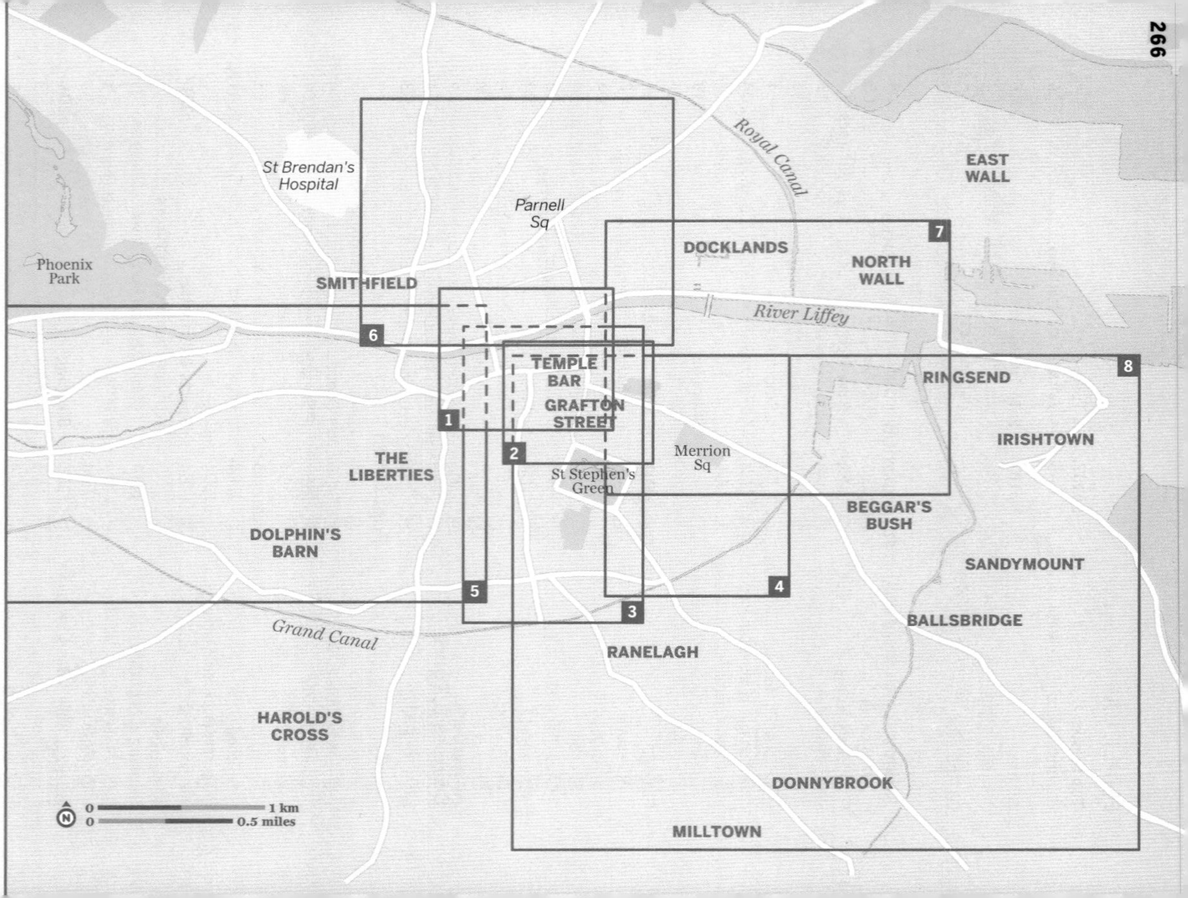

TEMPLE BAR *Map on p268*

Top Sights **p107**
1 Christ Church Cathedral....A5

Sights **p110**
2 Contemporary Music Centre....B4
3 Dublinia: Experience Viking & Medieval Dublin....A6
4 Gallery of Photography....D4
5 Handel's Hotel (Site of Neal's New Musick Hall)....B5
6 Ha'penny Bridge....E3
7 Icon Factory....G3
8 Mosaic....A5
9 National Photographic Archive....D4
10 National Wax Museum Plus....G2
11 Sunlight Chambers....C4
12 Temple Bar Gallery & Studios....E3

Eating **p111**
13 Al Vesuvio....D4
14 Banyi Japanese Dining....F3
15 Beef and Lobster....C5
16 Bison Bar & BBQ....C4
17 Bunsen....D4
18 Chameleon....E3
Cleaver East....(see 78)
19 Dollard & Co....C4
20 Elephant & Castle....F3
21 F.X. Buckley....E4
22 Klaw....F4
23 Music Cafe Dublin....C4
24 Queen of Tarts....C5
25 Queen of Tarts....B5
26 Roberta's....C4
27 Sano Pizza....C5
28 Seafood Cafe....E4
29 Temple Bar Food Market....D4
30 Zaytoon....C4

Drinking & Nightlife **p114**
31 Auld Dubliner....F3
32 Brogan's....D4
33 Darkey Kelly's Bar & Restaurant....B5
34 Fitzsimons....D3
35 Liquor Rooms....C4
36 Octagon Bar....C4
37 Oliver St John Gogarty....F3
38 Palace Bar....G3
39 Porterhouse....C4
40 Street 66....C4
41 Temple Bar....E3
42 The Oak....C5
43 Turk's Head....C4
44 Vintage Cocktail Club....E4

Entertainment **p115**
45 Ark Children's Cultural Centre....D4
46 Button Factory....E4
47 Chaplins Comedy Club....H3
48 Ha'Penny Bridge Inn....E3
49 Irish Film Institute....D4
50 Mother....C5
New Theatre....(see 58)
51 Olympia Theatre....D4
52 Project Arts Centre....D4
53 Smock Alley Theatre....B4
54 Workman's Club....D4

Shopping **p118**
55 All City Records....E4
56 Claddagh Records....E4
57 Claddagh Records....G2
58 Connolly Books....D4
59 Cow's Lane Designer Mart....B4
60 Cow's Lane Designer Mart....B5
61 Find....B4
62 Flip, Sharpsville & Helter Skelter....E4
63 Folkster....D4
64 Gutter Bookshop....B4
65 Jam Art Factory....E4
66 Library Project....E3
67 Lucy's Lounge....E4
68 Rory's Fishing Tackle....F3
69 Scout....B4
70 Siopaella Design Exchange....E4
71 Tamp & Stitch....B4
72 Temple Bar Book Market....E3
73 Urban Outfitters....E4

Sports & Activities **p120**
74 Christ Church Guided Tours....A5
Dublin Musical Pub Crawl....(see 37)
75 Melt....E4

Sleeping **p204**
76 Ashfield House....H3
77 Barnacles....E4
78 Clarence Hotel....C4
79 Dublin Citi Hotel....E4
Gogarty's Temple Bar Hostel....(see 37)
80 Kinlay House....B5
81 Morgan Hotel....F3
Oliver St John Gogarty's Penthouse Apartments....(see 37)

Key on p267

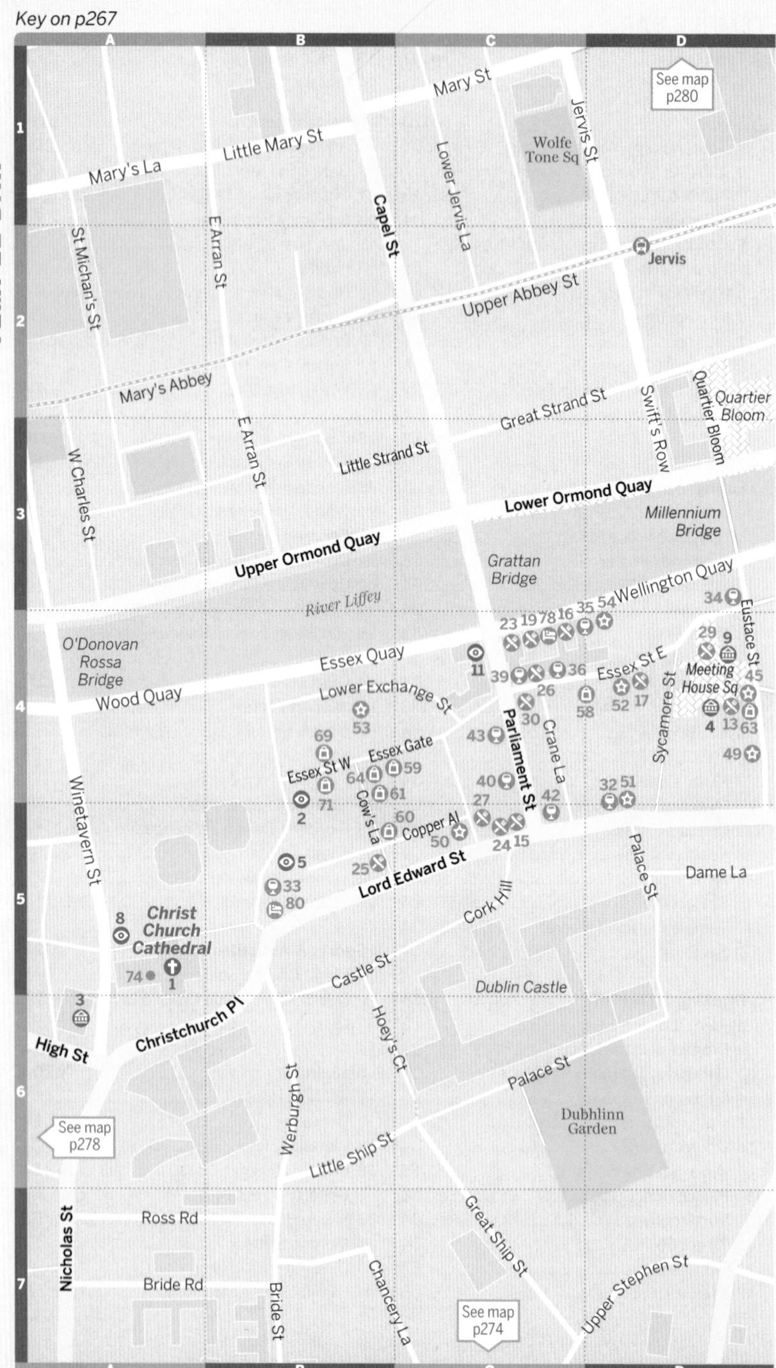

A
B
C
D
1
2
3
4
5
6
7
See map p280
Mary St
Little Mary St
Mary's La
Wolfe Tone Sq
Jervis St
Lower Jervis La
Capel St
E Arran St
St Michan's St
Jervis
Upper Abbey St
Mary's Abbey
Great Strand St
Swift's Row
Quartier Bloom
Little Strand St
W Charles St
Lower Ormond Quay
Upper Ormond Quay
Millennium Bridge
Grattan Bridge
River Liffey
Wellington Quay
O'Donovan Rossa Bridge
Essex Quay
Wood Quay
Lower Exchange St
Essex St E
Meeting House Sq
Eustace St
Sycamore St
Parliament St
Crane La
Essex St W
Essex Gate
Cow's La
Copper Al
Winetavern St
Lord Edward St
Dame La
Palace St
Cork Hill
Christ Church Cathedral
Castle St
Dublin Castle
Christchurch Pl
High St
Hoey's Ct
Werburgh St
Palace St
Dubhlinn Garden
See map p278
Little Ship St
Nicholas St
Ross Rd
Bride Rd
Bride St
Chancery La
Great Ship St
Upper Stephen St
See map p274

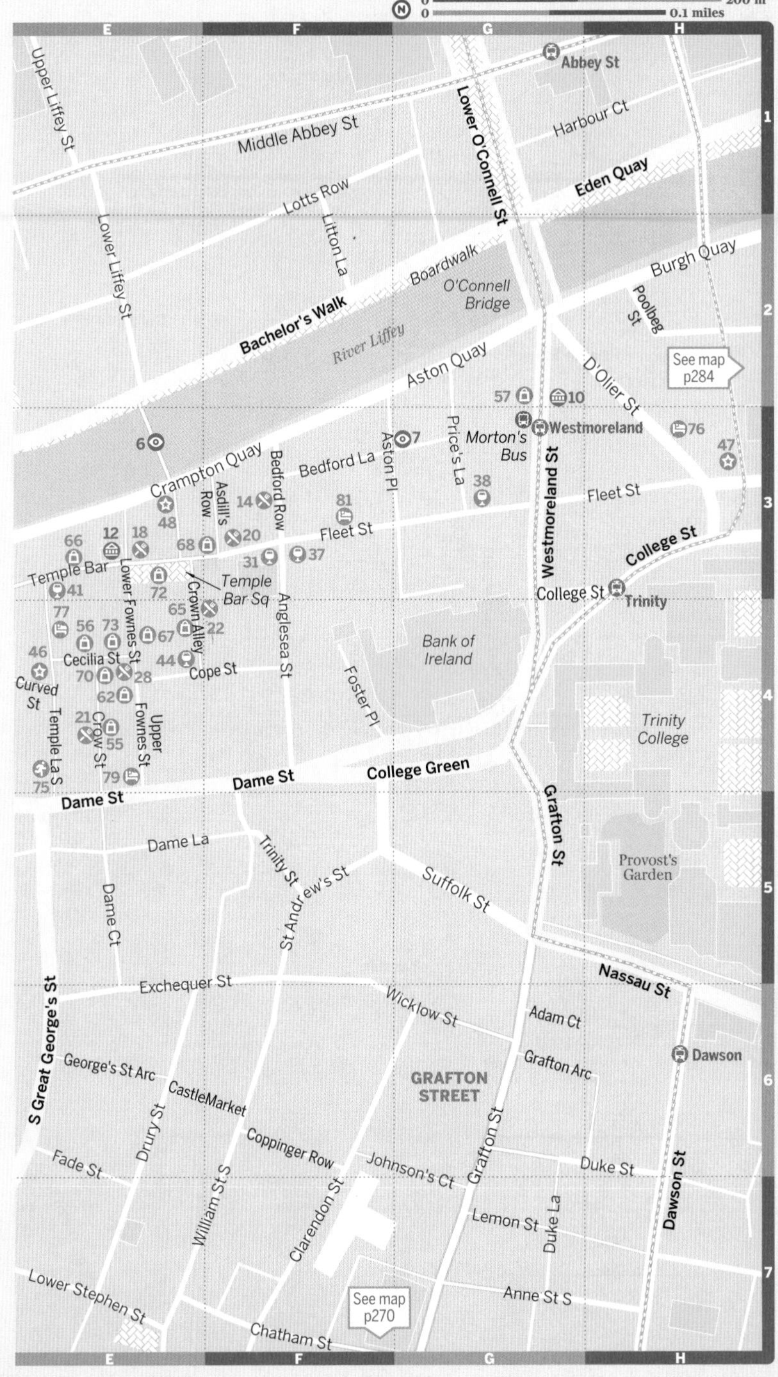

TEMPLE BAR
0 200 m
0 0.1 miles
Abbey St
Upper Liffey St
Middle Abbey St
Harbour Ct
Lower O'Connell St
Eden Quay
Lotts Row
Litton La
Lower Liffey St
Boardwalk
O'Connell Bridge
Burgh Quay
Poolbeg St
Bachelor's Walk
River Liffey
Aston Quay
D'Olier St
See map p284
Westmoreland
Morton's Bus
Aston Pl
Price's La
Crampton Quay
Bedford La
Bedford Row
Asdill's Row
Fleet St
Westmoreland St
College St
Temple Bar
Lower Fownes St
Crown Alley
Temple Bar Sq
Anglesea St
College St
Trinity
Bank of Ireland
Cecilia St
Cope St
Curved St
Foster Pl
Temple La S
Crow St
Upper Fownes St
Trinity College
Dame St
College Green
Grafton St
Dame La
Trinity St
Provost's Garden
St Andrew's St
Suffolk St
Dame Ct
Nassau St
Exchequer St
Wicklow St
Adam Ct
S Great George's St
George's St Arc
Grafton Arc
Dawson
CastleMarket
GRAFTON STREET
Drury St
Coppinger Row
Fade St
Johnson's Ct
Duke St
William St S
Clarendon St
Lemon St
Duke La
Dawson St
Lower Stephen St
Anne St S
See map p270
Chatham St

Key on p272

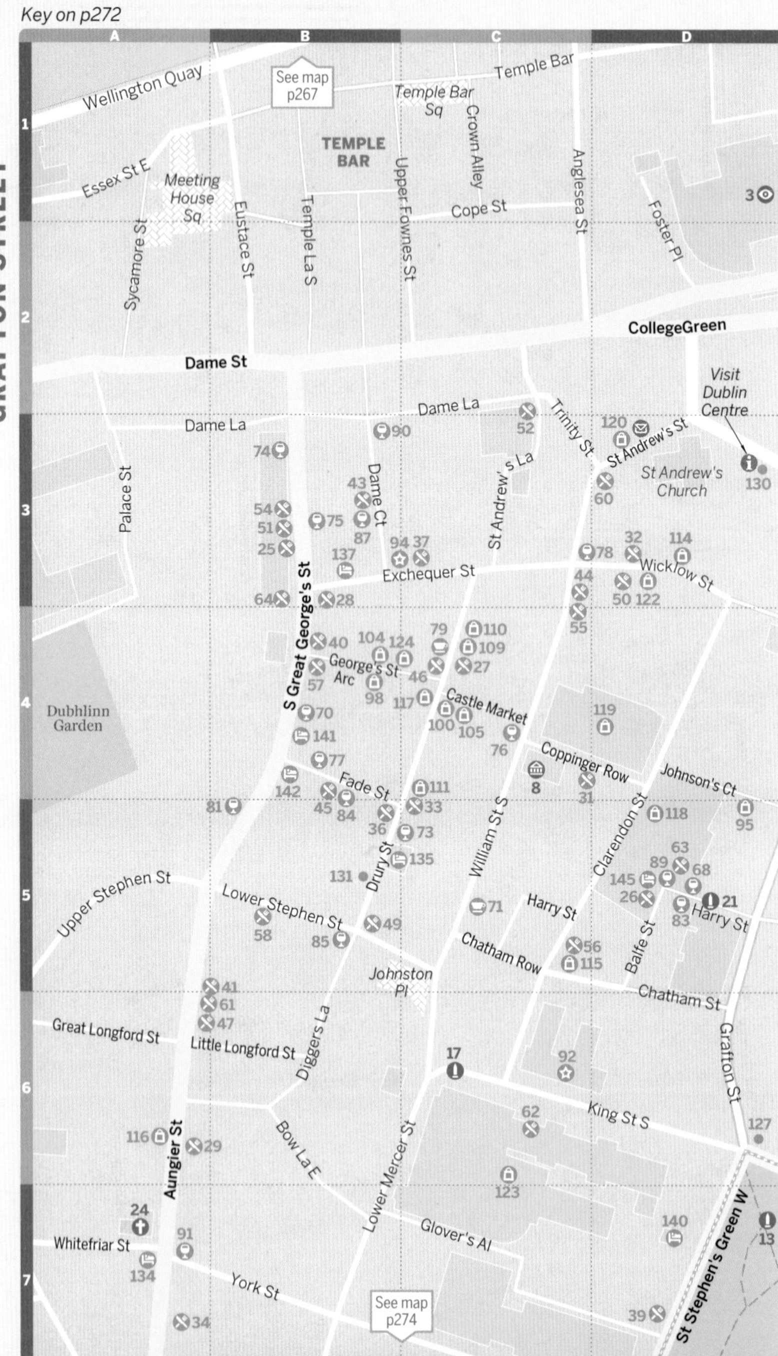

Wellington Quay
Temple Bar
See map p267
Temple Bar Sq
TEMPLE BAR
Crown Alley
Essex St E
Meeting House Sq
Upper Fownes St
Temple La S
Eustace St
Cope St
Anglesea St
Foster Pl
Sycamore St
Dame St
CollegeGreen
Visit Dublin Centre
Dame La
Dame La
Trinity St
St Andrew's St
St Andrew's Church
Palace St
Dame Ct
St Andrew's La
Exchequer St
Wicklow St
S Great George's St
George's St Arc
Castle Market
Dubhlinn Garden
Coppinger Row
Johnson's Ct
Fade St
William St S
Clarendon St
Drury St
Upper Stephen St
Lower Stephen St
Harry St
Harry St
Chatham Row
Balfe St
Johnston Pl
Chatham St
Great Longford St
Little Longford St
Diggers La
Grafton St
King St S
Bow La E
Aungier St
Lower Mercer St
Glover's Al
Whitefriar St
St Stephen's Green W
York St
See map p274

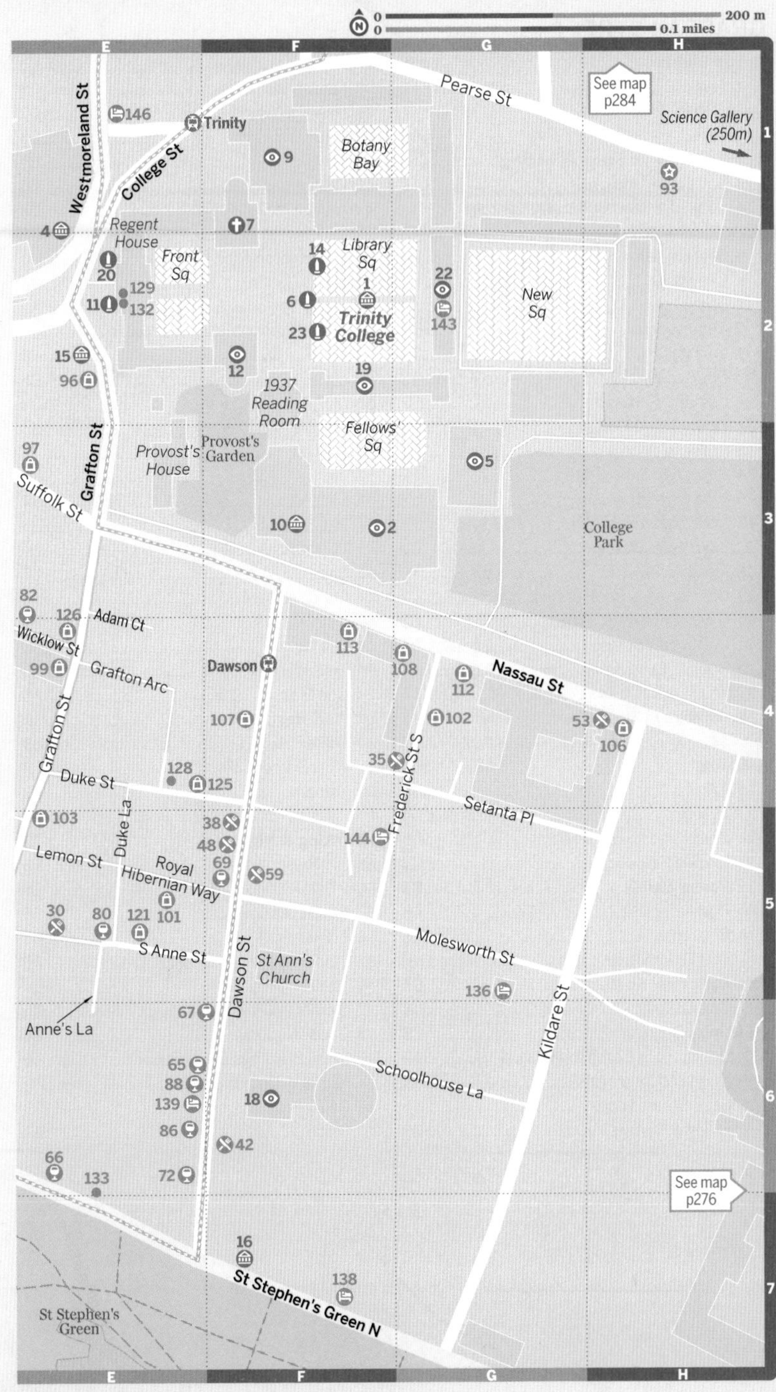

GRAFTON STREET
0 200 m
0 0.1 miles
See map p284
See map p276
Science Gallery (250m)
Pearse St
Trinity
Westmoreland St
College St
Botany Bay
Regent House
Front Sq
Library Sq
Trinity College
New Sq
1937 Reading Room
Fellows' Sq
Provost's Garden
Provost's House
Grafton St
Suffolk St
College Park
Adam Ct
Wicklow St
Grafton Arc
Dawson
Nassau St
Frederick St S
Duke St
Setanta Pl
Duke La
Lemon St
Royal Hibernian Way
Molesworth St
S Anne St
St Ann's Church
Dawson St
Anne's La
Kildare St
Schoolhouse La
St Stephen's Green N
St Stephen's Green

GRAFTON STREET *Map on p270*

Top Sights **p56**
1 Trinity College F2

Sights **p66**
2 Arts & Social Science Building F3
3 Bank of Ireland D1
4 Bank of Ireland Cultural & Heritage Centre E1
5 Berkeley Library G3
6 Campanile F2
7 Chapel F1
8 City Assembly House C4
9 Dining Hall F1
10 Douglas Hyde Gallery of Modern Art F3
11 Edmund Burke Statue E2
12 Examination Hall F2
13 Fusiliers' Arch D7
14 George Salmon Statue F2
15 Irish Whiskey Museum E2
16 Little Museum of Dublin F7
17 Luke Kelly Statue C6
18 Mansion House F6
19 Old Library & Book of Kells F2
20 Oliver Goldsmith Statue E2
21 Phil Lynott Statue D5
22 Rubrics Building G2
23 WEH Lecky Statue F2
24 Whitefriars Street Carmelite Church A7

Eating **p71**
25 777 .... B3
Avoca .... (see 97)
26 Balfes D5
27 Blazing Salads C4
28 Bonsai Bar B3
29 Bow Lane A6
30 Bunsen E5
Cliff Townhouse .... (see 138)
31 Coppinger Row C4
32 Cornucopia D3
33 Drury Buildings C5
34 Dublin Pizza Company A7
35 Dunne & Crescenzi G4
36 Fade Street Social B5
37 Fallon & Byrne C3
Fallon & Byrne Restaurant .... (see 37)
38 Featherblade F5
39 Glovers Alley D7
40 Good World B4
41 Govinda's B5
42 Greenhouse F6
43 Honest to Goodness B3
44 Lemon C3
45 L'Gueuleton B4
46 Loose Canon C4
47 Lucky Tortoise A6
48 Marco Pierre White Steakhouse & Grill F5
49 Masa B5
50 Murphy's Ice Cream D3
Pepper Pot .... (see 119)
51 Pi Pizza B3
52 Pichet C2
53 Pig's Ear H4
54 Pitt Bros BBQ B3
55 Port House C4
56 Saba C5
57 Simon's Place B4
58 Sisu Izakaya B5
59 The Ivy F5
60 Trocadero D3
61 Uno Mas A6
62 Wagamama C6
63 Wilde D5
Wow Burger .... (see 82)
64 Yamamori B3

Drinking & Nightlife **p79**
65 37 Dawson Street E6
66 9 Below E6
67 Bestseller F6
68 Bruxelles D5
69 Café en Seine F5
70 Chelsea Drug Store B4
71 Clement & Pekoe C5
72 Dawson Lounge E6
73 Drury Buildings Cocktail Bar C5
Farrier & Draper .... (see 119)
74 George B3
75 Globe B3

76 Grogan's Castle Lounge....C4
Hogan's....(see 142)
77 Idlewild....B4
78 International Bar....C3
79 Kaph....C4
80 Kehoe's....E5
81 Long Hall....B5
82 Mary's Bar....E3
83 McDaid's....D5
84 No Name Bar....B4
85 P.Mac's....B5
86 Peruke & Periwig....E6
Pygmalion....(see 119)
87 Rí Rá....B3
88 Sam's Bar....E6
89 Sidecar....D5
90 Stag's Head....B3
91 Swan....A7

Entertainment p84
92 Gaiety Theatre....C6
93 Samuel Beckett Theatre....H1
Ticketmaster....(see 123)
94 Ukiyo....B3

Shopping p84
95 Appleby....D5
96 Aran Sweater Market....E2
Article....(see 119)
97 Avoca Handweavers....E3
98 Barry Doyle Design Jewellers....B4
99 Brown Thomas....E4
Chupi....(see 119)
100 Costume....C4
101 Danker Antiques....E5
Design Centre....(see 119)
102 Designyard....G4
103 Dubray Books....E5
104 George's Street Arcade....B4
105 Harlequin....C4
106 Heraldic Artists....H4
107 Hodges Figgis....F4
108 House of Names....G4
109 Industry....C4
110 Irish Design Shop....C4
111 Jenny Vander....C4
112 Kilkenny Shop....G4
113 Knobs & Knockers....F4
114 Louis Copeland....D3
115 Loulerie....C5
MoMuse....(see 119)
116 Nowhere....A6
117 Om Diva....C4
118 Parfumarija....D5
119 Powerscourt Townhouse....D4
120 Rhinestones....D3
121 Sheridan's Cheesemongers....E5
122 Siopaella....D3
123 St Stephen's Green Shopping Centre....C6
124 Stokes Books....C4
125 Ulysses Rare Books....E4
126 Weir & Son's....E4

Sports & Activities p78
1916 Rebellion Walking Tour....(see 78)
127 Carriage Tours....D6
128 Dublin Literary Pub Crawl....E4
Green Mile....(see 16)
129 Historical Walking Tour....E2
130 Pat Liddy Walking Tours....D3
131 See Dublin by Bike....B5
132 Trinity College Walking Tour....E2
133 Viking Splash Tours....E6

Sleeping p201
134 Avalon House....A7
135 Brooks Hotel....B5
136 Buswell's Hotel....G5
137 Central Hotel....B3
138 Cliff Townhouse....F7
139 Dawson....E6
140 Fitzwilliam Hotel....D7
141 Grafton Guesthouse....B4
142 Kelly's Hotel....B4
143 Trinity College....G2
144 Trinity Lodge....F5
145 Westbury Hotel....D5
146 Westin Dublin....E1

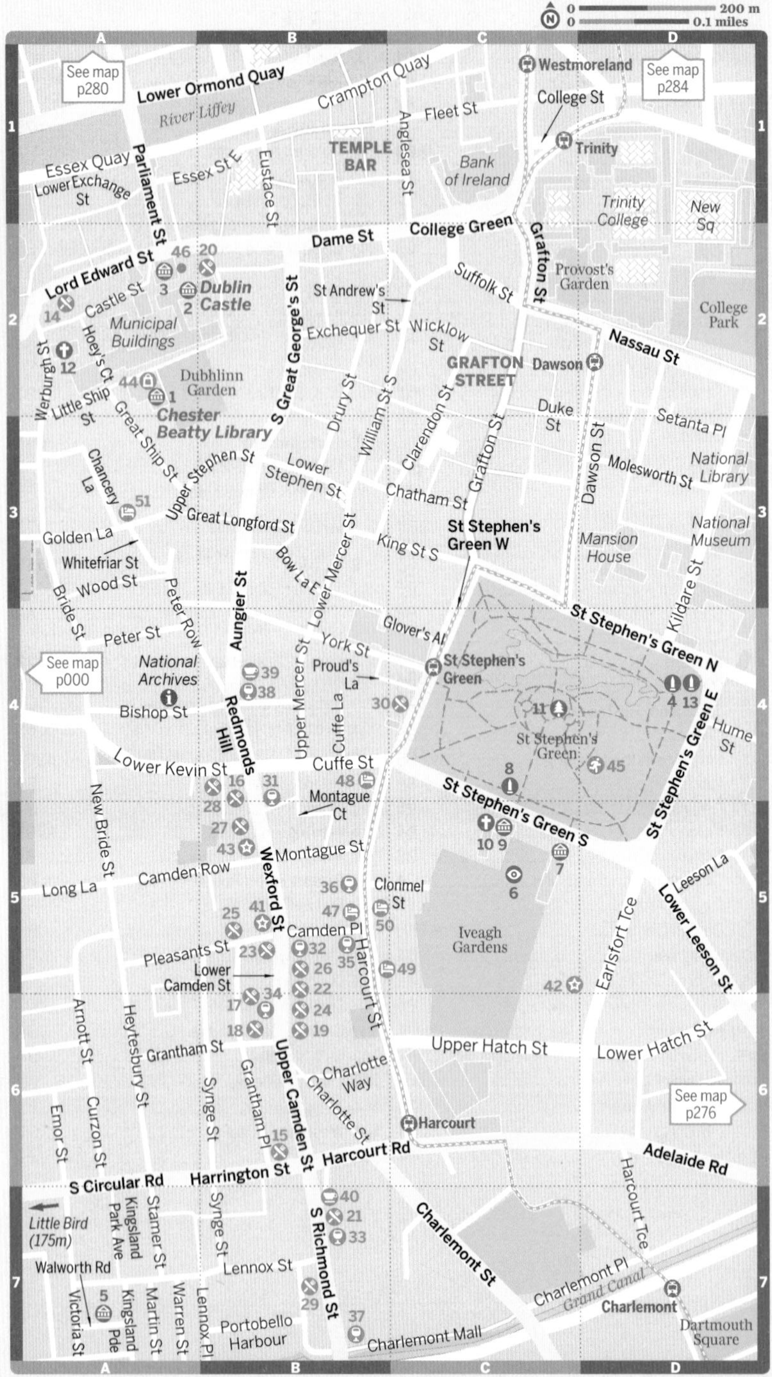

GRAFTON ST & ST STEPHEN'S GREEN
200 m
0.1 miles
See map p280
See map p284
See map p000
See map p276
Lower Ormond Quay
River Liffey
Crampton Quay
Westmoreland
College St
Trinity
Fleet St
TEMPLE BAR
Anglesea St
Bank of Ireland
Essex Quay
Lower Exchange St
Parliament St
Essex St E
Eustace St
Trinity College
New Sq
Dame St
College Green
Grafton St
Lord Edward St
Dublin Castle
Castle St
Suffolk St
Provost's Garden
St Andrew's St
College Park
Municipal Buildings
Exchequer St
Wicklow St
Nassau St
Werburgh St
Hoey's Ct
S Great George's St
GRAFTON STREET
Dawson
Little Ship St
Dubhlinn Garden
Drury St
William St S
Clarendon St
Duke St
Setanta Pl
Chester Beatty Library
Great Ship St
Dawson St
Chancery La
Upper Stephen St
Lower Stephen St
Molesworth St
National Library
Chatham St
Great Longford St
National Museum
Golden La
Bow La E
King St S
St Stephen's Green W
Mansion House
Whitefriar St
Lower Mercer St
Wood St
Peter Row
Aungier St
Kildare St
Bride St
Glover's Al
St Stephen's Green N
Peter St
York St
National Archives
Upper Mercer St
Proud's La
St Stephen's Green
Bishop St
Redmonds Hill
Cuffe La
Hume St
Lower Kevin St
Cuffe St
St Stephen's Green E
St Stephen's Green S
Montague Ct
New Bride St
Wexford St
Montague St
Camden Row
Long La
Clonmel St
Leeson La
Iveagh Gardens
Camden Pl
Earlsfort Tce
Lower Leeson St
Pleasants St
Harcourt St
Lower Camden St
Arnott St
Heytesbury St
Grantham St
Upper Hatch St
Lower Hatch St
Charlotte Way
Synge St
Grantham Pl
Charlotte St
Upper Camden St
Emor St
Curzon St
Harcourt
Harcourt Rd
Adelaide Rd
S Circular Rd
Harrington St
Harcourt Tce
Charlemont St
Little Bird (175m)
Kingsland Park Ave
Stamer St
S Richmond St
Walworth Rd
Lennox St
Charlemont Pl
Grand Canal
Charlemont
Victoria St
Kingsland Pde
Martin St
Warren St
Lennox Pl
Portobello Harbour
Charlemont Mall
Dartmouth Square

GRAFTON STREET & ST STEPHEN'S GREEN

Top Sights **p61**
1 Chester Beatty Library ... A2
2 Dublin Castle ... A2

Sights **p66**
3 City Hall ... A2
4 Famine Victims Memorial ... D4
5 Irish-Jewish Museum ... A7
6 Iveagh Gardens ... C5
7 Iveagh House ... C5
8 James Joyce Bust ... C4
9 Museum of Literature Ireland ... C5
10 Newman University Church ... C5
11 St Stephen's Green ... C4
12 St Werburgh's Church ... A2
13 Wolfe Tone Monument ... D4

Eating **p71**
14 Azteca ... A2
15 Brother Hubbard South ... B6
16 Bunsen ... B4
17 Cake Café ... B6
18 Camden Kitchen ... B6
19 Camden Rotisserie ... B6
20 Chez Max ... B2
21 Eatyard ... B7
22 Hang Dai ... B5
23 Jerusalem Restaurant ... B5
24 Listons ... B6
25 Meet Me in the Morning ... B5
26 Neon ... B5
27 Opium ... B5
28 Pang ... B4
29 Richmond ... B7
30 Shanahan's on the Green ... C4
Silk Road Café ... (see 1)
Sophie's @ the Dean ... (see 47)

Drinking & Nightlife **p79**
31 Against the Grain ... B4
32 Anseo ... B5
33 Bernard Shaw ... B7
34 Camden Exchange ... B6
35 Copper Face Jacks ... B5
36 Dicey's Garden ... B5
37 J. O'Connell ... B7
38 Lucky Duck ... B4
39 Network ... B4
Opium ... (see 27)
40 Wall and Keogh ... B7

Entertainment **p84**
41 Devitt's ... B5
42 National Concert Hall ... C5
43 Whelan's ... B5

Shopping **p65**
44 Chester Beatty Library Gift Shop ... A2

Sports & Activities **p78**
45 Children's Playground ... D4
46 Sandeman's New Dublin Tour ... A2

Sleeping **p201**
47 Dean ... B5
48 Green ... B4
49 Harrington Hall ... B5
50 Iveagh Garden Hotel ... B5
51 Radisson Blu Royal Hotel ... A3

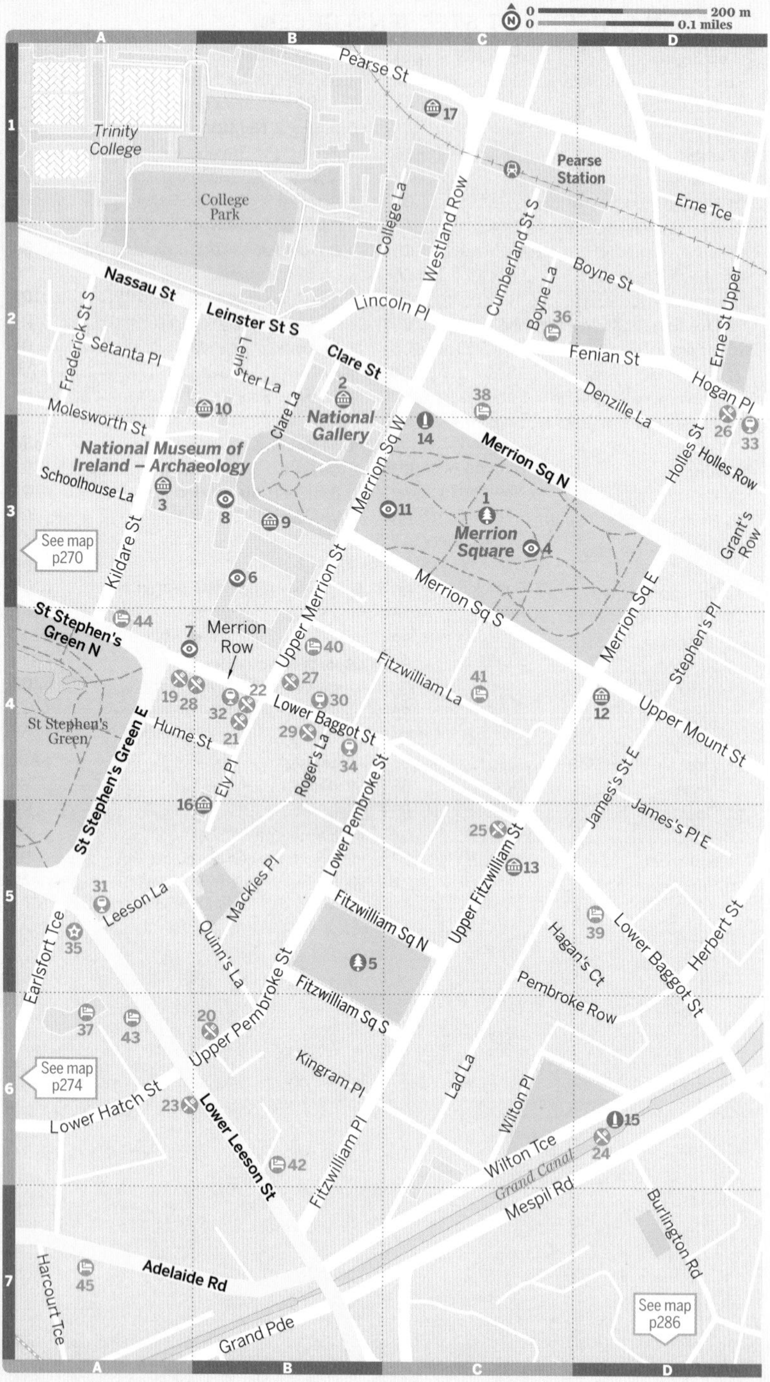

MERRION SQUARE & AROUND

0 200 m
0 0.1 miles

A B C D

1 2 3 4 5 6 7

Pearse St
17
Trinity College
Pearse Station
College Park
Erne Tce
College La
Westland Row
Cumberland St S
Boyne St
Nassau St
Lincoln Pl
Boyne La
36
Erne St Upper
Frederick St S
Leinster St S
Fenian St
Setanta Pl
Leinster La
Clare St
2
National Gallery
Hogan Pl
Denzille La
38
10
Molesworth St
Clare La
14
Merrion Sq W
26
33
National Museum of Ireland – Archaeology
Merrion Sq N
Holles St
Holles Row
Schoolhouse La
3
8
9
11
1
Merrion Square
4
Grant's Row
Kildare St
Upper Merrion St
6
Merrion Sq S
Merrion Sq E
44
St Stephen's Green N
7
Merrion Row
40
Stephen's Pl
Fitzwilliam La
19 28
32
22
27
30
41
12
Upper Mount St
Lower Baggot St
St Stephen's Green
Hume St
21
29
34
Roger's La
Ely Pl
James's St E
16
Lower Pembroke St
St Stephen's Green E
James's Pl E
25
Upper Fitzwilliam St
13
Mackies Pl
31
Leeson La
Fitzwilliam Sq N
39
Lower Baggot St
Herbert St
35
Earlsfort Tce
Quinn's La
5
Hagan's Ct
Upper Pembroke St
Fitzwilliam Sq S
Pembroke Row
37
43
20
Kingram Pl
Lad La
Wilton Pl
Lower Hatch St
23
Lower Leeson St
15
Wilton Tce
24
Grand Canal
42
Fitzwilliam Pl
Mespil Rd
Burlington Rd
Adelaide Rd
45
Harcourt Tce
Grand Pde

See map p270
See map p274
See map p286

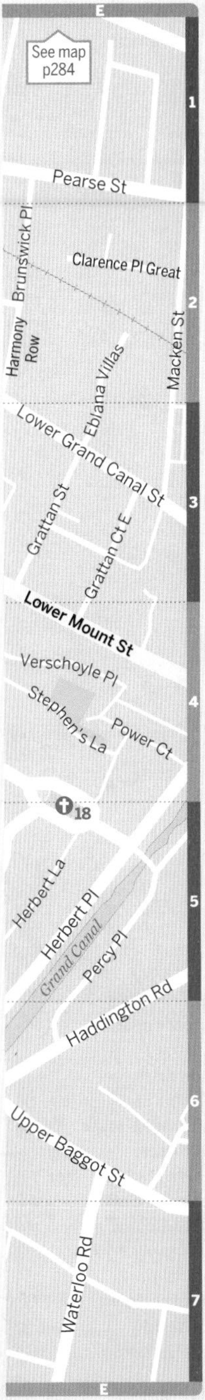

E

See map p284

Pearse St
Brunswick Pl
Clarence Pl Great
Harmony Row
Macken St
Eblana Villas
Lower Grand Canal St
Grattan St
Grattan Ct E
Lower Mount St
Verschoyle Pl
Stephen's La
Power Ct
18
Herbert La
Herbert Pl
Grand Canal
Percy Pl
Haddington Rd
Upper Baggot St
Waterloo Rd

E

Top Sights **p90**

1 Merrion Square ... C3
2 National Gallery ... B2
3 National Museum of Ireland – Archaeology ... A3

Sights **p97**

4 Art Market ... C3
5 Fitzwilliam Square ... B5
6 Government Buildings ... B3
7 Huguenot Cemetery ... A4
8 Leinster House ... B3
9 Museum of Natural History ... B3
10 National Library of Ireland ... B2
11 National Memorial ... C3
12 Number 29 Lower Fitzwilliam Street ... D4
13 Origin Gallery ... C5
14 Oscar Wilde Statue ... C3
15 Patrick Kavanagh Statue ... D6
16 Royal Hibernian Academy (RHA) Gallagher Gallery ... B5
17 Science Gallery ... C1
18 St Stephen's 'Pepper Canister' Church ... E5

Eating **p101**

19 Bang Café ... A4
Brambles ... (see 3)
Coburg Brasserie ... (see 37)
20 Dax ... B6
21 Ely Wine Bar ... B4
22 Etto ... B4
23 House ... A6
24 La Peniche ... D6
25 L'Ecrivain ... C5
26 Musashi Hogan Place ... D2
27 Restaurant Patrick Guilbaud ... B4
Science Gallery Café ... (see 17)
28 Unicorn ... B4
29 Xico ... B4

Drinking & Nightlife **p103**

30 Doheny & Nesbitt's ... B4
31 Hartigan's ... A5
House ... (see 23)
32 O'Donoghue's ... B4
33 Square Ball ... D3
34 Toner's ... B4

Entertainment **p104**

O'Donoghue's ... (see 32)
35 Sugar Club ... A5

Sports & Activities **p104**

Guided Tour of Oireachtas ... (see 8)

Sleeping **p203**

36 Alex ... C2
37 Conrad Dublin ... A6
38 Davenport ... C2
39 Latchfords ... D5
40 Merrion ... B4
41 Merrion Mews ... C4
42 Number 31 ... B6
43 Premier Suites ... A6
44 Shelbourne ... A4
45 Wilder Townhouse ... A7

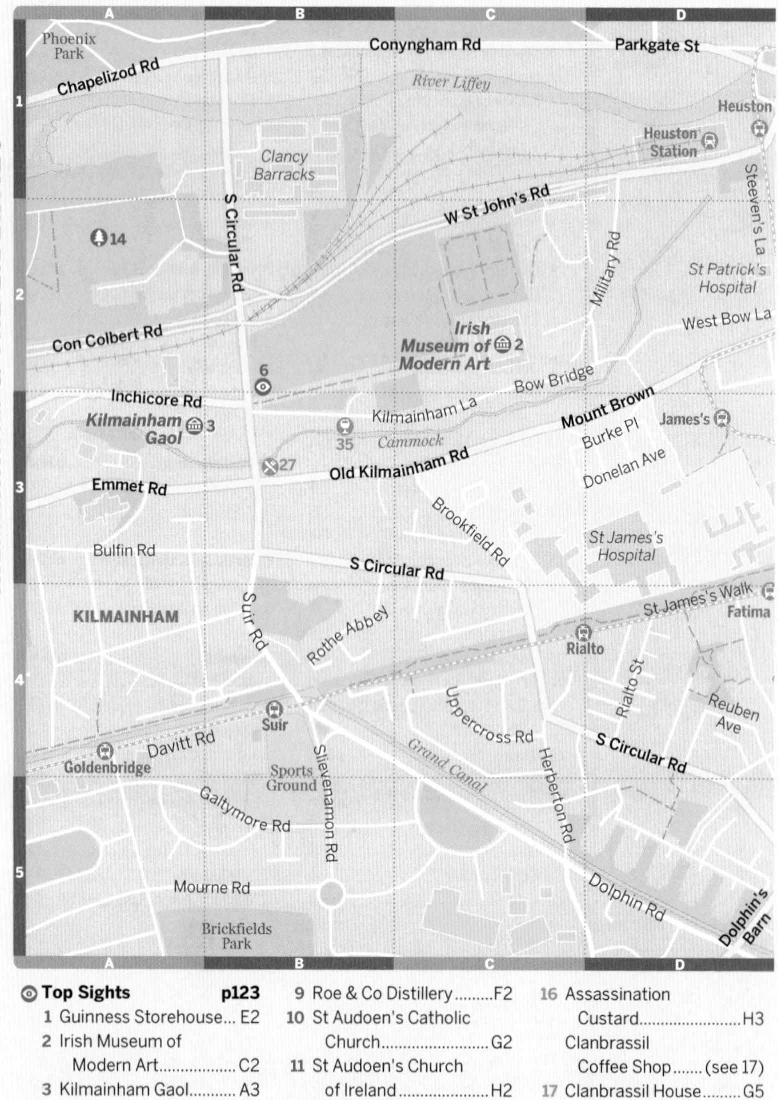

Top Sights **p123**
1 Guinness Storehouse... E2
2 Irish Museum of Modern Art.................. C2
3 Kilmainham Gaol........... A3
4 St Patrick's Cathedral .. H3

Sights **p133**
5 Dublin Liberties Distillery G4
6 Kilmainham Gate B2
7 Marsh's Library H3
8 Pearse Lyons Distillery E2
9 Roe & Co Distillery F2
10 St Audoen's Catholic Church........................ G2
11 St Audoen's Church of Ireland H2
12 St Patrick's Tower F2
13 Teeling Distillery G4
14 War Memorial Gardens...................... A2

Eating **p136**
1837 Bar & Brasserie.............. (see 1)
15 57 The Headline G5
16 Assassination Custard......................... H3
Clanbrassil Coffee Shop....... (see 17)
17 Clanbrassil House......... G5
Coke Lane Pizza .... (see 34)
18 Container Coffee............F2
19 Dublin Cookie Company......................F2
20 Fumbally......................... H4
21 Gaillot et Gray................ G5
Itsa@IMMA ....(see 2)
22 Legit Coffee Co.............. G3

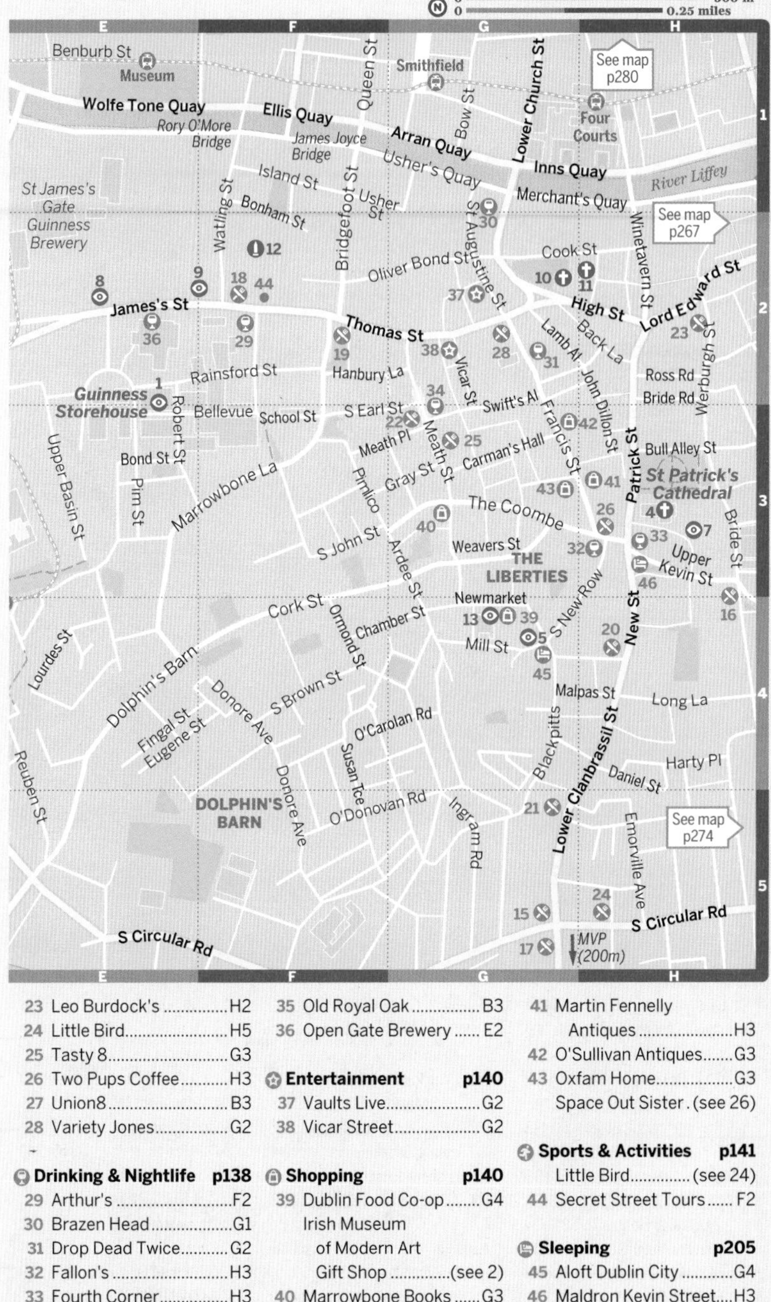

23 Leo Burdock's H2
24 Little Bird H5
25 Tasty 8 .... G3
26 Two Pups Coffee H3
27 Union8 .... B3
28 Variety Jones G2

Drinking & Nightlife p138
29 Arthur's F2
30 Brazen Head G1
31 Drop Dead Twice G2
32 Fallon's H3
33 Fourth Corner H3
34 Lucky's G3
35 Old Royal Oak B3
36 Open Gate Brewery E2

Entertainment p140
37 Vaults Live G2
38 Vicar Street G2

Shopping p140
39 Dublin Food Co-op G4
Irish Museum of Modern Art Gift Shop .... (see 2)
40 Marrowbone Books G3
41 Martin Fennelly Antiques H3
42 O'Sullivan Antiques G3
43 Oxfam Home G3
Space Out Sister . (see 26)

Sports & Activities p141
Little Bird .... (see 24)
44 Secret Street Tours F2

Sleeping p205
45 Aloft Dublin City G4
46 Maldron Kevin Street H3

Key on p282

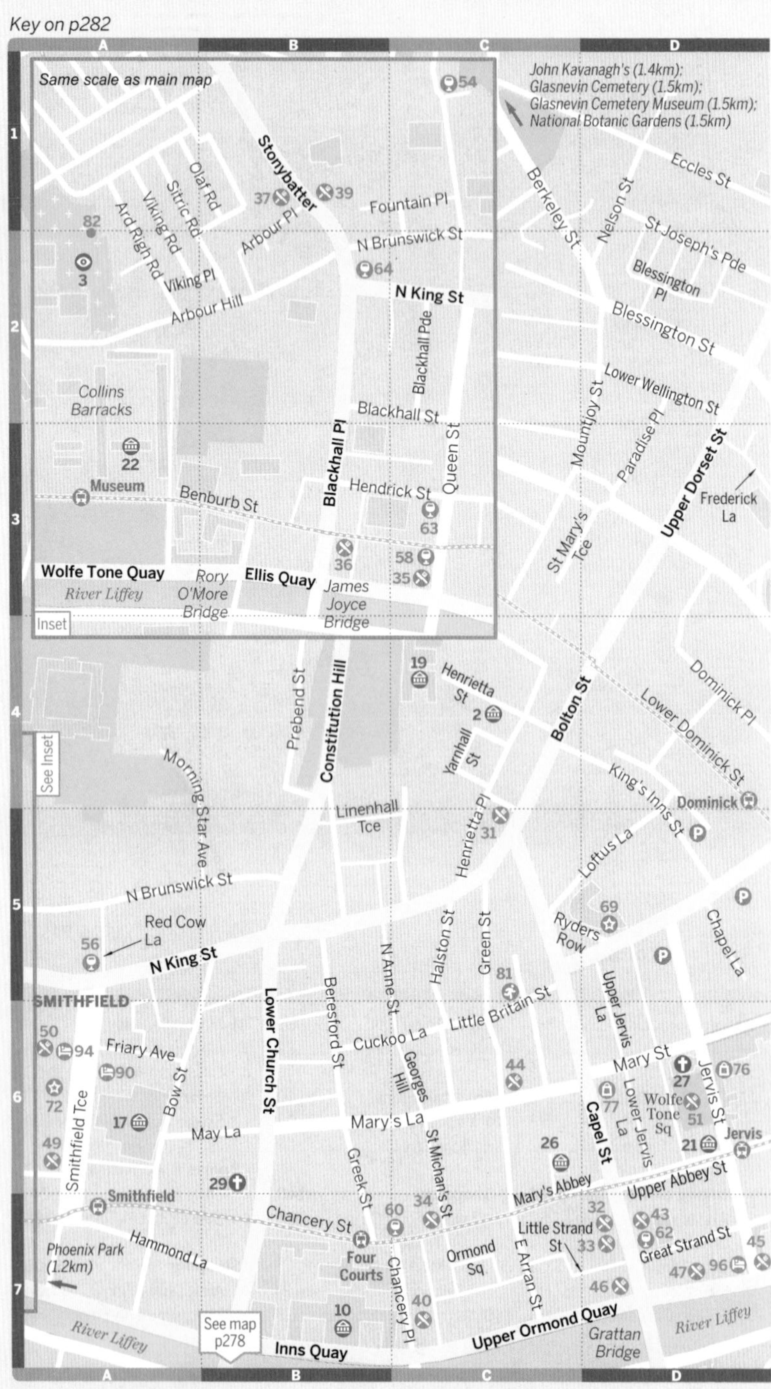
NORTH OF THE LIFFEY
Same scale as main map
Inset
See Inset
John Kavanagh's (1.4km); Glasnevin Cemetery (1.5km); Glasnevin Cemetery Museum (1.5km); National Botanic Gardens (1.5km)
Phoenix Park (1.2km)
See map p278
Stonybatter
Olaf Rd
Sitric Rd
Viking Rd
Ard Righ Rd
Viking Pl
Arbour Pl
Arbour Hill
Fountain Pl
N Brunswick St
N King St
Blackhall Pde
Blackhall St
Blackhall Pl
Queen St
Hendrick St
Collins Barracks
Museum
Benburb St
Wolfe Tone Quay
River Liffey
Rory O'More Bridge
Ellis Quay
James Joyce Bridge
Berkeley St
Eccles St
Nelson St
St Joseph's Pde
Blessington Pl
Blessington St
Lower Wellington St
Mountjoy St
Paradise Pl
Upper Dorset St
Frederick La
St Mary's Tce
Dominick Pl
Lower Dominick St
Dominick
King's Inns St
Loftus La
Bolton St
Henrietta St
Yarnhall St
Henrietta Pl
Prebend St
Constitution Hill
Linenhall Tce
Morning Star Ave
N Brunswick St
Red Cow La
N King St
SMITHFIELD
Halston St
Green St
Ryders Row
Chapel La
Upper Jervis La
Little Britain St
N Anne St
Beresford St
Lower Church St
Cuckoo La
Georges Hill
Friary Ave
Bow St
Smithfield Tce
May La
Mary's La
Mary St
Lower Jervis La
Wolfe Tone Sq
Jervis St
Jervis
Capel St
St Michan's St
Greek St
Mary's Abbey
Upper Abbey St
Smithfield
Hammond La
Chancery St
Four Courts
Chancery Pl
Ormond Sq
Little Strand St
E Arran St
Great Strand St
Upper Ormond Quay
Grattan Bridge
Inns Quay
River Liffey

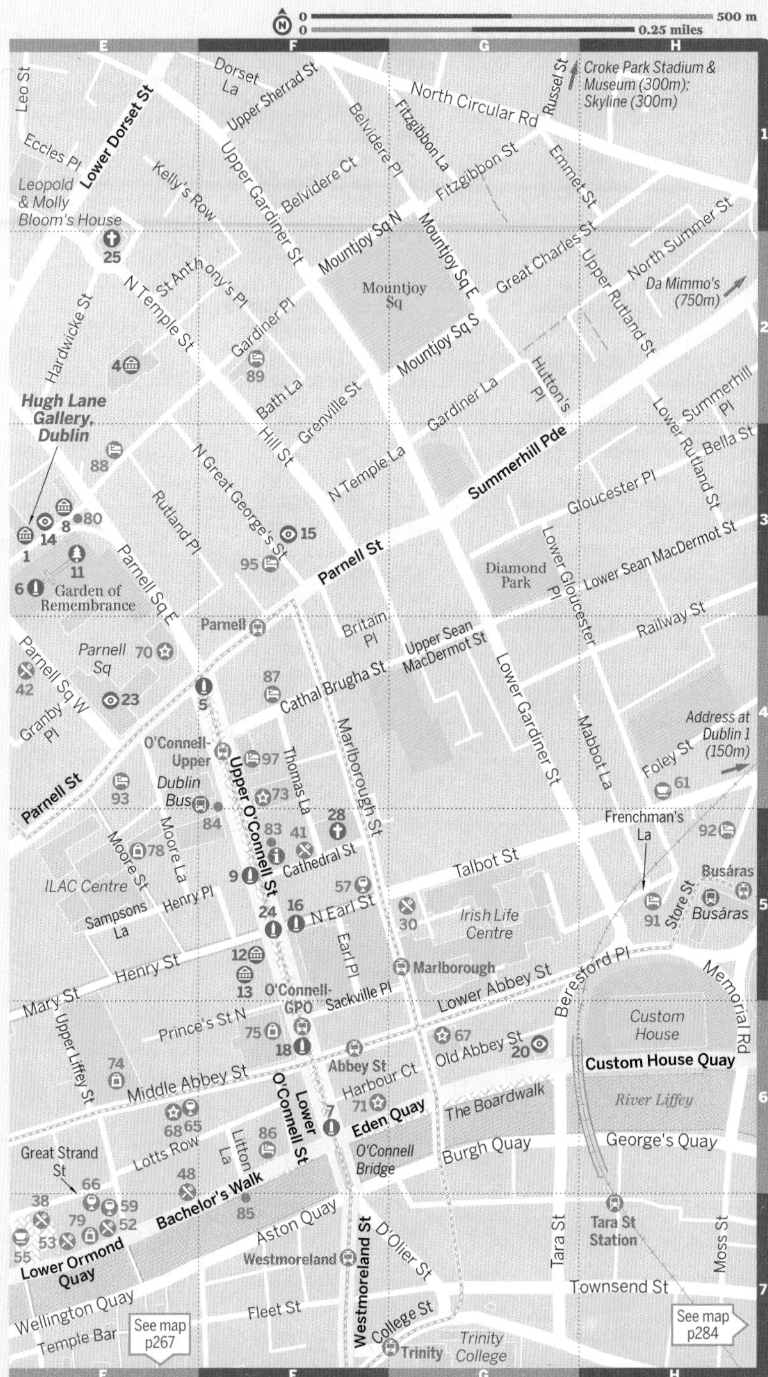

0 500 m
0 0.25 miles
Croke Park Stadium & Museum (300m); Skyline (300m)
Da Mimmo's (750m)
Address at Dublin 1 (150m)
North Circular Rd
Lower Dorset St
Upper Gardiner St
Mountjoy Sq
Hugh Lane Gallery, Dublin
Leopold & Molly Bloom's House
Garden of Remembrance
Parnell Sq
Parnell St
Summerhill Pde
Diamond Park
Upper O'Connell St
Lower O'Connell St
Lower Gardiner St
Talbot St
Irish Life Centre
ILAC Centre
Henry St
Mary St
Lower Abbey St
Middle Abbey St
Custom House
Custom House Quay
River Liffey
Eden Quay
Burgh Quay
George's Quay
Bachelor's Walk
Aston Quay
Lower Ormond Quay
Wellington Quay
Westmoreland St
D'Olier St
Townsend St
Trinity College
Busáras
Tara St Station
See map p267
See map p284

NORTH OF THE LIFFEY *Map on p280*

Top Sights p144
1 Hugh Lane Gallery, Dublin E3

Sights p149
2 14 Henrietta Street C4
3 Arbour Hill Cemetery A2
4 Belvedere House E2
5 Charles Stewart Parnell Statue F4
6 Children of Lir Monument E3
7 Daniel O'Connell Statue F6
8 Dublin Writers Museum E3
9 Father Theobald Mathew Statue F5
10 Four Courts B7
11 Garden of Remembrance E3
12 General Post Office F5
13 GPO Witness History F5
14 Irish Writers Centre E3
15 James Joyce Cultural Centre F3
16 James Joyce Statue F5
17 Jameson Distillery Bow Street A6
18 Jim Larkin Statue F6
19 King's Inns C4
20 Liberty Hall G6
21 National Leprechaun Museum D6
22 National Museum of Ireland – Decorative Arts & History A3
23 Rotunda Hospital E4
24 Spire F5
25 St George's Church E2
26 St Mary's Abbey C6
27 St Mary's Church D6
28 St Mary's Pro-Cathedral F5
29 St Michan's Church B6

Eating p156
30 101 Talbot G5
31 Boco C5
32 Brother Hubbard D7
33 Camerino D7
Chapter One .... (see 8)
34 Fegan's 1924 .... C7
35 Fish Shop C3
36 Fish Shop B3
37 Grano B1
38 Han Sung E7
Hatch & Sons .... (see 1)
39 L Mulligan Grocer B1
40 Legal Eagle C7
41 M&L F5
42 Mr Fox E4
43 Musashi Noodles & Sushi Bar D7
44 Oxmantown C6
45 Panem D7
46 Soup Dragon D7
47 Tea Garden D7
48 Terra Madre E6
49 Third Space A6
50 Thundercut Alley A6
51 Tram Cafe D6

Winding Stair .... (see 79)
52 Woollen Mills E7
53 Yamamori Sushi E7
Yarn .... (see 52)

Drinking & Nightlife **p159**

54 Barbers C1
55 Caffe Cagliostro E7
56 Cobblestone A5
57 Confession Box F5
58 Dice Bar C3
59 Grand Social E7
60 Hughes' Bar C7
61 Laine, My Love H4
62 Pantibar D7
63 Token C3
64 Walshs B2
65 Wigwam E6
66 Yamamori Tengu E7

Entertainment **p161**

67 Abbey Theatre G6
68 Academy E6
69 Cineworld Multiplex D5
70 Gate Theatre E4
71 Laughter Lounge F6
72 Light House Cinema A6
73 Savoy F4

Shopping **p162**

74 Arnott's E6
75 Eason's F6
76 Jervis Centre D6
77 Louis Copeland D6
78 Moore Street Market E5
79 Winding Stair E7

Sports & Activities **p163**

80 1916 Easter Rising Coach Tour E3
81 AdventureRooms C5
82 Arbour Hill Guided Tours A2
83 City Sightseeing F5
84 Dublin Bus Tours F4
85 Dublin Discovered Boat Tours F7
Glendalough & Powerscourt Tour .... (see 84)
James Joyce Walking Tours .... (see 15)

Sleeping **p206**

86 Abbey Court Hostel F6
87 Academy Plaza Hotel F4
88 Castle Hotel E3
89 Clifden Guesthouse F2
90 Generator Hostel A6
91 Isaacs Hostel H5
92 Jacob's Inn H5
93 Jury's Inn Parnell St E4
94 Maldron Hotel Smithfield A6
95 MEC Hostel F3
96 Morrison Hotel D7
97 Riu Plaza Gresham Hotel F4

DOCKLANDS

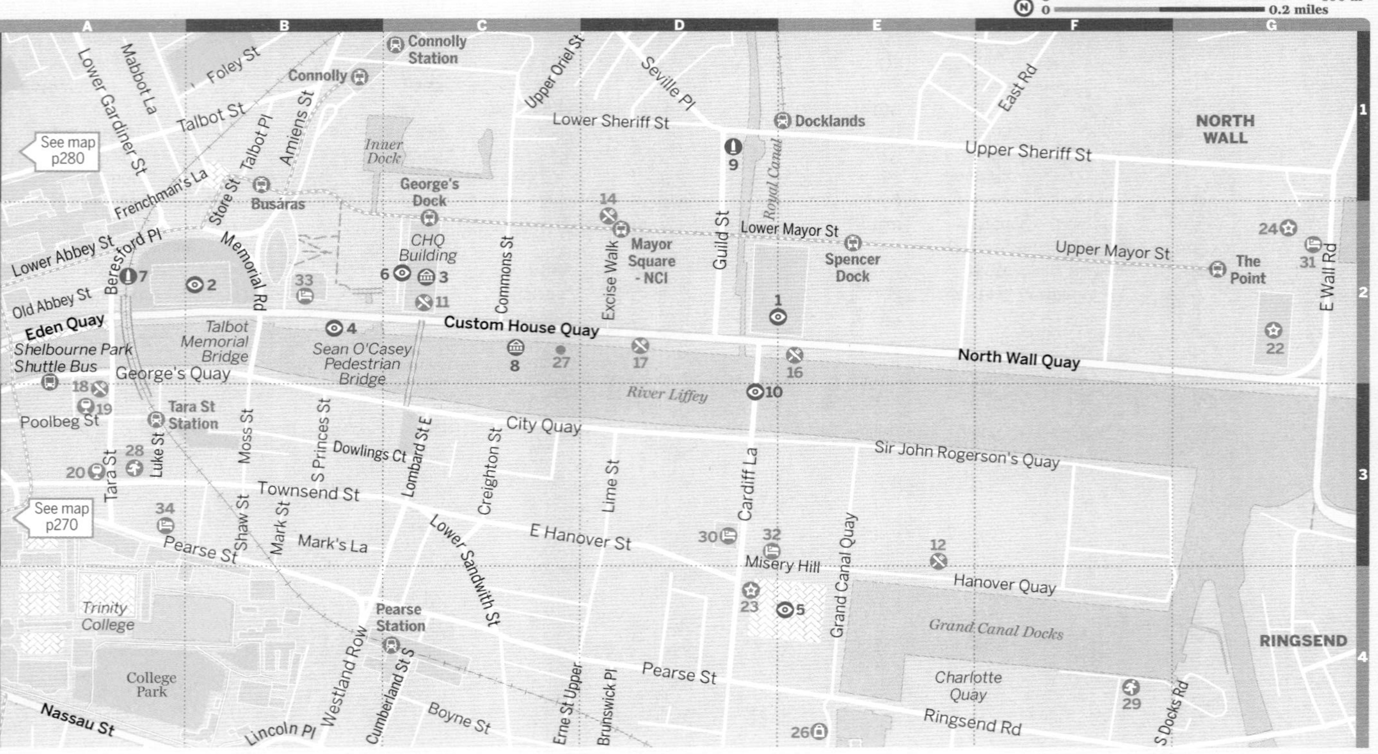

0 — 400 m
0 — 0.2 miles
Connolly Station
Connolly
Foley St
Mabbot La
Lower Gardiner St
Talbot St
Talbot Pl
Amiens St
See map p280
Upper Oriel St
Seville Pl
Lower Sheriff St
Docklands
East Rd
NORTH WALL
Upper Sheriff St
Inner Dock
George's Dock
Busáras
Frenchman's La
Store St
Royal Canal
Lower Abbey St
Beresford Pl
Memorial Rd
CHQ Building
Commons St
Excise Walk
Mayor Square - NCI
Guild St
Lower Mayor St
Spencer Dock
Upper Mayor St
The Point
E Wall Rd
Old Abbey St
Eden Quay
Custom House Quay
North Wall Quay
Shelbourne Park Shuttle Bus
Talbot Memorial Bridge
Sean O'Casey Pedestrian Bridge
George's Quay
River Liffey
Poolbeg St
Tara St Station
Moss St
S Princes St
Lombard St E
City Quay
Sir John Rogerson's Quay
Dowlings Ct
Creighton St
Lime St
Cardiff La
Luke St
Tara St
Townsend St
See map p270
Shaw St
Mark St
Mark's La
Pearse St
Lower Sandwith St
E Hanover St
Misery Hill
Grand Canal Quay
Hanover Quay
Trinity College
Pearse Station
Grand Canal Docks
RINGSEND
College Park
Westland Row
Cumberland St S
Boyne St
Erne St Upper
Brunswick Pl
Pearse St
Charlotte Quay
Ringsend Rd
S Docks Rd
Nassau St
Lincoln Pl

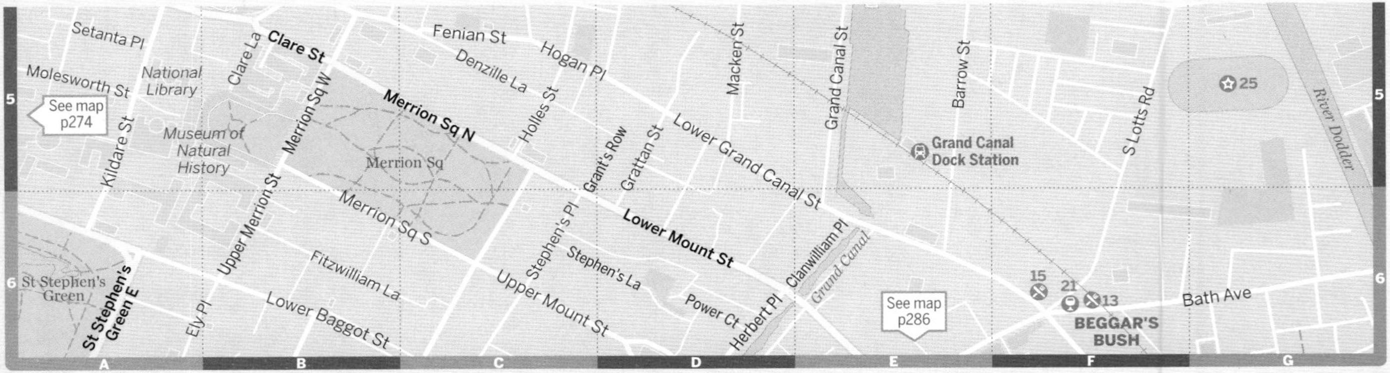

See map p274

See map p286

Sights p166

1 Convention Centre ... E2
2 Custom House ... B2
3 EPIC The Irish Emigration Museum ... C2
4 Famine Memorial ... B2
5 Grand Canal Square ... E4
6 Irish Family History Centre ... C2
7 James Connolly Memorial ... A2
8 Jeanie Johnston ... C2
9 Luke Kelly Bust ... D1
10 Samuel Beckett Bridge ... D3

Eating p167

11 Ely Bar & Grill ... C2
12 Herbstreet ... E3
13 Juniors Deli & Cafe ... F6
14 Musashi IFSC ... D2
15 Paulie's Pizza ... F6
16 Quay 16 ... E2
17 Rocket's ... D2
18 Workshop Gastropub ... A3

Drinking & Nightlife p168

19 John Mulligan's ... A3
20 Ruin ... A3
21 Slattery's ... F6

Entertainment p169

22 3 Arena ... G2
23 Bord Gáis Energy Theatre ... D4
24 Odeon Cinema ... G2
25 Shelbourne Park Greyhound Stadium ... G5

Shopping p169

26 Design Tower ... E4

Sports & Activities p169

27 City Kayaking Dublin ... C2
28 Sports and Fitness Markievicz ... A3
29 Wakedock ... F4

Sleeping p207

30 Clayton Hotel Cardiff Lane ... D3
31 Gibson Hotel ... G2
32 Marker ... D3
33 Spencer Hotel ... B2
34 Trinity City Hotel ... A3

THE SOUTHSIDE

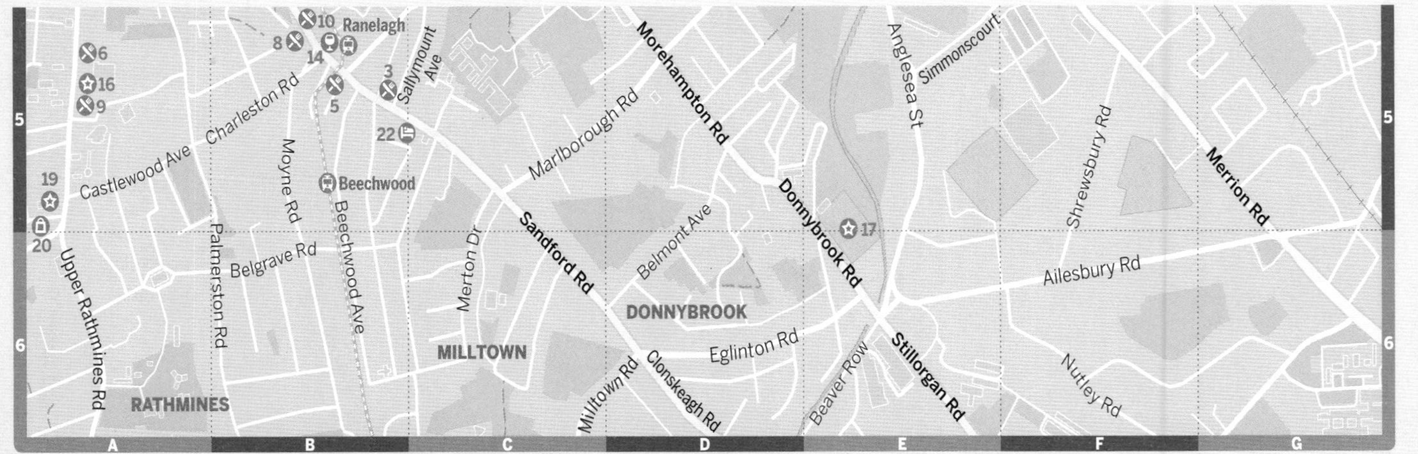

Sights p172
1 Herbert Park D4
2 National Print Museum D2

Eating p172
3 Butcher Grill B5
4 Chophouse E2
5 Dillinger's B5
6 Farmer Brown's A5
7 Farmer Brown's E2
8 Kinara B5
9 Manifesto A5
10 Nick's Coffee Company B5
11 Saba C3
Stella Diner .... (see 19)

Drinking & Nightlife p174
12 Beggar's Bush D2
13 Blackbird A4
14 Taphouse B5

Entertainment p175
15 Aviva Stadium E3
16 Bowery A5
17 Donnybrook Stadium E5
18 Royal Dublin Society Showground E4
19 Stella Theatre A5

Shopping p175
20 April and the Bear A5

Sleeping p208
21 Ariel House E3
22 Devlin B5
23 Dylan D3
24 Herbert Park Hotel E4
25 Intercontinental Dublin F4
26 Pembroke Townhouse D3
27 Schoolhouse Hotel D2
28 Waterloo House C3

Our Story

A beat-up old car, a few dollars in the pocket and a sense of adventure. In 1972 that's all Tony and Maureen Wheeler needed for the trip of a lifetime – across Europe and Asia overland to Australia. It took several months, and at the end – broke but inspired – they sat at their kitchen table writing and stapling together their first travel guide, *Across Asia on the Cheap*. Within a week they'd sold 1500 copies. Lonely Planet was born.

Today, Lonely Planet has offices in Franklin, London, Melbourne, Oakland, Dublin, Beijing and Delhi, with more than 600 staff and writers. We share Tony's belief that 'a great guidebook should do three things: inform, educate and amuse'.

Our Writers

Fionn Davenport

Irish by birth and conviction, Fionn has spent the last two decades focusing on the country of his birth and its nearest neighbour, England, which he has written about extensively for Lonely Planet and others. In between writing gigs he's lived in Paris and New York, where he was an editor, actor, bartender and whatever else paid the rent. When he returned to Ireland in the late 1990s he tried his hand at radio, which landed him a series of presenting gigs, most recently as host of Inside Culture and regular travel contributor to the mid-morning Sean O'Rourke Show, both on RTE Radio 1. He moved to Manchester a few years ago where he lives with his wife, Laura, but he commutes back and forth to Dublin, only 40 minutes away. Fionn posts his travel shots on instagram - @fionndavenport

Contributing Writer

Catherine Le Nevez wrote the Brú na Bóinne, Enniskerry and Glendalough sections of the Day Trips chapter. She has traveled to around 60 countries and completed her Doctorate of Creative Arts in Writing, Masters in Professional Writing, and postgraduate qualifications in Editing and Publishing along the way. Her work has also appeared in numerous online and print publications.

Published by Lonely Planet Global Limited
CRN 554153
12th edition – February 2020
ISBN 978 1 78701 820 4

10 9 8 7 6 5 4 3 2 1
Printed in China